Holy Fairs

The Frank S. and Elizabeth D. Brewer Prize Essay of the American Society of Church History

Holy Fairs

SCOTTISH COMMUNIONS AND AMERICAN REVIVALS IN THE EARLY MODERN PERIOD

Leigh Eric Schmidt

PRINCETON UNIVERSITY PRESS

PRINCETON, NEW JERSEY

Library of Congress Cataloging-in-Publication Data
Schmidt, Leigh Eric.
Holy fairs : Scottish communions and American revivals in the early modern period /
Leigh Eric Schmidt.
p.   cm.
Includes index.
ISBN 0-691-04760-X (alk. paper)
1. Lord's Supper—Presbyterian Church—History. 2. Presbyterian Church—Scotland—
History. 3. Presbyterian Church—United States—History. 4. Revivals—United States—
History. 5. Scotland—Church history. 6. United States—Church history—Colonial period,
ca. 1600–1775. 7. United States—Church history—18th century. 8. United States—
Church history—19th century. I. Title. BX9189.C5S36   1989
269'.24'09411—dc20   89-31642
                                                                                      CIP

This book has been composed in Linotron Sabon

TO MY GRANDPARENTS

Ada Lee and George Mattison

Cleo and Roland Schmidt

Contents

viii · Contents

Illustrations

Acknowledgments

THE EIGHTEENTH-CENTURY devotional writer John Willison said that he found the subject of communions "very large and copious." Though he had written abundantly and lucidly on the topic, he noted that "after all that hath been said and written" there still seemed "room for much more." With Willison I have found a well-nigh inexhaustible depth in the Scottish communions and in their American counterparts. What success I have had in fathoming these sacramental solemnities and revivals has emerged out of long, insightful tutelage and rich collegiality.

Edwin S. Gaustad of the University of California at Riverside initiated me into the field of American religious history when I was an undergraduate, and one of his works, *The Great Awakening in New England*, inspired my first look into revivalism in American culture. Specifically I owe him thanks for his comments upon this manuscript—broadly for nearly a decade of profound instruction, solid advice, and steady encouragement.

At the next stage of my academic preparation, Albert J. Raboteau and John F. Wilson of Princeton University guided my research into American religious history. As advisers on the dissertation that is the basis of this work, they were simultaneously very supportive and rigorously challenging. Both, I confess, recognized the potential in these festal communions before I did and helped focus my energies on them when I thought I would rather be working on another Christian festival, namely Christmas.

Horton M. Davies helped guide me in my first year at Princeton and kindly found time amid his very active retirement to read and comment upon this manuscript; his great knowledge of the history of Christian worship charted my way in that field. Janet Fishburn of Drew University, whose interest and insight has been important from the first stages of this project, offered me wise counsel based on her own research into early American Presbyterianism. Similarly, Jon Butler, Charles Hambrick-Stowe, and Eugene Lowe each offered an incisive reading of this manuscript, posing important questions and suggesting different angles from which to view my materials. Also a number of scholars long familiar with Scottish history and culture—notably James Cameron, Ian B. Cowan, Lindsay Errington, Richard Sher, and T. C. Smout—helped me, through correspondence or conversation, to get my feet planted firmly on their turf. On this count, Ned Landsman in particular offered helpful advice as well as measured readings of different drafts of my work.

I would also like to thank three scholars whose influence on this book was indirect. At Princeton Chava Weissler and Mary Douglas got me thinking more seriously about ritual and about the interrelationship between history and anthropology. Such prompting proved important for the course of this study. Also Michael McGiffert of the Institute of Early American History and Culture put an earlier work of mine through his editorial wringer and squeezed out an important lesson about tireless revision and the arduousness of getting something right. It is a lesson from which this work has profited repeatedly.

Outstanding institutional backing for five-plus years has allowed me to proceed apace on my work. Princeton University generously supported my graduate study for three years, and the Whiting Foundation munificently funded my research and writing for a fourth year. The Andrew Mellon Foundation and the Religious Studies Department at Stanford University made a valuable year of research and teaching possible through a generous postdoctoral fellowship. Also the American Philosophical Society has helped fund my research abroad; for that essential support I am grateful. Finally, the American Society of Church History supported publication of this manuscript through the Frank S. and Elizabeth D. Brewer Prize.

In the course of my research I have been very fortunate to have access to a number of important libraries, collections, and archives. In America I am particularly beholden to the library staffs of Princeton University, Princeton Theological Seminary, Stanford University, the University of Oregon, Washington and Jefferson College, Pittsburgh Theological Seminary, the Kentucky Historical Society, the Presbyterian Office of History (formerly the Presbyterian Historical Society), and the Presbyterian Study Center (formerly the Historical Foundation of the Presbyterian and Reformed Churches). I was particularly gratified by the interest shown in my work by Jerrold Brooks, William Bynum, and Mary Lane at the Study Center in Montreat. Abroad I have found welcome at the National Library of Scotland, the New College Library, the Edinburgh University Library, the Scottish Record Office, the Strathclyde Regional Archives, the Mitchell Library, and the British Library. On a personal note, Mrs. Helen Treasure kindly opened both her home and her collection of John McMillan manuscripts to me.

A number of friends and colleagues at Riverside, Princeton, Stanford, Eugene, and Drew have over the years made the pursuit of scholarship more pleasurable, more leisurely, and more worthwhile. I thank them for the evenings of conversation and conviviality, for the sharing of food, drink, and thought. Perhaps these evenings left a mark on my understanding of these holy fairs: the wonders of conviviality and commensality are themes that I thankfully sound from experience.

Throughout the best and most influential friend I have had in the academy has been my wife, Linda Tyler, whose dedication to her own scholarship has kept me going on my own. Her commitment, in learning and in love, has buoyed me up.

Finally, I thank my parents, Roger and Ann Schmidt, and my brother, Jeffrey. My great indebtedness to my whole family is, I trust, expressed in the dedication of this project to my grandparents.

Holy Fairs

Prospect

IN THE AUTUMN of 1785 Robert Burns, bard of Scotland, composed one of his most renowned poems, "The Holy Fair." In a note appended to the work in 1787, an incidental observation was made explaining the title of the poem: "*Holy Fair* is a common phrase in the West of Scotland for a sacramental occasion." Whether the expression was indeed in general usage or whether Burns' own artifice gave it currency is a small concern; for, whatever the case, the phrase was certainly striking, suggestive, and apt. Sacramental occasions in Scotland were great festivals, an engaging combination of holy day and holiday. They were, as one divine said, "fair-days of the gospel," festal events in a Reformed calendar otherwise dominated by the week-to-week observance of the Sabbath. In them religion and culture, communion and community, piety and sociability commingled. Regularly times of renewal and revival, they were the high days of the year.[1]

Lengthy events, usually lasting four days, these evangelical festivals had burgeoned in post-Reformation Scotland and throve there. In due course these occasions were celebrated with similar fervor among Presbyterians who left the homeland, first in Ulster and then in North America. Spanning more than two centuries, these holy fairs were interwoven with religious awakenings on both sides of the Atlantic—an interweaving that only came unraveled with the demise of the festal communions in the nineteenth century. Rich in spirituality and ritual, these solemnities were at the center of evangelical Presbyterian culture. Great public celebrations, often attracting thousands, they were important events in the religious history of early modern Scotland and America.

Burns might have found this assessment of the importance of these sacramental occasions misguided. Imbued with Enlightenment sentiments toward popular evangelicalism, Burns watched the communion seasons in his native Ayrshire in the 1780s with bemusement. Of the vehement outdoor preaching at these events, for example, he wrote in derisive tones:

> Hear how he clears the points o' Faith
>   Wi' rattlin' an' thumpin!
> Now meekly calm, now wild in wrath,
>   He's stampan, an' he's jumpan!
>
> His lengthen'd chin, his turn'd up snout,
>   His eldritch squeel an' gestures,

> O how they fire the heart devout,
>   Like cantharidian plaisters
>   On sic a day!

To the poet, the sacramental occasion was an ungodly mixture of superstition and hypocrisy, of pious presumption and outright depravity:

> On this hand sits a Chosen swatch,
>   Wi' screw'd-up, grace-proud faces;
> On that, a set o' chaps, at watch,
>   Thrang winkan on the lasses

In the eyes of the enlightened, satire more than significance should be accorded these holy fairs.[2]

The learned of later periods have often followed Burns in his sardonic evaluation of this popular festival, his poem setting the tone for their estimations of these sacramental occasions. Though worrying at times that Burns had "mingled unseasonable levity with his caustic wit," liturgical reformers and church historians often thanked him for helping bring such sacramental gatherings into disrepute. His poem, it was said, did "a world of good all over the country." As a "prophet of religious reform," Burns had performed "a great service to Scottish religion." He had assisted those who were altogether uncomfortable with the indulgence of evangelical fervor and popular festivity to put behind them such "eccentricities" and "singularities"—"our forefathers' superstitions." Whether Burns' poem had as much to do with the decline of "these rude festivals" as his grateful heirs often thought is doubtful, but his poem nonetheless came to embody one of the dominant views later generations had of these communion seasons: They were a terrible embarrassment to Reformed Christianity.[3]

Surprisingly few historians have challenged this enlightened perspective or gone on to ponder at any length the importance of these sacramental occasions. One of the great Scottish historians, Henry Grey Graham, though he still thought these "pious saturnalia" had "passed away not too soon," did insist that all other aspects of religious life in eighteenth-century Scotland "sink into insignificance" when compared with these eucharistic solemnities—occasions that he was quite willing to acknowledge were of "transcendent importance" for the evangelicals. Nothing else in the calendar of religious events, Graham observed, aroused "the feelings of the people" more than did these summer and early fall gatherings for the celebration of the Lord's Supper. Despite his claims, made in 1899 in a book that attained the level of a minor classic in Scottish historiography, no one took up the gauntlet that Graham had seemed to lay down. Few would take these popular festivals seriously, and no one would bring them out into the thick of cultural history where they belong. The holy fair, the great religious festival of Presbyterian Scotland, would remain too often cloaked in condescension.[4]

A few church historians, usually within the evangelical tradition, have over the years come to the defense of these sacramental festivals. Esteeming these occasions as historic times of revival, they have highlighted the powerful spiritual responses that these events evoked. "No one can read the story of revivals in Scotland," Reverend W. J. Couper observed early in this century, "without noting how closely they are associated with sacramental occasions." Couper voiced a conviction that went back to nineteenth-century evangelical historians, such as Duncan MacFarlan, who in turn echoed earlier apologists. No matter what the critics said of these communions, MacFarlan concluded, "it is of itself an important fact, that most of the remarkable revivals which have occurred in Scotland have been more or less in connection with these [sacramental occasions]—have been eminently forwarded by them." Few scholars outside the fold of evangelical historians have borne this point in mind or explored this coincidence of sacrament and revival. Interest in Scottish revivalism has been limited, and interpretive insight into the most distinctive and important form of Scottish Presbyterian renewal, the sacramental season, has been even more sparing.[5]

In the United States, where so much has been made of revivalism, this evangelical festival—prominent in America throughout most of the eighteenth and early nineteenth centuries—has surprisingly not fared much better. Though bemusement at these "*gala day*[s]" or "Religious Fairs" has been less, scholarly attention has not been any greater. At times denominational historians, such as Mary McWhorter Tenney and Ernest Trice Thompson, have recognized the importance of the communion season in America and its substantial ties with revivalism. Other historians of American Protestantism have on occasion glimpsed in these communions a forerunner of the camp meetings, while students of Reformed worship have noticed the liturgical richness of these eucharistic celebrations. Most recently, Marilyn J. Westerkamp in her book *Triumph of the Laity* has taken note of these communions, particularly those of seventeenth-century Ulster, and commented briefly on their transplantation to the middle colonies. But these various recognitions, important though they are, have only begun the process of redescription and interpretation. For America, as for Scotland, these holy fairs or sacramental festivals have yet to have their history told with fullness.[6]

In attempting to bring fullness to this interpretation of these sacramental occasions, a variety of questions about revivalism have been posed and several different angles explored. In studying revivals, scholars have generally emphasized questions of causation and consequence—why evangelical awakenings occurred and what social, economic, and political consequences such movements had. This is true of the most far-ranging interpretation of American revivalism, William G. McLoughlin's *Revivals, Awakenings, and Reform*, as well as a number of more specific studies. Speculation on the causes of evangelical awakenings—for example, economic changes, political crises, frontier conditions, anxieties over affluence—has often eclipsed scrutiny of the events themselves. And the case is much the same when pondering the consequences of revivalism—for example, the legitimation of a free-labor economy or the forwarding of revolutionary principles: evangelical ritual and experience too easily become of secondary importance. Indeed, McLoughlin and others have expressly attempted to shift attention away from the parochialisms of "revivalists and revival meetings" to the broader cultural stresses and changes that produce such figures and events. Broad questions about cultural revitalization and epochal awakenings are thus seen to be the most fruitful lines of inquiry. This work, however, has taken a different tack. Striving for a fine-grained understanding of the revivals themselves, it has sought full engagement with the evangelicals and their gatherings, working out from there to the culture in which these events were interwoven.[7]

As part of this shift of emphasis, this work has sought to open up Scottish and American revivalism to "ethnographic history" and the theories of cultural performance and ritual that inform that history. Out of this "retrospective ethnography," as practiced by such diverse historians as Peter Burke, Robert Darnton, Natalie Zemon Davis, and Rhys Isaac, emerges a different set of questions from the traditional ones of causation and consequence: How did the revivals help the participants give shape to their world? What did they mean to those amid them? How were such festal occasions interrelated with community and the boundaries that defined it? How did specific rituals or cultural performances contribute to the formation of different social relationships, patterns of authority, and webs of meaning? How were various media—actions, objects, words, images, or music—employed in the rituals as symbols and forms of communication? Such interpretive questions make revivals the stuff of cultural history. This history encourages us to focus our attention on particular rituals and performances within a past culture and through interpretation of them to gain access to that distant world. The communion season is well-nigh ideal for such a pursuit. As a set of intricate rituals and as an embodiment of a complex symbolic universe, this lost evangelical festival is a fertile field for the retrospective ethnographer.[8]

To do this "history in the ethnographic grain"—to use Robert Darnton's phrase—requires a studied eclecticism, both in employing a wide variety of sources and in exploring a range of interpretive perspectives.

This has certainly been the case in attempting to tease out the diverse meanings of these holy fairs. For sources, not only have sermons, theological treatises, catechisms, and directories of worship been important, but also critical have been popular devotional manuals, spiritual biographies and autobiographies, prayers, meditations, psalms, diaries, letters, poems, revival narratives, church records, and travelers' accounts. Additionally, material evidences—for example, communion tokens, eucharistic vessels, contemporary sketches and paintings—have provided inlets into these sacramental occasions. An openness not only to diverse sources, but also to disparate disciplines has given the interpretation whatever fullness it possesses. The history of worship, theology, and spirituality has been brought into conjunction here with social history, anthropological approaches to ritual, histories of popular culture, and studies on ethnicity, gender, and material culture. The potential danger of such diversity is a mishmash of perspectives, but the possible benefit is a livelier conversation among historians in different areas and even among scholars in other disciplines, especially among those in religion, history, and anthropology. Certainly this potential benefit has been one of the larger aims of this study.[9]

Another ambition of this work, again inspired by ethnographic history, has been to make the study of revivalism less an examination of the exploits of great evangelists and more an exploration of the mental world of all the participants, women and men, saints and sinners, pastors and people. In attempting this, the study has tried to disclose continuities and discontinuities between elite and popular religion. It has sought to explore the dynamic, interactive relationship between ministers and congregants, between clerical expectations and lay experiences. These efforts to penetrate the mental world of pastors and people have not proceeded so much from a desire to fathom what some, with leanings toward structuralism, would call a collective *mentalité*. Instead the design of this study has been to appreciate not only what was common about the experiences of these evangelicals, what indicated that they shared the same ideas and beliefs with those around them, but also what set particular saints or sinners apart. This aim was captured by revivalist William Tennent, Jr., when he marvelled at the "beautiful Variety, and yet sweet Harmony" of the spiritual "Relations" recounted to him by evangelicals he visited in central New Jersey in the 1740s. To have pursued the "sweet Harmony" without the "beautiful Variety" would have meant losing sight of an essential feature of these sacramental solemnities—the variegated, finely textured fabric of experience at these events.[10]

This effort to get at these occasions not only at a prescriptive, official, or ministerial level, but also at a popular level has meant pursuing the experiences of a variety of laypeople, those of idle spectators as well as those of devout communicants. Clearly an attempt has been made to tell the stories of those saints who were transported to heaven or who were betrothed to the Bridegroom or who received visions of the suffering Christ through these rituals. But the stories of those who got drunk on these occasions and rarely, if ever, came near the communion table or the tent, except perhaps to scoff, have also been kept in mind. There are stories too of the indifferent, the distracted, the fearful, and the failing. And there are stories as well of change from communion to communion: how people's minds sometimes wandered when they were at the Lord's table or at other times were so focused that they fainted away or trembled or cried uncontrollably. In other words, the design in interpreting these festal communions has been to probe not only the collective and the corporate, but also the individual and the idiosyncratic, not only the devout, but also the diverted. The aim, in short, has been to disclose both commonality and divergence, never to let the one swallow up the other.

In the four chapters that follow, such ethnographic interpretations—of mental worlds and ritual actions—have been balanced by more traditional narrative and analysis. Chapter 1 gives a broad-ranging historical account of the development of the sacramental occasion in post-Reformation Scotland through perhaps its grandest display of power, the Great Revival in America. The first chapter provides an indication of the extent of this festival in the Old World and the New and offers a narrative framework for the interpretations of ritual in chapter 2 and of piety in chapter 3. These two middle chapters are where the ethnographic questions are most fully broached, where the rituals of the occasion are explored both for their religious and social significance and where the mental world of pastors and people is unfolded. The synchronic orientation of the central portion of the study—its analysis of ritual structures and patterns of piety that endured through time—is followed by a closing chapter that shifts back to a diachronic perspective, to full engagement with the question of change over time: Why did this sacramental festival decline in the first half of the nineteenth century? Why were enlightened critics of popular religion, such as Burns, amused or even outraged by these holy fairs? What happened to religion once such popular festivals had been reformed? In offering interpretations of both historical changes and persisting traditions, I have tried to gain both historical knowledge and anthropological understanding of these events. Chapters 1 and 4 are thus historical bookends that provide support for the ethnographic interpretations of chapters 2 and 3. Finally, an afterword, drawing out various strands from the study of these holy fairs, brings the work full circle.

Subordinating chronology to structure—even for half of a study—is something a historian does with reluctance. In organizing the work in this way I have taken heart from the early eighteenth-century editorial policies of George Wemyss. In compiling a collection of sermons that had been delivered at these occasions over the course of four decades, Wemyss arranged them, he said, "without regard to the order of time." Rather he organized the sermons around the structure of the sacramental season itself: fast day sermons, Saturday preparation sermons, Sabbath action sermons, speeches at the tables, thanksgiving and exhortation sermons. Though surely not a blueprint for most historical writing, Wemyss's editorial decision nonetheless suggests a point with which I had to grapple: The sacramental season is to be understood not only through "the order of time," but also through the enduring patterns of its ritual and piety. Upon such ordering principles—whether for good or ill—this study has been built.[11]

Whatever fullness the four chapters that follow may possess, no pretension to finality is harbored here. The caveats and doubts of past observers of these sacramental revivals are enough to keep us who depend on such sources humble in our own claims. "I can give you no suitable description of it," James McGready, a prominent leader of the Great Revival, confessed of his inabilities to depict one particularly powerful sacramental occasion, "neither could you form an adequate idea of it, unless you had been present." The admonition of another observer, a wide-eyed missionary in western Pennsylvania, was even more sobering: "The sacramental occasion was the most solemn scene I ever witnessed. I shall not attempt the description. . . . The solemnity, the impression, the evidence of the divine presence, were such as is not to be told. . . . [T]his work is in many respects mysterious and extraordinary. And after the most careful observation, long experience and inquiry, there are some things which cannot be understood. . . . [T]here are things to be seen, which are not to be described. After all that could be told or written, your conceptions would be far short of the reality." Such confessions of inadequacy pointedly remind us of our own limitations as we build on the "faint description[s]" of those who lamented their own "incapacit[ies] in seeing through the mysterious parts" of the communion season. Perhaps what we strive for finally is a rendering that evokes the mysteries of the sacramental occasion, not one that solves them.[12]

Despite prospects at once bleak and daunting, a worthy description, a detailed interpretation, a fitting evocation of this complex and powerful evangelical festival has been attempted. Making this description as stippled as the less than perfect sources permit has been a constant challenge. Such efforts to disclose other cultures in prose culminate finally—as Rhys Isaac assures and demonstrates—in careful presentation, in whatever art we can bring to history. Playing with the particular bits of a past culture, as the *mosaicisti* might have worked with fragments of glass, the historian tries gently to piece together a distant world. What follows is one mosaic—an attempt to recapture bit-by-bit, fragment-by-fragment the meanings of the holy fair, its history and its power.

CHAPTER 1

From Reformation to Revival: Sacramental Occasions in Scotland and America

"I HAVE the happiness to inform you, that the Lord is yet doing wonders in our country," the Reverend James McGready reported from Logan County, Kentucky, in 1803. "Our Sacramental occasions are days of the Son of Man indeed, and are usually marked with the visible footsteps of Jehovah's majesty and glory. . . . [A]t the Sacrament in the Ridge congregation, . . . [t]here were upwards of five hundred communicants; and at the tables, through the evening, and during the greater part of the night, the people of God were so filled with such extatic raptures of divine joy and comfort, that I could compare it to nothing else than the New Jerusalem coming down from heaven to earth."[1] Thus did one of America's leading revivalists describe the pentecostal outpourings during the Great Revival that affected a substantial part of the new republic between 1790 and 1810. At the center of his account stood the sacramental season, a four-day evangelical festival with a long history intertwined from the first with revival. McGready stood near the end of a tradition that had its inception in post-Reformation Scotland; he with many others was a guardian of a set of venerable rituals that had arisen and throve over the past two centuries. The American revivals that he and others like him led take much of their meaning from this long history. Influenced by the Catholic and Protestant divide of the sixteenth century and shaped further by the Episcopalian and Presbyterian strife of the next century, the sacramental occasions that would make McGready famous on the American frontier emerged out of a troubled past and only came to fruition in the evangelical awakenings of the eighteenth century. To this mottled history of the rise and flourishing of the sacramental season this chapter is devoted.

INNOVATIONS AND LEGACIES: THE AGE OF REFORM IN SCOTLAND

In April 1565, five years after the ascendancy of Protestantism in Scotland, a Catholic priest named James Carvet celebrated a Mass in Edinburgh about the time of Easter. Shortly after he had finished the rite, as he was trying to make a surreptitious departure from the town, he fell into the hands of a riled group of Protestants. They put all his priestly vestments back on him, tied him up with his eucharistic chalice in his hand, and "set him on high" in the center of town where eggs were rained upon him for about an hour. The next day the priest was subjected to similar abuse "for the space of three or four hours" before "some Papists . . . stopped [it] as far as they could." One no doubt exaggerated report indicated that in all ten thousand eggs were hurled Carvet's way; another noted sardonically that "the boys and others" in the town had "served him with his Easter eggs." Though the Protestants were of the opinion that Carvet for his offense had "deserved death," they had to rest content with this dramatic desecration. Carvet escaped with his life, but the Romish idolatry of the Mass, the reformers could rejoice, had been dealt another blow by "the Brethren."[2]

Carvet's treatment by the agitated Protestants was fraught with symbolic power. Eggs, at once symbols of the Catholic customs surrounding Easter as well as emblems of derision and detestation, were turned upon this cleric, his sacral garments, and his chalice—all three embodying for the offended Protestants the blasphemies of Rome. This decidedly violent, strangely creative mockery of James Carvet suggested in stark action the Protestant revulsion from Catholic forms of worship, particularly the Mass, from the Catholic calendar of holy days, notably Easter, and from Catholic clericalism, especially ecclesiastical vestments and the reservation of the cup for priests alone. John Knox, the furious trumpet of the Scottish Reformation, had said that "one Mass . . . was more to be feared than . . . ten thousand armed enemies"; it was, he thought, "the fountain and spring of all other evils that now abound in this Realm." This Protestant crowd in their scorn for James Carvet and his Catholic Mass acted to purge their land of such a danger.[3]

For James Carvet, as he was mercilessly pelted by eggs, the world must have looked out-of-joint, twisted, upside down. To celebrate a rite that had for centuries been at the center of Christendom he had been forced to risk his life and had ended up a besmirched, splattered spectacle. Not many years before in Scotland, he could have been assured that at Easter people would have flocked to his Mass to receive the consecrated Host. Now the Mass was outlawed; the whole notion of holy days such as Palm Sunday, Good Friday, and Easter was suspect; and the only crowd he collected was one that hardly came in reverence. Protestantism was changing the face of the Scottish church. James Carvet must have wondered what was going on in Scotland, where would such forces lead, would there be any of the old faith left.

These dramatic changes must have been all the more disorienting to the likes of Carvet since in Scotland they had come on rather suddenly. The Protestant movement had been somewhat slow in gaining momentum in Scotland and was without extensive support before the 1550s. From the

1520s efforts to curb the circulation of Lutheran works attested to growing fears of the spread of Protestant views, and earlier still the infrequent
auto-da-fé or more frequent admonition of an occasional heretic pointed
to the presence of heterodoxy, particularly Lollardry. But these were isolated instances of suppressed dissent; even after the field preaching of
George Wishart in the 1540s, the Protestant cause in Scotland was carried
on mainly through loosely knit conventicles. Though critics within the
Scottish church itself suggested that such abuses as pluralism, simony,
absenteeism, and undiscipline needed correction, little evidence before the
mid-1550s indicates that the old church was gravely imperiled by Protestantism. The seaport towns of Ayr in the west and Dundee in the east
had become beachheads of sorts for the Protestants, but even in such
places as these the popularity of the insurgents was mixed.[4]

The prospects of Scottish Protestantism soon improved, however. Under the passionate leadership of John Knox, who returned to Scotland
briefly in 1555–1556 and permanently in 1559 after sojourns in England
and on the Continent, the movement for reform was given new scope.
Political circumstance joined with deepening religious and intellectual
backing to propel Protestantism forward. French political domination
over Scotland, embodied in the regent Mary of Guise, had become increasingly burdensome to a number of Scottish nobles. Linking their political campaign with Knox's religious crusade, they were able with the
backing of Elizabeth, England's Protestant sovereign, to take Scotland
out from under Catholic France and to align it with Protestant England.
In the process Knox and his compatriots were transformed in the years
from 1555 to 1560 from defiant insurgents to the bold leaders of the Scottish church. Ushered into power on the wings of political and religious
change, Knox and his party issued their Reformed *Confession of Faith* in
1560.

The consolidation of this victory was no small challenge. The prevalence of Catholic recusancy into the 1580s and beyond kept the reformers
ever vigilant. Even when they obtained tacit conformity to Protestant beliefs and worship, the persistence of Catholic practices in many areas for
decades to come made evident that the Protestants did not have full hold
on the people. Equally divisive and problematic was disagreement among
the reformers themselves. By the early 1580s sharp contention over
church polity, embodied especially in the debates of arch-Presbyterian
Andrew Melville and Archbishop Patrick Adamson, foreshadowed lingering controversy. Though cooperation and compromise on issues of
church government were at times notable, struggle between advocates of
presbyterian forms and those defending episcopacy was evident and
would become more so. The movement for reform in Scotland with the
growing tensions within Protestantism and the ongoing confrontation

with Catholicism was thus characterized as much by troubling division as clear triumph.

For all the problems the new Church of Scotland faced it moved forward with many of its reforms with alacrity. It set up kirk sessions, composed of the minister and elders of a congregation, to oversee the social, moral, and spiritual discipline of the community. Through this local church court, the Reformed Kirk would make perhaps its most direct impact on the laity and its strongest bid for hegemony over the mores of the people. The church moved swiftly as well to install their own ministers in parishes throughout the land and with few exceptions, notably in the Highlands and Islands, succeeded in doing so by the end of the sixteenth century. Committed to reshaping the religious knowledge of the laity, the church instituted as well new standards of catechesis and religious education. Among its most sweeping changes would be in the area of worship. If the Protestants had their way, the whole devotional rhythm of the late medieval church would be transformed. The veneration of saints, five of the seven sacraments, prayers for the dead, devotions to the Virgin, relics, pilgrimages, festivals, monastic orders, and the reservation and adoration of the Host—to make only a partial list—would all be eliminated. Many of the patterns of Catholic spirituality, however, were not easily or simply displaced by Protestant forms. This conflict between the legacies of Catholic devotion and the innovations of Protestant worship is important for understanding the later emergence of the sacramental occasions.

As the experience of James Carvet suggested, much of the hostility between Catholics and Protestants was focused on the celebration of the eucharist. At no point did the Protestant leaders, such as Knox and George Hay, bristle more than at the thought of the Catholic Mass. The "stinking and filthy masse" epitomized for them "the darknesse of superstition" that had come to cloud the purity of apostolic Christianity; it was "damnable idolatrie," a profanation of the central rite of the Christian church. This revulsion involved both the theology and the ritual of the Mass. Doctrinally the Protestants condemned the Catholic idea of the Mass as a reenactment of Christ's sacrifice, for they viewed this as a "derogation to the sufficiency of his only sacrifice." They were equally, if not more offended by the Catholic notion of transubstantiation which they saw as illogical and damnable, as a carnal misinterpretation of the true mode of Christ's presence in the sacrament. At the same time the Scots were careful to guard the elements of bread and wine from being treated as "naked and bare signs." While rejecting Catholic transubstantiation as well as Lutheran consubstantiation, they averred with Calvin that Christ's presence, mediated through the Holy Spirit, was real. The Lord was manifest in the true, divinely instituted performance of "that mystical action." At the table the faithful fed upon Christ's body and blood, were made one with him, "flesh of his flesh, and bone of his bones." The Scottish reformers wanted to distance themselves from transubstantiation without compromising the awesome power of the eucharist. Like Protestants everywhere, they were contemptuous of Catholic ideas of transubstantiation and sacrifice, but they maintained all along a distinctive appreciation of the sacramental presence and mystery.[5]

If doctrinal differences fueled conflict between Protestants and Catholics, debates over ritual observances were even more volatile. The Scottish reformers strove to rework the essential actions, language, and setting of the Catholic Mass. They dedicated themselves to eliminating the elaborate ceremonies of the Mass and to re-creating Christ's Last Supper as they envisioned the Evangelists and Paul having received it. To this end, they changed the focus of the rite from a sacrificial altar to a communion table and the standard posture at the reception of the elements from kneeling to sitting. They argued, too, that Christ had not distributed the bread and wine to each of the disciples individually, but that the apostles had divided the elements among themselves. This example, the Scottish reformers believed, ruled out priestly distribution to each of the communicants; instead those seated at the table were to handle the sacred elements themselves, passing the bread and wine from one to another. They also insisted that Christ had intended both the consecrated bread and wine to be shared in by all communicants, that the Catholics in allowing the laity the Host alone were "stealing from the people . . . the blessed cup." Differences over the cup were matched by differences over the element of bread; for the reformers moved away from discrete, unleavened hosts, substituting instead shared, leavened loaves. They eliminated as well altar screens and rails that separated the priests from the laity and replaced them with "fences"—usually made out of words, but sometimes out of wooden palings—that separated the faithful as a whole from the ungodly. In such changes, Reformed notions of commensality, of the communion as collective meal, supplanted Catholic ideas of adoration and priestly sacrifice.[6]

In addition to transforming eucharistic ritual, the Scottish reformers sought to restructure the Catholic calendar in which the Mass fit. Believing that Christ had not instituted special periods for lay reception of this feast, they sought to make lay participation in it a regular, or at least semiregular, part of Christian worship. Though their plans to insure the frequency of the Lord's Supper were riddled with difficulties from the first, their larger aim of separating lay reception of the eucharist from Catholic holy days, principally Easter, was more successful.[7] For the reformers, holy days—such as Pasch, Yule, or Good Friday—were superstitious, unwarranted by Scripture, and thus best eliminated. This was clearest in Protestant disdain for Catholic festivals. They spurned the "fond feastes" that "the Papists have invented" as debased superstitions, as debauched, idolatrous revelries. Processions with the Host in particular, such as those during the feast of Corpus Christi, were "a verie masse of all heresie and error; As the adoration of that bread, the bearing about and closing up of it, as it were in a prisone, and then to convoye it to the feilds, to take the aire." For the Protestants such processions and festivals suggested a superstitious, misplaced veneration of the blessed sacrament. They recoiled at the thought of Catholic adoration of the Host, "how it was gazed upon, kneeled unto, borne in procession, and finally worshipped and honoured as Christ Jesus himselfe." They would eliminate such grand occasions—and the devotional objects that went with them such as pyxes, monstrances, and reliquaries—and return to a simpler, more frequent celebration of the Lord's Supper.[8]

The Scottish reformers in recasting Christian worship—and eucharistic practice in particular—faced a number of obstacles, not the least of which was the fact that many Scots were still enamored with much of the old faith. The Protestants, at least the more stringent who shared in Knox's Genevan rigor, had a vision of reform that outran what most people were prepared for. In 1587 one Protestant report found that all over the country Catholic practices were persisting, despite systematic Protestant opposition. At Dumfries it was reported that "holie dayes" were kept "by plaine commandment" as well as "all superstitions, ryotousnesse, at Yuile and Pasche, &c." At Stirling it was found that "the Sabbath there is everie where abused" and that "superstitious ceremoneis, pilgrimages to Christ's Well, fasting, festives, bone-fires, girdles, carralls, and suche like" prevailed in abundance. At Dumbarton it was feared that the Catholic laird there had "stollin away the heart of the commouns, by banketting at Yuile, continuing three dayes, enduring which tyme all Papistical ceremonies were used." Even in Ayrshire, a Protestant stronghold and one of the centers for the radical Presbyterian movement in the next century, Catholic practices were still in evidence. In 1581 the Scottish Parliament issued a general lament that "the dregges of idolatrie yitt remaine in diverse parts of the realme, by using of pilgrimages to some chappells, wels, croces, and suche other monuments of idolatrie, as also, by observing of the festivall dayes of sancts, sometimes named patrons, in setting furth of bone fires, singing of carrells, running about kirks at certane seasons of the yeere, and observing of suche other superstitious and Papisticall rites." Protestant visions of transformed devotion collided with many people's obvious fondness for the old ways.[9]

For all the continued popularity of many Catholic forms of devotion and for all the Protestant complaints about this, the reformers were clearly advancing their faith year by year. Not only were their teachings becoming more entrenched, but also their coercive power was becoming more effective. In 1577 at Perth, for example, several inhabitants were bold enough to celebrate the pageant of Corpus Christi, bearing the consecrated Host through the town and acting out plays that went along with the procession—all this "to the great slander of the Church of God and dishonour of this haill town." The kirk session moved quickly to discipline these "Corpus Christi players" and forced confessions from as many as they could "never to meddle with such things again" lest they face more severe censure. After successfully suppressing the feast of Corpus Christi, the church officers went after another festival, a local one known as St. Obert's Eve. Conducted on the tenth of December, this elaborate folk drama was replete with dancing, drumming, piping, and costumes. By 1588 St. Obert's Eve was reportedly a thing of the past. Though the session continued to have trouble with Yule day celebrations, it had managed by 1600 to chasten the most visible, dramatic Catholic festivals and holy days. The situation at Perth is a good index for the situation throughout most of Scotland at 1600. After a little more than a generation of reform the Protestants had largely succeeded in levelling the religious rhythm of late medieval Catholicism.[10]

By 1600 the age of reform in Scotland had transformed the Catholic holy year into a Reformed one in which there were few, if any, high days aside from the weekly observance of the Sabbath. The Protestant movement had resulted, as Charles Phythian-Adams has observed in his study of the communal year at Coventry, in the "obliteration of the established rhythm of life itself." The sacral and festal events that had marked this rhythm either went uncelebrated, like the feast of Corpus Christi, or at minimum, as was the case with Yule, had been severely undermined. Religious festivals and processions, critical for the maintenance of community under the old order, had all but disappeared. Though Catholic traditions persisted in places and some episcopal moderation on the issue of holy days was evident at times, the Reformed program proved durable. In Scotland, as in Coventry, the processions and pageants of the old way were at an end.[11]

What the Reformed Church offered in the place of the old calendar and the traditional festivals was a spiritual life of sustained discipline and devotion. One Knoxian Protestant, for example, contrasted the corrupt observance of "festivall and superstitious dayes" with the Reformed ideal of keeping "perpetuall and spiritual festivities with Christ and his saints."[12] Day-in, day-out, Sabbath after Sabbath, the Reformed saints were to strive after joyful, harmonious communion with their God and their fellow Christians. Demanding great steadfastness and perseverance, this ideal, as grand as it was, often proved unrealistic. It displayed, as Steven Ozment has suggested, a "naïve expectation that the majority of people were capable of radical religious enlightenment and moral transformation," a vision that cut against the Reformed conviction of the incorrigible depravity of humankind.[13] The hope for a community of saints who year-round were diligent, self-controlled, sober, prayerful, and devout within their families and outside of them ran up against an older way of organizing devotional life around festal public events. In the traditional society of early modern Europe people could live their lives "in remembrance of one festival and in expectation of the next."[14] The reformers sought to end this cycle, to make life a perpetual festivity with Christ.

That the reformers found realizing their ideal hard-going was clear enough. Most simply pressed on and refused to compromise with the old way, having no inclination to ask whether there was any room for the tradition of popular religious festivals in the Reformed faith. The result, as John Bossy has recently remarked, was that Protestant communities throughout Europe largely failed "to create a symbol of social unity as powerful as the Host, or a celebration of togetherness as popular as the feast of Corpus Christi." The reformers had dismantled the rituals of community of the medieval church without creating replacements that could rival such great corporate events as the community-wide participation in the Easter season or the full, intricate processions of Corpus Christi. With the dissolution of such "mysteriously integrative" festivals and spectacles, religion became less interwoven with the public realm. As sacramental festivity diminished, family devotions grew in importance; religion became more of a domestic affair than it had been before, more private in its emphases, less explicitly communal. Thus the Reformed movement with its moral rigor and disciplined Sabbatarianism chastened not only those aspects of the medieval church that many agreed needed renewed discipline, but also several parts of it that had offered popular devotional and communal events. Reformed religion, distancing itself from such popular festivals and public displays of piety, was more privatized than its older counterpart had been.[15]

By the early seventeenth century there were discernible signs that a growing group of fervent Presbyterians was ready to counter these oft-noted trends within the Reformed faith. These evangelicals seemed prepared to step into the breach created by the elimination of the high days of medieval Catholicism and offer in their stead a great public event centered on the celebration of the Reformed Lord's Supper. These Presbyterians, of course, never would have admitted that in creating a sacramental festival they owed anything to Catholic tradition. They defended the Knoxian liturgical and theological changes down-the-line as gospel truths and spurned Catholic belief and ritual as hopelessly tainted. They had absolutely no truck with the traditional Catholic festivals and were extremely contemptuous of Catholic vestiges still evident among the practices of their Episcopal opponents. If anything, these Presbyterians made the early Reformed agenda appear compromising. Yet paradoxically these evangelical Presbyterians, in originating the sacramental occasion, were successful as much because of Catholic legacies as Protestant innovations. The rise of festal communions early in the next century suggested that the old rhythm that went along with the popular festivals of late medieval Catholicism was not as easily eradicated as the early reformers had hoped.

The Reformed Scots had set out in their eucharistic theology and ritual to re-create a purely biblical and apostolic feast without any dregs from Catholicism. Yet the reality from the first clearly fell short of such wholesale transformation. If discontinuities were legion, continuities were also evident, many of which were conducive to the reemergence of sacramental festivity. For example, the Scottish Protestants, like the Catholics before them, continued to see the eucharist as the most solemn and august act of Christian worship. Though the two defined the nature of Christ's presence differently, both remained steadfast in the belief that Christ was present in the eucharist—a presence that was real, powerful, overwhelming. Seeking to allay fears of unworthiness and to prevent the physical and spiritual dangers associated with an unworthy approach, both prepared for this extraordinary event through penitential devotions such as fasting, prayer, and meditation. The Catholic pattern of fasting followed by feasting would be long preserved in the Presbyterian tradition. The Protestants, again following their Catholic forebears, covered the eucharistic elements and the place of celebration with fine cloth to suggest the solemnity of the event. Also both Catholics and Protestants focused on Christ's redemptive sufferings and death, on re-presenting them in ritual and in meditation. Indeed, the devotionals of a sixteenth-century Scottish Catholic, Alexander Barclay, and those of a seventeenth-century Scottish Presbyterian, Daniel Campbell, were consonant—at times almost identical—in their dramatic evocation of Christ's sufferings. The similarity of the meditative images of Barclay and Campbell bespoke the Protestant inheritance of a devotional tradition focused on the Passion. The sufferings of Christ, envisioned in lurid detail in meditative reflection, were long at the center of both Catholic and Protestant spirituality. In various ways, Catholic legacies lingered amid Protestant innovations.[16]

With their Catholic enemies the evangelical Presbyterians ended up sharing a great deal. This became altogether clear in their rejuvenation and perpetuation of sacramental festivity. The entrenched Catholic assumption that the sacrament warranted, as the Council of Trent put it, "a special festive solemnity," would long remain evident in popular Presbyterian practice. As with Easter and Corpus Christi, the Presbyterian sacramental occasion was to attract great crowds and to evoke great public displays of piety. The sixteenth-century reformers had lamented "how superstitiously the people runne to that action at Pasche." In the next century critics would bemoan the multitudes—"indigested, disorderly, confused, and mixt Convocations"—that ran after Presbyterian sacraments. These evangelicals were accused, as their Catholic opponents before them, of indulging popular superstitions about the power of the sacrament and encouraging a wanton mixture of piety and sociability. On another point, those who had blasted the Catholics had railed against the consecration of certain days and seasons. But by the end of the seventeenth century this attack had turned on the Presbyterians, for they had virtually transformed summer and early fall into one long sacramental season in which the communions were openly hailed as the high days of the year. The early reformers had criticized the Catholics for turning the Host into a spectacle, an object of veneration because of its infrequent distribution to the laity and because of its awe-inspiring place in the procession of Corpus Christi. In turn the Presbyterians found themselves holding annual communions as spectacular in many ways as those eucharistic festivals held by the Catholics before them. "What would the Ancient *Lights* and *Guides* of the Christian Church . . . say, if they saw such *promiscuous Routs* assembled, and mostly, for no other end, than making a *Spectacle* of such a *Venerable Mystery*?" one Episcopalian critic of the Presbyterians queried in the 1690s. "Is not such unaccountable *Parade* much liker to the *Popish Processions*, than the *Devout Performances* of the *purer times* of *Genuine Christianity*?" In an ironic twist the evangelical Presbyterians, the most Puritan group in Scotland, wound up recovering much of the eucharistic festivity of late medieval Catholicism in their own sacramental occasions.[17]

By the close of the eighteenth century it was well-nigh accepted wisdom—not only among enlightened opposers of revivalism, but also among many of the evangelicals themselves—that the Presbyterians had created a festival that paralleled older Catholic practices. "The annual celebration of the *Sacrament of the Lord's Supper*, in the rural parishes of Scotland," a biographer of Robert Burns observed matter-of-factly in 1797, "has much in it of those old *Popish* festivals, in which superstition, traffic, and amusement, used to be strangely intermingled." Another eighteenth-century critic noted that "in Scotland [people] run from kirk to kirk, as it were, after the host, and flock to see a sacrament, as those to share in the procession." Such observers, though clearly making such points for purely polemical purposes, nonetheless suggested a larger truth: the Presbyterian communion occasions in many ways paralleled the eucharistic traditions of late medieval Catholicism. Scottish revivalism, as it would emerge in the early seventeenth century, had as its most immediate cultural parallel the sacramental festivals and holy days that the early reformers had taken great pains to dismantle. These evangelical

Presbyterians thus would build their success on a tradition of popular festivity that they repudiated only to rehabilitate.[18]

The age of reform provided the ferment out of which the sacramental occasion would emerge in the early seventeenth century. The Scottish Protestants had established a distinctive form for celebrating the Lord's Supper—a set of Reformed rituals that provided the central actions for the later communion seasons. At the same time the reformers were effectively countering the traditional Catholic holy days and holidays that had given shape to much of popular piety. The more successful the reformers were in suppressing such Catholic "superstitions" the greater the danger that they would create a gap between their own spiritual demands and what most people were interested in performing. Into this gap between Reformed expectations and popular desires entered a Presbyterian solution. Evangelical preachers and their people would join together to create a distinctive Reformed festival.

PRESBYTERIAN AWAKENING: THE RISE OF A POPULAR FESTIVAL

Between 1625 and 1630 John Livingston, a young Presbyterian preacher who because of his zealous opposition to episcopacy had never been allowed to hold a parish, itinerated his way around much of southwest Scotland. In 1630 one of his stops was at the kirk of Shotts for the celebration of a "solemn Communion." There he joined with a handful of the most popular ministers the Presbyterians could boast for a series of meetings that reportedly went on "almost day and night, for four or five days" together. These highly charged meetings found culmination on Monday in an extraordinary "down-pouring of the SPIRIT." On that Monday, outdoors in "the Church-yeard," Livingston preached a sermon he always considered the most powerful he ever delivered. As he exhorted the "great multitude . . . there convened" for two-and-a-half hours in "a soft shouer of rain," his words had "a *strange unusual* MOTION on the hearers"; it was even said that many were so overwhelmed by his performance that they fainted away and laid upon the ground "as if they had been dead." One chronicler concluded that "near 500 had at that time a discernible *change* wrought on them, of whom most proved lively Christians afterward: it was the sowing of a seed through *Clidesdeal*, so as many of the most eminent Christians in that country, could date either their *conversion*, or some remarkable *confirmation* in their case, from *that day*." This "solemn Communion at the Kirk of the *Shots*" capped a decade of Presbyterian revivification in Scotland. More than any other event, the impressive revival at Shotts indicated that the sacramental occasion had come into its own and was helping foment a Presbyterian awakening.[19]

Legendary in evangelical annals ever afterward, the Shotts sacrament was regularly pointed to by later revivalists as one of the great heralds of the eighteenth-century evangelical movement. Some historians have been misled by the primacy accorded this revival in evangelical histories into thinking that it somehow marked the beginning of the extended, effervescent sacramental occasions, that before Livingston's success at Shotts these events were basically unknown. This revival and Livingston's singularly powerful sermon are often credited with originating many aspects of the communion season, particularly the Monday thanksgiving service. Some have gone as far as to see this occasion as an aberration in Scottish eucharistic practice essentially (and they would add thankfully) without parallel again until the 1650s. Such perceptions, however, are ill-founded and often are indicative more of a liturgical bias against these lengthy and large communions than a close look at the sources. Shotts was indeed a high point in an extensive Presbyterian awakening, but the rituals performed there were not spontaneous creations of the moment. With roots in the growing Presbyterian and Episcopalian struggles of post-Reformation Scotland, sacramental occasions burgeoned in the 1620s into great evangelistic events. In a climate of marked religious and political unrest, communions among the most fervent Presbyterians were transformed from parochial events into massive evangelical gatherings.[20]

The thronged communions of the radical Presbyterians in the 1620s and 1630s arose out of a larger context of Presbyterian resistance to episcopacy. Committed to reconstructing episcopal power and authority in Scotland, King James VI waged a sustained campaign, evident as early as the 1580s, against Presbyterian polity and worship. Erastian in outlook, the king particularly wanted to curb the most ardent Presbyterians whom he rightly perceived as enemies to royal and episcopal authority within the church. After becoming king of England in 1603 James became all the more wary of Puritan influences and sought to bring the churches of his two kingdoms more in line with one another, mostly at the expense of Scottish Presbyterianism.[21] In postures of defense and opposition, the Presbyterians would challenge the king's agenda to anglicize the Scottish church. From as early as the 1590s, Presbyterian resistance found partial expression in popular religious gatherings that were heralds of the later revivals and sacramental occasions.

In the face of persecution in the decades preceding the full-fledged awakening of the 1620s, a handful of the most zealous Reformed ministers began to enhance the popular pull of Presbyterianism, its Word and sacraments. One of the earliest and most renowned of these ministers was Robert Bruce, whose venerable presence at Shotts contributed substantially to that meeting's success. Bruce, who because of his devoted Presbyterianism and consequent political indiscretions had fallen out of the good graces of James VI, was a highly followed preacher. Throughout his career that spanned the years 1587 to 1631—whether in Edinburgh, Inverness, or the southwest—Bruce's preaching was exceedingly popular. "He made alwayes ane earthquake upon his hearers," the seventeenth-century historian James Kirkton commented, "and rarely preached but to a weeping auditory." John Livingston, one of his closest disciples, was convinced that "never Man spake with greater power since the Apostles Days." Famed for his conversionist preaching, Bruce was also a sacramentalist. His first celebration of the communion in Edinburgh in 1588 had reportedly resulted in "elevated affections among the people, as had not been seen in that place before"; indeed, one subsequent chronicler, Robert Wodrow, would claim that it had been accompanied by an "extraordinary effusion of the Spirit." Two years after this communion, in 1590, Bruce published his *Sermons upon the Sacrament of the Lords Supper* which became a standard for eucharistic expression among the Scottish Presbyterians. Dedicated to both the Word and the sacraments, to leading people "to Christ be the ear" as well as "be the eie," Bruce represented an early synthesis of conversionist preaching and fervent eucharistic piety.[22]

As a powerful preacher, Bruce built a considerable following of ardent Presbyterians alienated from the episcopal designs of James VI. Displaced from St. Giles in Edinburgh on account of his suspect loyalty to the crown, Bruce often found himself under royal confinement as he was in Inverness from 1605 to 1609 and at other times thereafter. When not confined, Bruce's ministry was often peripatetic and frankly subversive. In 1605 he came under the king's wrath not only for "his hearty zeal" against prelacy, but also for "his entertaining a frequent resort of the ministry and people," both to the detriment of religious peace and unity. In 1613, when at large in Kinnaird, Bruce was criticized for "going from place to place" in his ministry and was noted for preaching "at communions." All along he looked threatening to bishops and king because of the "multitudes [that] came from all corners to hear him." In 1622, exasperated anew with Bruce's antiepiscopal stringency and his popular preaching, the king declared that he would no longer tolerate "Popish pilgrimages" among the people to hear Bruce; James once again confined the preacher to Inverness. Bruce's participation in the meetings at Shotts in 1630 thus capped a long career of Presbyterian advocacy and evangelical fervency. Indicative of his sustained popularity, when he died the next year in 1631, his body was "accompanied to the grave with four or five thousand persons" in attendance. The great Presbyterian revivalists of the 1620s and 1630s—David Dickson, John Livingston, and Robert Blair—would all look to Bruce as a spiritual father.[23]

If Bruce was the most important figure preparing the way for the awakening of the 1620s, John Welsh, son-in-law of John Knox, was not far behind. Another Presbyterian whose zeal got him into trouble with the king, Welsh was actually banished to France in 1606 and was never able to return to Scotland. But his decade-and-a-half ministry in the southwest before his expulsion was widely famed for its evangelistic successes. Said to have reaped "a harvest of converts" in Kirkcudbright by the early 1590s, Welsh then moved on to Ayr where, according to the seventeenth-century historian James Kirkton, "his fruitfulness in converting souls . . . will be found unparalleled in Scotland." Indeed, David Dickson, a primary leader of the revivals and communions of the 1620s, apparently deprecated his own successes in light of Welsh's accomplishments. Robert Wodrow reported that Dickson was wont to observe that "the vintage" in his own parish at Irvine "was not equal to the gleanings, and not once to be compared to the harvest at Ayr, in Mr John Welch's time, when indeed the gospel had wonderful success, in conviction, conversion, and confirmation." The heralded evangelistic efforts of Bruce and Welsh evidently had few equals before the 1620s. Pastors such as Robert Rollock, John Davidson, and William Livingston also made substantial contributions to the Presbyterian cause and received a fair amount of attention. In particular Rollock, who in 1616 published a collection of lectures on Christ's Passion, gained the encomium of John Livingston who grouped him with Bruce, Welsh, and Dickson as the preachers most profoundly influencing him. All the same, Bruce and Welsh were seen as the leading figures. Though in a sizable company of fervent Presbyterian preachers, they most clearly portended things to come.[24]

How much the early evangelistic activities of Bruce, Welsh, and other preachers contributed to the development of the sacramental occasion is difficult to determine. Certainly many features of the later communions were simply standard parts of the Reformed tradition. Such things as preparatory services, sitting to receive the elements, self-examination, careful fencing of the tables, and communion tokens were all evident in one form or another from the early years of the Reformation in Scotland. Bruce, Welsh, and their partners hardly had a definitive influence on these aspects of Presbyterian practice. What separated the festal communions from earlier sacraments were such characteristics as outdoor preaching, great concourses of people from an extensive region, long vigils of prayer, powerful experiences of conversion and confirmation, a number of popular ministers cooperating for extended services over three days or more, a seasonal focus on summer, and unusually large numbers of communicants at successive tables. The task of establishing whether the evangelistic gatherings of Bruce, Welsh, and company helped forge any of these specific attributes remains obstructed by lack of evidence, but at minimum their activities laid a foundation for the popular sacramental gatherings that were to come. Their meetings and preaching set a precedent for ministers and people gathering from over a wide area, often in the face of royal opposition, for intensive religious fellowship. Their evangelistic activities from the 1590s on were prologue to the full-blown awakening of the 1620s and 1630s.[25]

Still the connection between the earlier meetings and the later communions may have been more direct than vague precursor. One revealing shard of evidence to this effect comes in John Livingston's autobiography. In commenting on his childhood over the years 1603 to 1613, he observed: "I had the advantage of the Acquaintance and Example of many gracious Christians, who used to resort to my Father's House, especially at Communion-occasions: such as Mr. *Robert Bruce*, and several other godly Ministers." Livingston made no distinction between these "Communion-occasions" and the ones that came a decade or so later. The nomenclature, the fact that Bruce and other ministers came to assist at these events, and the indication that many saints gathered at them suggest sacramental occasions that were kin of sorts to Shotts. The famed zeal of John's father, pastor William Livingston, adds to this surmise. Long despised by royal and episcopal forces as "a fyrebrand of discorde and dissensioun," the elder Livingston was restrained in 1607 from his "too muche wandering and travelling abroade" in his ministry. Other bits of evidence—such as Bruce's assistance at various communions before 1620 and John Livingston's description of his overwhelming religious experience at the Lord's table about 1615—suggest that the powerful sacramental occasions of the 1620s and 1630s were not wholly new. These sacramental events may have been taking initial shape in the south and west of Scotland in such places as Kirkcudbright, Ayr, Irvine, Lanark, and Kilsyth from the 1590s, under the likes of Bruce, Welsh, and William Livingston. At minimum it seems unwise to continue to view these communion occasions as an outright invention of the radical Presbyterians of the 1620s and 1630s. Though historians have long assumed this—usually to criticize these events as departures from the Reformed tradition—the creation of such festal occasions was clearly not ex nihilo. The evangelicals of the 1620s were beholden to a long tradition of sacramental festivity as well as more recent developments in Presbyterian evangelism and worship that arose out of growing conflict with an Erastian, anglicizing monarch.[26]

Before the full-fledged awakening of the 1620s the Presbyterian cause in Scotland appeared to be in trouble. Between 1605 and 1607 James dealt a serious blow to the most ardent Presbyterians by exiling six of their leaders, including John Welsh, and imprisoning their foremost theorist and apologist, Andrew Melville, in the Tower of London before banishing him for good to the Continent in 1611. In 1610 the king reestablished full episcopal authority within the Church of Scotland and created as well the Courts of High Commission to discipline religious malcontents, especially recalcitrant Presbyterian ministers. In 1614 James appointed the Lord's Supper to be celebrated at Easter; in 1615 he made this observance obligatory "in all tymes comming."[27] In 1618 he offered the substance of his liturgical reforms for Scotland in the Five Articles of Perth. These required receiving the Lord's Supper kneeling, permitted the private dispensing of the eucharist to the infirm, accepted private baptisms, enjoined catechetical instruction of the young which would be capped by confirmation by a bishop, and reinstituted a number of holy days—such as Good Friday, Pentecost, and Christmas—even as "the superstitious observation of Festivall dayes by the Papists" was warned against. Forced to acquiesce to the king's bidding, the General Assembly accepted the articles in 1618; ratification by Parliament followed three years later. Passage of the Articles of Perth, despite considerable opposition, made it look as if the king and his Episcopal party were capable of riding rough-shod over their Presbyterian adversaries.[28]

What the prelatical party had not foreseen was the lasting indignation that these articles would arouse. Resentment centered above all on the first article, the injunction to kneel when receiving the eucharist. The arch-Presbyterian David Calderwood, venting tract after tract, led the opposition. Repulsed by kneeling, Calderwood saw it in good Puritan fashion as "conformitie with the Papists in a ceremony, which hath been abused by them to the vilest idolatry that ever was in the world, the worship of the bready God." Kneeling and the consequent reception of the elements "out of the ministers hand," both proscribed from the first by the Scottish reformers, would again make the Lord's Supper "an Idoll feast." Contrasting "the Antichrists gesture of kneeling" with "Christs gesture of sitting," Calderwood saw this decretal as undermining the whole edifice of the Scottish Reformation. The Reformed eucharistic rituals—as developed by Knox, his compeers, and his successors—were of divine, scriptural foundation. Abandonment of them and return to the vitiated practices of Rome and Canterbury would leave the Scots prey to God's wrath, to "darkness . . . inundation . . . hunger and cold . . . sickness and death."[29]

The outrage of Calderwood and his fellow Presbyterian ministers was matched by popular displeasure. Though in some areas the articles were calmly accepted, notably in the northeast, in others, especially around Edinburgh and in the southwest, public opposition ran high. The celebration of the Lord's Supper was repeatedly turned into an occasion of open dissent. From 1618 on people "withdrew themselves in great numbers" from several kirks whose ministers had accepted the articles and "ran to seek the communion from other ministers they knew to be refractory." These "mutinous people," encouraged by their dissenting ministers, "travelled abroad to seeke the Communion where it was ministred in puritie." In Edinburgh in 1619 the people reportedly "went out at the ports in hundreths and thousands, to the nixt adjacent kirks" where they could find ministers who would celebrate the Lord's Supper in the Reformed way. Similarly, in the same year at Glasgow John Livingston and a group of his student friends publicly challenged the bishop and refused to kneel at the sacrament; they resorted instead two or three weeks after their protest to a Presbyterian communion at Govan. Popular antipathy to the injunction to kneel was epitomized in the woman who told her minister in 1621, "I will either receive it sitting, or not at all."[30]

The Articles of Perth had obviously introduced "great confusion and disorder" into several parishes. Those kirks under Episcopal guidance often found themselves plagued by recalcitrant Presbyterians or even deserted by them. In such congregations the communions were often "cold and graceless," hampered by a "confusion of gestures," with some communicants kneeling, some sitting, and some refusing to come at all in order to avoid being "accessorie to the sinne of the kneeler." The first article effectively made the Lord's Supper a rallying point for Presbyterian dissent. Careful preservation of Reformed eucharistic ritual, as "delivered . . . by the Fathers" of the Scottish Reformation, became a banner of the Presbyterian movement of the 1620s. Popular resistance to altering the sacred rite, to substituting kneeling for sitting, gave the embattled Presbyterian party a tremendous boost. Having made the Lord's Supper a vehicle of Presbyterian protest and solidarity, the Five Articles of Perth helped prepare the way for a Presbyterian awakening that not surprisingly would receive much of its energy from sacramental occasions.[31]

Adversity was a blessing for these Scottish Puritans; James' efforts "to establish the English ceremonies in worship" had clearly backfired. In 1621 David Dickson, when he heard of Parliament's ratification of the Five Articles, was "made bold to prophesie" the imminence of a Presbyterian awakening. "From that discouraging day and foreward," he reportedly surmised, "the work of the gospel should both prosper and flourish in Scotland, notwithstanding all the laws made to the prejudice of it." Though by 1621 it took little of the Puritan spirit of discerning to make such a prediction, Dickson's premonition was accurate. Soon thereafter, largely under his leadership, "that wonderful exercise of conscience amongst the people in Stewarton paroch, and divers other places" broke out. This revival, typically dated as beginning "about the year 1625," was actually already in evidence by 1622. Robert Blair, a leading evangelical preacher, reported revivalistic successes at Stewarton in the year preceding his departure for Ulster in 1623. "The Lord had a great work in converting many," he reported. "Numbers of them were at first under great terrors and deep exercise of conscience, and thereafter attained to sweet peace and strong consolation." The awakening continued to grow "for some YEARS continuance; yea, like a spreading moor-burn, the power of *Godliness* did advance from one place to another." From 1622 into the 1630s, one portion of the southwest or another was aflame with revival.[32]

Reports on these revivals rarely descend to particulars, preferring grandiose, sweeping phrases about the great outpourings of the Spirit to gritty details about what pastors and people were doing. That communion occasions were an important part of the awakening emerges clearly enough, however. David Dickson's sacraments at Irvine, for example, were regularly thronged, so much so that an "Irvine sacrament crowd" reportedly became a commonplace. "People, under exercise and soul concern, came from every place about Irvine," Robert Wodrow wrote of Dickson's parish, "and attended upon his sermons; and the most eminent and serious Christians, from all corners of the Church, came and joined with him at his communions, which were indeed times of refreshing from the presence of the Lord." Dickson, as did his cohort Samuel Rutherford, also left a number of sacramental sermons that attest to the prevalence and importance of these events by the early 1630s. Their sermons, sounding themes that became familiar parts of these events, attested to the growing significance of these communions as evangelistic occasions. The sermons of Rutherford and Dickson—as well as the *Letters* of the former—testified to the emergence of awesome, powerful sacramental assemblies.[33]

Still more concrete testimony about the revivals of the 1620s is available from John Livingston, who began his ministry in 1625. In mid-1626 he noted in his autobiography that on a Monday at a sacramental occasion he had discovered for the first time the power of extemporaneous preaching. Until then he had written out his sermons "word by word"; after that evangelistic success he "never wrote all at length but only Notes." Also in 1626 Livingston reported that he "Preached at a Communion in *Borgue*, where were many good people that came out of Kirkcudbright." From 1626 to 1630 Livingston's itinerant ministry centered on these sacramental occasions. "Most parts of these Summers," he attested, "I was travelling from Place to Place, according as I got invitations to Preach, and especially at Communions in *Lanerk, Irvin, New-milns, Kinniel, Culross, Larbour,* and the *Shots,* and several other places." Livingston's autobiography, more than any other source, reveals the centrality of sacramental occasions in the awakening of the 1620s and 1630s. Outdoor extemporized preaching, extended services from at least Saturday through Monday, great crowds, multiple ministers, lengthy prayer meetings, numerous conversions, and blissful confirmations of salvation were all in evidence. Though the forms were still evolving—a set day for a public fast preceding the communion, for example, was yet to be formalized—most of the rituals were in place. The awakening of the 1620s in the southwest set the initial pattern for a revivalistic form that would overspread most of Scotland by the early eighteenth century. The coincidence of communion and evangelical renewal had been established.[34]

Even as the movement swelled in the southwest, exiled and immigrant Scots in Ulster were fomenting a Presbyterian revival there. From the early seventeenth century James I had sought to strengthen England's hold on Ireland by planting English and Scottish settlers in the north of Ireland. By the 1620s the Scots dominated a number of counties, particularly those on the east coast of Ulster, such as Antrim and Down, which were readily accessible from the ports in the southwest of Scotland. The early Scottish colonists had little professed religious mission in Ulster. The majority of them were there in hopes of finding better land and "better accommodations." "Little care was had by any," Robert Blair lamented, "to plant religion." This disregard for the evangelical faith was soon to change as zealous Scottish pastors, who fell out of favor with James and his bishops, sought refuge in the slightly freer air of Ulster. By the mid-1630s these transplanted Scottish Presbyterians would find Ulster as stifling as Scotland, and many would return home. Still their mission of the 1620s successfully planted evangelical Presbyterianism in Ulster for good. Indeed, Ulster became an embattled but enduring stronghold of Presbyterian dissent.[35]

The religious mission to the Scottish settlements in Ulster was initially led by a core of Presbyterian ministers—Robert Blair, James Glendinning, and Robert Cunningham who were all active there by 1623. John Livingston, who came over to Ulster on the back of his success at Shotts in 1630, and Josiah Welsh, son of the exiled minister John Welsh of Ayr, would also leave profound marks. Other Scottish ministers, such as Andrew Stewart, George Dunbar, and Edward Bryce, joined as well in the revivals. Of these pastors Glendinning with his passionate preaching was the first to attract extensive attention. By about 1624 Glendinning, "having a great voice and vehement delivery," had "roused up the people" around Antrim and "wakened them with terrors." He proved, indeed, such a powerful preacher that one eyewitness had seen many "stricken, and swoon with the Word—yea, a dozen in one day carried out of doors as dead, so marvellous was the power of God smiting their hearts for sin, condemning and killing."[36]

Soon, however, Glendinning—much to the chagrin of his supporters—passed that fine line separating the prophet from the madman. Fasting for days on end and sleeping little, Glendinning settled "upon a day that would be the day of judgment." This and "other conceits" left many convinced that he was a deluded enthusiast. At one point, making a valiant attempt to persuade Robert Blair that he was right about the apocalypse, Glendinning ended up only confirming Blair's worst fears about him. "He asked me," Blair related, "if I would believe he was in the right, if his foot could not burn in the fire?" Before Blair could answer, Glendinning's foot was headed for the flames. Blair immediately wrestled him down, preventing Glendinning from proving his point one way or the other. Failing to convince his colleagues and yet refusing to give up his vision, Glendinning went "from error to error" until at last he ran away "to see the seven Churches of Asia," apparently never to be heard from again. Glendinning's fall was a setback for the evangelicals in Ulster, but the other ministers rallied together and managed to build on the "anxiety and terror of conscience" that Glendinning's apocalyptic gospel had aroused.[37]

Whether Glendinning's revivalistic preaching took place in the context of sacramental occasions was not noted by Blair or others, but what is clear is that his compeers regularly put forth their greatest evangelistic efforts at such events. Blair and Cunningham, for example, resolved in 1624 on the unusual design of celebrating the Lord's Supper eight times in the year, four in each of their parishes, in hopes of promoting moral and spiritual renewal. With both congregations coming together for these occasions, these sacraments proved exceptionally popular. "These communions became so edifying, and were so blessed," the seventeenth-century historian Patrick Adair claimed, "that multitudes of professors from all places of both counties ordinarily resorted to them, and some from Tyrone—there was such a spirit of zeal and power of God poured forth at that time." After these communions in 1624 the revival continued to spread through monthly meetings for preaching and prayer and through further sacramental occasions. These communions, drawing great numbers together for an extended series of meetings, were developing in much the same way as coeval events in the west of Scotland.[38]

By the 1630s these events were major ones in the lives of many people both in Ulster and in the southwest. Congregants regularly came to these occasions with "a great zeal and a vehement appetite" ready for days of communal devotion. "The people so hung upon us still desirous to have more;" Blair said of one of these assemblies in 1630, "no day was long enough; no room was large enough." At a communion in 1632 Blair was forced to keep up an exhausting pace as he preached ten sermons in three days. What was draining for the ministers demanded equal spiritual vigor on the part of the laity. "I have known them that have come several miles from their own Houses," John Livingston related, "to Communions to the Saturdays Sermon, and spent the whole Saturday night in several companies, sometimes a Minister being with them, sometimes themselves alone, in Conference and Prayer, and waited on the publick Ordinances the whole Sabbath, and spent the Sabbath night likewise, and yet at the Mundays Sermon were not troubled with Sleepiness, and so have not Sleeped till they went Home." In the late 1630s, after Livingston had resettled at Stranraer on the west coast of Scotland and after many of the most zealous preachers had been ousted from Ulster, people used to flock to his communions from "out of *Ireland*." At one of them alone five hundred people were said to have migrated across the water to celebrate the sacrament with Livingston, his congregants, and no doubt other visitors and ministers. By the 1630s communion occasions had clearly been established as important popular events for the evangelical Presbyterians of Ulster and the southwest. One Scottish antiquarian, who had few kind words for these sacraments, concluded that "instead of the people being lifted up to the level of the Communion, it was brought down to the level of the people." This thrust was incisive in spite of its rather dull critique, for it hints at what had happened. These evangelicals—pastors and people—had begun to turn the Reformed Lord's Supper into a popular sacramental festival.[39]

As these sacramental gatherings grew more popular and influential, they attracted increasing opposition from miter and crown. Between 1631 and 1635 the bishops in Ireland cracked down on the evangelical preachers there. Blair, Livingston, Josiah Welsh, and George Dunbar, for example, were all deposed. Such preachers were accused of stirring "up the People to Extasies and Enthusiasms," teaching their congregants such heterodox ideas as "the necessity of a new birth by bodily pangs and throes," and encouraging defiance of episcopal and royal authority. While these evangelicals denied such charges, the dangers they and their meetings posed for the king and his bishops were becoming progressively clear. In 1634 Charles I, who succeeded his father in 1625 and who had even grander designs for bringing the Scottish church into line with Canterbury, backed an act that sought to curb these communions. Mandating that people communicate only in their own parishes, it attacked those "dissobedient people, who ordinarlie, when the communion is ministrat in thair parishes and at all other tymes when thair occasions and their humor serves thame, not onelie leaves thair awne parish kirkes bot runnes to seeke the communion at the hands of suche ministers as they know to be disconforme to all good order, which is the meanes of thair dissobedience to his Majesteis lawes." Charles hoped to curtail "all suche wandrings of the people" to these dissent-filled communions. This act, coupled with the deposing of ministers, nevertheless failed to undercut the popularity of these sacramental occasions.[40]

If anything, the opposition of the 1630s only fueled the Presbyterian movement. Deposing Livingston, for instance, only turned him once again into a roving itinerant who went "from Place to Place" and from communion to communion, no doubt reaching more people than if he had been saddled with the responsibilities of a normal parish ministry. The same went for the attempt to curb David Dickson and Samuel Rutherford by uprooting them. This only had the undesired effect of allowing them to disseminate their ideas elsewhere and of making their original charges all the more devoted to them. More reluctant than Charles II to turn such figures into martyrs, Charles I in his relative moderation found himself awash in dissenters. By the mid-1630s communion occasions had become an important means by which the most zealous Presbyterians were forwarding their cause. Rallying people behind the power of their gospel and the purity of their eucharistic ritual, the radical Presbyterians were by 1635 beyond suppression.

The Presbyterian movement had gained such momentum by the mid-1630s that an outright challenge of their Episcopal opponents became increasingly feasible. With the mistimed attempt of Charles I to impose a new Prayer Book on Scotland in 1637, the Presbyterians seized the initiative. Forcing Charles to call a General Assembly in 1638, they ousted the bishops, repudiated the Articles of Perth, and prohibited the new liturgy. The Presbyterian revolt in 1638 ushered Scotland into more than a half-century of intensified strife and division. The sacramental occasion, which had largely come into its own by 1638 and had helped foster this Presbyterian awakening, would take further shape in the ensuing era of religious and political tumult.

Covenanters and Communions, 1638–1688

Gilbert Burnet, a Scottish minister who eventually became bishop of Salisbury, described at some length the peculiar liveliness and solemnity of the communions of the extreme Presbyterians in the 1650s. "They were in nothing more singular," he insisted, "than in their communions":

> On the *Wednesday* before they held a fast day with prayers and sermons for about eight or ten hours together: On the *Saturday* they had two or three preparation sermons: And on the Lord's day they had so very many, that the action continued above twelve hours in some places: And all ended with three or four sermons on *Monday* for thanksgiving. A great many Ministers were brought together from several parts: And high pretenders would have gone 40 or 50 miles to a noted communion. The crouds were far beyond the capacity of their churches, or the reach of their voices: So at the same time they had sermons in two or three different places: And all was performed with great shew of zeal. They had stories of many sequal conversions that were wrought on these occasions.

Burnet went on to note that it was "scarce credible what an effect" these activities "had among the people."[41] While he eschewed all these Presbyterian doings, Burnet could not help but marvel at the unusual power and popularity of these sacramental occasions.

The prominence of the communions of the 1650s, like the salience of the revival at Shotts, has led some historians to credit—or more often blame—the most zealous Presbyterians of this decade with the invention of the sacramental season. "Church historians are practically unanimous," one of the more recent scholars attested, "that these mass Communions originated with the Protesters [as the most ardent Presbyterians were then known] in the early 1650's. [These communions] constituted a deliberate break with tradition, in opposition to the law and usage of the Reformed Church. . . . There was nothing incidental about them as at Shotts."[42] Developments in the 1650s were indeed important. The number of sermons typically delivered at these events grew as did the number of ministers that were likely to be on hand; midweek fast days became increasingly prominent; and the emphasis on extemporaneous prayer and preaching was solidified. But such developments were elaborations on the popular sacramental events of the preceding decades, extensions of an already burgeoning evangelical tradition, not a new and heedless abandonment of Reformed principles. The festal communions that were largely in place in Ulster and in the southwest by the revolt of 1638 continued to develop and prosper in the turmoil of the 1640s and 1650s and even survived after the Restoration despite the violent opposition of Charles II. In that half-century between the rebellious General Assembly of 1638 and the Glorious Revolution of 1688, the sacramental occasion became by degrees a fixed, yet ever more complicated part of the world of these evangelicals.

As part of their revolt in 1638 against the ecclesiastical policies of Charles I, the Presbyterians drew up a National Covenant that was intended to bind Scotland both to the Presbyterian cause and to God. Though the document was circumspect in its wording, especially in its profession of loyalty to the Crown, subscription to it nonetheless helped consolidate the radical Presbyterian movement as well as enhance the party's strength outside the traditional stronghold in the southwest. In 1643 the Scottish Presbyterians extended their influence further when they joined in the Solemn League and Covenant with English Parliamentarians and Puritans. The Covenanters, as these vehement Presbyterians came to be known, saw themselves more and more as the leaven that would raise Scotland—and perhaps England and Ireland as well—to a level of purity befitting a covenanted people.

Fiercely Scottish and Presbyterian, the Covenanters were suspicious of all things English and Anglican. Their suspicions extended as well to the English Independents whose eucharistic practices in particular troubled the Scots of the 1640s. When Presbyterians and Puritans came together between 1643 and 1645 at Westminster to try to formulate unified standards for the purified Churches of Scotland, Ireland, and England, the Lord's Supper was a consistent sticking point. The divines spent three weeks, for example, debating where the communicants were to sit when receiving the Lord's Supper, whether they should simply remain in their pews as the English would have it or come forward to a table as the Scots insisted. Robert Baillie, one of four Scottish commissioners at the Assembly, revealed how deep-seated the differences between the two parties were. "The unhappie Independents," he charged, "would mangle that sacrament. No catechizing nor preparation before; no thanksgiving after; no sacramental doctrine, or chapters, in the day of celebration; no coming up to any table; but a carrying of the element[s] to all in their seats athort the church: . . . We must dispute every inch of our ground." To all these quarrels was added the debate over whether noncommunicants should be dismissed before the administration of the sacrament. The Scots thought that everyone should observe the solemnity through to its finish whatever their spiritual state, while the English tended to sanction a more closed, cloistered communion at which only the saints would be present. On this point, as on several other issues—such as partaking at a table—the Presbyterians and Independents never resolved their differences.[43]

In the 1640s the Covenanters found that working out an agreement with English Puritans was about as difficult for them as co-existing with their Episcopal opponents. The debates of the 1640s, centered on Westminster, revealed the extent to which the Scottish Presbyterians were devoted to a certain way of celebrating the eucharist. The rituals of the Lord's Supper, once unified in the Latin Mass, had become a way of defining one religious community over against another. Sitting at a table to receive communion, for example, had become a distinctive ritual act that divided the Scottish Presbyterians from Anglicans and Independents. For all its pretension to unifying Puritan worship, the Westminster Assembly had ended up only making the Scottish Presbyterians more committed to their own Reformed way. The stands the Scots took there accentuated the differences between them and the English.

Of the four Scottish divines at the Westminster Assembly only Samuel Rutherford, when pastor at Anwoth in Galloway, had been extensively involved in the sacramental occasions as they had developed over the past two decades in the south and west; none of them had taken part in those that had arisen in Ulster. The Westminster Directory and the Act of the General Assembly that adopted it in 1645 reflected the distance of many Presbyterian leaders from the revivals of the 1620s and 1630s. Indeed, the General Assembly through endorsement of the Directory appeared to put a check on several aspects of the sacramental occasions. The General Assembly left Monday services unrecognized, put a limit of three on the number of pastors allowed to minister at these events (and actually preferred that just the minister of the parish and one assistant be involved), endorsed only a single service for preparation, and pushed for greater frequency of celebration which ran counter to the infrequent, festal pattern that was emerging. Though there was qualified acceptance of outdoor preaching when parishioners were "so numerous that thair paroch kirk cannot contain them," such preaching was to be cautiously ordered and was not to take place simultaneously with the service within the church. The adoption of these recommendations was an early sign that there were to be tensions between official policy and popular practice. Such tensions occupied discussions of the sacrament for a good part of the next two centuries before finding resolution on the side of the church's governing body. In the meantime the evangelicals and their preachers went on all but impervious to calls to bring their communions in line with such official directions. The Westminster Directory, as it handled the celebration of the Lord's Supper, was a portent of a division between official prescription and popular practice that would become altogether clear in the sacramental debates of the next two centuries.[44]

Between the National Covenant of 1638 and the triumph of Oliver Cromwell over the Scottish army in 1651, the communion occasions remained strong in those areas where their power had first been felt—the southwest and Ulster. In the latter many of the communions were held by itinerant preachers who were sent from Scotland to minister to the vacant, desolate Presbyterian kirks there. Among those sent were Robert Blair and John Livingston whose popular followings remained as strong as ever. "Sometimes," Livingston related of his four summer sojourns in Ulster between 1643 and 1648, "there would be four or five Communions in severall Places in the three Months time." The meetings continued to be large, all the more no doubt because of their rarity and the long-standing celebrity of Blair and Livingston. After 1648 enough ministers had settled anew in Ulster that the Presbyterian mission there could go on without the visits of the likes of Livingston and Blair. The former, for example, evidently returned to Ulster only once more—in the summer of 1656—to preach and lead communions. In the southwest the story was similar. A number of evangelical preachers, such as Livingston, William Guthrie, and James Guthrie, bridged the revivals of the 1630s and 1650s with their intervening activities. Livingston, for instance, could list eight pastors with whom he had led communions between 1638 and 1648 in the vicinity of Stranraer alone, and at one turbulent communion at Mauchline in 1648 eight ministers and two thousand people were said to be on hand, with services stretching from Saturday to Monday. In the 1640s the sacramental occasions, despite political unrest and civil war, remained important religious events.[45]

During Cromwell's seven years of dominion over Scotland after his victory in 1651, the sacramental occasion reached a new height despite—or perhaps because of—rancorous division among the Presbyterians. The

Covenanters, confused about how they should respond to the efforts of Charles II after 1649 to reclaim the thrones of Scotland and England for the Stuarts, disintegrated into factions. The Remonstrants or Protesters, as the more radical Presbyterians came to be known, suspected Charles of duplicity, of only swearing support for the Covenants as a political stratagem. They forestalled backing Charles until they could receive more assurances of his sincerity. The Resolutioners, as the more moderate Presbyterians were called, backed Charles II in hopes of restoring royal authority and preventing Cromwell's subjugation of Scotland. The attempts of the Resolutioners to restore the king in 1650 and 1651 failed and ended instead in Cromwell's triumph. The Protesters, lukewarm about Charles in the first place, found Cromwell's Protectorate more congenial than did the Resolutioners. Though political strife continued to run high between the two parties, the discord did not dampen the religious zeal of the Protesters. In fact, the division only hardened their resolve to win the people over not only to Christ, but also to their party. The sacramental occasion would be one of their main instruments in this contest.

The communions of the Protesters, as Bishop Burnet's account suggested, were both powerful and popular. John Livingston, who aligned himself with the Protesters, reported in the mid-1650s "some reviving of the Work of God in the Land," noting in particular that "in *Tiviotdale* and the *Merse*, Communions were very lively and much frequented." Another contemporary noted in his diary in 1654 that in Galloway in the southwest there was "never a greater outletting of God's presence in comunions; tuo congregations, befor dead, falling in great love of the ordinances." In the same year this diarist confided that "Christ was at the communion in Fennik and that it was a refreshing day" and that in the "north syde of Fyfe" there was "a great resort to comuniones, and ministers [speak] much of people getting good theirat." To the north Protester Thomas Hog in the late 1650s was part of a similarly successful sacramental solemnity at Kiltearn: "*The Lord bowed his Heavens and came down*, and displayed his saving Power on that Occasion most comfortably and signally." The seventeenth-century historian James Kirkton, reflecting on the religious life of Scotland in this period, revelled in the successes of the Protesters. "I verily believe," Kirkton gloried, "there were more souls converted to Christ in that short period of time, than in any season since the Reformation. . . . Nor was there ever greater purity and plenty of the means of grace than was in their time." Sacramental occasions in particular were blessed events, according to Kirkton. "If a man hade seen one of their solemn communions, where many congregations mett in great multitudes, some dozen of ministers used to preach, and the people continued, as it were, in a sort of trance (so serious were they in spiritual exercises) for three dayes at least," Kirkton continued, "he would have thought it a solemnity unknown to the rest of the world." Kirkton's account, though no doubt given a roseate hue by his looking back at this decade from the persecution of the late 1670s, still broadly captures what the accounts of sacraments in Merse, Teviotdale, Galloway, Fenwick, Fife, and Kiltearn suggested more narrowly: the Protesters were leading revivals that had as one of their mainsprings the communion occasion.[46]

Critics of the Protesters were quick to denigrate these evangelistic successes. The Resolutioners were convinced that their opponents were using these sacramental events manipulatively "for strengthening of their party and faction," that their "clear design in all this" was "to set up themselves as the only pious and zealous people, worthy to be trusted and followed in our publique differences." The Protesters were in many ways vulnerable to such charges. In places they openly excluded any from the Lord's Supper who did not follow their rigid political line and everywhere they sought proselytes for their "new refyned congregation" of saints. They went out of their way to appeal to the people, evidently adopting at times a distinctively fervent style of prayer and preaching—"a strange kind of sighing"—as well as holding their boundless communions in which "great confluences from all the Country and many Congregations about are gathered." The Protesters were also not above attempts to undermine the ministry of their opponents as they often produced through their popular sacraments "great animosities and alienations in simple People, against those Ministers who will not imitate these irregular courses." The revivalistic, politic activities of the Protesters were enhancing the popularity of the sacramental occasion, even as it was being employed designedly to sap the following of their opponents.[47]

For all this party spirit the revivals of the 1650s should not be identified solely with the Protesters or confused wholly with factionalism. The moderate Resolutioners, who included among their ranks David Dickson and Robert Blair, were not without their own evangelical preachers. Blair, for example, was "a chief actor and prime instrument" at a number of sacramental gatherings in these years. "At these solemn occasions," his son-in-law William Row observed, "many souls got much good by his ministry. It was the Lord's wonderful condescension and kindness to his own in Scotland, that, while they were under the feet of usurpers [Cromwell and the English], the Lord sweetened the bitterness of their bondage, by blessing the labours of his faithful servants of the ministry, . . . in several parts of the kingdom." The Resolutioners may never have gone to such great lengths to spur revival as did the Protesters, but neither were they without their own evangelistic successes. In the face of the political uncertainty and religious strife of the 1650s, the communion occasion provided a powerful source for religious renewal and assurance, and such spiritual comforts were not wholly confined to the Protesters. The sacrament was an occasion in which to find strength and security, one way of sweetening the bitterness of division and subjugation.[48]

The Restoration of Charles II in 1660 spelled disaster for the Protesters whose suspect loyalty and sectarian spirit provided the king with ample reason to suppress them. Reinstituting episcopacy and reestablishing the Crown as the supreme head of the church, he wished to curtail the Covenanters once and for all. To this end, he executed such arch-Protesters as James Guthrie and Archibald Johnston, exiled other leaders such as Livingston and Robert McWard, deposed around three hundred Presbyterian ministers—the preponderance of whom were from the southwest—and then filled these kirks with his own curates. Though Charles brooked no compromise with the more extreme Covenanters, he did try to appease the more moderate Presbyterians. For example, he did not attempt to reassert the Articles of Perth or to impose a Prayer Book. Even as he refused to accept the General Assembly, he kept the kirk sessions, presbyteries, and synods. Such efforts at conciliation were successful in a number of areas, particularly in the northeast where the most zealous Covenanters had never been that strong in the first place. In the southwest, however, where the extreme Presbyterians had long been powerful, the Covenanters were ready to resist Charles, his bishops, and his curates to the death.[49]

With the ousting of their ministers, the Covenanters were forced to conduct most of their meetings in private houses. Despite act after act and proclamation after proclamation, king and Parliament never managed to suppress these conventicles. While such small, private meetings were of necessity the devotional staple of these harried Presbyterians, clandestine communions were important as well. Often these sacraments grew to such a size that they were not secret at all, but openly defiant of authority. Throughout these decades the government was plagued not only by the smaller conventicles, but also by "seditious and tumultuous communions." Led by such Covenanting stalwarts as Gabriel Semple, John Blackader, and John Welsh—the grandson of the exiled Presbyterian pastor of the same name—these conventicles and communions were a constant challenge to royal and episcopal authority. "These meetings, ye know, are forbidden by authority," Welsh preached at one of the sacramental occasions in 1678, "but there is one greater than they that commands the contrary of what they command, and his command must be obeyed." In the years following the Restoration, the communion occasion became wrapped up with ever more militant resistance to king and bishop.[50]

The fullest account of these illicit communions comes in the memoirs of the diehard Covenanter John Blackader. From the early 1660s Blackader and other deposed ministers had joined together with their people for improvised worship in private houses and in the fields. By the mid-1670s, conventicles were legion, and "Meetings of several Thousands in the fields" were not uncommon. In these years Blackader reported that among the greatest religious occasions these persecuted Covenanters had were "several great solemn dayes in sundry parts of the Land for publick fasts, and Celebrating the Communion of the Lords Supper in open fields"; "greater multitudes," Blackader related, were at these communions "than ever was at any such meetings before." These meetings, stretching from at least Saturday to Monday, demanded careful planning in order to avoid their disruption by the king's dragoons, and often people had to come "in some posture of Defence" to prevent "any affront to so solemn and sacred a work." At a massive communion at East Nisbet in 1678, for example, the Covenanters had to prepare for attack, for it "was rumoured that the Earle of Hume (as ramp a youth as any in [t]his Countrey) was intend[ing] to assault the meeting with his men & Militia. . . . It was also said, they profanely threatned to cause their horse[s] [to] drink out the Communion wine." Despite such dangers and insecurities, multitudes continued to draw together for these sacramental occasions.[51]

The work at East Nisbet, the threats of the Earl of Hume notwithstanding, went on smoothly and solemnly. "Tho' the people at first meeting were something apprehensive of hazard," Blackader related, "yet from the time the work was Entered, till the Close of it, they were neither alarm'd nor affrighted: But sat as composed and the work as orderly gone about, as it had been in the Days of the greatest peace and quiet." Blackader had singled out five or six communions as the most impressive, but closely described only this sacrament at East Nisbet. His depiction was unusually full, a tessellation of illuminating details. "The place where they Conveen'd," Blackader reported, "was most Commodious, as [if] it had been formed at first for the same purpose, being a pleasant Haugh, hard by Whitater water side, with a spacious brae in form of a half round, all green Grass, and of a Considerable Height. The Multitude sat in the Haugh, the Communion Tables set in the midst, and a Large greater Multitude on the face of the brae from the bottom to the Top." The people came not only to sit upon the hillside listening, but also to sit at the Lord's table partaking. "At this occasion there was two Long Tables," Blackader detailed, "with seats on every side of each Table, and a shorter Table at the head, as use to be: At every Table was supposed to sit about 100 persons. Fifteen or 16 Tables in all were serv'd that Day." Such a spectacle of thousands coming together to celebrate the sacrament in open defiance of the law presented a powerful, animating scene. Blackader related how "the Glorious presence, & powerfull grace of Christ" pervaded the gathering:

There indeed was to be seen the goings of God, Even the goings of their God and King in that sanctuary. . . . This Ordinance of preaching & Administration of his Last Supper, that Love Token Left for a memorial of him till his coming again, was so signally Countenanced, backed with power, and refreshing Influences from heaven, that It might be said Thou O God didst send out a plentifull rain whereby thou confirmed thine Inheritance when it was weary. The Table of the Lord was covered avowedly in the open fields in presence of the raging Enemies, many great dayes of the Son of man have been seen in the . . . Desolate Kirk of Scotland Even Since the Last Invasion of that monstrous prelatick party, smitting shepherds and scattering the flocks at first, But few the Like of this, either before or after.

The East Nisbet communion, like a handful of others that approached its size, was a pinnacle in the Covenanters' struggle.[52]

Similar in magnitude to the communion at East Nisbet was one conducted a short time later at Irongray. Blackader, his wife, and their son journeyed sixty miles in order to participate in this occasion. As they traveled thither "they found all the way full of people, many on horse, others on foot" coming to this communion gathering. "The Assembly was Large," Blackader reported, "greater Than at East Nisbet, mo[r]e gentlemen and strangers from [far] and near. . . . There was 2 Long Tables, Longer than at East Nisbet, and mo[r]e Communicants." Care had been taken as usual to guard the gathering from disruption, and despite a number of alarms the solemnity proceeded without a hitch. "The whole work from the beginning on Saturday till the Close on Munday about one in the Afternoon," Blackader averred, "was much Countenanc'd & the people much refresh'd in their spirits Notwithstanding of all the occasion their poor bodies had to be wearied thro' sore travell, watchings[,] Alarms[,] other straitnings & Dissaccommodations which could not be shun'd among such a Multitude keeping so closely together among Moors, and Mountains." The sacramental occasions of the mid-1670s were powerful displays of religious fervor as well as formidable vehicles of protest. Religious experience at the sacramental occasions of the post-Restoration period was inextricably bound up with political and ecclesiastical allegiance.[53]

After the communion at Irongray few sacramental occasions were allowed to reach such proportions again. Blackader did note a massive communion at Colmonell in Ayrshire in 1679, but he was ill at the time and unable to attend. All he was able to report in his memoirs was that "there were many min[iste]rs there, much preaching, the greatest Multitude that ever I heard was on the fields in Scotland, before or since."[54] Shortly after this communion the Covenanters' cause was decisively defeated at Bothwell Bridge in June 1679 by the king's army led by the Duke of Monmouth. Efforts at suppression were stepped up in the wake of this battle. More and more the Covenanters were fined, banished, imprisoned, or even executed as the authorities went "Hunting for them as for wild beasts of the Forrest." Blackader was himself finally captured and imprisoned in 1681 at the Bass where he spent all but the last few months of his life. Until the Glorious Revolution of 1688, repetition of scenes like those at Irongray and East Nisbet would apparently be rare. Conventicles and communions, fraught with risk in the first place, were forced to become all the more clandestine after 1679. Still after all the bloodshed and conflict such meetings were never completely suppressed.[55]

The suffering and sacrifice of the Covenanters lingered long in the memory of Presbyterians. The heirs of this heritage would often glory in the steadfastness of their ancestors and would often lament that they failed to manifest strength equal to these pillars of the past. Even a distant heir like James McGready would remember, in a sermon to one of his congregations in Kentucky, "the sufferings of the people of God in Scotland" under Charles II and James II. He would remember the secret meetings "in thickets and desert places," the hounding by dragoons, the prisons, and the tortures—"their thumbs screwed off—their legs put into iron boots and wedged until the bone was shivered to pieces." And he would wonder if his people were worthy to lay claim to this heritage of sacrificial faith that he celebrated.[56]

Others would be less grisly and more matter-of-fact in their remembrance. John Willison, preaching at a sacramental occasion in the early eighteenth century, recalled in particular the dangers that the Covenanters braved when they gathered for the Lord's Supper. "These are precious seasons," he related, "which our fathers sometimes would have prized at a high rate, when they were put to seek their spiritual bread with the peril of their lives, because of the sword in the wilderness." The comments of McGready and Willison were indicative of the legacy of the Covenanters. Hallowed by retelling and enlargement, the story of the Covenanters— their conventicles, sufferings, and clandestine communions—became a noble, at times almost sacral part of the Presbyterian past. The communion seasons, high points in the militant struggle and long endurance of the Covenanters, had become wrapped up in that hallowed history. Participation in them had become part of what it meant to be a Scottish Presbyterian. The Covenanters had added the glorious history of Presbyterian sacrifice to the sacred history of Christ's sufferings and death.[57]

SACRAMENT AND REVIVAL: HIGH DAYS IN SCOTLAND, 1688–1750

In August 1742 at Cambuslang, a parish a few miles outside of Glasgow, the evangelical awakening in Scotland surged to a new high. There a communion season, the second in a month's time, was so thronged that "the lowest estimate" of "this vast concourse of people" was "upwards of thirty thousand"; other assessments ran as high as fifty thousand. Communicants, numbering "about three thousand," filled table after table from morning to evening on the Sabbath, and still it was conjectured that a thousand more would have come forward, if only "there had been access to get tokens." Thousands more, who for one reason or another did not make it to the Lord's table, flocked to hear the Word expounded from a number of makeshift pulpits, or "tents" as these outdoor stands were called. It "was computed that above twenty-four ministers and preachers were present." Still "what was most remarkable," the host minister, William McCulloch, averred, "was the spiritual glory of this solemnity, I mean the gracious and sensible presence of God. Not a few were awakened to a sense of sin, and their lost and perishing condition without a Saviour. Others had their bands loosed, and were brought into the marvellous liberty of the sons of God. Many of God's dear children have declared, That it was a happy time to their souls, wherein they were abundantly satisfied with the goodness of God in his ordinances, and filled with all joy and peace in believing."[58]

A good sense of the grandness of the sacramental occasions at Cambuslang comes in an account penned by John Scot, a layman who came to the revival from Monkland with his father. The event, its bustle and energy, left a deep impression on Scot, a boy of thirteen at the time:

> There were two sacramental occasions at Cambuslang s[ai]d year[.] [T]he last was about the first of A[u]gust where was many ministers from distant parts and such a multitude of folk from distant parts as far as Edinburgh, Stirling, Air, Pasley, & the agasant country in this nighbourhood that I never expect to see such a multitude again in one place in this world[.] [T]here was three tents up that day two for sermon & one for dispensing the sacrament and as many at each tent as could hear besids grate numbers seated in the fields & goeing from one place to another. The work began at 8. o'clock & the sun was set before the tables were finished.

In the revivals at Cambuslang, evangelicalism in Scotland experienced some of its highest days. Culminating in the grand sacramental occasions of the summer of 1742, the Cambuslang revival gave evangelical Presbyterians considerable cause to rejoice.[59]

The evangelicals were given further occasion for exultation in early October when a communion season at Kilsyth, not far from Cambuslang, wonderfully capped a revival that had been brewing in that parish over the past few months. With a dozen or more ministers in attendance and "near fifteen hundred" communicants, this sacramental occasion, though about half the size of the Cambuslang communion six weeks earlier, was nonetheless eminently blessed. "The spiritual fruits of this solemn and extraordinary dispensation of word and sacrament" were, Kilsyth pastor James Robe assured, bountiful beyond measure. Many "christless and secure sinners" were prodded out of complacency; others "when at the Lord's table, and at other times" were overwhelmed by the love of God. The Kilsyth sacrament, coming on the tail of the mammoth meetings at Cambuslang, gave the evangelicals an additional boost at a time when they could hardly get any higher this side of heaven or the millennium.[60]

The revivals at Cambuslang and, to a slightly lesser degree, those at Kilsyth have always loomed large in histories of the evangelical movement in Scotland. This is in great part because these revivals were indeed extraordinarily powerful, but it is also because the ministers of these parishes, McCulloch at Cambuslang and Robe at Kilsyth, took unusual care to document the course of the awakening in their congregations. "I had a prevailing inclination from the beginning," Robe confessed, "with all the exactness I was capable of, to observe every thing that past, and with the most scrupulous niceness to examine every uncommon circumstance, and to take down notes of what appeared to me most material." McCulloch was similarly exacting in examining converts and in chronicling the awakening in his parish. Recording the spiritual experiences of over one hundred people, McCulloch left, as we shall see, a voluminous amount of material for historians to draw on in reconstructing the piety of the laity at these communions and revivals. At one point James Robe had lamented "the omission of our worthy forefathers to transmit to posterity a full and circumstantial account . . . of the extraordinary outletting of the Holy Spirit in the West of Scotland" in the 1620s. Together Robe and McCulloch made sure that such an omission could never be charged against them.[61]

The abundance of good material available on the Scottish evangelicals at Cambuslang and Kilsyth in the early 1740s has at times been allowed to obscure the longer history and wider extent of sacramental revivals in the eighteenth century. Cambuslang and Kilsyth were important centers for the evangelical movement in Scotland, but the revivals and sacramental occasions in those places were interwoven with a much larger tradition. Like the revival at Shotts or the communions of the Protesters, the sacramental seasons at Cambuslang and Kilsyth were peak events in a tradition long familiar with such high days. Between 1688 and 1750 the sacramental occasion, as the festal event in the Reformed calendar, became ever more central to the religious culture of Presbyterian Scotland.

With the Glorious Revolution the Presbyterians were vindicated. Those ministers who had been deposed at the Restoration and who had managed to outlive the years of persecution—of whom there were about sixty—were now able to set the tone for the newly established Presbyterian Church. Though it took some years for the Presbyterians to wrest a number of parishes out of Episcopalian hands, especially in the northeast, even before the Revolution Settlement in 1690 the Presbyterians managed to take over most of the kirks of the southwest through the "rabbling" of the curates. The triumph of the beleaguered Presbyterians after more than a century of struggle with advocates of episcopacy gave them their best opportunity yet to shape the religious life of Scotland.

With the vindication of the Presbyterians came the vindication of their worship. The years immediately following the Glorious Revolution witnessed in particular the solidification of the sacramental practices that had been developing from at least the 1620s. Presbyterian zeal ran high in the wake of victory, and communion seasons provided a suitable occasion in which to display that fervor and at which to stoke it further. "[A]bout the Time of our late happy Revolution . . . there were such vehement Desires among the People, after the Ordinances, and lively Preaching of the Word, that had been scarce for so many Years before," John Willison sketched, "that it was necessary to gratify them with much Preaching, at these solemn Occasions." Or, as another Presbyterian apologist remarked early in the eighteenth century, "Communicants have been very numerous . . . ever since the *Revolution*." Between 1688 and 1710 the festal communions became at once a settled, but dynamic part of the social and religious life of Scotland. What had had an often subversive role through most of the seventeenth century became a standard, if still controversial, part of the Presbyterian order by the early eighteenth century.[62]

The quickness with which this eucharistic festival became an established feature of evangelical life after 1688 was suggested by a variety of commentators. The lampoons of Episcopalian critics and the fears of more moderate Presbyterians provided one kind of testimony. In the mid-1690s the Episcopalian John Sage, for example, blasted these sacramental occasions, their "*strange Pomp*," the "*thousands of Spectators*," "the solemnity of *Church-yard Sermons*," the "*long Harangue*[s], . . . supplyed from the *stores* of the *Extemporary Spirit*," the lengthy preparatory and thanksgiving services, the successive tables, and the numberless ministers and sermons. "How *Glorious* and *August* are their *Communions*!" Sage exclaimed sardonically. "What *singular preparations* have they! How many *Powerful Prayers*! How many *Soul-searching Sermons*! Who can compare with them for *fervour* and *zeal*, for *Graces* and *Gifts*, for *special marks* of Gods *peculiar favour* and *assistance*?" "All this *Parade*," Sage was sure, was a device "for *catching* the *Populace*" and sealing Presbyterian popularity at the further expense of the Episcopalians. Even a number of more moderate Presbyterians worried from the first about the "great confluences of people" at these communions and the disorders that could result from such "exorbitant crowds." Though their reservations would have only limited effect on these popular sacramental practices before 1800, their qualms, registered regularly from the 1690s on, attest to the immediate popularity of these communion seasons after the Revolution.[63]

The ministerial writings of the evangelicals provide another witness to the rapid establishment of these sacramental occasions after 1688. For example, the diary of George Turnbull, pastor at Alloa and "a steady friend" of the great evangelical preacher Thomas Boston, is sprinkled—in entries spanning the period 1688 to 1704—with references to the sacramental occasions as "sweet gospel day[s]," "great day[s] of the gospell," or "sweet time[s] of the gospell." Similarly, Robert Wodrow in his voluminous correspondence, though occasionally overwhelmed to the point of annoyance with the throngs at these summer sacraments, nonetheless attested to the popularity of "those fair-days of the Gospel." An avid historian of the church, Wodrow also collected valuable evidence in his *Materials for a History of Remarkable Providences*. At a communion at Earlston in 1688, for instance, "there wer one thousand Communicants, several thousands hearing, and twelve Ministers." To take another example from forty years later, Wodrow reported "vast confluences" at communions with people coming from fifty miles to these festal occasions. In between the report of 1688 and that of 1728, similar occurrences were common. Year-in, year-out the communion season was a high point in the religious life of the community, and in one parish or another, in any given year, it was well-nigh certain to issue in "an extraordinary stirr" among the people.[64]

By 1703 George Wemyss, in the preface to a popular collection of sermons and exhortations preached at these events, could justifiably proclaim: "Communions in *Scotland* are for the most part very solemn, and the great Master of Assemblies is pleased so far to countenance them with his presence and power, that many hundreds, yea thousands in this Land, have dated their conversion from some of these occasions." By 1720 one zealous advocate of these extended festivals simply lauded them as "the good old Way"; for bootless opponents of these sacramental practices it was all too clear that these "eminently blessed" sacramental occasions had become something of a "Divine, Infallible, and Unalterable" institution in Scotland.[65]

The devotional literature in the decades following the Glorious Revolution also reflected—and helped sustain—the growing centrality of these sacramental occasions in the religious culture of the evangelicals. With establishment came renewed access to the Scottish press, a tool the Presbyterians readily employed. Since the Reformation the Scottish Presbyterians had borrowed much of their devotional literature from the likes of

William Perkins, Thomas Shepard, and Lewis Bayly. Though the Scots had produced an isolated devotional classic or two earlier in the seventeenth century—notably William Guthrie's *The Christian's Great Interest* and Samuel Rutherford's *Joshua Redivivus*—only after 1688 did they begin in earnest to build up a literature to undergird their own practice of piety. The sacramental season, as the keystone in their spirituality, was the focus of many of these new devotionals. For example, Robert Craighead, a Scottish Presbyterian pastor who spent much of his life ministering in Ulster, published in 1695 his *Advice to Communicants* which had gone through at least two more editions by 1698. Another Scot, Daniel Campbell, added his *Sacramental Meditations on the Sufferings and Death of Christ* in 1698, a work that was in its fourth edition by 1703. In that year Campbell contributed another devotional work on the eucharist, *The Frequent and Devout Communicant*. John Spalding's *Synaxis Sacra* also in 1703 and James Webster's *Sacramental Sermons* in 1705 added to the surfeit of devotional works that were to be used as aids in the preparation for sacramental occasions. Though the Scots continued to borrow from the English—for example, Thomas Doolittle's *Treatise Concerning the Lord's Supper* was frequently reprinted in these years—they had managed by 1705 to establish their own devotional literature, a good part of which was dedicated to enhancing the piety that went along with the sacramental season.[66]

In the next generation this devotional tradition continued to develop and find further expression. The literature reached its apogee in the work of John Willison of Dundee. Between 1716 when he published his *Sacramental Directory* and 1747 when he published his *Sacramental Meditations*, Willison established himself as the consummate Scottish catechist and spiritual writer. Indeed, his exhaustive *Sacramental Catechism* combined with his concise *Young Communicant's Catechism* to forge for Presbyterian eucharistic doctrine a rough equivalent to the Larger and Shorter Catechisms of Westminster. No one in Scotland wrote more on the Lord's Supper; no one gave fuller expression to the piety connected with the festal communions. Through catechisms, meditations, devotional directions, sermons, and songs—among his works were *One Hundred Gospel-hymns, . . . much Adapted to Sacramental Occasions*—Willison articulated the range, scope, and power of the Scottish sacrament. His works, popular and influential in America as well as in Scotland, were by turns systematic and fervent, didactic and visionary. Though hardly an innovative thinker, Willison codified the eucharistic spirituality of the evangelical Presbyterians and further solidified their sacramental devotions. The sacramental occasion was central to Willison's world; in turn, the works of "the all-popular Mr. Willison" are crucial to the study of Scottish sacramentalism and revivalism.[67] Willison's voluminous writings, all accomplished in the first half of the eighteenth century, were ample testimony that the sacramental season was at its meridian.

While the devotional work of ministers in the decades following 1688 attests to the triumph of this evangelical festival, the experiences of laypeople offer the best evidence of the central importance that these events had come to hold. A number of memoirs from the late seventeenth and early eighteenth centuries demonstrate this significance. For example, the spiritual relations of Mary Somervel, who was born in 1678 into a Covenanter family, described a religious life that found its experiential height in eucharistic participation; she discovered in the communions "sweet refreshing from the presence of the Lord." Similarly, seamstress Elizabeth Cairns made clear in her memoirs that "Communion-Times" were the high days of the year, times of renewal, vision, illumination, and transport. "I have been when sitting at a Communion Table, taken up as it were to the Top of Mount-*Pisgah*," she related, "and allowed to view the promised Land; yea, I may say more, . . . I had not only the far off Views, that I should get Heaven at the End of Time, but at the present Time the Vail has been drawn aside, and I allowed to behold, embrace, and solace my self in the Contemplation of these glorious Objects, and Mysteries wrapt up within the Vail." Other memoirs, such as those of John Ronald and Margaret Bruce, offered similar testimony.[68]

The most influential and popular of the published memoirs, however, was that of Elisabeth West, a devout servant who left a detailed account of her spiritual journeys from about 1690 to 1707. In its fifth edition by 1733, her narrative stood as a standard of evangelical Presbyterian devotion. Her pilgrimages led her to one impressive sacrament after another. In 1698, for example, she reported "a glorious work" at one of these communions; there was "great weeping" and "travailing of the new birth" among the people. The popularity of her account, however, stemmed not only from its evangelical fervency, but also from its nationalistic Presbyterianism. For West the communions reenforced her deepseated aversion to episcopacy. At one sacrament, for instance, she noted with approval an exhortation that enjoined all "to hold fast the profession of the Presbyterian government, so that none of us should ever consent to the inbringing of prelacy again, which Scotland hath spued out." The sacramental occasions and the published memoirs that gloried in them helped undergird the Presbyterian hold on Scotland.[69]

A final, similarly revealing memoir comes in the spiritual relations of Elizabeth Blakader. Less nationalistic, more strictly inward-looking than Elisabeth West's account, Blakader's journal, unlike the other narratives, survives in what is apparently her own hand. Moving from her youth during the last years of persecution under the Stuarts through her "old age" in the 1720s, the account of her spiritual life carries a good deal of warmth and power. Her struggles to come to terms with the death of "my greatest earthly Comfort, my Husband" and "my heavy Charge of seven fatherless Children" are especially poignant. Only after the deepest despair is she able "to attain unto submission unto the will of my God in removing my dearest comfort from me," and even then submission is painful, perhaps incomplete.[70]

Her descriptions of her experiences at sacramental occasions reveal that her moments of bliss could be as profound as her darkest periods of despair. During one "kind visit from Heaven" on the Saturday night of a communion season about 1689, she had the "prevailing deadness and Carnality" of her heart and the "deep Soul perplexity" over her fitness to come into the presence of the Lord at "that holy table" dramatically swept aside:

I had Cause to say, It is the voice of my Beloved, Behold he commeth—Skipping over the Mountains & leaping over the Hills: And I believe he never leapt over higher hills. I was so much ravished with his Love, that I scarce knew where I was, Mean while there was a Scripture brought to my mind with irresistable power, I Sam. 1.15. The woman went away & did eat & was no more sad. By free Grace I found a blessed change on my frame, and my Soul was Swallowed in the Love of God. On the morrow I went to the Table of the Lord, & found it a good day indeed.

Consistently Elizabeth Blakader found that these "Extraordinary Solemnities" were the occasions in which Christ provided her with "Soul transfiguring views of him." In them she found "unexpressible Comfort," even "health & Cure to Soul & Body." As her "wilderness journey" drew to a close, with the Lord "Graciously (not violently) loosing the pins of this Clay Tabernacle," she could look back on these "great Gospel Solemnities" as pinnacles of rest and light in a steep, arduous pilgrimage. Her religious experiences—along with those of her many counterparts—suggest how the devotions connected with the sacramental occasion had come to be a dominant part of lay spirituality.[71]

By the time Elizabeth Blakader closed her account in 1724, any number of indices indicated the prominent place the sacramental season had come to hold in the religious culture of post-Revolution Scotland, a place it would hold into the next century. The ascendancy of this summer and early fall festival had been rapid and essentially smooth. Fluctuations in the vitality of these festivals were, of course, noticeable throughout the eighteenth century. Wodrow, for example, often made observations to this effect: "Communions this year are more then ordinarly sweet," he might note, or "Our communions this summer are sweet. The number of communicants is rather mo[re] than usuall." Yet even in years lamented by Wodrow for their darkness and declension—a recurrent, if not chronic, complaint—the sacramental occasions were still recognized as times of "quickening" and "upstirring." What emerges finally is an image of continuity: summer-in, summer-out in parish after parish these sacraments were the high points in the year.[72]

In the course of more than a hundred summers and thousands of sacramental occasions, some were bound to stand above the rest. Those at Cambuslang and Kilsyth in 1742 were obviously among the most salient. But it is important to keep these extraordinary moments of revival in perspective. Five years before the tumultuous events of 1742, a sacramental occasion at Dunfermline attracted "betwixt four and five thousand communicants," a number that surpassed both Cambuslang and Kilsyth; tables were served from nine in the morning "till about twelve at night." "The Lord," pastor Ralph Erskine recorded simply in his diary, "owned the occasion. Ministers were well helped, and many people heartened." Looking back over his thirty-year ministry at Dunfermline, Erskine remembered "solemn sacramental occasions" as having consistently been "times of refreshing from the presence of the Lord." "From sacrament to sacrament," he averred, "God hath been pleased to show forth something of his glory." Even John Scot, the layman who was understandably overawed by the second sacrament at Cambuslang in 1742, went on to describe other communions that were similarly "sweet and comfortable season[s]," one from which in 1749 amid the tent preaching he dated his conversion. The evangelistic events of 1742 were the culmination of more than a century of evangelical renewal and revival in Scotland. The sacramental occasion from the awakening of the 1620s through that of the 1740s and beyond into the early nineteenth century provided the primary means for Presbyterian renewal, for a long and well-developed tradition of revivalism.[73]

This long history of sacramental revivals bespoke the power of the communion season to renew Presbyterian communities, to invigorate flagging saints, and to transform flagrant sinners. Over the years the sacramental occasion had come to embody an evangelical synthesis of conversionist preaching and eucharistic practice. In the sacramental occasion the salvation of sinners was coupled with the confirmation of saints as complementary processes in the revivification of a community. The "travailing of the new birth" joined with "the work of confirmation" at these communions. These sacramental revivals were never aimed simply at the unconverted; they were for the whole community, churched and unchurched, sinners and saved. The new birth was the point of entry into a long journey heavenward upon which the pilgrim was in need of repeated renewal, reconfirmation, and perhaps even reconversion. The communion season drew people into the pilgrimage and kept them going once on the journey. For these evangelical Presbyterians salvation and the sacrament were intimately related, even inseparable. Conversion and communion had flowed together in this tradition.[74]

By the 1740s the power of this sacramental revivalism to convert and to renew was being tested in the new environs of colonial America. Elizabeth Blakader, when she thought one of her husband's business ventures would force the family to move to London, viewed the prospect of losing out on these "great Gospel Solemnities" as "one of the greatest Causes of my grief in parting from Scotland."[75] Of the many worries facing Presbyterian immigrants to America, this was not one over which they needed to expend much anxiety. These "Extraordinary Solemnities," which had developed into a vital part of evangelical Presbyterian culture, would be readily re-created in the colonies. These high days in Scotland would have a heyday in America.

SCOTTISH COLONIALISM AND PRESBYTERIAN MISSION: THE SACRAMENTAL SEASON IN EARLY AMERICA

Late in the summer of 1636 Robert Blair and John Livingston, two of the foremost leaders of the Presbyterian awakening of the 1620s, set sail on "the *Eagle-Wing*" with about one hundred and forty parishioners for New England. Overburdened by "the Yoak of the Prelates tyranny" in Scotland and in Ulster, they were ready to cast their lot with the English Puritans who were peopling Massachusetts Bay Colony. "We set to Sea," Livingston reported, "and for some space had a fair Wind, till we were between three and 400 Leagues from *Ireland*, and so nearer the Bank of Newfoundland, than any place of *Europe*. But if ever the Lord spake by his Winds and other Dispensations, it was made evident to us, that it was not his Will, we should go to *New-England*." Forced to turn back by "the swellings of the sea [that] did rise higher than any mountains we had seen on the earth," pastors and people resettled in Ulster or Scotland and continued the struggle. What effect this boat full of zealous Presbyterians, coming off a decade of sometimes ecstatic revivals, would have had on a colony caught up in the Antinomian Controversy is interesting to ponder, if hard to conceive. What is certain is that the frustration of the hopes of Blair and Livingston "to spread and propagate the gospel in America" marked an early setback for the Presbyterian mission—a failed attempt at Scottish colonization that was not without company in the seventeenth century.[76]

Blair and Livingston, before they ever embarked for New England, had been part of another more successful colonial venture in Ulster. Close to the homeland and regularly fed by new immigrants, the Scottish settlements there were largely dominated by Presbyterians of the western Lowlands. These communities proved that the religious culture of the southwest was transplantable, that a colonial situation, if an impediment, was nonetheless a viable context for Presbyterian mission. Still the proximity of the southwest to these counties in the north of Ireland—particularly Londonderry, Antrim, and Down—made this extension of Scottish social and religious patterns a fairly simple colonial undertaking. Ministers from Scotland, for example, could easily settle there and prospective preachers from Ulster could readily seek training in the Scottish universities, as William Tennent, Sr., did to name one exemplar. The strength of the Scottish communities in Ulster may have boded well for later settlements much farther from home, but nonetheless the difficulties of transatlantic colonization remained imposing and were only rarely surmounted by the Scots in the seventeenth century.[77]

About 1620 the Scots made plans to found their own colony in America, to enter the imperial race alongside England, Holland, France, Sweden, Spain, and Portugal. In 1621 the Scottish adventurer Sir William Alexander received a charter from James I for Nova Scotia. The first expedition set sail from Kirkcudbright in 1622 for this New Scotland, but ended up landing in Newfoundland instead. Only in 1629 were small settlements at Port Royal and Cape Breton finally established. Neither lasted long, and in 1632 Charles I destroyed what remaining hopes there were for Nova Scotia by signing it over to France in the Treaty of St. Germain-en-Laye. The clear failures of the 1620s, coupled with continual political and religious strife at home, put a check on Scottish colonial ambitions for the next half-century. In the 1680s Scottish proprietors, particularly the Quaker Robert Barclay, took a prominent part in the colonization of East Jersey, but by 1702 this colony had been merged with its western half to form the Crown colony of New Jersey. In 1684 a group of Covenanters, hoping to find relief from intensified persecution by Charles II, settled at Stuart's Town in South Carolina, but all they found was more violence. The Spanish, coming up from St. Augustine in Florida, destroyed the settlement in 1686.[78]

The Spanish also loomed large in the failure of Scotland's most ambitious colonial scheme of the seventeenth century, the attempt between 1698 and 1700 to found a colony at the Isthmus of Panama or what the Scots called Darien. Spearheaded by the Company of Scotland Trading to Africa and the Indies, the Darien enterprise was intended to provide a colonial base from which Scotland could forward its mercantile interests. Orchestrated in the wake of the Presbyterian triumph, it took on as well the spirit of a religious mission. The General Assembly mobilized and found six ministers and two divinity students to oversee the spiritual well-being of the colony—a ministerial group that included the arch-Covenanter Alexander Shields. The religious concerns of these spiritual guides were quickly discovered to be at cross-purposes with the commercial aspirations of the leaders of the venture. Far from heeding these watchmen who went "crying and roaring every day among them," the seamen, settlers, and officers were at best indifferent to these emissaries of the "Church of *New-Edinburgh*" and at worst openly contemptuous.

More dismal still was the mission of these spiritual watchmen to "the *Natives*" of the region. The ministers had come to "these remote ends of the Earth" with the hope that "the light of the Gospel might shine in these dark Regions where it did never yet shine" and that "the poor Heathens might be brought to see and walk in this Light." Possessing almost no ability to communicate with the indigenous people, all they could do was bemoan Satan's hold on his "Vassals and slaves" and lament the injustices of their countrymen who made the Scottish religion "odious" to this "poor naked People." For the eight spiritual leaders of this expedition—two of whom died before landing at Darien and only one of whom made it back to Scotland—this whole mission to the New World proved a giant cross. Their prayers, fasts, and solemn gospel ordinances were neglected; their evangelical faith was given no heed. By March 1700 disease, poor provision, lack of royal support, and the hostility of the Spanish all compelled the abandonment of Scotland's grandest colonial scheme. "All places in *America* are not alike fit to plant Colonies in," minister Francis Borland concluded of the mishap in which he had shared. The same was the case it turned out for the planting of evangelical Presbyterianism.[79]

The failure of Darien essentially ended the independence of Scottish colonialism. The Act of Union of 1707 that brought Scotland under the political control of England made certain what had already become clear: Scottish immigrants to the New World, no matter how much they disliked their southern neighbors, would have to make their way in English colonies. Though settlers from Scotland and Ulster had already begun to trickle over to America in the seventeenth century, only in the early eighteenth century did Scottish and Ulster Scottish emigrants begin to embark for the British colonies in heavy numbers. By the 1730s Scottish settlements were sprinkled throughout the colonies from Maine to the Carolinas with the middle colonies—Pennsylvania, Delaware, New Jersey, and New York—the center of the movement. Pulled to America by hopes for better land and provision and pushed there by rising rents, poor harvests, and other crises—one of which by the eighteenth century was rarely religious persecution—the emigrants made their exodus from the Old World.[80]

The Scots and Ulster Scots who came to colonial America were largely Presbyterian, but that religious identity was not necessarily secure. There were a good number of Scottish Quakers and Episcopalians among the immigrants, and, once in the colonies, interaction with other groups was as inevitable as it was extensive. As Ned Landsman has observed, the

consolidation of Scottish Presbyterian identity in the New World was often forged out of confrontation with ethnic and religious diversity.[81] Also,
even though Presbyterianism was the predominant religious tradition the
settlers brought with them, it remained to be seen whether the church
could keep up with its people when they were scattered in a wilderness.
While Francis Mackemie, a founding figure of colonial Presbyterianism,
managed with the help of a handful of other ministers to organize a presbytery in 1706, it was a constant struggle to solidify the church and to
find enough pastors to minister to a dispersed people. Nonetheless, by the
1720s, Presbyterian churches had been established as a vital part of many
Scottish and Ulster Scottish settlements.[82]

With the transplantation of Presbyterianism to the American colonies
came Old World ways of organizing worship and devotion. The sacramental occasion, as one of the most prominent features of the evangelical
Presbyterian tradition, was soon re-created in America. In New England,
for example, enclaves of Presbyterian immigrants almost immediately
staged sacramental occasions fully reminiscent of Scotland and Ulster. As
early as 1724 at Londonderry, New Hampshire, only four years after the
formation of a church there and only five after settlement of the town,
over two hundred saints were said to have partaken at the "communion
season." A decade later the number of communicants at a similar event
had grown to seven hundred, many evidently flocking to Londonderry
from other Presbyterian settlements. These "sacramental seasons" were,
as one nineteenth-century chronicler of Londonderry observed, "something like the assembling of the ancient tribes, on their national festivals";
these evangelicals, scattered on the frontier and dispersed in small agrarian hamlets, came together and reaffirmed who they were and what they
believed. This was true not only of the Presbyterians in and around Londonderry, New Hampshire, but also those a short distance away on the
frontier at Booth Bay, Maine. There the Presbyterians experienced one
powerful communion after another following the founding of the church
in the mid-1760s. The clerk of the church session described one such occasion in late April 1769 as "one of the most glorious days of the divine
presence and power we have hitherto seen in this place; the comforts of
the Lord were strong to many souls, His power appeared evident on all
the days of this solemnity, especially on the Sabbath and in the time of
the administration in particular. O that we may ever walk worthy of such
favors and that such days of the Son of man may be often seen in this
Church to all generations." In the far-flung Presbyterian communities
along the edges of Congregational New England these evangelicals cultivated their own traditions and often held aloof from the dominant religious culture.[83]

In the middle colonies, where Presbyterian immigration was much heavier than in New England, sacramental occasions were proportionally larger and more pronounced. The communion seasons—prevalent, powerful, and well-attended—figured prominently in the religious life of the Presbyterian immigrants throughout the region. In 1744, when the evangelist William Tennent, Jr., visited "a new erected Congregation in the Towns of *Maidenhead* and *Hopewell*" in New Jersey, one of his first aims was to celebrate the Lord's Supper. The congregation, being without a settled pastor, happily embraced this opportunity. "The *Sacramental Season*," Tennent rejoiced, "was blessed to the refreshing of the LORD's dear People there, as well as to others of them which came from other Places. So that some who had been much distressed with Doubts about their State, received Soul-satisfying Sealings of GOD's everlasting Love: Others were supported and quickned, so that they returned Home rejoicing and glorifying GOD." The communion season, though far removed from Ulster or Scotland, invigorated this newly gathered congregation in this distant patch of New Jersey.[84]

Tennent's experience in Maidenhead and Hopewell had plenty of parallels. His brother Gilbert, for instance, reported similar sacramental revivals in his congregation at New Brunswick, New Jersey. "Frequently at *Sacramental Seasons* in *New-Brunswick*," Gilbert Tennent informed readers of *The Christian History* in November 1744, "there have been signal Displays of the divine Power and Presence: divers have been *convinced* of Sin by the Sermons then preached, some *converted*, and many much affected with the *Love* of GOD in JESUS CHRIST. O the sweet Meltings that I have often seen on such Occasions among many! *New-Brunswick* did then look like a *Field the LORD had blessed*: It was like a little *Jerusalem*, to which the scattered Tribes with eager haste repaired at Sacramental Solemnities; and there they fed on the *Fatness of God's House*, and drunk of the *River of his Pleasures*." As in New England, "the scattered Tribes" in the middle colonies reassembled and renewed their faith through these eucharistic festivals. To the west at Fagg's Manor, Pennsylvania, the Reverend Samuel Blair offered this summary assessment: "Our *sacramental Solemnities* for communicating in the *Lord's Supper* have generally been very blessed Seasons of Enlivening and Enlargement to the People of GOD." From at least the 1730s, the evangelical movement had been gaining momentum in the middle colonies; the sacramental season, a traditional source of revitalization for the Presbyterians, provided a notable portion of that impetus.[85]

One of the best indications of the place the sacramental occasion occupied in the evangelistic mission of the middle-colony Presbyterians comes from an unlikely source, the New Englander David Brainerd. A fervent Congregationalist by background, Brainerd had been commissioned by the Society in Scotland for the Propagation of Christian Knowl-

edge to spread the gospel among the Delaware Indians. In moving southward under the auspices of this Scottish missionary group, Brainerd was
earmarked to be an ally of the leading Presbyterian revivalists in the region. In this he did not disappoint; he readily joined in the evangelistic
meetings of his Presbyterian hosts, particularly their communion seasons.
Early on he was exposed to the power of the Scottish communion, when
in June 1745 he assisted Charles Beatty at a sacramental occasion in Ne-
shaminy, Pennsylvania. With "three or four thousand" people in attendance, this communion was a grand event; Brainerd was deeply affected
by this "sweet melting season." Not long after Brainerd was exposed to
the blessings of these solemnities, he began to incorporate those Indians
whom he was proselytizing into such proceedings. Thus the next time he
was invited to assist at a communion occasion he brought "the Indians
along with me . . . near fifty in all, old and young." The occasion, Brainerd believed, markedly increased their spiritual concerns, and similar
effects were reported at the next sacramental solemnity that he and his
converts attended in October.[86]

Buoyed by these assemblies and the impact they had on his congregants, Brainerd prepared to hold his own sacramental season among
those whom he was trying to save from "the grossest Darkness and Hea-
thenism." Having first "taken Advice . . . in this solemn Affair" from his
"Reverend *Correspondents*," Brainerd followed the Scottish pattern basically to the letter: Friday was "set apart for solemn *Fasting* and *Prayer*";
Saturday was given over to further preparations and exhortations; Sunday brought the Lord's Supper and more sermons; Monday concluded
"the Sacramental Solemnity" with praise, thanksgiving, and calls for sustained moral discipline. "This appear'd to be a Season of divine Power
among us," Brainerd summarized. "The religious People were much refreshed, and seem'd remarkably tender and affectionate, full of Love
[and] Joy, . . . Convictions also appear'd to be reviv'd in many Instances;
and divers persons were awakened whom I had never observ'd under any
religious Impressions before." In particular affections were raised during
"the Performance of the *Sacramental* Actions, especially in the Distribution of the *Bread*." At that point the people "seem'd to be affected in a
most lively Manner, as if *Christ had been* really *crucified before them*."
This sacramental revival—with all the "Affectionate Sobs, Sighs and
Tears" it engendered—truly overjoyed the often disconsolate Brainerd.
"O what a sweet and blessed Season was this!" he exulted. "God himself,
I'm persuaded, was in the midst of his People!" This sacramental season
proved to be among the most satisfying events in Brainerd's life; indeed,
the "sweet Union, Harmony and endearing Love" he experienced there
was "the most lively Emblem of the heavenly World, I had ever seen."[87]

After this epiphanal communion Brainerd continued his devotion to the sacramental season. Two months later, in June 1746, he gathered his congregation together again, and they traveled en masse to a sacramental occasion led by William Tennent, Jr., at Freehold. Though this solemnity did not attain the power of his own in April, it nonetheless was "a season of comfort to the godly, and of awakening to some souls." Many of "my People who communicated," Brainerd related, were "agreeably affected at the Lord's Table, and some of them considerably melted with the Love of Christ." In the next two months he participated in similar sacramental revivals at Cranbury, New Jersey, and Charlestown, Pennsylvania. Again and again he found these occasions to be glorious seasons of "divine Power and Grace."[88]

The power of the sacramental occasion confessedly carried mixed blessings in the context of Brainerd's mission. Brainerd, after all, employed this Christian feast to undermine the traditional religious beliefs of the Delaware, their "idolatrous *Feast*[s] and *Sacrafice*[s] in Honour to *Devils*." The sacramental season could be one more battering-ram used by white Christians to burst a religion they considered heathenish. Conversion, in this context, entailed not a renunciation of sin, but of culture. Brainerd's mission fully revealed the ambiguities of Presbyterian expansion and revivalism. At the same time his revivals suggested the significance of the sacramental season for the strengthening of evangelical Presbyterianism in the colonies. The great works of grace Brainerd documented in his journals in the 1740s were regularly tied to these sacramental occasions. In Brainerd's account the sacramental season coalesced with revival and mission. Through it, the evangelical Presbyterians were helped to tighten their hold on their own people and to widen their arms outward to embrace others.[89]

To the south, in Virginia and the Carolinas, a somewhat similar story unfolded. The sacramental season strengthened traditional Scottish evangelicalism, while at the same time helping these Presbyterians bring others outside their own religious and ethnic group into the faith. Though the Presbyterian movement in the South was slowed by the opposition of the Anglican establishment, by the mid-1740s these evangelicals were making significant inroads, especially in Virginia. One of the early centers for the Presbyterian mission in Virginia was Hanover County, where a growing group of dissenters, led by the layman Samuel Morris, had been part of a "Revival of Religion which began in the Year 1743." As this work of grace spread, these dissenters increasingly hooked up with the Presbyterian revivalists in New Jersey and Pennsylvania. In the course of these refreshings William Tennent, Jr., and Samuel Blair visited for a fortnight and offered Scottish and Ulster Scottish immigrants in the area a rare opportunity to celebrate the eucharist. At the same time they introduced Anglicans and English dissenters there to the sacramental rituals of Scottish Presbyterianism: "The Assembly was large, and the Novelty of the Mode of Administration did peculiarly engage their Attention. . . . It appeared as one of *the Days of Heaven* to some of us; and we could hardly help wishing we could with *Joshua* have delayed the Revolutions of the Heavens to prolong it." The occasion was an important part of the revival then going on in Hanover; it was "a most glorious Day of the Son of Man." In 1747 Presbyterian Samuel Davies picked up where Blair, Tennent, and others, such as William Robinson and John Roan, had left off. In his missionary work in Virginia he reported similarly effervescent communions that gradually extended their power beyond the white dissenters to a growing group of black Christians. "I had the pleasure," he noted in 1756, "of seeing the table of the Lord adorned with about forty-four black faces." Repeatedly in the Virginia revival the Presbyterians aimed their meetings not only at their own people, but also at English dissenters and black slaves.[90]

Samuel Davies, far from being a singular Presbyterian hero in the Virginia revival in the 1750s and 1760s, had plenty of assistance. John Todd, John Wright, and Robert Henry were similarly successful as evangelists, and other ministers, such as John Brown and John Craig, also led important, stable pastorates in the region. Wright, for example, found his sacramental occasions to be times of "special outpourings of the spirit." "I had the sacrament of the Lord's supper administered the last Sunday of July, in my infant congregation," Wright commented in 1755, "which proved a solemn season. There was a vast concourse of people, about 2000 I daresay." Todd noted in the same year that at a sacrament "we preached Thursday, Friday, Saturday, Sabbath, and Monday, when there was comfortable evidence of the power of God with us every day. Believers were more quickened, and sinners were much alarmed." From the mid-1750s the sacramental season was an established, vital part of evangelical Presbyterian life in Virginia. By the 1760s the communion occasion was also apparently growing in importance in the Carolinas. In Guilford County, for example, David Caldwell was heralded for his evangelistic meetings and communions, perhaps helping to prepare the way for a host of Presbyterian revivalists from that area in the next generation—James McGready and Barton Stone included. By then the Scottish sacramental occasions would be flourishing not only "in Virginia and the Carolinas," but "indeed in the whole South and West."[91]

A half-century after Scottish and Ulster Scottish immigration to the colonies had begun in earnest, much of the religious culture of the Old World had been re-created in America. The sacramental occasion in all its patterned richness had been transplanted and had begun to flourish in its new environment. Long accustomed at home to traveling great distances to these events, these immigrants were unusually prepared for preserving this traditional festival within a dispersed, largely agrarian culture. The sacramental occasion was ideally suited to this colonial situation, to holding an immigrant group together in the face of the fragmenting effects of having been uprooted. In Scotland these events helped knit together regional communities out of small, scattered "farmtouns," and in America they held the potential to do much the same thing.[92] As the testimonies of Blair or the Tennents or Todd suggest, they often managed to fulfill that potential. In fact, sacramental occasions—unlike issues over ministerial education, enquiry into the religious experience of others, subscription to the Westminster Confession, or psalmody—were not in themselves a source of division among Presbyterians in early America. Though strife from these other issues at times filtered into the communion season, these rituals were essentially a point of agreement, activities in which the Scottish and Ulster Scottish Presbyterians in America could share as they attempted to put aside the discords that characterized so much of ecclesiastical and social life. For colonial Presbyterians they were an opportunity to come together, to heal breaches between neighbors, and to invigorate a camaraderie that made their dispersed, regional communities work.

What success the sacramental occasion had in renewing these immigrant communities was based not on its exceptionalism, but on its predictability. These were not spontaneous, unusual, or infrequent awakenings, but part of the very fabric of religious and social life. Year-in, year-out the sacramental season would be celebrated; people would reassemble; new communicants would be received; old saints revived; sinners awakened. Down years, of course, there were for whatever reason—from the weather to war. (An outpouring of rain often greatly dampened the outpouring of the Spirit at these outdoor meetings.) Still the sense of continuity dominates over that of dramatic discontinuity.

An illustration of this continuity is found in the sparse, but nonetheless revealing diary of Reverend John Cuthbertson, roving minister to a number of scattered Presbyterian immigrants along the Pennsylvania frontier from 1751 to 1774. Week after week, year after year Cuthbertson made his exhausting round from settlement to settlement, from family to family, preaching, praying, marrying, and baptizing. Each year, come late summer or early fall, he celebrated the Lord's Supper. Though Cuthbertson never described these occasions at any length, his terse, abbreviated notes suggest how the events were woven into this agrarian world. Dispersed clusters of Presbyterians came together—Cuthbertson already had two hundred and fifty communicants in 1752 at what was only his second sacrament—and participated in the familiar rituals. They fasted, received tokens, prayed, listened to sermons and exhortations from "the tent," heard the words of institution, came forward to sit at the table of the Lord, watched the bread blessed and broken and the wine poured out, partook of the sacred elements, sang traditional psalms, and praised God. For the 13th to 17th of August 1761, Cuthbertson entered one of his typical notations of a sacramental occasion into his diary:

13. f[as]t-Day, prayed, pr[eached] ps. 79.8— & pr[eached] Hos. 14.8. g[ive] a[ll] [praise to God]
15. pr[eached] ps. 15. pr[eached] Hos. 14.8. Con[vened] Sess[ion]: Distrib[uted] Tokens
16. S[abbath] pr[eached] ps. 22.28-1. pr[eached] Mat. 22.4. . . . Deb[arred]; & Invited, Sung ps. 24. c[ame] down [out of the pulpit], r[ead] I Cor. 11.23-27. Blyssed Bread, took, broke; distributed it & wine. 260 Com[municants] & 9 hours. g[ive] a[ll] [praise to God]
17. pr[eached] ps. 23. pr[eached] Tit[us] 2.11,12. dismissed Singing ps. 101. & Bap[tized] Jean and Sarah, Wife & D[aughte]r to Adam Ricky

The sacramental occasions were both extraordinary and ordinary times: they were special periods of sustained communal devotion, high days in the year, but they were also a prescriptive part of the calendar. Cuthbertson, in his compact diary entries, suggested both the unusual solemnity and the wonted familiarity of the sacramental season in colonial America.[93]

In the half-century preceding the American Revolution the colonial Presbyterians established a durable, largely continuous tradition of revival and renewal. From Londonderry, New Hampshire, to New Brunswick, New Jersey, to Cub Creek, Virginia, the sacramental occasion was re-created in the colonies. If not yet Cambuslang or Cane Ridge, these early meetings were impressive miniatures of coeval events abroad and notable portents of revivals to come on the frontier. These evangelical Presbyterians of the colonial era managed to lay the foundation upon which the next generation would build.

Communions and Camp Meetings: James McGready and the Great Revival

The American Revolution severely jolted what stability and strength the various churches had managed to develop in the colonial era. Disrupting congregations, pulling pastors and people alike away to war, undermining or even overthrowing established churches, riveting public attention on political issues, the conflict had a highly unsettling effect on American religious life. Yet if the years of war were disquieting ones for the churches, the evangelicals proved strikingly resilient, quickly regrouping and moving forward with revivals that in a number of places, especially in Virginia, had been in evidence right up to 1776. Some Presbyterians indeed had looked even amid war in the late 1770s to the sacramental solemnities for "a great reviving of Religion amongst us," and by the mid-1780s and early 1790s another series of revivals—in Virginia, North Carolina, and western Pennsylvania—had cropped up in connection with these communions.[94] By the turn of the century this latest evangelical awakening had found a new center on the frontier in Kentucky and Tennessee. At the same time back over the mountains and up in western Pennsylvania, the awakening continued to grow. By 1810 the Great Revival, as this religious tumult has come to be known, had affected a sizable portion of the new republic.

To tell the story of this complex revival and to delineate the place the old Scottish sacramental practices had in it is a difficult task. The movement was highly diffuse geographically, important actors innumerable, and denominational involvement far from limited to the Presbyterians.[95] The prevalence of the communion occasion in this period adds to the difficulty, for the generation from 1785 to 1815 saw the Scottish revival pattern peak in significance for American religious history. The traditional rituals that the Scots and Ulster Scots had brought with them to America were the basis of revivals from western Pennsylvania down through Kentucky and over to Virginia and the Carolinas. To bring focus to this account of the Great Revival and the part the sacramental season played in it, the narrative has been organized largely around one important figure—James McGready—who participated in sacramental occasions and revivals wherever he traveled. He stands as an embodiment of a particular movement and a longer tradition, both of which were far larger than himself.

McGready, born about 1758 in Pennsylvania, was raised in Guilford County, North Carolina, a regional stronghold for Presbyterianism in the South. After the Revolution he began his training for the ministry under the guidance of two leading lights in western Pennsylvania, Joseph Smith and John McMillan, both College of New Jersey graduates and both fully within the evangelical Presbyterian tradition. While under their tutelage, McGready found himself amid a series of revivals that had begun as early as 1781 and that continued through his departure for the South about 1788. Within these years of revival in western Pennsylvania, "there were many sweet, solemn sacramental occasions. The most remarkable of these was at Cross-Creek, in the spring of the year 1787.—It was a very refreshing season to the pious, a time of deliverance to a number of the distressed, and of awakening to many. The Monday evening was peculiarly and awfully solemn; some hundreds were bowed down and silently weeping, and a few crying out in anguish of soul." The year before this notable sacrament at Cross Creek McGready himself was among the transformed at another one of these occasions. There, "on the Monongahela, . . . at a Sacrament on the morning of a Sabbath in 1786," he "first felt the all-conquoring power of the love of Jesus, which to all eternity I shall never forget." McGready's participation in these early sacramental revivals in western Pennsylvania set the tone for his later career.[96]

These powerful communions in the 1780s helped mark out the region as one of the centers for evangelical Presbyterianism. By 1802 the congregations of Smith, McMillan, Thaddeus Dodd, and Elisha Macurdy, among others, were common locales for revivals, particularly for sacramental seasons that at times came close to rivalling those in Kentucky for extent and size. In particular Macurdy—known popularly as the preacher "who knocked the people down"—displayed an evangelistic prowess akin to McGready's on these occasions, events that attracted as many as ten thousand people on the Pennsylvanian frontier. Equally notable to the evangelical power of the meetings was the precision with which the Scottish traditions were maintained. The basic forms of a Thursday fast, a Saturday meeting of preparation, the lengthy Sabbath exercises, and a Monday thanksgiving service were clearly preserved. But more than that, such customs as the use of "the old tunes" with the Scottish psalms, the practice of "fencing the tables," or the use of communion tokens—"none may come to the tables without their tokens"—were also interwoven with the narratives describing these extraordinary "times of awakening" in the region. From the early 1780s well into the nineteenth century, western Pennsylvania would be a preserve for the traditional sacramental occasions of the evangelical Presbyterians. Few places in the late eighteenth century could have better prepared James McGready for his subsequent revivals in the South and West.[97]

After leaving western Pennsylvania and his theological and evangelistic mentors, McGready made his way back toward Guilford County, North Carolina. On his way he stopped at Hampden-Sydney College in Virginia where another revival was in progress under the leadership of President John Blair Smith. That McGready played anything more than a supporting role in the awakening that stirred a large section of Virginia from 1787 to 1789 is doubtful. He left no account of the revival, and other chroniclers only briefly noted later that he had been on hand for at least part of the work. This revival, as with those in western Pennsylvania, was obviously not under his guidance; instead it offered him additional exposure to the evangelistic efforts of others. For further refinement of his revivalistic training he had arrived in the right place.

Spiritual concern at Hampden-Sydney was initially sparked by private prayer meetings among four devout students, but the revivalistic hopes of these young men soon engaged the attention of Smith and eventually other pastors and people in the area as well. By 1788 Charlotte, Prince Edward, and Cumberland Counties were all caught up in what had become "a general awakening." The Reverend Robert Smith, who had immigrated to Pennsylvania as a child in the early 1730s, said of this revival that he had "seen nothing equal to it for extensive spread, power, and spiritual glory, since the years '40 and '41. The work has spread for an hundred miles, but [it is] by far the most powerful and general in John Smith's congregations, which take in part of three counties." Again sacramental occasions contributed to the revival and as at Cambuslang capped the growing ferment. The concourses of people at these events were large; sermons went on "almost all day out of doors"; tables were served "till near sundown." Regularly God's presence was felt in these "most sweet, solemn, and powerful" assemblies. "Two-hundred and twenty-five hopeful communicants" were added to John Smith's charge "in the space of eighteen months" in 1787 and 1788. Robert Smith, concerned that his son might "wear his life to an end too soon" because of all his spiritual labors, worried particularly that the whole summer his son would be "riding to sacraments, and preaching every where. For the importunities of the people are pressing, and his desires are strong." The sedulous John Smith received needed support at these sacramental occasions from a number of other ministers, including William Graham, Nash Legrand, and perhaps McGready. Together they forwarded a tradition of sacramental revivalism in Virginia that stretched back to the 1740s and that would continue into the nineteenth century. The revivals around Hampden-Sydney once again revealed the power of "this affecting festival."[98]

After his short sojourn at Hampden-Sydney, McGready finished his trek back to North Carolina where he took charge of the congregations of Haw River and Stoney Creek. By the early 1790s this austere, prophetic preacher had awakened many congregants throughout Guilford and Orange Counties and in the process emerged as a prominent revivalist in his own right. McGready, in forwarding Presbyterian revivalism in North Carolina, followed such preachers as David Caldwell and James Hall, both of whom preceded him as successful evangelists in the region. Hall, in particular, was said to have led sacramental revivals in Iredell County from the early 1780s. McGready not only had the efforts of the likes of Hall and Caldwell upon which to build, but also benefited from the spread of the Hampden-Sydney revival. Many from North Carolina—"multitudes" was one chronicler's vague estimation—evidently journeyed up "into Virginia to attend the sacramental seasons in Prince Edward and Charlotte." With western Pennsylvania and the valley of Virginia, backcountry North Carolina became a center for evangelical Presbyterianism. Not surprisingly the sacramental occasion, given this milieu, would flourish there well into the nineteenth century. Indeed, as late as 1866, one reform-minded observer wrote a series of articles for the *North Carolina Presbyterian* urging restraint of the festal communions.

"The crowds and the attendant excitement of the communion season," familiar by then in the area for about three-quarters of a century, remained in this critic's mind distressingly excessive. Though the inroads of reform were clearly evident in these articles in the 1860s, sacramental occasions, fraught with religious and social excitement, were of long endurance in the region.[99]

By 1796 McGready had moved on again, this time from North Carolina to Kentucky, where the need for ministers was pressing among a rapidly growing frontier population. Settling in Logan County, he took up pastoral care of the Gaspar River, Red River, and Muddy River congregations. These infant churches in the Cumberland region would be engulfed from 1797 to 1805 in some of the most tumultuous revivals in American history. Yet, throughout this awakening, the traditional pattern of the sacramental season would provide the guiding form. These frontier revivals, famed as the first camp meetings, were also the latest communion seasons.

To read McGready's narratives of the Kentucky revivals is to read what was, after more than a hundred and seventy years of similar outpourings, a somewhat standard litany of the wonders of the Scottish communion season. "In June [1800], the sacrament was administered at Red River," McGready reported. "This was the greatest time we had ever seen before." "In July," he noted the next month, "the sacrament was administered in Gasper River Congregation. Here multitudes crowded from all parts of the country to see a strange work, from the distance of forty, fifty and even a hundred miles; . . . [In August] Muddy River Sacrament, in all its circumstances, was equal, and in some respects superior, to that at Gaspar River." And so went McGready from communion to communion throughout the summer and into the fall, bringing people to God and enlivening those already in the fold. Repeatedly he related how "a most remarkable season of the out-pouring of the Spirit of God" was connected with these communion occasions. Indeed, in this particular narrative McGready mentioned eighteen revivals between 1797 and 1800, sixteen of which were directly linked to these sacramental solemnities. "What is truly matter of praise, wonder and gratitude to every follower of Christ," McGready concluded of the intense revivals of 1800, "is, that every sacramental occasion in all our congregations, during the whole summer and fall, was attended with the tokens of the sweet presence and power of the Almighty Jesus." When it came to describing the revivals in 1801, instead of basically repeating his narrative for 1800, he simply provided "a list of our sacraments, . . . held at different places" as a fair, if sparse, summation of the work for that year. By 1803, even more immersed in these ecstatic communions, McGready could only marvel at "God's power and presence" at these occasions. "So many souls happy in the love of God, I never saw upon earth before," he exulted over the Red River sacrament in 1803. "The exercise at the tables was indeed a heaven upon earth. Christians at the tables, almost universally, from first to last, were so filled with joy unspeakable, and full of glory, that they might, with propriety, be compared to bottles filled with new wine." The glories of these occasions had come to resemble for McGready the descent of the New Jerusalem.[100]

The sacramental revivals, initially centered on Logan County, were matched by similar occasions northward around Lexington. There the revivals were spearheaded by one of McGready's colleagues from North Carolina, Barton Stone. Though Stone ultimately moved away from Presbyterianism, impelled by a restorationist Christian vision, his early revivals were founded upon the evangelical Presbyterian tradition. The mammoth meeting at Cane Ridge in August 1801 with perhaps as many as twenty thousand people in attendance was set up as a traditional Presbyterian "communion occasion," swollen to such a size that it rivalled Cambuslang and whipped to such a fervor that it continued for two or three days beyond the Monday services. Eighteen Presbyterian ministers were on hand as well as a number of Baptist and Methodist preachers. Preaching, singing, and praying went on for days on end, but amid the ecstasy and fervor the traditional rituals remained in place. Minister John Lyle, for example, noted in his diary on this occasion that after "the action Sermon," which was delivered as usual from "the Tent" before the eucharist itself, "I . . . sat down at the first table which Mr Blythe serv'd[.] I had some reviving clearer veiws of divine things than I had before [or] after[.] In time the tables were serving Mr Sam'l Finley preach'd on How shall we escape if we neglect so great salvation. I heard a part of that & then went to serve tables. When I spoke I felt uncommonly tender &c. There were eleven hundred communicants according to the calculation of one of the elders." The action sermon, the tables, the tent, the successive servings, the large number of ministers coming together to assist each other, and the role of the elders were all suggestive of the Scottish tradition.[101]

What was true for "Cain Ridge Sacrament" was also the case for slightly less spectacular revivals in northern Kentucky: the Scottish rituals underpinned these works of grace. Sacrament after sacrament attracted three to five or even eight thousand people. John Lyle, for example, calculated "about 4000 people" at the Lexington sacrament in 1801 and a similar number in the same place for another "solemn affecting season" the next year. Of one sacrament at Paris in August 1801 he recalled the great strain of preaching the action sermon to "7 or 8 thousand people." "I extended my voice so loud," he said, "that I was soon exhausted & thought I would have died or fainted away yet notwithstanding spoke above an hour." Another observer in the region, who made it a point to visit a number of these meetings, detailed a whole series of communions; finally, as McGready did, he simply made a bald list of "like occasions, . . . all similar to those I have described." "The work is greatest," he concluded bluntly, "on Sacramental occasions."[102]

Scottish traditionalism, of course, was not the whole story of the Great Revival, even for the Presbyterians. Revivalism in the new republic was becoming ever more complicated and heterogenous. Methodist and Baptist influences were clear amid these traditional Presbyterian gatherings for the sacrament, and even Shaker contributions in certain ecstatic forms of behavior were evident at times at the height of the revival. While religious ecstasy, such as visions and fainting away, had been fairly common in the evangelical Presbyterian tradition, the sacramental occasions of the Great Revival, at least in several instances, markedly exceeded former communions in the range and prevalence of ecstatic behavior. Also, people were increasingly camping outdoors rather than depending on local hospitality—a definite innovation, though in Scotland such arrangements on an informal basis were not unknown.[103] This logistic change, if by no means universal, did turn many of the communion seasons into "sacramental camps" and prepared the way for the full-fledged camp meetings of the Methodists, Cumberland Presbyterians, and others.[104]

Still what historians have long seen simply as the first flowering of America's own camp meetings—as the supreme example of what Peter Mode called the "frontierization" of American Christianity—from a different angle and longer historical view looks decidedly less distinctive, less exceptionally American. At minimum an Old World festival was facilitating the emergence of this American form of renewal, the camp meeting. Old World influences on American revivalism were profound, and of all places such influences were particularly notable on the frontier. The Great Revival was a grand display of the creative powers with which the Scottish sacramental occasion had come to be imbued in America. Indeed, the importance of these communions in the new republic suggests the Old World texture of a significant strand of American revivalism.[105]

If in places in this awakening the older forms were ultimately transformed into something new, in other places tradition was maintained and defended. Clear innovators within Presbyterianism—such as Stone or Richard McNemar, a Presbyterian turned Shaker—left the ranks, while the more tradition-minded, such as McGready, John McMillan, or John Lyle, stayed in the fold and generally held to the familiar forms. Throughout much of the West and South—including western Pennsylvania, the valley of Virginia, backcountry North Carolina, Kentucky, and Tennessee—the old forms of renewal, based upon the sacramental practices of Scotland and Ulster, were often preserved for another generation or more.

Agrarian settlements in these areas, removed from the older, more developed communities of the eastern seaboard, tended to become the bearers of Presbyterian tradition.[106] The old rituals and customs—the fencing of tables, communion tokens, Scottish psalmody, preparatory meetings, fast days, thanksgiving services, action sermons, sitting at the long linen-covered tables, the great crowds, outdoor preaching from the tent—often endured in these regions into the 1820s and 1830s and in some cases even longer. For the Presbyterians, the South and West were indeed bastions for this Old World festival.

An indication of the prominence and persistence of these sacramental revivals in the South and West comes in two nineteenth-century drawings of these events. One, depicting a "sacramental scene in a western forest," suggests the impressive size and solemnity of these gatherings, if in an idealized way. The image also roots these activities in the West, in this case in western Pennsylvania, and suggests again how the famed frontier revivals need to be envisioned not only as camp meetings, but also as communion seasons.[107] The other drawing shows one of these gatherings, once again set in a grove, with the Lord's Supper in progress. The cabins around about the communicants suggest the durability of the communion season. "The custom of spending three or four days encamped at the place of worship, during communion occasions," pastor William Henry Foote explained of Presbyterians in Orange and Granville Counties in North Carolina in the 1840s, "extensively prevails to this day." "Cabins are built for the accommodation of the worshippers, and for the season [the people of] the whole neighborhood give themselves up to the exercises of the meeting." Flourishing still in the 1840s in North Carolina, the communion season had incorporated the logistic arrangements of the camp meeting and had even formalized these patterns with cabins for lodging. In such cases the sacramental occasion became not only an allied form of the camp meeting, but perhaps even a springboard to later Presbyterian retreats. The communion season thus long continued to tie American Presbyterians to Scottish tradition, even as it facilitated change and the emergence of new forms. Through the early decades of the nineteenth century, the sacramental season remained a notable part of the religious culture of the South and West.[108]

In his last years James McGready, living up to his reputation as the consummate frontier preacher, headed still farther west into mission territories that revealed once more the power of this Old World festival in such regions. Before his death in 1818 McGready had founded churches as far west as Indiana where he organized one of the earliest congregations in the territory. This sparsely settled country proved, like Kentucky or Tennessee before it, to be fertile ground for the old sacramental practices. In 1828 a New England missionary to early Indiana felt compelled

1. *Sacramental Scene in a Western Forest.*

2. *A Communion Gathering in the Olden Time.*

"to disclose some customs about holding meetings, existing there, which may seem a peculiarity in the northern states." Though he did not set out the whole history, this wayfaring minister offered a good final indication of the persistence of the Scottish tradition:

> As the Presbyterians there are chiefly from the southern states, they have brought with them the customs of the Presbyterians of Virginia and Carolina; and these have brought them from the mother church in Scotland. One of these customs is, to have a sacramental meeting consist of several successive days, including a Sabbath. At this meeting it is common to have a plurality of ministers. . . . The meeting begins either Friday or Saturday, and closes Monday;— Sabbath is the communion. Preaching everyday is at the same place, which is either a meeting-house, or a stand in some piece of woods; and often where there is a meeting-house, the house is so small, and the assembly so large, that they have to go to the woods. The congregation consists of the people of the congregation, where the meeting is held, and numbers, from others round about. . . . Some of these c[o]me 25, and others 30 miles, purposely to attend the meeting.

Though changes in American revivalism and in American culture were becoming increasingly apparent by the 1820s and 1830s, this account suggests the pertinacity of tradition. The communion season, two decades after the Great Revival and two centuries after Shotts, was yet to have spent all its energy. From John Livingston's generation to that of James McGready, sacramental occasions were indeed fair-days of the gospel— vital celebrations long at the core of evangelical Presbyterian culture.[109]

As this early missionary to Indiana described the sacramental season, he was quite specific. He noted, for example, the long tables at which successive groups of communicants sat, observed how the sermon immediately before the Lord's Supper was still popularly known as "the action sermon," and commented upon the deliberate motions of the ministers as they took the bread, blessed, broke, and distributed it.[110] Though he had himself participated in a number of these Presbyterian sacraments and though he was clearly impressed by the power of the Scottish mode, the whole remained somehow peculiar, foreign, something the people back home at the Connecticut Missionary Society needed explained to them. His knowledge that these occasions had a long history stretching back to Scotland was one way of coming to terms with this popular festival unfamiliar to his own tradition, but his description of the intricate rituals of these occasions suggested that understanding the history of the sacramental season was only a first step, that much remained to be disclosed. As this Christian traveler intimated, understanding these festal occasions requires close attention to the rituals that patterned them.

CHAPTER 2

"A Visible Gospel": The Rituals of the Sacramental Season

IN HIS POPULAR *Sacramental Catechism*, devotional writer John Willison gave a standard explanation of why God had "*adjoined Sacraments to the Word.*" "*Sacraments,*" he related, "are as it were a *visible Gospel*, the Offers of free Love, and Benefits of Christ's Purchase, are thereby exposed to the *Eye*, as the Word doth found them in the *Ear*. God knows our Stupidity and Dulness, that we are much more affected with Things that we see with our Eyes, than that which we only hear." People need their faith strengthened by "sensible Signs" and "visible Pledges," Willison averred; only through "*Signs and Wonders*" would people believe. Though Protestants generally and evangelicals particularly are often seen as having so aggrandized the preached Word that sacramental actions paled in comparison, faith in the unsurpassed power of the eucharist was forever central to the revivalism of the evangelical Presbyterians. Embodied in measured gestures and tangible elements, the gospel was caught up in the mystical actions of the Lord's Supper and set forth for all to see. "Looking upon these elements hath done more good than many Sermons," John Livingston testified; "the substance of the whole Bible is in these sacramental elements; the whole covenant, a whole Christ in a state of humiliation and exaltation." Or, as one preacher proclaimed at a Saturday preparation service on the eve of eucharistic celebration: "The Lord . . . hath been calling to you by the still calm voice of the word, the trumpet will sound louder to morrow, he hath been speaking to you this day by his word, but to morrow he will speak by his bloody wounds." As words gave way to eucharistic actions, people saw the gospel.[1]

Sacrament and Word coalesced in the communion season; both were part of the rich pattern of activities, part of the spectacle to be watched, part of the drama in which to participate. The standard forms of address, the careful movements of the eucharist, as well as the duties of the participants were all ritualized. The well-known suspicions of evangelicals toward the rituals of Rome or Canterbury should not obscure their devotion to their own patterned actions; such "antiritualistic" sentiments did not diminish the abundant and variegated meanings that evangelicals regularly expressed through ritual. For the evangelical Presbyterians, God was present above all in the "*visible Gospel*" that was enacted in the sacramental season. It is this visible gospel, this drama of communion and community, sin and salvation, that this chapter attempts to unfold.

John Beath's Session Records and the Historical Interpretation of Ritual

John Beath, clerk of the church session for the Presbyterians of Booth Bay, Maine, in the late 1760s, had an ethnographer's eye for detail. Charged with "recording the history of the Church"—all three years of it—he seems to have taken on the task with zeal and received thirteen pounds, ten shillings for his efforts. Beath repaid his fellow congregants with a richly detailed account of the church's calling of the Ulster Scot John Murray as pastor, his eventual acceptance of the call after much temporizing, the commitment of the church to Presbyterian ecclesiology, its studied avoidance of Congregational polity, Murray's careful catechizing of his new flock, and the process of electing the elders and deacons. In all Beath's account ran to twenty-five manuscript pages and covered the years 1764 to 1767. Read before the deacons, elders, and minister, it was declared by all "to be a true and faithful history of fact from the first steps to the settlement of the Church down to this day." Beath continued to clerk for the session, and two more years of his attentive observations survive. For all five years, he showed a keen eye not only for the formal workings of church polity and discipline, but also for ritual, for baptism, marriage, and the Lord's Supper. The communion occasion, as the high point in the church's life, received particular attention. In what is an unusually detailed piece—right down to how the cups and platters were symmetrically arranged on the communion table—Beath went step-by-step through the rituals of the sacramental season. Much of the patterned intricacy of the event is revealed in Beath's text.[2]

Shortly after the church was formed, a sizable collection was taken up for "provision of vessels . . . instruments and utensils" for the Lord's Supper. The six cups, three large flagons, six platters, and four large dishes that were bought were "all of the best hard metal, and most elegant fashion." Linen to cover the tables was also acquired, and arrangements were made for the supply of bread and wine. Though Beath did not describe the architectural setting, the church itself, as other Presbyterian ones were, had to be organized to accommodate such gatherings with aisles suitable for placement of the tables and benches.[3] Announcement of the communion was made a number of weeks in advance, and Murray set about examining the candidates as to their qualifications for this "sacred feast." Did they possess sound, catechetical knowledge of the doctrines of the faith and the meaning of the sacrament? Had they experienced "a work of grace in their souls"? Were they living a godly life? Catechesis and examination were careful and extensive.

As the sacrament approached, preparations increased. A "numerous congregation" gathered a little over a week before the fast day at the home of William Fullerton for a special meeting of prayer and instruction. Already, Beath noted, "evident tokens of God's gracious presence were seen and felt by many." On "the preparation Sabbath"—that is, the Sunday preceding the sacramental Sabbath—Murray devoted both the morning and afternoon services to expounding on the Lord's Supper, its powers for the worthy and its dangers for the unworthy. The following Wednesday was appointed as "a day of public fast and humiliation in this town." Sins were reviewed; each of the Ten Commandments expounded; "the great work of self-examination, and secret personal renewing their Covenant" enjoined; psalms sung; and confessions of iniquity made. At the close of this solemn, penitential service all were to return home, continuing their "fast without touching any refreshment till after the Sun was down, as it had begun at that hour preceding day."

Preparations were to go on privately in family worship, secret prayer, self-examination, personal covenanting, and meditation. Public readying for the sacrament resumed on Saturday afternoon with a sermon on "the dying love of Christ" and further elaborations of who was invited to the feast and who was not. Near the close of the service Murray came down out of the pulpit, stood by the communion table, and "then poured out on the table a great number of small square pieces of lead," tokens for admission to the Lord's Supper. Handing these with great solemnity to each communicant one-by-one as they came forward to the table, Murray went over the importance of the token as a guard against the unworthy, a sign of the covenant, and a pledge of steadfast devotion. The next day the tokens would then be given to the assisting elders as a surety of one's qualifications to be at the table. Again psalms were sung, and a blessing as usual closed the service.

The careful construction of the ritual reached its apogee on Sunday. The tables, carefully arranged and "decently covered with clean linen," "all met and joined in the midst, just before the pulpit; in the centre was set a square table to which the others joined." Here on this central table the sacramental bread and red wine were set, punctiliously ordered, and "covered from public view" by fine napkins. Prayer, psalm singing, and a sermon were followed by the words of institution, Paul's account of Christ's origination of this ritual from 1 Corinthians 11. This passage was read and then explicated at length—"verse by verse"—to suggest once again the various meanings of the feast. Then with an awful solemnity the minister fenced the table; that is, he debarred "in many particulars all those characters he understood comprehended under the three classes, ignorant, unbelieving and prophane." Again "the ten commandments were run over" in an exhaustive listing of the unworthy. At the same time Murray "freely invited" all believers and "true penitent[s]" to come and partake at the Lord's table.

After the table was fenced, a psalm was sung, and the worthy came to sit at the long tables. When they had seated themselves, the pastor "descended from the pulpit with his Bible and Psalm book in his hands and took his seat at the element table in the centre." The elders now uncovered the bread and wine; then the pastor read the words of institution again, "pausing at each part until he had endeavored to imitate the divine examplar." Murray thus "took the bread and then the cup in his hand and held them up in view of all" and offered "meditations" on these elements. With the whole congregation standing and watching, the minister then consecrated the bread and wine, setting them apart "from a common to a sacred use by solemn prayer." The bread was broken and the wine poured out from a flagon into cups. At the central table the minister and elders communed; from them the bread and wine were passed along the tables until all had partaken. Murray then rose and offered further meditations and comforts as well as reminding the communicants of their "vows and resolutions" to live holy lives. As a psalm was sung, these communicants retired to their seats, and a new group filled up the tables again. The rituals of dispensing the elements were repeated as many times as necessary until all had been served.

The rituals of the sacramental season, though focused on the Lord's Supper, continued after this central celebration. After the lengthy service of successive tables Murray gave "a solemn exhortation" to all in the assembly. He addressed the communicants in their varying states—from the most unworthy to the most comforted saint. He also exhorted "the spectators" as either unprepared Christians who had missed a great blessing or as unconverted sinners who should hasten to the blood of Christ for regeneration. The exhortation also moved the congregation into eucharistic thanksgiving. This became the dominant theme of the services that afternoon and on Monday. Thanksgiving sermons were preached on both occasions; the blessings of the great feast were enumerated and extolled. Finally, the solemn work closed.

John Beath went through this careful description without remarking at the time on the effect of this communion on the church. Only a bit later, as he reviewed the spiritual life of the congregation, did he comment on its power. Through the first months of Murray's pastorate the congregants had solemnly attended Sabbath worship, but "nothing very remarkable of a public nature" visited the church "until the sacrament." "Then there were such symptoms of the powerful and special presence of God of grace," Beath happily narrated, "as every one might discern and we can never enough be thankful for; it was a solemn, sweet and glorious season; many of God's children were filled with the joys of the Lord and many poor souls brought to see their need of that Saviour they had shamefully neglected, and wickedly crucified." The sacramental season affected these Presbyterians at Booth Bay the way it affected so many other congregations. It brought renewal and revival. God's people were refreshed and the unconverted awakened. The spiritual power generated at the occasion radiated outward to "neighboring towns" as Murray itinerated for two weeks, preaching every day as he sought to further this little awakening. The whole community, Beath assured, and many of the surrounding settlements had been rejuvenated; "thus it continued thro' all the Summer amongst us." Quite caught up in this refreshing, Beath hoped "the awakening" would "continue and increase until the whole earth bow to the conqueror Christ."

This local revival in Booth Bay in 1767 was in evidence through the remainder of Beath's account. The sacramental occasion continued as the well-spring of much of its power. In October 1767, six months after the first celebration, the sacrament was administered again "in the presence of a great concourse of people to about 220 communicants." It was another "glorious Season of Grace" in which several persons were "remarkably awakened & many comforted in a surprizing manner." The next October "a great multitude" again assembled, and the number of communicants had grown to two hundred and forty. The powerful effects yet again awed Beath as well as those around him; indeed, three communicants, "their cup running over," were "so overpowered with the joys of the Lord that they fainted away." By the standards of Cambuslang or Cane Ridge, of course, these were hardly grand sacramental occasions, but within this small community and "this infant Church" these were the high days of the year.[4]

The elaborateness of Beath's description of the first communion in Booth Bay suggests how densely patterned, richly symbolic the sacramental season was. This intricacy was clearly revealed, even though the communion was relatively small with no other ministers assisting Murray and a crowd that was evidently containable in the church. The bigger events were no doubt still more spectacular with services outdoors, sermons by the dozens, and crowds in the thousands. Yet the pattern, moving from penitence on the fast day through thanksgiving on Monday, was essentially the same from place to place and from sacrament to sacrament. If Beath's account of the modest communion seasons at Booth Bay did not capture the potential magnitude of these occasions, it certainly suggested the subtlety and complexity of the rituals.

While Beath described in detail the rituals that undergirded these occasions, he offers us little help in interpreting them. What are we to make of these intricate, carefully orchestrated, scrupulously guarded rituals? How are these various symbols and patterned actions to be interpreted? How were these rituals interwoven with the communities which they re-vivified? The sacramental occasion was, indeed, "a *visible Gospel*," a spectacle, a drama set out as much for the eyes as for the ears. In it Christ spoke "a Sacramental Dialect," to use another phrase of the popular cat-echist John Willison, a language of action, symbol, and ritual. Historians at times have slighted this sacramental dialect and instead given priority to the spoken or printed word over ritual action. With the communion occasion this emphasis has to be shifted. Here historians need to under-stand sacraments as readily as sermons, to interpret actions as carefully as words.[5]

The historical interpretation of ritual is no easy task, and historians who attempt this sort of "retrospective ethnography" are bound to face several problems. Unlike field workers, historians must interpret rituals they themselves have not observed, actions that distant figures have crys-tallized in words—the very medium ethnographic historians want to sup-plement and enrich. If historians are fortunate, they may have some visual evidence—sketches, engravings, or paintings, for example, that may cap-ture actions, even as they freeze them. Historians confessedly face a range of such source problems in their attempt to interpret ritual, but the diffi-culties with sources do not make the endeavor impracticable. Beath's text offers a ready example of a chronicle that can be considered in a sense as a set of ethnographic "field notes." While he failed to record a number of things, as would any observer, he provided a basic description of the rit-uals that invites interpretation. His account, though an unusually full one, has considerable company. Taken together, these accounts provide adequate, if qualified, access to these rituals. Given such sources, the problem shifts from how these past actions can be recovered for interpre-tation to how such interpretation should proceed.[6]

Interpretation of the rituals of the sacramental season could proceed variously, but the approach taken here has aimed at disclosing in detail both the religious and social meanings of the rituals of these occasions. Interpreters have often given the social, instrumental dimensions of ritual the lion's share of attention. Intertwined with a community, rituals are understood to reflect and sustain social structure and to generate solidar-ity. They prescribe and reinforce relations between the sexes, between parents and children, and between superiors and subordinates. From this angle of vision ritual is primarily interesting in so much as it resolves ten-sions within the social structure, patterns social relations, or solidifies the community. Even when this angle of vision is reversed and questions of how rituals of inversion could challenge the existing order are asked, the focus tends to remain on the social impact of ritual.

This dominating concern with the relationship of ritual to community is evident even in the work of Rhys Isaac whose writing has been of critical importance in forwarding an ethnographic history of early American culture. Isaac, when discussing the Baptist movement and "the richness of its rituals," assesses these worship patterns almost exclusively in terms of community and collectivity. Isaac's work is clearly among the best, and yet when it comes to evangelical ritual, the discussion revolves around the social significance of these actions rather than their multilayered expression of various religious meanings. Kisses of peace, love feasts, watch nights, and foot washings, no doubt, were essential for creating "*a* community within and apart from *the* community" in colonial Virginia, but what did these activities mean to those who performed them?[7] What meanings, besides notions of community, did these actions evoke? As with the rituals of the Baptists or Methodists, so it is with those of the Presbyterians: social implications are only one cluster of meanings present in the rituals of the sacramental season. Sorting out the import of ritual for community is a critical task, but the larger ambition of interpretation should be to see that "the fan of meanings" is spread as widely as possible and not constricted to the narrower span of social significations. Complex and polysemous, the rituals of the sacramental season embodied a way of looking at this world and the next, a way of understanding the past and the future, a way of giving meaning to human lives and relationships in the present, as well as a way of ordering and reordering communities. Unfolding "the fan of meanings" has been the watchword for the interpretation of these expansive rituals.[8]

In interpreting the rituals of the festal communions, the focus in this chapter is on public worship, on concerted action. Though these meetings were laden with private devotions—such as secret prayer, personal covenanting, self-examination, and meditation on Christ's sufferings—practices that were as ritualized as the public activities, such private forms of piety are mainly addressed in the next chapter as aspects of each saint's spirituality. In this chapter attention is given primarily to corporate ritual, to collective action. In concentrating on public worship the intent has not been to suggest that all participants shared equally in the range of meanings that these rituals entailed. The relationship of any given individual to the group was complicated, variable. That will become altogether clear in the next chapter. This chapter attempts to get a handle on the collective and the corporate with full recognition that individual actors drew on the powers of the sacramental season selectively and unevenly.

What is said here about the rituals and symbols of these festal communions is said in a very broad way. This makes the analysis applicable in many instances to the sacramental occasions generally. That there were differences and changes within these rituals from place to place and over time is quite openly acknowledged; the importance of context, variability, and development is warmly affirmed. That affirmation should be clear in part from the historical treatment of this tradition in the first chapter and should be evident as well in the evaluation of change in chapter 4. Still the aim in this chapter is to say something about the rituals and symbols of the sacramental season that to a degree transcends particular evangelical Presbyterian communities and specific celebrations of the sacrament. Yet the interpretations are always rooted in the particular, in broodings on the likes of John Beath, clerk of the church session in Booth Bay, Maine, in the 1760s.

The ruminations in this chapter have been on segments of these sacramental festivals—reflections on fragments that when joined together are intended to form a tessellation illumining the whole. Many different cantles and corners of these rituals have been explored in an effort to evoke the events in something approaching their fullness and power. The bits and pieces have been fitted into a pattern that roughly follows the movement of the communion seasons themselves from purification and penance to thanksgiving and affirmation. The chapter first considers rituals and symbols of repentance and cleansing—such things as fasting, mourning, pure language, clean clothes, and white linens. Then attention is turned to processes of transformation—for example, initiation, confirmation, and conversion—to thresholds that were crossed on these occasions. Finally, rituals of communion and community are explored—the dispensing of tokens, the fencing of tables, the singing of psalms, the sharing of elements. Throughout the aim has been to fathom an array of meanings, to see these communions in the round, or, more basically and directly, to understand them.

These evangelicals, of course, would have questioned whether anyone who came to these occasions as a spectator to observe rather than as a communicant to worship would ever really understand these fair-days of the gospel. They would have wondered about a spectator who talked about their worship as ritual, instead of as divine ordinance. They would also have been quick to point out the distance between the spectator and the table, and they would have been dubious that cultural analysis and redescription, rather than experience, would close that gap and make the power of this festival somehow understandable. Still they would have known that there was always a place for spectators at their festal communions; for, after all, these evangelicals performed this drama of salvation in part for them.

Preparation, Penitence, and Purification

Preparation for the sacramental season involved extensive efforts at purification. Beath had emphasized the long preparatory process, the lengthy confessions of sin, the tireless efforts to guard the table from the impure, the fasting, and the penitential duty of self-examination. Such cleansings were an essential, ubiquitous part of the sacramental occasions. In these efforts, culminating in the Lord's Supper itself, the saints all fled "to Christ's fountain for washing," for Christ's purifying blood that washed away the corruptions of the flesh and the heart. Though various activities led up to the sacramental occasion—examination, catechesis, prayer meetings, preparatory Sabbaths—the communion season itself began with a fast day. It began, in other words, in humiliation and penitence.[9]

Beath recorded that the congregation spent twenty-four hours from sunset on Tuesday to sunset on Wednesday without refreshment. Many other churches held this fast on Thursday or Friday. While Thursday appears to have been the most common, it was by no means prescriptive.[10] What was prescriptive was the fast itself and the service that marked it. Joel 1:14 often stood as the text of inspiration for this day: "Sanctify ye a fast, call a solemn assembly, gather the elders, and all the inhabitants of the land, into the house of the Lord your God, and cry unto the Lord." In the sanctification of a fast, as in the sanctification of the Sabbath, worldly business and profane activities were suspended. "A Religious Fast requires total abstinence, not only from all food," the Westminster Directory read, "but also from all worldly labour, discourses and thoughts, and from all bodily delights." Gathered in corporate humiliation and in sustained discipline, the people turned to the Lord "with fasting, with weeping, and mourning."[11]

Beath revealed the penitential air that pervaded the occasion when he reported that all united in "spreading our iniquities before [Almighty God] . . . accusing, judging and condemning ourselves for them, and especially laying open that miserable state whereby our hearts were rendered unfit, and ourselves unworthy to make so near an approach to him as we had the prospect of attempting on the ensuing Sabbath." Even the psalms that were sung, Beath noted, were chosen for "the same purpose" of confession and repentance. The fast day service was a corporate act of penitence. It was, colonial pastor John Brown explained, "a Day of Solemn and Extraordinary Devotion; Confession, pray[e]r & Humiliation, and abstinance, . . . a Day [of] Sorrow & Mourning." All sins, private and collective, that threatened to disrupt relationships within the community and with God were confessed and abhorred. The community had to be chastened before it could be renewed.[12]

The fast itself revealed the penitential aspect of this first part of the sacramental occasion most fully. This abstinence was cast as "a holy Revenge upon the Flesh or Body for its former Excesses." This renunciation of sustenance for a day not only disciplined the body, placing it "more in subjection to the soul," but also was an important symbol of inward repentance and humiliation. Such a physical act of renunciation reified a spiritual state. The evangelicals always insisted that the fast itself could never "make satisfaction to divine justice for the least sin." Its importance was as a symbol, not as an efficacious act that merited God's grace. The fast concretized in a symbolic act that deep sense of guilt the saints had for sin, for all that disordered their lives and estranged them from their neighbors and their God, for all their thanklessness and disobedience. It was "a plain acknowledgement of our unworthiness of the least mercy," Willison said, "or even of the common necessaries of life, and far less of the heavenly manna that God provides for his children in the sacrament." The chastened body was an emblem of the humbled heart. A body that hungered and thirsted suggested a soul that was "hungering, thirsting, panting, fainting and almost dying" to meet with Christ in the Lord's Supper. Such parched, starving souls, James McGready assured, would be "feasted at Christ's table on the hidden manna" and "refreshed with the new wine of Canaan." The direction to "empty thy stomach" went hand-in-hand with the advice to "make ready to feast with thy Redeemer." Empty stomachs symbolized empty souls longing to be filled with the bread of life and the cup of salvation.[13]

The disciplining of individual bodies was wrapped up with the disciplining of the community. As each soul was humbled and each body brought under renewed control, the community was purged of worldly distractions and brought into closer union with God. Through fasting, pastor John Brown related, congregations were prepared for "higher & gr[ea]ter Degrees o' Communion [&] fellowship with G[o]d." The ordinary world of work and pleasure—its duties and routines, its food and drink and other "bodily delights"—was put aside as the saints readied themselves for the festal occasion of the sacrament, for communion with God and extended fellowship with one another. The fast was prologue to greater spiritual attainment and communal affirmation.[14]

These penitents gathered not only "with fasting," but also "with weeping and mourning." Though weeping could hardly be formally required in the way that fasting was, such mourning for sin and over Christ's painful death was nonetheless a ritualized part of these communion services. Tears might come at any time—in private prayer or meditation—but more often they were part of the public assemblies; hence the sacramental meetings regularly "became a Bochim—a place of tears—sweet tears of penitence." Particularly during the administration of the Lord's Supper itself the communicants often "dissolve[d] into tears at the sight of so sad a spectacle as the sight of Christ hanging crucified on the cross for our sins." "At the Table," one Scottish evangelical reported characteristically, "I saw many shedding tears in abundance." John Willison suggested the importance of weeping during the sacrament in a meditation he composed that was "proper in time of Partaking, or in time of Serving the Communion Table": "O NOW let the sight of a bleeding Saviour make me a weeping sinner! . . . Oh! can I see this blood run down in streams, and my eyes not pour out some drops! Shall I not give drops of water for streams of blood? . . . Lord, pity my hard heart, and give me such a look as thou gavest Peter, that may cause me weep, and weep bitterly at the remembrance of my sins, my pride, my passion, my disobedience which pierced my dearest Lord. . . . Now is the time to weep."[15]

Though evangelical Presbyterians were careful to distinguish between the tears and "the frame of heart that produces them," they nonetheless accorded unusual importance to these "drops of water." While God could look beyond such "outward expressions" to the "inward frame," the saints themselves could not. The tears made visible a humbled heart. By them sincere penitents were made known to all; without them there was "much Ground to suspect that our Repentance is not true." Weeping and mourning were essential public displays of repentance (Willison came close to calling tears "absolutely necessary"). Through tears, the abstract theological concept of repentance became at these sacraments something to be seen, something very tangible. People were then able to see repentance on the faces of their neighbors—in rivulets on their countenances. A minister in colonial Virginia, for example, could tell that a man at one of these communions had repented of his sins because he "saw him leaning upon [his wife's] shoulder, pale as death, with the tears running in abundance." Similarly, a skeptic at one of these events wondered why "all the people look as solemn as if they were afraid of thunder and lightning; and added he could not see how people could weep and look so." The tears, the sobbing, the sighing, the solemn visages were part of the spectacle, part of the drama of the communion season, part of the way these evangelicals displayed their deepest feelings of repentance and forgiveness to one another. Being bathed in tears and being washed in the blood of Christ were, in sum, often tandem events. The one made manifest the other.[16]

Weeping and fasting were two dramatic actions that helped reify for these evangelicals the inward process of purifying the heart. Other less dramatic, but equally important symbolic acts testified to the purgation of sin in preparation for this near approach to Christ in the sacrament. "There is a washing which concerns all before they meddle with holy services," Willison attested, "and especially such as the sacrament of the Lord's Supper." Certain common forms of uncleanness in particular were singled out as in need of "this cleansing" as the eucharist drew nigh. Though the whole body was to be chastened, some of the most proscribed defilements were "the sins of the tongue." At all times saints were to be careful in their use of language, but at no time more than on the hallowed occasion of the communion. Giving themselves over wholly to spiritual concerns, these evangelicals were to "speak the language of the heavenly Canaan" in marked contrast to the worldly who spoke "the language of hell." To sanctify the sacrament they were to "turn from all tongue-sins, rotten discourse, and corrupt communication." They were to put aside all jesting, cursing, backbiting, and storytelling. The sacrament required a special, godly language—a clean, heavenly speech. Conversation on these days had to be pure and undefiled.[17]

This requirement that all communicants should strive to speak in this heavenly tongue arose in a large part out of a stark sense of the filthiness of the mouth. "You would reckon it a sad disease," Willison observed, revealing his awareness of the mouth's pollution, "to have your excrements come out at your mouth; and yet, alas! this is the disease of many." This defilement was doubly alarming, given the mouth's reception of the holy elements. "Mouths that are polluted by swearing and evil speaking," Willison warned, "are not fit to eat and drink the sacred symbols of Christ's body and blood." The interdiction against ungodly speech thus helped guard the sacred elements from defilement and at the same time helped protect the community from the disruptive, evil influences of such speech. Reenforced in church sessions that often formally suspended those guilty of "profane, obscene, & filthy talking" from participation in the Lord's Supper, this requirement of saintly speech carried considerable weight and was important both for the hallowedness of the sacrament and for the harmony of the community. Backbiters and gossips, libellers and scolds, liars and swearers would all have to cleanse their mouths before they could approach the holy table. As the consecrated bread and wine were protected from polluted mouths, so was the community rid of the canker of rancorous speech.[18]

This clean, chastened language was also, like tears and fasts, a critical outward sign that helped the evangelicals distinguish themselves from the worldly. The person who vented such expressions as "I'll be damned" or "God damn his soul if it was not so and so" or who engaged in frothy, divisive discourse at these sacraments was evidently not among God's people. After all, the streams of language that came from the mouth, these saints were convinced, had their fount in the heart. Vain, worldly, or contentious speech before or after the sacrament was a telling sign of carnality and reprobation. The seventeenth-century pastor Zacharie Boyd made this point in clear, startling tones:

By the savour of your breath it shall bee knowne heereafter what yee have eaten this day. Yee who shortly after the Communion begin to raile, scold, lye, and braule, beguile not your selves: these rotten words are but *stinking belchs*, which proceede from the *rotten meate of damnation*: If the *bread Lord* . . . were in such mens hearts, the savour of life would be in their words, for wordes doe proceede from that whereof there is abundance in the heart.

The way people talked, especially in the proximity of the sacred, was a critical gauge of their spiritual state. Purity of heart, in sum, was manifested in a variety of ways. Clean, heavenly speech was among the clearer signs.[19]

Clothes were another. Like the appropriate language, the right clothes were integral to the occasion. Though hardly as ritualized as such sacral garments as mourning dress or baptismal robes, the garb of sacramental occasions was nonetheless distinctive. The best clothes the saints had were the ones usually chosen for the occasion. New clothes might even be acquired or made for the event. At Cambuslang saints occasionally expressed a worry that they could not come to church for lack of clothes that were "clean & neat enough." Such worries in Kentucky gave McGready cause to warn that those who stayed away from the sacrament for fear that "new clothes are necessary" and the expense too great were succumbing to a suggestion from the devil. Willison similarly suspected that "most people on the Sabbath are concerned to adorn their bodies with their best clothes," and in doing so neglected to attire their souls adequately. The ministers were well aware that the concern over clothes for Sabbaths and sacraments could get in the way of piety, that they might be worn to accentuate social standing or stratification as much as to suggest the event's spiritual significance. The ministers knew too that certain clothes might be worn, especially by the youthful, to enhance the attractiveness of the wearer and to distract others from pious concerns. Still pastors readily recognized the importance of correct dress for sacred occasions. People were to take care that their bodies were "gravely and decently apparelled," that pride and show were avoided, but that at the same time earnest devotion was displayed in the clothes worn on these holy days.[20]

Shoes and stockings in particular could take on devotional significance in the context of the sacramental occasion. In western Pennsylvania, for example, shoes and stockings, an early chronicler noted, were at times carried to the meeting, kept clean by being wrapped in kerchiefs, and were then put on only upon arrival at the sacrament. In Scotland, as in the colonies, barefootedness was common; in both places wearing shoes at these events became one way to indicate the hallowedness of the proceedings and to show that what transpired there was out-of-the-ordinary, that the sacrament warranted special forms of dress. People communicated the uncommon solemnity of the sacrament in a variety of ways; taking care to wear shoes and stockings was one way of suggesting its gravity.[21]

For the devout, clothes could be symbols of piety, outer garments that revealed an inner faith. Just as removing one's hat in these services could be a sign of reverence, wearing clean, decent clothes was an indication of solemn devotion. This was suggested in a passage of Scripture often cited when these evangelicals were attempting to cleanse themselves of all pollution for their near approach to God: "And the Lord said unto Moses, Go unto the people, and sanctify them to-day, and to-morrow, and let them wash their clothes, and be ready against the third day; for the third day the Lord will come down in the sight of all the people upon mount Sinai" (Exod. 19:10–11). If clean clothes revealed a readiness to meet God, the opposite was true as well. "Filthy garments" or "nasty clothes" could be "emblematical" of sinfulness and unpreparedness. All clothes, but especially such dirty ones, were reminders of sin, the original source of the "body's need of apparel." Negatively as well, rich, gaudy garments were symbols of pride and vanity. "Velvets, silks, and satins" were "but the excrements of a vile worm." These fine fashions were defiling, emblems of a pride that consumed the heart. They stood directly opposed to the ideal devotional dress of the evangelical—plain, neat habiliments. In wearing clothes that suggested their movement away from the pedestrian, labor-filled world and that made their devotional frame apparent, the saints revealed their readiness for the feast.[22]

Being dressed in "their best Sunday clothes" for the sacramental occasions was a preparation that these saints performed as a matter of course. Dressing this way communicated a seriousness and solemnity that was distinct from any verbal articulation. "A church-going people are a dress-loving people," a mid-nineteenth-century heir of these evangelical Presbyterians affirmed; "The sanctity and decorum of the house of God are inseparably associated with a decent exterior." He applauded the attentiveness of his Presbyterian forebears to dress. "In their approach to the King of Kings, in company with their neighbors," this chronicler observed, "the men, resting from their labors, washed their hands and shaved their faces, and put on their best and carefully preserved dress." Likewise "wives and daughters" were "attired in their best." For Sabbaths and sacraments people showed the importance of the occasion in the clothes they wore and in the neatness of their appearance—in washed hands and shaven faces. Evangelical culture may have been a culture of the preached Word, but its resources for communication clearly extended far beyond that medium.[23]

Not only were the bodies of these evangelicals bedecked in clothes that revealed the solemnity of the occasion, their communion tables as well were covered with special cloths. Clean, white linens were the ubiquitous covering for the long communion tables. These linens were matched by immaculate white napkins that covered the sacred elements. One commentator described these coverings as "snowy linen"; another noted that the cloths were "bleached and washed into spotless whiteness"; still another that "all the tables were decently covered with clean linen." White, being in this Christian symbolic world "the most perfect colour" and "a token of innocence," suggested holiness and purity to these saints. Not surprisingly the whiteness and cleanness of these cloths and napkins were carefully maintained. "If the linen on the communion table, or the vessels that contain the elements, were foul," Willison remarked, "you would be ready to cry out, It is a horrid shame and abomination to see them in such a case; and so, indeed, it would, for there ought to be an outward decency in these things: our Lord would have the very room in good order, where he was to eat the passover." "A foul cloth or vessel" would have been an offense against the very purity the saints were striving to attain. The scrupulously clean linen was thus a symbol of purity, a tangible object that revealed the sanctity of the communion table and set it apart from common tables. The long tables covered with fine white linen communicated holiness and purity to the eyes of the faithful. What the saints saw helped them believe.[24]

But these white cloths meant more than purity; their potentiality to symbolize elements of the faith went beyond notions of consecration. These spotless cloths—the analogues of "the fine linen of the saints," the glorious robes of heaven, "clean and white"—could evoke the heavenly communion of the saints. Or these linens could speak to Christ's death and resurrection. Willison took this line, reminding his readers that "when Mary came to the sepulchre, looked in and saw the linen, but not the Lord, she presently fell a weeping." Likewise saints in coming to the Lord's table should long to see more than the linen. Weeping over Christ's death and absence, symbolized in the linen, the saint might then meet with Christ as Mary did. Thus could sacral symbols of purity, such as these spotless coverings, evoke other meanings. Rituals and symbols of purity and preparation ultimately opened outward into fuller emblems of the faith.[25]

THRESHOLDS AND TRANSFORMATIONS

Preparation and penitence were prologue to transformation. The rituals of the sacramental season carried people through a variety of passages and transitions. Congregants were moved from penitence to thanksgiving, from repentance to new birth, from conversion to confirmation, from youth to adulthood, from this world to "the gate of heaven." It is hard to imagine that more thresholds within the Christian faith could be crossed or more transformations effected in one event than were in the Scottish sacramental occasion. This forceful condensation gave the rituals of the communion season an unusual power and intricacy. As Willison said, participating in the Presbyterian sacrament was "a *complex* Act, and a very great Work," for to these evangelicals it was the most august, compact ordinance under heaven—"a bright representation and compend of the whole christian religion." As a crystallization of their religious world and a celebration of it, the communion season compressed into a few days a series of transformations that helped give order, meaning, and definition to the lives of the faithful.[26]

One of the most important transitions the sacramental occasion could mark was the passage from youth to adulthood. A first communion was considered "the Threshold" of faith through which young people entered "the State of Adult Church-membership." Thus the communion season acted as a ritual of confirmation that attested to the spiritual maturation of the children of these evangelicals. Most young people, though some exceptions for precocity were acknowledged, were not admitted to the Lord's table until they were "above Twelve Years of Age." At Cambuslang in the 1740s, of those whom pastor William McCulloch examined, the age at the time of the first communion centered on fifteen and sixteen, though some came slightly earlier and some either through scrupulosity or indifference waited longer. If "the choicest season" for admission to the Lord's Supper for the first time proved to be the mid-teens, this parameter nonetheless remained fairly broad and flexible. A young person could be ready at twelve or twenty. This flexibility allowed the evangelical Presbyterians to maintain their ideal of the Lord's Supper as an ordinance for the already redeemed, while at the same time preserving the ritual as a traditional Christian rite of confirmation and youthful maturation.[27]

Coming to a first communion regularly entailed careful catechetic instruction by the minister and elders who conducted special sessions for the youth in order to prepare them fully for this solemn event. These preparatory meetings themselves could become times of revival, accompanied as they often were, "with great Tenderness, and many Tears, among the young People; one of them helping to affect another, yea and make very moving Impressions upon the whole Audience." Catechesis and closing with Christ joined in these preparatory sessions, further readying the youth for their confirmation as adult members. In this rigorous, invigorating process leading up to the first communion and in the rite itself the young gained recognition as "rational men and women" who now made the choice for themselves whether to affirm the baptismal covenant that had been made for them by their parents. At this "most critical juncture" in their lives, the young laid the foundation for their further spiritual growth and were confirmed as members of Christ's family.[28]

The rituals of confirmation through the first communion were by no means perfunctory endeavors, but carried considerable power. This was true foremost for the "young folk" themselves; as one said, when "I first communicated . . . I went trembling to the Lords table," or, as another said of her first communion, "that Sacrament-occasion was a most sweet time to my Soul." But this ritual of confirmation also presented an engaging scene for those who watched these young communicants seal their faith for the first time. An early American Presbyterian, John Leyburn, described one of these occasions in Virginia:

> When the invitation was given to the young converts to assemble around the table spread before the pulpit in the cross aisle, there was a spectacle which moved every heart, and drew tears of joy from many an eye. Fathers, mothers, ministers, Christian friends at last saw the answer to their prayers. Those who had been dedicated to God in infancy, and re-dedicated a thousand times since in the closet, at the family altar, and at this very sacramental table, had now . . . come forward to avouch Jesus as their new Lord and Master.

The critical passage into adult membership was concretized in the act of coming forward; as the young moved toward the long table, the others watched and wept as they witnessed this active profession of faith.[29]

The eighteenth-century Scottish pastor James Oliphant similarly attested to "the Solemn Mode of public admission of young Communicants to the Lord's Table." On Saturday he called each young person by name, and all stood up "immediately before the pulpit" where Oliphant exhorted them upon the great significance of the first communion. Finally he dispensed sacramental tokens to each of them, leaden emblems of the covenant that provided tangible evidence of their full membership in this evangelical community. Such rituals—whether in the Old World or the New—were intended to solemnize a mighty transition from "the course of this world" to "a holy and religious course." Between their baptism as infants and their confirmation as adult members lay an ambiguous period in the lives of these evangelicals, a time when they were "halting between two opinions," when their souls were caught "betwixt sinking and swimming." Through the rituals of the sacramental season, evangelical youths resolved the ambiguity of their spiritual state and navigated the passage into fuller religious union with the saints. At the same time they signalled that they had "come to years of discretion." For these evangelical Presbyterians, there was understandably "no Time in Youth so critical as the time of our first communicating."[30]

This rite of confirmation could extend beyond the young to those who were newly converted and who wished to confirm their place among God's people. Thus not only the young were initiated into the church's communion through the Lord's Supper, but also those who only belatedly turned to Christ. For these people the first communion was as important as it was for the young. They, too, took on this seal of Christian member-

ship and passed from the world of the unconverted to that of a covenanted people. "You may profess the christian religion," Willison
warned, "but you are never christians by an act of your own, until you
present yourselves at the Lord's table." Until people went through the
rituals of the sacramental season and then came forward to Christ's table,
they were without "the appointed badge of the christian profession."
They had not passed over this threshold of faith.[31]

The motif of confirmation at these sacramental occasions might be
pushed back a step to initiation through the rite of baptism. Though not
integral to these communions, baptisms were nonetheless celebrated at
times during the course of the event, particularly on Mondays. In such
instances people were provided with an opportunity to witness another
passage, for baptism was "the Door of Christ's House." The rite, of
course, evoked far more than initiation. It suggested as well purification,
regeneration, and sanctification and could open outward to engage all
present in a corporate remembrance of their baptismal covenant and their
own part in assisting the newly baptized to grow in grace. Parents in particular were to gain a renewed awareness of their obligations to make the
household a nursery for their children's salvation. Additionally, in its solemn invocation of the Father, the Son, and the Holy Ghost, the rite could
add to the sense of divine presence and power that often characterized the
Monday meetings. When occasion arose to celebrate a baptism in conjunction with the eucharist, the richness of the communion rituals was
further enhanced. This "Sacrament of Initiation," when merged with the
communion occasion, added another important ritual of passage to that
series of thresholds crossed at these events.[32]

The sacrament spoke not only of initiation and confirmation, but also
of death. As a re-presentation of Christ's death, the Lord's Supper was in
part a ritual of mourning. A primary communion frame was one of
"godly sorrow" over Christ's sufferings and death; these were "the days
of mourning for my Redeemer's death," Willison attested. In reliving
Christ's crucifixion through ritual the saints were confronted as well with
their own death and the question of their salvific standing as they faced
eternity. This contemplation of death was enhanced at those communions
held outdoors in the churchyard where the saints worshiped near or even
upon the graves of their forebears. "The field of death" with its "green
graves" and "gray tombstones" provided a setting for the sacramental
rituals that made reflection upon death, heaven, and "the great resurrection" almost inescapable. Yet, whatever the setting, participating in the
Lord's Supper and preparing for it helped ready these evangelicals for
death; for to be spiritually ready to partake of the communion was to be
spiritually ready to face final judgment. "Now, if you would take time
duly to prepare for the Lord's Supper," Willison instructed, "you should

not be found unprepared for death; for the same preparation is needful for both." The sacrament, a potent re-presentation of Christ's death, helped the saints be ready for their own death.[33]

Not only did the sacrament lead the saints to mourn, it also provided them with assurances that were comforts when facing death. In the eucharist they reaffirmed the great Christian paradox that Jesus in dying had conquered death, that Calvary had been a victory, that death had lost its sting. "The last enemy is death," one minister exhorted communicants as they sat at the table, "but be of good chear . . . you shall live in glory. You shall be crowned in the new Jerusalem with a crown, under which sit no cares, no fears, no pains, no sorrows: for sorrow and sighing, and dangers and trials, are all passed away—and shall return no more." To the various passages that the sacrament spoke, death was another; the saints, when on "the Threshold of Eternity," could look to their experiences at sacramental occasions as having provided "Cordials against that critical Time."[34]

The sacramental occasion could involve or evoke various thresholds that potentially spanned from birth through youth and adulthood to death. Scottish Presbyterianism, having shorn Christianity of its medieval sacramentalism, tended to condense in the communion season a number of traditional Christian rituals of passage. At the same time the Presbyterians added a quintessentially evangelical rite of transformation to their composite of the older sacramentalism: for one of the central transformations that took place during the communion season was the process of conversion. During these solemnities people regularly closed with Christ for the first time. Sinners, long strangers to the fullness of evangelical faith, were transformed into saints. More than sparking conversion, the communion rituals also facilitated the complementary process of renewal. Saints whose faith had slackened were rejuvenated; the process of conversion was retraced as old experiences were made new. Dramatic renewal and conversion were the fundamental transformations sought in these events. As complex, personal, and interior as these experiences were, they were nonetheless shaped by the ritual context in which they occurred. Ritual in its various components—actions, objects, words—facilitated the processes of conversion and renewal.

The rituals of the sacramental occasions gained their power to convert or revive people from the whole plexus of activities that made up these events. From preparatory meetings for prayer and catechesis to days of fasting, feasting, and thanksgiving, the communion season entailed a wide range of activities all dedicated to effecting conversion and renewal. Yet few aspects of the solemnities were as important as the dramatic preaching of the Word for leading people to close with Christ or to renew their earlier avowals. To say this is not to point us away from ritual or spectacle, but instead it is to suggest how the preaching of the Word was itself part of the ritual, how its success was related to delivery, cadence, gesture, setting, and time-honored patterns of speech, and how it was often intimately connected with the elements and actions of the sacrament. From fast day sermons to Saturday preparatory sermons to action sermons to addresses for fencing the table to meditations during the celebration, to thanksgiving sermons, to prayers and benedictions, preaching and speaking were critical parts of the ritual. At these festal gatherings, performed words were always a powerful medium of communication—a fundamental part of the process that led to conversion and renewal.

Robert Burns, in depicting evangelical preaching at sacramental occasions, contrasted the "eldritch squeel an' gestures" of a popular preacher with the "English style, an' gesture fine" of a moderate cleric. Other observers likewise regularly commented on the "frantic action" of evangelical preachers at communions. Delivery and performance were of critical importance, for the preachers were indeed a large part of the drama. The people crowded around them to "stare" as well as to hear, to watch "the parson . . . sweating, bawling, jumping, and beating the desk" as well as to hear the Word proclaimed in "the deepest, *strangest*, and most hollow *tone*." The "tent"—the outdoor pulpit from which they preached—was the stage upon which the ministers performed. Raised above their audience, the preachers with dramatic movements, solemn cadences, demonstrative facial expressions, and charged words made clear the way of salvation. Through the drama of the Word, people were revived and reborn.[35]

The transformative power of the Word on these occasions was often closely tied to the central rite of the Lord's Supper. An example of this interpenetration of Word and sacrament comes from John Leyburn's description of a sacrament in early nineteenth-century Virginia:

> One of the ministers . . . held up the sacramental cup, and asked, in language that went to every unconverted heart, "Can you, will you longer reject and trample on this precious blood, poured from the wounds of a dying Saviour?" "I call God and this great assembly to witness," said he, "that it is offered you afresh this day. Again dare to spurn it from your lips, and the record will be written against you on high, which, in the terrible day of God's coming judgment, will flame out to your astonishment and dismay in letters of fire." Not a few, who felt the power of that appeal, were soon after drinking of that cup, in memory of Him who had washed them from their sins, and given them a hope, through grace, of drinking it with him hereafter in his heavenly kingdom.

The minister, holding up the sacramental cup, joined the visual with the aural and thus succeeded in making regeneration all the more tangible and all the more imperative.[36]

Another example of how the Word was not so much preached, but performed on these occasions and how it commingled with the sacrament comes from William Wirt's description of the "performance" of the colonial pastor James Waddell:

> As he descended from the pulpit, to distribute the mystic symbols, there was a peculiar, a more than human solemnity in his air and manner. . . .
>
> He then drew a picture of the sufferings of our Saviour; his trial before Pilate; his ascent up Calvary; his crucifixion, and his death. . . . His enumeration was so deliberate, that his voice trembled on every syllable; . . . His peculiar phrases had that force of description that the original scene appeared to be, at that moment, acting before our eyes. . . .
>
> But when he came to touch on the patience, the forgiving meekness of our Saviour; when he drew, to the life, his blessed eyes streaming in tears to heaven; his voice breathing to God, a soft and gentle prayer of pardon on his enemies, "Father, forgive them, for they know not what they do"—the voice of the preacher, which had all along faltered, grew fainter and fainter, until his utterance being entirely obstructed by the force of his feelings, he raised his handkerchief to his eyes, and burst into a loud and irrepressible flood of grief. The effect is inconceivable. The whole house resounded with the mingled groans, and sobs, and shrieks of the congregation.

"Never before," Wirt commented, "did I completely understand what Demosthenes meant by laying such stress on *delivery*." As Christ's sufferings were re-acted in Word and then in sacrament, people were caught up in the drama of the Passion. Gestures, "air and manner," handkerchiefs and clerical dress, tears and intonation, cups and loaves, words and images—all this and more could contribute to the process of communication, to the solemnity and power of the occasion. During such charged, complex performances, people were transformed or invigorated by the spectacle of the Word.[37]

If the performed Word was particularly critical to the process of conversion at these events, at the center of the process of renewal was the Lord's Supper. The eucharistic rituals were at the core of the sacramental season, the axis upon which the whole turned. To understand the compact symbols and layered meanings of the sacramental elements, actions, and words is to move closer to fathoming why these occasions contained such transformative power.

Bread and wine constituted the feast of the Lord. Often brought forward to the table by the elders in solemn procession, the elements in their fine vessels presented to the eyes of the faithful, even before their consecration, emblems of sacramental blessing and solemnity. As one Scottish evangelical reported of a sacrament at Campsy, "W[he]n I saw the Elders [bring] forward the Elements, my heart was melted down with love to Christ." The very gravity of this procession, as the bread and the wine were introduced into worship, heightened the awe and expectation of the onlookers. All along the elements remained hidden from view by fine white napkins, only to be unveiled as the ministers prepared to celebrate the eucharist. Consecrated through prayer, the bread and wine were no longer "common things"; they were holy objects, the central symbols of the rite. Blessed, the bread was broken and the wine poured out. In the act of breaking the bread, the sufferings of Christ—"the breaking and tormenting of Christ's body"—were vividly displayed. Similarly, when the red wine in large flagons was poured out into cups, Christ's flowing blood on the cross was re-presented. In these two actions all of the sufferings of Christ were condensed; "the bloody Tragedy of Christ's Sufferings" was, as Willison said, "represented and re-acted." Here Christ crucified was "set forth before your eyes, in the bread broken and the wine poured out." Christ was lifted "up on high, upon the pole of the cross and of the sacrament, that you may look to him." "O take a fixed look of him now," Willison exhorted, "and let your eye affect your heart." As a visible gospel, the elements and the various actions performed with them were to be understood through the eyes, not the ears.[38]

Not only the actions of breaking and pouring, but the preparation of the elements also suggested the Savior's Passion. Bread, Willison reminded, "ere it be fit to nourish us, must be first sown, and die in the earth; then it must be thrashed, grinded in the mill, baken in the oven, broken, and eaten." Wine, too, was subject to the same kind of torturous preparation. It "must be squeezed out of the grape, and this must be trodden and bruised in the wine-press: so Christ was crushed in the wine-press of his father's wrath, till the blessed juice of his body, his precious blood, did gush out in abundance for the redemption of our souls." Both bread and wine were thus full symbols of Christ's sufferings. At the same time these elements suggested the blessings of Christ's atoning death. The bread suggested not only grinding and threshing, but also nourishment and strength; it was "the Support of human Life." Likewise Christ was the basis for the eternal life of the soul. Wine offered similar benefits of refreshment. As it warmed the cold stomach, so did Christ warm the cold heart. Christ's bloody sacrifice and its salvific blessings found concentrated expression in these elements and the sacramental actions that were performed with them.[39]

Sacramental words were conjoined with the eucharistic actions and elements. Though these Presbyterians adamantly resisted a fixed liturgy or set prayers, their sacramental language on these occasions was highly ritualized. Among the most ritualized parts were the speeches accompanying the administration of the Lord's Supper itself. These meditations, as Beath's narrative readily suggested, focused on the words of institution from 1 Corinthians 11:23–26:

For I have received of the Lord that which also I delivered unto you, That the Lord Jesus, the same night in which he was betrayed, took bread: And when he had given thanks he brake it, and said, Take, eat; this is my body, which is broken for you: this do in remembrance of me. After the same manner also he took the cup, when he had supped, saying, This cup is the new testament in my blood: this do ye, as oft as ye drink it, in remembrance of me. For as often as ye eat this bread, and drink this cup, ye do shew the Lord[']s death till he come.

These words—ones that were at the very foundation of the whole occasion—were carefully explicated by the ministers. These sacramental words and their exposition once again recapitulated the sacramental piety and theology of the occasion. The meanings of the actions and elements were reviewed. Reflection was fully concentrated on the drama at hand. The meditations were aimed at drawing the participants further into the tragedy that was being re-acted in order to stay any wandering minds, to situate the whole assembly on Golgotha at the foot of Christ's cross. The traditional words combined with the actions and elements to heighten this dramatic re-presentation of Christ's Passion.[40]

The Lord's Supper—its ritual actions, language, and objects—drew people into a direct confrontation with a forceful, highly paradoxical drama; for here they saw "the Creator of all worlds a mangled, bloody corpse." McGready cited a hymn in one of his sermons that suggested the powerful pull of this drama:

Around the bloody tree,
They pressed with strong desire,
That wondrous sight to see—
The Lord of Life expire.

As they witnessed that "wondrous sight" of the Passion, they were confronted with images grown familiar from re-presentation year after year. Yet the sense of wonder seemed always fresh. "Behold the circumstances of his sufferings and bloody death," McGready preached, "and wonders are unfolded which afford a theme which shall be new throughout eternity."[41]

As they watched the drama unfold, the people faced the paradoxes of their salvation. These are the hands that uphold the world bound and nailed to the cross? This is the King of kings mocked with a purple robe and a crown of thorns? This is the great Judge of all the world arraigned as a criminal and condemned to die? Christ drinks the cup of wrath, so that the saints may drink the cup of salvation? He is crowned with thorns, so that they may be crowned with glory? He suffers this death, so that they might have life? The reenactment of Christ's Passion in the sacrament confronted these evangelicals with a series of such paradoxes. Willison once used the word *strange* eighteen times in the course of one short sacramental meditation. The whole was "a strange Mystery!" or "a strange Thing!" or "a strange Sight!" or "a strange Act!" or simply "strange!" Through the ritual of the Lord's Supper, communicants were engulfed in "an ecstacy of wonder" and mystery. Out of this paradoxical drama emerged transformative power. Filled alternately with awe, fear, penitence, thankfulness, ecstasy, submission, assurance, praise, love, and hope, the saints found in this complex rite renewal and transformation. They witnessed the paradoxes of their redemption.[42]

As the communicants partook of the Lord's Supper, a critical transition in the rituals of the occasion took place. The temper of the assembly shifted from its dominant early frames of preparation and penitence to praise and thanksgiving. The sacramental actions of the ministers that vividly re-acted Christ's death gave way to the sacramental actions of the communicants themselves. As they took the bread and cup into their own hands, they expressed their acceptance of Christ as their Savior. As they ate the bread and drank the wine, the communicants feasted on the sacred symbols of Christ's body and blood and were conjoined with their Redeemer. Tears of joy now mixed with tears of repentance. Atonement was accomplished. The sacrificial, penitential sides of the ritual gave way to its eucharistic dimensions. They celebrated a "eucharistical feast . . . a thanksgiving to God for redeeming love." As they rose from the table, a song of praise was regularly sung, thus further marking the transition from repentance to rejoicing. "You ought to go from this table in the eunuch's frame," Willison advised, "who, after sealing a covenant with God, 'went on his way rejoicing,' Acts viii.39. God's people are frequently in scripture called 'to rejoice and be glad in the Lord:' and, to be sure, there is not a more fit season for it than now." Engendered by the reception of the elements and confirmed in the singing of psalms, thanksgiving characterized the remaining rituals of the occasion. The people had been transformed from penitents to celebrants.[43]

One example of the transformative power that the act of receiving the elements could hold comes from an account penned in 1757 by the colonial pastor John Wright. He spoke in particular of one communicant whose feelings of unworthiness made him extremely reluctant to come to the table. Though this confused penitent eventually "accepted a token trembling" and managed to sit down at the table, he did not take a piece of bread when it was passed to him. Seeing this, Wright confronted him:

> I took bread and went to him, but he told me that he could feel no faith. I dare not take, said he. But don't you want a Saviour, said I? O yes, O yes, said he; but I am not worthy of him. But are you not needy? O yes, said he, I am lost without him. But are you not labouring and heavy laden, said I? O yes, O yes, said he, I am crushed under the load of sin. Well, then, said I, Christ calls you

by name to come to him, upon which he took the bread into his hand and stood upright, and being a tall man, all the assembly almost could see him, and stretched forth his hands as far as he could, and looked with the most affecting countenance that ever I saw on the symbol of Christ's body, and wept and prayed to this purpose: "Lord Jesus, I am lost without thee," looking intensely at the bread; "I come trembling; I would fain be a partaker of thy broken body, for I am undone without thee; Lord Jesus, have mercy on me.["] He then attempted to put the bread into his mouth, but, by the trembling, could hardly get the bread into his mouth. He then sat down, and with all imaginable sedateness, partook of the wine. You would never forget the solemn transaction between Christ and that poor sinner, if you was [a] spectator as I was. I know I never shall in this world, as long as I can remember anything.

Though no doubt an exceptional case in the form that it took, the spectacular potentialities of the sacramental season are nonetheless altogether clear in a passage like this one. Gestures, facial expression, tears, dialogue, bread and wine all contributed to the drama. As this man looked at his salvation in "the symbol of Christ's body," in turn the congregants—spectators all—watched this "solemn transaction." "The whole day," Wright concluded, "was one of the days of the Son of Man; when Christ was lifted on the cross, he seemed as if he would draw all unto himself." At such moments sinners and saints saw and experienced transformation through the Presbyterian sacrament.[44]

The reception of the elements moved this man, as it did many others, from anxious penitence to solemn thanksgiving. After the celebration of the Lord's Supper, the services on Sunday evening and Monday confirmed that the threshold from penitence to joy had been crossed. Monday often became the great culmination of the work. Duncan MacFarlan, a Scottish evangelical chronicler of the early nineteenth century, observed this feature of the sacramental revivals: "We have been very much struck with the fact observable in Scottish revivals, that the services of the *Monday* after the communion were usually, more than those of other days, eminently blessed." McGready and other narrators of the Great Revival confirmed this pattern as well. At the sacrament at Red River in July 1799, McGready noted that it was "a very solemn time throughout. On Monday, the power of God seemed to fill the congregation." Similarly, the Gaspar River sacrament the next month "was one of the days of the son of Man, indeed, especially on Monday." The rituals of the sacramental season thus carried congregants from repentance to affirmation, from humiliation to rebirth with the Lord's Supper acting as the fulcrum for this shift. The Monday services capped the processes of conversion and renewal. Solemn, thankful, and at times even joyous and ecstatic, the Monday meetings often confirmed the transformative power of the festal communions.[45]

As this threshold from penitence to thanksgiving was crossed, these evangelicals seemed at times poised to make a final passage, a triumphant transcendence of the mire of this world. The communions were often described as "days of heaven upon earth" or "seasons of special intercourse with heaven" or as emblematic of "the New Jerusalem coming down from heaven to earth." The saints rejoiced that they were brought closer to heaven on these occasions than at any other time. Two couplets from "A Parting Hymn, for a Sacramental Occasion" suggested the sacrament's conjunction with this heavenly realm:

> 'Tis heav'ns, rich earnest sure we taste,
> While, clinging round the Cross, we feast;
>
> The world retires—Lo! heaven is near;
> 'Tis good, O Lord, to shelter here.

Another versifier sang a similar song "while setting around thy board":

> On wings of love our spirits rise,
> And heav'n begins below the skies.

McGready, too, regularly employed this diction. "At the table of the Lord," he noted at one point, "they appeared to feel heaven upon earth." These sacraments, most all agreed, were tokens of heaven, if not quite outright transports there.[46]

McGready, in a provocative sacramental meditation, reflected on the nearness to heaven attained through the sacramental season. Taking Genesis 28:17 as his text—"How dreadful is this place! This is none other but the house of God, and this is the gate of heaven"—McGready marvelled at the strange solemnity of the occasion that lifted people above the world to the threshold of heaven. "When Christians are seated at a communion table, and are near Christ," he preached, "they are at the gate of heaven, for Christ is at that gate." During the Lord's Supper and in the thanksgiving that followed, the gathering verged on the heavenly community. Final passage into heaven, of course, would have to wait, but the sacrament at least allowed these evangelicals a foretaste of "the sweet fruits of the heavenly Canaan." Here they had "a Pisgah's view of the promised land." Situated on that last threshold, the saints found that the transformative power of the sacramental season allowed them inklings of final transcendence.[47]

COMMUNION AND COMMUNITY

The rituals of the communion occasion spoke not only to the transcendent, but also to the temporal, not only to heavenly communities, but also to earthly ones. The sacramental occasions, Willison attested, helped create "a bond of mutual love and unity among believers themselves"; it was, he said, "an excellent mean for procuring and advancing unity and love among the saints and servants of God." One woman at Cambuslang gave clear, colorful expression to this sense of union and love that arose out of the sacramental occasion: "My heart was so filld with love to Christ & the Souls of others that I could have been content if it had been possible to have taken all the multitude on the Brae in my arms & to have carried them all up to Heaven." The communion ideally would not only enkindle such love, union, and mutuality, but also reconcile enemies and sustain the moral order. How did the sacramental season promote such community? What was it about these occasions that strengthened the bonds that held the saints and their society together? What sort of community was to emerge out of these festal gatherings?[48]

At a very basic level the power of the sacramental season to promote community came from its gathering together people in great numbers from over a wide area. When the time of the sacramental occasion arrived, people pilgrimed to the meeting from twenty, thirty, and even fifty miles or more. This very act of pilgrimage was generally a corporate endeavor, an opportunity for fellowship, conviviality, and shared devotion. An excellent example of this comes in the experiences of Archibald Alexander, a founder of Princeton Theological Seminary, who made the large sacramental occasions of late eighteenth-century Virginia a devotional staple of his youth. He regularly traveled great distances with other Christians in order to attend the communions and reported that at the approach of one of these outdoor solemnities in Briery that "the roads were covered with multitudes flocking to the place of worship." Himself journeying with others to this communion, he long remembered several religious conversations that he had along the way and fondly spoke of the acquaintances he had made. Besides noting the religious sociability of his own party, he recalled seeing "a large company of young people on horseback, . . . engaged in singing hymns" as they traveled. "Young converts" from North Carolina, this group pilgrimed "fifty or sixty miles to attend the sacrament, and were full of zeal and affection." Similarly, at another communion, Alexander noted a group of thirty people "from Rockbridge who had come over to the sacrament." "They seemed already," he said, "under a solemn impression, even before attending any services." Thus could the journey to the festal communions foster a sense both of spiritual expectancy and enlarged camaraderie. Fellow travelers to the communion, people could grow closer to God and to each other through pilgrimage. Singing, talking, praying, and socializing along the way, the saints experienced increased piety as well as heightened love and union.[49]

Once the pilgrims arrived, the hosting community warmly welcomed and accommodated the hundreds, if not thousands, who journeyed there. "The people who belong to the congregation where the meeting is," missionary Thomas Robbins reported, "all keep open houses for any that come." Houses and barns were regularly crowded with visitors and friends from the surrounding area. This hospitality was obviously conducive to fellowship and social intimacy. Isaac Reed, early missionary to Indiana, believed that the sacramental season of the Presbyterians was especially important for creating such communal bonds: "This practice," he said, "leads the Christians to know and love one another, all around a large tract of country, and cherishes this spirit and practice of hospitality." Broad geographical communities could thus be forged out of isolated farms and hamlets through this festal gathering for the sacrament. Summer-in, summer-out, these Presbyterians assembled and reaffirmed the bonds that made them a covenanted people. Dispersion in these high days yielded to community.[50]

Even when "sacramental camps" at times replaced the hospitality of open homes, the potential for intimacy, sharing, and mutuality was hardly lessened. As Presbyterians around 1800 in certain areas, such as western Pennsylvania or Kentucky, began to camp in the grove rather than retire in the evenings to local houses, the reasons given were twofold. "The practice of camping on the ground," it was said, was "introduced partly by necessity, and partly by inclination. The assemblies were generally too large to be received by any common neighbourhood. Every thing indeed was done, which hospitality and brotherly kindness could do, to accommodate the people.—Public and private houses were both opened, and free invitations given to all persons who wished to retire. . . . But notwithstanding all this liberality, it would have been impossible to have accommodated the whole assembly with private lodgings. But besides, the people were unwilling to suffer any interruption in their devotion, and they formed an attachment for the place." Thus in the sacramental camps the older patterns of hospitality were supplemented by even more intense forms of fellowship. Necessity and inclination combined to add to the communal power of the sacramental season. Whether lodging together in local homes or camping together in the sacramental grove, these evangelicals often found that gathering for the communion bred amity, friendship, and community.[51]

If community could be fostered in part merely in the act of coming together, it was specific rituals and symbols within the communion season itself that made manifest the communal power of these effervescent gatherings. One of the most basic of these rituals was taking a collection; for few acts more clearly expressed mutuality and social obligation than giving alms. Collections, of course, were a familiar part of ordinary Sabbath services, but at communions the offerings usually grew significantly in size. Taken by the elders on each day of the communion, collections at these events often ran ten, fifteen, and even twenty times higher than on ordinary Sabbaths. Church session records provide abundant testimony to this. In Paisley, for example, the communion occasion in August 1713 brought in 145 pounds, sixteen shillings, and eight pennies. On ordinary Sabbaths in the same year collections hovered between about eight and fifteen pounds. This sort of pattern was repeated year after year in Paisley and in other parishes. At Cambuslang in 1742 the collection at the communion in July was over 250 pounds, and the total at the second sacrament a month later was even larger. These sums were all the more remarkable, since a typical Sabbath collection in the parish consisted in a few pounds. This pattern, though on a much smaller scale, was also evident in John McMillan's congregations in western Pennsylvania. As early as 1778, collections that were in the one-to-three-pound range mushroomed to twelve pounds at the sacramental occasion. The crowds at these gatherings obviously account for part of the increase in the collections, but not for all of it. Communion seasons, as the high days in the year, were also high days of charity and mutuality. These occasions stood out in church records as periods of particular care and concern for "the poor of the parish." In collecting alms and disbursing them the saints displayed their fundamental social obligations to the indigent. The communion collection not only suggested mutuality, it provided for it.[52]

Community could be fostered not only in taking collections, but also in singing psalms. Indeed, singing was perhaps the most all-embracing activity of the communion rituals. All could sing, even those who were not quite ready to face the awesome responsibilities of the Lord's Supper or who were still struggling to close with Christ. Both psalms and hymns were impressive collective expressions of the faith. Singing, Willison said, "helps excite and accentuate the graces; it is the breath or flame of love or joy; it is the eternal work of heaven, the music of saints and angels there." Of all occasions the sacrament was the time in which song was to be most prevalent and jubilant. "If ever the heart be tuned for the work of praise," observed Willison, who himself composed over a hundred sacramental hymns, "it should be now; for greater matter for it you cannot have this side of heaven, than on this occasion." Through such praise, the saints not only glorified God, but also "edif[ied] one another." Binding them to the community of saints above, song nurtured love and unity on earth as well. "The melody and conjunction of many serious souls," Willison said, "tend to raise and elevate the heart." Psalms and hymns were often the sparks that served to enkindle the flame of love among the saints. At no time was there more communal singing than during the extended devotions of the sacramental season.[53]

The importance of congregational singing to these evangelicals is further seen in their disdain for those who did not sing. Warmth and vigor in singing praises to God, these evangelicals believed, were incumbent upon all. Those "who sit dumb in the congregation, while their neighbours are praising God, as if the devil had tackt their tongues to the roof of their mouths" were the subjects of repeated reproof. Singing heartily was yet another outward indication of inward devotion. "Look well then to your hearts in singing," Willison advised, "mind the matter more than the music, the cleanness of the heart more than the clearness of the voice." Singing praises to God was thus the duty of all in the congregation, whether they had good voices or not, whether they were sinners or saints. Those who did not sing were not truly part of the community. Instead, like Judas who absented himself from the psalm sung after the first communion, they were betraying Christ and were revealing their lack of commitment to him and his church. Joining in praise was thus an essential activity for "the whole Congregation." Through "united voices" the evangelicals expressed their union one with another.[54]

The very familiarity of the psalms that were sung during the communions added to their communal significance. Again and again the same psalms were performed from communion to communion. This was especially true of Psalm 24 which was regularly sung after the action sermon just before the celebration of the Lord's Supper. The colonial Presbyterian pastor John Cuthbertson revealed the ritualized place of this psalm in these communions in his terse diary entries: "prayed[,] sang[,] discoursed of the Sacrament, debarred, invited, sang Ps. 24" ran a characteristic note. Though this psalm was not set or prescriptive, its liturgical importance was nonetheless great. The familiar words and cadences reminded the assembly anew of the solemnity and purity with which they needed to approach God:

> Who is the man that shall ascend
>   into the hill of God?
> Or who within his holy place
>   shall have a firm abode?
> Whose hands are clean, whose heart is pure,
>   and unto vanity
> Who hath not lifted up his soul,
>   nor sworn deceitfully.
> He from th' Eternal shall receive
>   the blessing him upon,
> And righteousness, ev'n from the God
>   of his salvation.
> This is the generation
>   that after him enquire,

> O Jacob, who do seek thy face
>> with their whole heart's desire.

One saint at Cambuslang reported that before singing Psalm 24 she had been in a dead frame, but then in singing it in preparation for the eucharist "a power came along that filled me with love and joy." In singing such praises, whether Psalm 24 or another, the saints discovered "great power & sweetness." Giving expression to various parts of the evangelical faith, the familiar Scottish psalms and their performance helped knit together a covenanted people—a people that was bound together through shared forms of worship.[55]

Traveling and lodging together as well as taking collections and singing psalms were all examples of corporate activities that could heighten community. Fasting and praying as a congregation, standing or sitting in unison, listening and watching together were still further examples of collective acts that could help make a community of believers out of a scattered people. Even moments of shared quiet in the midst of prayer or eucharistic celebration, when the "words die . . . in expressive silence," were important not only for private supplication or meditation, but for corporate identity.[56]

Yet for all the little bits of the communion season that intertwined with community, the ritual of the Lord's Supper remained the central event. "One great Design of this Ordinance," all commentators agreed, was to forward "the Union and Communion of Christians one with another." The sacramental bread in particular was a primary symbol of this union. Just as it was "made up of many Grains compacted together," so too were believers bound together into "one mystical Body." In this regard 1 Corinthians 10:17 was always close at hand for eucharistic meditation: "For we, being many, are one bread, and one body: for we are all partakers of that one bread." The Lord's Supper, more than any other part of the sacramental season, was understood as the consummate ritual of community. Here "Amity and Friendship with our Brother" were enjoined, illwill and malice proscribed. Anyone in the community who had fallen out with another was to heal this breach before coming to the table. Harmony with neighbors was an essential qualification for communion; for, as one communicant said, the sacrament represented "a Communion of Saints" in which no one participating was to "harbour Malice & Envy in their hearts against their Brethren." Those who did not put aside their "unchristian quarrel[s]" and "seek peace and friendship with all" were debarred from the Lord's table. This initial demand that all be reconciled before communing was but preparation for the great rejuvenation of the community that came in the Lord's Supper itself. This feast was where the formal requirements of reconciliation were to give way to genuine rapprochement and renewed fellowship.[57]

A number of features of the ritual were particularly vital for giving the Presbyterian eucharist its communal cast. The organization of the sacramental tables, for example, could contribute to it. Converging on the table that held the sacred elements, the communion tables were regularly joined together in such a way that rendered the unity of those feasting together explicit. Beath observed how "the tables all met and joined in the midst, just before the pulpit; in the centre was set a square table to which the others joined." Outdoor services often followed a similar pattern. One commentator said that the tables converged "to a point some six or eight feet in front of the pulpit," where the table with the elements occupied "the point of convergence." The tables, all joining together and "all radiating from the large common table" with "the sacred symbols," suggested a communal feast. The communal quality of this organization of space was further suggested by what was absent: no railing around an elevated altar separated the people from their cleric or from the bread and wine. The minister, in fact, descended from the pulpit, sat at the table with his people, and feasted with them. This organization of the tables— whether within a church or outside in a grove or on a brae—provided a distinctive setting for the central ritual of the sacramental season. Long, joined tables were a forceful symbol of a community feasting together.[58]

Two other aspects of this ritual in particular suggest how the saints were bound together through the Lord's Supper: first, they were seated around the tables, and second, they divided the elements among themselves. The seated posture at communion, long a distinctive badge of Scottish and Ulster Scottish Presbyterians, was viewed as critical not only because it was seen as apostolic, but also because it suggested a mode of fellowship. This posture, as opposed to kneeling, indicated that the sacrament was "a blessed Love-feast" through which the communicants could experience a "holy Familiarity" with Christ and with each other. Sitting at the communion table helped these saints communicate their close, even convivial relationship with their God and with their fellows. Not only "Table-posture," but also "Table-gesture" contributed to making this a communal feast. The saints were to hand the elements "about from one to another." They were to receive the elements into their own hands, taking a piece of bread from the sacramental loaf and lifting the cup to their own lips. Thus the elements were divided and shared, passed from one saint to another all the way down the long tables. In partaking, the communicants were united through these shared actions and elements and became "one bread." These actions among the saints, Willison averred, showed "their mutual Christian Love and Union among themselves, and their Communion and Fellowship one with another." "Table-gesture" and "Table-posture" were potent symbols of commensality, mutuality, and community. Such subtle symbolic actions—small, simple, specific—were the sorts of things out of which such a grand thing as community was created.[59]

Such small actions were joined with notions of a transcendent, ideal community—the communion of the saints—that tied the local congregation's celebration of the eucharist into a much larger and resplendent community. Willison, in a striking passage, emphasized the continuity in the activities of the saints gathered for communion below with those feasting above:

> O there is rare Company at this Feast. . . . Christ himself is there present, and the Father also; for in this Feast we have Fellowship with the Father and the Son, thro' the holy Spirit. Here the Children of God, yea the glorious Saints above sit at this Table, and share with us in this Feast. It is true, they sit at the upper end of the Table, and we at the lower End.—They have better Appetites better Musick; they feed on a naked Christ, we by Signs and Symbols; but we have all the same Cheer. O what a great and good Company is here!

The long, connected tables on earth were extensions of that great table in heaven. The community of saints in the world was linked through the sacrament to a perfect community—an ideal community by which they could judge their own and one they could attempt, however imperfectly, to emulate. Through the Lord's Supper, the saints were conjoined with a transcendent community that validated their own efforts in the wilderness of the world to make their little society conform as much as possible to that ideal. Such an eschatological vision of the interrelatedness of their ritual acts with those of the saints in heaven gave an ultimate focus to the communal actions of the Lord's Supper. The communion of saints gave transcendent meaning to the celebration of Presbyterian community in this world.[60]

McGready in one of his sacramental sermons also reflected on this theme of the communion of the saints. In discussing how the sacramental occasion bore "some faint resemblance" to "the heavenly city of the New Jerusalem," he noted:

> It will be a heavenly meeting. . . . Christ is there, and his presence constitutes heaven. The whole Trinity will be there; and I have no doubt multitudes of the inhabitants of heaven will be there. . . . And when our Lord's table is spread in the wilderness, and he holds communion with his saints, I think it is rational and scriptural to suppose that the angels are hovering over the table and the assembly, rejoicing with Christ over the dear bought purchase of his blood, and waiting to bear joyful tidings to the heavenly mansions. And while they are sitting at this table, and communing with their Lord, it is more than probable,

that some of their christian friends and brethren, who once sat with them at the same table, and under the same sermons—with whom they spent many happy days and nights before, but now have left the world and gone home to the church triumphant above;—I say it is more than probable, that some of these will be mingling with the angelic band around the *"heirs of salvation."*

Such a passage is highly evocative. The cadences of McGready's powerful sermons—for example, the repetition of the understated phrase *it is more than probable*—come alive in such an excerpt. More directly, he displayed here a deep sense that all of the divine world came together for the sacrament and was present through the ritual. Small, isolated groups of saints, when they banded together for the sacrament, became part of a larger community with a divine foundation. As they shared in these venerable rituals, they gained as well a sense of the continuity of the faith and the generations. Those who had gone on to heaven before them, they could be assured, were still part of their community, forever engaged in this communion of saints. Through the sacrament, through sitting together at the Lord's table and sharing the bread and wine, these evangelicals affirmed their part in a longer history and a larger community.[61]

What was this ideal community like that these evangelicals were attempting to create through the sacramental season? Was it really that much different from the fallen world in which they lived? In some ways these sacramental rituals were quite in harmony with the society around them. The social distinctions between whites and other racial groups, for example, were often preserved in the ritual. When David Brainerd brought his Indian converts to the sacrament at Freehold, they were only served after all white members had communed. They were seated, it was said, "by themselves at the last table." Likewise black communicants were, at times at least, admitted only after white members had partaken. As one minister noted at the "Walnut Hill Sacrament" in Kentucky in 1802, "the 12 blacks who communed" were served "at the last table." Also at least one Presbyterian church in South Carolina had special tokens of "a baser metal" made for blacks that readily marked out their lower status from the white members with their finer tokens.[62]

Other forms of subordination also might apply to newer or younger members of the church. One later chronicler suggested, for instance, that "deference was paid to age" in the order of communicating with "the older members" gathering "around the sacred board" first. Such seating patterns—whether based on age, economic status, or race—were admittedly rarely reported.[63] Perhaps the ideal that the "Order of Sitting" at the Lord's table would be "without Difference of Degrees or Respect of Persons" did generally prevail. Perhaps explicitly hierarchical pew assignments, common within Presbyterian churches on both sides of the Atlantic, were regularly dissolved in the eucharist and in the outdoor tent preaching. But enough exceptions survive to indicate that the ideal was not uniformly maintained. Even in the egalitarian wide-openness of the tent preaching, distinctions in seating might persist. As Robert Burns noted in his description of this outdoor preaching at Mauchline, "Here, stands a shed to fend the show'rs, / An' screen our countra Gentry." At Mauchline the gentry evidently were shielded from the rain; the common people were not.[64] The communion of saints, no matter how loving and cohesive it was supposed to be, regularly retained the social and racial distinctions that were part of the larger society, and such distinctions could work their way into the sacrament. At such times the rituals of the sacramental occasion served to reenforce and perpetuate social and racial inequalities.

Among the best examples of how the sacrament might strengthen existing social distinctions comes in the relationship of husbands to their wives and fathers to their families. Many aspects of the sacrament were dominated by patriarchal metaphors and symbols. People gathered at their Father's house, learned to obey their Father's Law, and anticipated meeting their Father in heaven. On sacramental occasions the saints were invited to their Father's table by Christ who, like "an affectionate father," provided for them at this feast. Like a master who was at the head of his table, thus did Christ oversee his Supper. McGready, for example, compared the father's control over the earthly estate to God's power over the "heavenly inheritance." "When children are in their father's house, and seated at his table, . . . occasionally he shows them the patents which secure their interest in his estate. So, when the children of Christ are seated at a sacramental table, they often . . . are permitted to read their Father's testament which will shortly put them in possession of their heavenly inheritance." Sitting around the Lord's table was like sitting around the father's table. The metaphors of the Lord's Supper often meshed tongue-and-groove with the authority of the father over his wife, children, and servants.[65]

Patriarchy informed the devotional practice of the evangelical Presbyterians at nearly every turn. A father was supposed to "exert his authority" over those in his charge in order to bring them all under the sway of the gospel. As "head and master" of the family, he was to lead his household in prayer morning and evening and to superintend the spiritual lives of his wife, children, and servants. These religious efforts, Willison assured, would increase the dutifulness of those in the father's household and would make them "more observant of his other commands." Such patriarchal authority could seemingly only be enhanced by a feast that replicated the father's presiding place over the table at home. The rituals of the "communion-table" could be emblems of the patriarchal ceremonies of the "common-table."[66]

Male authority was no doubt further augmented by the dominance of men in the performance of the ritual. The ministers and elders who orchestrated the communions from beginning to end were always men—venerable, highly authoritative ones at that. Together they controlled admission to the sacrament: they conducted the examinations, they distributed and collected the tokens, and they kept the communion rolls. During the eucharist itself the ministers sat in Christ's place at the head of the table and performed the central actions, and the elders were their sole lay assistants. The active roles taken on by women in the sacrament were, by contrast, quite circumscribed. They might tend to the eucharistic linen—washing and spreading it, as one chronicler suggested—or they might make the clothes that the family would wear to these solemn occasions. Perhaps as well they would prepare the sacramental bread; Beath noted, for example, that a Mrs. Herrinden had been appointed "to provide the sacramental bread" for these events in the church at Booth Bay. Women would also have prominent roles in what one North Carolinian called "the rites of hospitality," the care of the "large number of guests" who thronged these communions, rites that clearly carried their own patriarchal assumptions as women were at times " 'cumbered with much serving.' " Besides these sorts of tasks, few responsibilities in the communion season came a woman's way. The sacrament in its performance and in its metaphors had a markedly patriarchal bent. The authority of men—fathers over children, husbands over wives, masters over servants, pastors and elders over congregants—might all be affirmed in the sacrament.[67]

The potential these communions possessed for renewing and sustaining the existing social order should not be overstressed. The drama of the sacramental season was rife with contradiction, ambiguity, and paradox. This conservative face is indeed only one side of the token. The reverse reveals a communal feast that in many cases challenged existing social relations and acted to reduce barriers between the sexes, between the races, and between people of different economic standing. A prophetic, egalitarian impulse often infused these occasions—one so strong that it could temporarily overwhelm many of the structures that raised one human being above another. In these instances the sacramental season might point to a heavenly community that was in direct tension with the world—a community that was closely knit, peaceful, and loving and one that was more egalitarian than it was hierarchical.

At the sacrament social distance between people might be dissolved in a variety of ways. As a communal feast, all members shared in its bounties equally. All feasted at the same tables, drank from the same cups, and broke bread from the same loaves. The same spiritual benefits—communion with Christ at his table—were available to all. God in this feast was indeed no respecter of persons. No one, however wealthy or eminent, received a choicer portion, a more delectable bread or a finer wine. In a world in which diet contributed to the definition of social status such a feast was a clear leveller. Certain foodstuffs—for example, tea or wheaten bread—were regularly consumed in the eighteenth century only by those well up the social hierarchy. Diet, Rhys Isaac has observed for eighteenth-century Virginia, was "consciously associated with the ordered ranking of society." A great common meal—and the Presbyterian sacrament was quite explicitly such a feast—could be a forceful contribution to a more cohesive, less stratified community.[68]

The egalitarian potentialities of this love feast could affect women in particular. In marked contrast to many other feasts in these societies—for example, those at house raisings or corn huskings in the southern back-country—women did not have to serve men their food, wait upon them, and clean up after them; all were Christ's guests equally at his table.[69] What was more the authority of men to preside over this feast could perhaps blur the lineaments of patriarchy as much as define them. Here, after all, men served women at the table, the elders replenishing, for example, the sacramental elements as the communicants passed the cups and bread down the long tables. Elders and ministers were cast as much as servants as patriarchs at this feast.

Perhaps, given the potential for equality and even inversion in this feast, it is not surprising that women often outnumbered men at the Lord's table, sometimes as much as—if not more than—two to one. This appears, for example, to have been the case at Cambuslang where about 70 percent of William McCulloch's spiritual narratives were from women. Others presented similarly lopsided numbers. A communicant list for Gilbert Tennent's church in Philadelphia in the 1740s shows 214 women and only 118 men. By the early nineteenth century, communions at the same church were wholly dominated by women: at one, the numbers stood at 244 females and a mere forty-four males. Likewise in Shelby County, Kentucky, one Presbyterian communicant list for the years 1819 to 1827 carried the names of ninety-eight women and only forty-eight men. At Booth Bay female communicants were comfortably in the majority from the first. In fact, in Beath's church, women clearly led the way to the Lord's table; thirty-one of the first forty-nine people accepted into full membership were women, and on the initial communicant lists in 1767 women outnumbered men forty-two to twenty-seven. Only at subsequent communions did this preponderance level off a bit. In the sacramental occasion women could potentially take the lead in bringing their husbands and children into the communion of saints. Thus what appeared a patriarchal feast could actually be subverted in a number of ways. Sharing in the elements equally and often numerically dominating the rite, women could turn the Lord's Supper into a love feast that provided a respite from the overbearing patriarchy of the rest of their culture.[70]

A concrete example of how participation in the rituals of the sacramental season could enhance the power of wives versus their husbands comes from one of McGready's narratives. At "the Ridge Sacrament" a woman had enraged her husband because she had "remained at the meeting-house all night" after the Sabbath services. Monday morning he showed up at the thanksgiving meeting "bitterly exasperated against his wife." "He ordered her home, but she refused to go," McGready narrated; "he then gave her very abusive language, and went home very angry. After he went home he was struck with deep conviction, and lay powerless on his own floor, and never rose, until, we have reason to believe, he obtained religion." The sacramental occasion reshaped the relationship between this husband and wife. Strengthened in her resistance by this spiritual fellowship, she emerged victorious. Her husband had been rendered "powerless" by God. This man's impotence in his struggle with his wife is suggestive of the potentially subversive power of the sacramental occasion. Regenerate wives could challenge—and subdue—unregenerate husbands through participation in the evangelical faith.[71]

The sacramental occasions could contain still more dramatic examples of the expansion of traditional roles. Women and children, for example, often expanded their religious spheres in such gatherings, especially at the larger, more effervescent communions. Though the actual administration of the Lord's Supper was carefully ordered, many of the surrounding meetings were more open to improvisation—to the movement of the Spirit. Groups regularly met before and after the eucharist for social worship and prayer. In such assemblies women and children often became the leaders of worship; offering prayers or even exhorting, they served, in the words of one woman who led devotions in a barn on a Sabbath night at a sacramental occasion, "as the Mouth of the Company." In several cases, however, the potential for social levelling suffused more than the improvisatory prayer meetings. In colonial Virginia, for example, the early sacramental gatherings were said to be dominated by "the common people and negroes"—meetings in which blacks and whites became "brothers and sisters in Christ." Not surprisingly, gentlemen were said to spurn such concourses religiously. During the Great Revival, McGready and others often reported sacraments in which blacks, women, and children took charge—preaching, exhorting, singing, and praying. McGready, no lackluster preacher himself, reported that he felt outdone by a number of "dear young creatures, little boys and girls" who spoke upon divine subjects "beyond what I could have done." "I felt mortified and mean before them," he said. He was impressed with one young girl in particular who, "turning to Christless sinners, addressed them in a language which God alone must have put in her mouth, which was sufficient to move the hardest heart."[72]

One eleven or twelve-year-old girl, "a daughter of a wealthy gentleman in our country," made it her mission at Red River sacrament to convert her father: "O! says she, if I had ten thousand worlds, I would give them all that my dear father could but see and feel in Christ what I do! She then ran to her father, and clasping her arms around his neck, she wept over him, and told him that he had no religion. . . . O my father, says she, Christ is willing to save you—O try to seek him, and you will find him—O! if you but saw that in Christ which I see—O! if you but saw his fullness and willingness, you would come to him. This seemed to pierce the old man like a dart, and made him weep like a child." Social roles could hardly have been more reversed. The daughter chastens the father for his irreligion, and he weeps like a child. Lines that defined boundaries between people of different ages, genders, races, and statuses were all blurred at the more powerful sacramental occasions; the conventions of deference and condescension could be undermined by the topsy-turvy energies of religious fervor. At such moments these evangelicals appeared indeed on the verge of a heavenly community—one in which all the saints loved and respected one another and one in which the inequalities, born of a hierarchical and patriarchal social structure, were dissolved.[73]

The relationship of the rituals of the sacramental season to social structure, it is clear, was not without ambiguity, contradiction, and paradox. Multivocal in their spiritual meanings, the rituals and symbols of the festal communions were similarly variegated in their social meanings. At times the rituals were clearly purveyors of stasis and tradition; at other points they appeared crucibles of change and ferment. As contexts varied, so also did the meanings. The rituals, for example, could simply mirror or reenforce long-standing social relationships, but they also held the potential to modify, challenge, or reenvision these configurations. People were able to lift out of these intricate dramas meanings relevant to the difficult and complicated human relationships in which they found themselves. A man might gain an enhanced sense of his own importance for the spiritual and temporal welfare of his household, but at the same time a woman might find ways to resist a wayward husband and bring him under her sway. Likewise a pastor might see in the eucharist or the tent preaching emblems of ministerial power, authority, and importance, but a layperson might find in this feast symbols of equality or visions of divine ravishment that transcended ministerial guidance. In their social implications, as in their spiritual meanings, the sacramental festivals were rich and polysemous.

This very ambiguity and paradox in the social import of these rituals extended to the whole notion of community that underpinned the communions. Though the sacramental occasions were designed to promote love and mutuality, they were also intended to maintain boundaries between members and nonmembers, between saved and unsaved. Themes of exclusion were as critical to the proceedings as those of inclusion. Perhaps no other aspects of the sacramental occasion pointed up the ambiguities of evangelical community more than did the communion tokens and the ritual of fencing the tables; for tokens and fences not only contributed to communal cohesion, but also made explicit the limits of inclusion.

Colorful bits of material culture, the communion tokens were important and pervasive parts of these sacramental celebrations. Beath reported, as already observed, that on Saturday the pastor at Booth Bay had ceremoniously distributed to the communicants "small square pieces of lead on which the initial letters of his name were stamped in capitals." The markings and shape of these tokens varied from place to place; often they were circular, oval, or rectangular, instead of square. Though the minister's initials were a common stamp, the tokens were regularly imprinted as well with letters that suggested the congregation in which the Supper was being administered or with dates that indicated the year of celebration. Often the tokens were more complex in their imprints: some bore a communion cup or loaf; others contained scriptural references or sacramental words. A few, such as that from Anwoth in Galloway in the 1750s, even carried such a dramatic emblem as a pierced heart which pointed to Christ's sufferings and sacrificial love. Some tokens—such as those from Strattonville, Pennsylvania, and Dunfermline, Scotland—also symbolized that love by having the token itself shaped as a heart. Another token from Dunfermline showed two hearts becoming one, emblematic both of the union of Christ and the believer that came in the Lord's Supper as well as the amity that was enkindled in the rite among the faithful. This amity was suggested too in the scriptural reference, Ephesians 4:2–3, that appeared on one of the heart-shaped tokens: "With all lowliness and meekness, with long-suffering, forbearing one another in love; Endeavouring to keep the unity of the Spirit in the bond of peace." The heart was indeed a rich symbol: it evoked Christ's suffering, sacrifice, and love; it suggested the loving relationship between the Bridegroom and his fair one; it was an emblem of repentance and regeneration and a call for purity of heart; and it marked the sacrament as a love feast among the saints. Potentially rich in their symbolism, the tokens could give added expression to various aspects of the eucharistic piety of the saints. What was said in words or symbolized in actions could be inscribed as well in things. Tokens could reiterate, echo, or even enlarge various meanings embodied in the eucharist.[74]

Whether plain or elaborate in their inscriptions, tokens were tangible objects that defined membership in the Presbyterian community. These small pieces of lead, distinctively marked, were badges that expressed belonging to a church. At a grander level, tokens were symbols of the covenant between God and his people. They helped define who were among God's covenanted people and who were not. They were visible emblems of membership in the invisible church, outward signs of those who had "inward tokens." Like the right language or the right clothes, the token was another way God's people concretized an interior, inscrutable state. It was a public emblem of their commitment to Christ. Without a token, no approach to God's table was possible. With one, access was gained. The token regulated membership in the community of saints. Those who had one, Beath noted, were knit "together in the bonds of love," but conversely those who did not have one were visibly excluded from the circle of faith. These leaden tokens were forceful symbols both of evangelical community and the boundaries that were drawn around it. They helped give hard specificity and careful definition to the membership of Presbyterian communities. Through them, the covenanted community was both knitted together and tightly bounded.[75]

The care with which the evangelical Presbyterians constructed the boundaries defining their community was even more evident in the solemn ritual of fencing the table. The minister, just before coming down from the pulpit to the tables, issued an elaborate warning to all those who were not fit to partake of the Lord's Supper. In a highly ritualized speech, the minister first reminded his auditory of the solemnity of the Lord's Supper: "This is the most solemn day of approaching to [G]od that we have while we are here travelling in this world," the minister would characteristically advise; "it is the most immediate approach to him, setting down at his table and partaking of his body and blood." The minister would then proclaim his obligation to "set a Rail about the Table, that none, who have no Right to the Table and Childrens Bread, may come near it." Debarring "in Christ's Name" all "prophane sinners," the minister enumerated with great care what sorts of people fell into this broad category. The ensuing litany, shaped by the Ten Commandments, had little of the Decalogue's terseness; by some accounts, it lasted "an hour or more." All atheists, deniers of the Trinity, enemies to Christ; all witches, charmers, and warlocks; all who were in "compact with the Devill"; all "ignorant Persons who know no God"—all these people were debarred through the first commandment. All "Worshippers of Images"; all who follow contrary ways of worship; all "Cursers, Swearers, Tearers of God's Name"; all Sabbath breakers of whatever stripe—all these people, arraigned by the second through fourth commandments, could "come not near" the holy table. Already the list grew compendious.[76]

3. Communion Tokens: (a) Chartiers, Pennsylvania. The *M* stands presumably for pastor John McMillan; (b) Junkin Tent, Pennsylvania. The *LS* is almost certainly an abbreviation for Lord's Supper; (c) Conecocheague, Pennsylvania. The year is indicated on what is one of the earliest surviving tokens for colonial America; (d) Anwoth, Scotland. This veined heart is among the most provocative emblems to be found on the tokens; (e) Dunfermline, Scotland. The two hearts are sided by two six-pointed stars; (f) Strattonville, Pennsylvania. This is a rare heart-shaped token from early America; (g) Dunfermline, Scotland. The *D* and the 1753 suggest place and date; (h) Dunfermline, Scotland. This is the obverse of the last token; the scriptural reference is Ephesians 4:2–3.

a) b)

c) d)

e)

f)

g)

h)
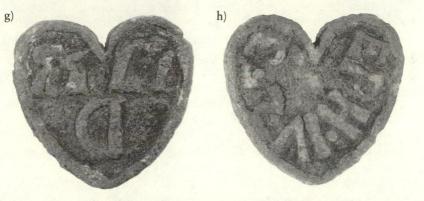

The fifth commandment—"Honor thy father and thy mother"—disqualified "all such as are disobedient to your naturall parents or civil parents" from the feast, and the sixth debarred all murderers. The seventh invited condemnation of sinners of the flesh—"all adulterers, unclean persons, effeminate, incestuous persons, guilty of bestiality, guilty of self pollution, or guilty of sodomy" as well as such sinners as "Gluttons," "Drunkards," and "promiscuous dancers." "All Thieves, Robbers, Oppressors, unjust Persons, Cheaters of their Neighbours"; "all Liars, Backbiters and Slanderers"; and finally "all covetous persons, that cannot be content with their own state and condition" were each condemned in turn by the eighth through tenth commandments. After this exhaustive enumeration the minister turned from debarring to inviting. "All penitent souls," all who were ready to part with their sins and "turn their Back on the Devil" were bid to come forward as were "all thirsty panting Souls" and "all poor cloudy Believers." "O come, come" was the strain of the concluding exhortation. The opportunity for repentance and salvation was held up to all.[77]

The long recital of sins that went with the fencing of the tables was a compendious catalog of evangelical morality. In this ritual these Presbyterians proclaimed to the world in precise detail who the unclean and wicked were and conversely who were the pure and godly. After the minister rehearsed this moral code, the congregants proceeded to act out their moral universe. The communicants came forward to the scrupulously guarded table as elders collected tokens and closely monitored entrance to this hallowed place. The saints—whether penitent, anxious, or already exultant—rose up and separated themselves from the crowd of spectators. One narrator observed that it was "like the division in that day when Christ shall separate the assembled multitude to the right hand and to the left." First in word and then in action these evangelicals created the boundaries that defined themselves over against the worldly. Through this ritual these evangelicals drew the lines that distinguished good from evil, the pure from the defiled. In a world where sinner and saint constantly had to intermingle and where it was difficult to distinguish between faith and hypocrisy, coming forward to the fenced table allowed the saints to proclaim a higher moral order where such confusions were cleared away. The fencing of the table was thus an occasion not only for the affirmation of evangelical morality, but for its very construction. In providing a glimpse of final judgment, this ritual helped create and sustain the boundaries that defined the moral order. It helped as well to establish the scope of evangelical Presbyterian community, its very parameters of inclusion and exclusion.[78]

At times themes of exclusion threatened to get the upper hand. Sacramental occasions always embodied at least a separation of saints from sinners, of those within the fold from those without, but often the Lord's Supper was used to draw still more divisive lines—ones that, instead of bounding and safeguarding Christian communities, cut through them. This was clearest, of course, in the lines that were drawn in eucharistic ritual to separate one type of Christian from another—Protestant from Catholic, Presbyterian from Episcopalian or Independent. But such lines were evident as well within Presbyterianism itself: Presbyterian community, even in Scotland after 1690, was never a whole. From their inception in the strife of the 1610s and 1620s the festal communions were caught up not only in community building, but also in community conflict. In the context of religious strife sacramental occasions could be used as "a wedge to drive on and fixe a rent" as they often were in the 1650s in the debates between Protesters and Resolutioners. In the eighteenth century a series of theological, political, and ecclesiological conflicts within the Presbyterian ranks—represented, for example, in the rise of the Seceders and in the debates between Jurors and Non-Jurors—revealed a divided Presbyterianism. Within such conflicts communion seasons could become "occasions of propaling our breaches" as much as healing them. In the summer of 1713, for example, Robert Wodrow at the height of controversy over the Oath of Abjuration (which required all ministers to disavow the Old Pretender) lamented that "Our Communions, that use to be our pleasantest and sweetest times, are times of distraction and discovering of our divisions." By the next summer when controversy over the oath had simmered down, communions were once again, Wodrow assured, sweet times of refreshing. Still the community fostered through the sacramental season always remained subject to disruption. More than that, the communions themselves could become the occasion for forwarding strife and division.[79]

The limits of Presbyterian communion and community were also evident in early America. In the 1740s conflict between Old Side and New Side Presbyterians, who were divided especially over issues of ministerial education and itinerancy, evidently percolated at times into the communions. Old Side minister John Craig, for example, reported New Side opponents who blasted him as "a Carnal Wretch" and lampooned his communion occasions as "Craig's frolick[s]." During the Great Revival similar conflicts boiled and were likewise given occasional expression at communions. In one Presbyterian church in Kentucky, for example, the congregation was beset by aggressive New Light sectaries from within their own body: "They would mingle in our Assemblies both when we met to hear the word preach'd & for social prayer & also on communion seasons on which occasion particularly they made it a point to be as troublesome to us as possible by making noice[,] Laughing[,] pointing & deriding[,] scofing & by every gesture of contempt of which they seemed capable." In such moments communions issued less in community than in strife and confusion. Old Side was set against New; one Presbyterian against another type of Presbyterian—whether Seceders, New Lights, Covenanters, or Cumberlands. Such sectarian divisions were pronounced for Presbyterians on both sides of the Atlantic. The festal communions often became interwoven with such controversies. As parties debarred one another from the Lord's table, communions could create communities in which those excluded far outnumbered those included.[80]

The rituals of the sacramental season fostered community, but not without qualification and irony. Gathering great numbers of people together for worship hardly ended ipso facto in solidarity. These rituals drew lines and set up boundaries, and such lines and boundaries were imposing and to various degrees divisive. Despite all the pilgrimages, psalms, and sacramental gestures, union and mutuality often remained elusive. Community was forged through communion, but so also at times were strife, discord, and faction. The communions were never simple events, and community was hardly the necessary upshot of this popular festival. Amity toward those within the fold often joined with enmity toward those without, and sometimes the latter was even more pronounced than the former. At times the festal communions did not so much resolve tensions within evangelical Presbyterian communities as heighten them. And always the ambiguities of inclusion and exclusion were there.

Despite the hard realities of divisiveness and the necessarily tough lines of exclusion, evangelical Presbyterians always held out hope that through their communions they would find lasting cohesion and community. In renewing the basic bonds that tied themselves to each other and to their God, the saints sought to revivify in an enduring way the communities in which they lived. Ultimately they hoped that the rituals of the sacramental occasion would extend outward and shape the way people lived day-in and day-out. A Scottish preacher, in commenting on the scriptural verse "This do in remembrance of me," suggested how the impressions created by the sacrament were supposed to linger: "This Remember is not confined . . . unto the very time we sit at the Lords table," he explained, "but in all the times of our life[.] [T]his Remember is not a bare naked historicall remembrance or a speculative remembrance as we may have of a history[,] but this remembrance is a practicall remembrance when you are going through your fields and when you are at your employments and at all times." The communion, having created "new bonds and engagements to a holy life," would have its fruition beyond Monday in renewed, purified, and godly lives. The saints were to go forth from the sacrament and live in holiness, love, and union. They were to live in perpetual remembrance of the sacrament.[81]

The rituals of the communion season ideally would have engaged people in the pursuit of holiness indefinitely, but experience showed that the force of these rituals was of shorter duration. As the sacrament came to a close, these evangelicals were compelled to reenter the world and to take up their temporal responsibilities that had been held in abeyance over the last week. As they came down from "Pisgah's top" into "life's darksome vale" and "scenes of toil," compromise all too often followed upon communion and community. A few of the saints, it was lamented, would remember their sacramental vows "no longer than the sacrament lasts." Some might fall away in "a day or two;" others would persevere until "the next month, or the next year."[82] If human weakness was inevitable, so was the approach of another communion. Though not always fulfilled, the promise of revival, renewal, and community was always harbored in the rituals of the sacramental season.

CHAPTER 3

The Mental World of Pastors and People: Sacramental Occasions, Eucharistic Devotion, and Popular Piety

IN DOCUMENTING the progress of the Great Awakening in his congregation from 1739 to 1744, Samuel Blair, pastor at Fagg's Manor in southeastern Pennsylvania, singled out one saint's journey as exemplary of the revival's effect on his parishioners. Just as Jonathan Edwards in his *Faithful Narrative* had lifted out the cases of Abigail Hutchinson and Phebe Bartlet, Blair took "the Soul Exercises and Experiences of one Person"— "a single *young Woman*"—to epitomize the revival's "blessed Work" at Fagg's Manor. As Blair related, the pilgrimage of this young woman began slowly. Having seen "others so much concern'd about their Souls," she wondered why she worried so little about her own. Gradually, pressed hard by her pastor's sermons, she became more uneasy about her eternal state and was "much troubled and cast down" for "a few Days" after each Sabbath. As her spiritual distress deepened, she joined for the first time "a *Society* of private Christians" for prayer, Scripture reading, and "religious Conference." Her anxiety over her own sin and corruption was only intensified by her meetings with those on similarly troubled journeys; indeed, her distress grew so marked at one point that she swooned away and fell "both Deaf and Blind" for a time. Regaining her senses, she continued to beg Christ for relief, but such relief still eluded her. Finally, after "*some Weeks*" in this "extreme Anguish," she came to "a Sacramental Solemnity" and there, on the Sabbath evening after the memorial of Christ's atoning death, she found reconciliation with God. As she listened to a psalm of the pilgrim—"My thirsty soul longs veh'-mently, yea faints, thy courts to see: My very heart and flesh cry out, O living God, for thee"—she finally found rest after weeks of longing. Christ had "put by the Veil" and allowed her a foretaste of the glories of heaven.[1]

The wayfaring hardly ended here. The glimmer of assurance faded, and she yearned anew to have Jesus as "her *own Saviour in particular*." This second round of "grievous Dejections" continued for "about *two Years*" with only intermittent periods of "Sweetness and Comfort." Sermons occasionally consoled her, but could as easily discourage. In these two years of distress the Lord's Supper as well offered her only mixed blessings. Though she regularly "found some Refreshing and Sweetness by that Ordinance," she remained unsettled by "much Fear and Perplexity" over her worthiness to partake. Finally, however, peace came. "After she had been so long under an almost alternate Succession of Troubles and Supports," Blair related, "the *Sun of Righteousness* at last broke out upon her to the clear Satisfaction and unspeakable Ravishment of her Soul, at a *Communion Table*. There her Mind was let into the glorious Mysteries of Redemption with great Enlargement." There, "meditat[ing] on the *Sufferings* of the LORD JESUS," she saw in an arresting moment of contemplation that Christ had "suffered for her Sins; that she was the very Person who by her Sins had occasioned his Sufferings, and brought Agony and Pain upon him." While at the table, she experienced simultaneously lamentation and joy; she both mourned for sin and delighted in God's presence. As a penitent, she had met with Christ at his table.[2]

Though her soul was ravished for a time, her pilgrimage necessarily continued. She pursued holiness with diligence and sought to fend off any doubts that persisted or returned. In her efforts she found "*Sacramental Seasons*" especially to be "blessed and precious Seasons to her" and a vital source of the Lord's "comforting Presence." At such occasions she continued to meditate on Christ's sufferings—for example, on "the *Blood* and *Water* that issued from the Wound made by the Spear in her SAVIOUR's Side"—and found invigoration in such prayerful contemplation. At one "*Communion Solemnity*" in particular she experienced anew the joys of union with the Bridegroom. Her spiritual life, though complex, centered on these communion occasions. Enmeshed in a web of spiritual duties—such as hearing sermons, attending prayer societies, observing family devotions, and retiring to secret prayer—the sacramental season was woven into the center of this web; all strands circled around it. The Lord's Supper, one Scottish divine intoned, "is the *Epitome* of the whole Christian Religion, both as to Doctrine and Practice." For Blair's exemplary saint, the sacrament—and the devotions surrounding it—were indeed very nearly the sum of Christian piety.[3]

This young woman's account, though straightforward enough, nonetheless raises a bundle of questions. Were her experiences in some way typical or were they exceptional? Blair, after all, set her up as a paragon and upbraided many of her fellow believers at Fagg's Manor for their indifference about "the great Concerns of Eternity," which he saw evidenced in their "very extravagant Follies, as *Horse-running, Fiddling* and *Dancing*."[4] Did such sinners fall well short of her saintly mark? Was the sacramental season for the less pious uninspiring or, if inspiring, did it inspire fear more than expectation, laxness more than ardor, or even licentiousness more than devotion? Did the rhythms and disciplines of this saint's piety mesh with the experiences of others at these communions? Were some given still more brilliant assurances of salvation or more intimate communion with Christ? And how all along did ministerial understandings of spirituality impinge upon or diverge from lay experience? This chapter attempts to answer such questions as it explores the mental world of pastors and people during these sacramental solemnities.

THE CAMBUSLANG NARRATIVES AND THE RECOVERY OF POPULAR PIETY

Even though Blair gave a rich description of the experiences of this young saint, there remain lingering questions about the fullness and the trustworthiness of his account. Did he abridge or alter what she told him for the sake of didacticism or for the sake of what he, as a minister, thought was sound, orthodox piety? Blair confessed outright that he did not "pretend to give her very Words for the most Part," though he remained "well satisfied" that "I don't misrepresent what she related" and said that "I was very careful to be exact" in writing down "the Account she gave me of herself." Blair's self-satisfaction notwithstanding, still one wonders what her very words were and why Blair failed to preserve them. Did lay experiences diverge from ministerial experiences and expectations? Were there gaps, large or small, between the mental world of pastors and that of their people? Such questions are difficult to answer, and they would perhaps be impossible to answer if all that survived were texts like Blair's where ministerial formulations and lay relations are inextricably wound together.[5]

Fortunately there are other sources—indeed ones of rare quality that allow unusual access to evangelical Presbyterian piety. In the first chapter mention was made of the great revivals at Cambuslang in the 1740s and the superlative cache of manuscripts that the pastor of the parish, William McCulloch, put together at that time. McCulloch's examinations record in detail the spiritual experiences of 108 people from in and around Cambuslang. As the awakening crested in his parish, McCulloch set about gathering testimony to the revival's influence on the lives of the renewed and the transformed. He intended to publish some of the most exemplary accounts as evidence that what was going on in Cambuslang was indeed a gracious outpouring of the Spirit. To that end he shared the manuscripts with a number of leading evangelical ministers who were to help him ready the accounts for publication. As part of the editorial process, the ministers bracketed material that they considered objectionable for later deletion. Despite all these preparations, the project never went to press. The result of their aborted plans was a unique collection of manuscripts running to about 1200 pages that are indeed a fertile source for understanding lay spirituality.[6]

Though no doubt as amanuensis McCulloch managed to screen some of the experiences of his saints, the texts nonetheless possess a first-person immediacy that suggests the filtering was minimal. Apparently he faithfully recorded the experiences of these evangelicals and only turned to editing what they told him later. And since the subsequent editing—accomplished only for the first of two manuscript volumes—consisted simply in bracketing the material that gave offense, little at all was lost. In fact, the editorial marks themselves only make the manuscripts doubly instructive, since they point us very directly to places where the mental world of the ministers may have diverged from that of the laity. The Cambuslang manuscripts, in sum, offer unique access to the mental world of the evangelical Presbyterians. Far from limited to the extraordinary revival in the parish, the accounts reveal the expanse of lay piety from family worship to sacramental occasions. The year-to-year rhythms of religious experience, the subtleties of the devotional life, as well as the grand moments of spiritual awakening are revealed in McCulloch's examinations. With these materials and other sources, such as published memoirs and church records, the piety of the laity may be carefully reconstructed.

Exploration of the Cambuslang manuscripts should help us understand the piety of the evangelical Presbyterians on both sides of the Atlantic. Interpretation of these rich materials from a Scottish parish on the edge of Glasgow in the 1740s should offer us insight into the experiences of Presbyterians at sacramental occasions elsewhere and at other times. Just as the rituals of the communion season were replicated from place to place, so was the spirituality. Blair's relation of the experiences of his young saint is one evidence of the transatlantic scope of the Scottish sacramental piety. Shared devotionals, sermons, catechisms, and psalms were further evidences. Evangelical Presbyterians, whether situated in the colonies or in the homeland, shared in common rituals and in a common piety. Thus the saints at Cambuslang should help illumine the faith of those communicants elsewhere who left little or no record. The experiences of New World Presbyterians, such as Blair's saint, find welcome expansion and nuance in the relations of these Old World counterparts.

To recount the experiences of one saint at Cambuslang is to reveal the rich potentialities of the McCulloch manuscripts for the recovery of popular piety. The spiritual relation of one young woman of eighteen years, Catherine Cameron, is especially suggestive. Her testimony confirms the richness of the Cambuslang manuscripts and offers, as did Blair's saint, an indication of the importance of sacramental devotion in the lives of the evangelical Presbyterians. Just as John Beath's session records served as a good point of departure for the discussion of ritual, so Catherine Cameron's account serves as a useful ingress into the mental world of the devout at the sacramental occasions.

Catherine Cameron, the daughter of a gentleman of some "fashion & station," was well educated and well instructed in the ways of Presbyterianism. Although she was a fairly pious child—praying in secret daily and attending church regularly—only when about fourteen did she begin to long for Christ in earnest. Her first notable religious experience occurred about that time during a sacramental occasion. "When I came to The Lords Table," she said, "I was much in weeping & trembling, and had a great desire to have ane interest in Christ." This early "Melting of heart" at a communion set the tone for her ensuing experiences. The sacramental season soon became a high point in the rhythm of her piety. "After that Sacrament, for some time I endeavoured to be more Circumspect in my walk; but after some time I began to forget my Engagements, & to return to former vanity & folly; and continued so till the next Sacrament occasion was . . . shortly in view." Within a couple of years her diligence increased and her early religious concern gave way to more profound convictions.[7]

As she journeyed the sacrament and the preparations for it became more and more important. In 1742 she attended "the Barony communion" not far from Cambuslang. Preparation began the Sabbath before and went on all week. She attended closely the sermons preached on "the preparation Sabbath" and discerned herself to be among "the number of the invited." With this resolve to come the next Sunday to the Lord's table, she dedicated the week to extensive prayer, devotion, and fasting. She meditated on the sufferings of Christ and gained an ever greater sense of her own sin. On the Saturday before the sacrament, she noted as her preparations peaked, "I slept none that night, but went out to the fields for secret prayer." The morning after her vigil she wept much during the sermon preceding the Lord's Supper and at the table she "felt much of a hungering & thirsting after Christ." His loving embrace, however, was yet to come.[8]

She followed up the Barony communion by attending the sacraments at New Monkland and Cambuslang. The preparations were repeated, and again she "got much of a weeping & mourning frame." At both her heart was "melted down into Godly sorrow, at the thoughts of Christs Sufferings, and of my sins whereby I had caused him to be pierced."[9] Still, she confessed, she had not yet "mett with Christ" at his table. Only during the thanksgiving service on Monday after the communion at Cambuslang was she filled with Christ's love. There she finally beheld Christ "with outstretched arms of Mercy."[10] Though the exalted joy resulting from this vision of the merciful Savior wore off in about five days and some doubts returned, she nonetheless had achieved a new closeness to Christ.

Her yearnings for Christ's love mounted anew as the second sacrament at Cambuslang drew near the next month. Again she spent a week in preparation, devoting much time in particular to secret prayer "out in the fields." On Tuesday night she received further assurances from God of her salvation. "I was so ravished with the Love of Christ that night," she exulted, "that I could sleep little, and all next Morning and day, I was in the same frame: and saying as the Spouse of Christ, My Beloved is Mine & I am his, My beloved is white and ruddy, the Chief among 10.000, yea Altogether lovely: and all the rest of that week, I continued rejoiceing in the near views of the Sacrament in that Place, hoping I would then get my Interest in Christ and my Marriage Covenant with him sealed there."[11] The images of marriage and union with the Bridegroom increasingly dominated her account. On Friday and Saturday she gained further tokens of Christ's love to her. Indeed, on Saturday, during a sermon preached by Alexander Webster, she was overcome by the "Preciousness" and "ravishing beauty" of her beloved and rejoiced that "my Soul was just married to Christ." That night out in the fields, in vigilant "praying, praising & pleading," she begged that "I might get a seal to my souls Marriage to Christ tomorrow at his Table." After all this near ecstatic preparation she was finally on the verge of meeting with Christ in the eucharist.[12]

On Sabbath morning the simple sight of "the Communion Table" filled her heart with sadness at the thought of Christ's sufferings and with joy at the thought of her near approach to him in this sacrament. When she sat down at the table and the elements were about to be distributed, she "burst out into a flood of tears" of gratitude and penitence. When she received the cup of "The Redeemers blood," she believed Christ spoke to her, saying, "My blood is sufficient to wash away all thy sins."[13] She was filled with peace at the knowledge of Christ's forgiveness and went from the table convinced of her salvation. Though some doubts returned in secret prayer that very afternoon, love and comfort predominated. She spent the rest of the day in singing psalms and in prayer and "every now & then I behoved to rise, and take another View of my Lords Table."[14] Immense power resided in this scene for her, and indeed sight as much as sound guided her experience. "I cannot express the joy with which I was filled, in time the Tables were serving," she jubilated, "and I could not endure to look down to the Earth, but look'd up—mostly to heaven, & thought, I heard Christ speaking to me from thence and saying, Arise my Love, my fair one, and come away: and saw him, as it were, reaching down his hand, & drawing me up to himself, and at the same time, I felt my heart powerfully drawn to him, with the cords of Love."[15] The whole communion occasion represented so much to her that she was moved to the gate of heaven, to the edge of final transcendence. Having met with

Christ in this love feast, she longed for the dissolution of her body and for final union with her beloved.

Again and again Catherine Cameron went through the week of preparations, listened to the sermons, partook of the bread and wine, and rejoiced in thanksgiving on Monday. In fasting on Thursdays she humbled herself anew and felt the pangs of humiliation for sin. "Being much cast down, I thought there was no comfort for me," she lamented on one fast day in particular, "and that The Redeemer would never return again, and That I durst not approach to his Holy Table." Friday and Saturday her spirits usually began to revive and soon she would become convinced that she was invited to this wedding feast. As she readied herself to approach the eucharist, she repeatedly merged mourning and rejoicing, weeping in contemplation of Christ's sufferings and celebrating in expectation of meeting "with Christ at his Table." The sight of the elements and Christ's table continued to imbue her with emotion; seeing and believing went hand-in-hand. "When I saw the Elements," she reported, "I was like to burst out, when I thought how the Body of Christ was broken for my sins. . . . When I took the Cup, I was made to believe, that He had pardoned all my sins: And I was made to sit as it were under The Redeemers Cross, and to behold him as crucify'd for them." Though the Lord's Supper itself was the culmination of all her preparations, devotions on Sunday evenings and Mondays were usually times of sweetness and power for her as Christ's presence continued to be felt long after he had finished presiding over his feast. These communion occasions wholly dominated her piety; they were the high days of her spiritual life; they marked its rhythm of doubt and assurance, of humiliation and ecstatic union.[16]

She longed, however, to escape this cycle. She yearned for grander vision, for the day when the shadows would give way to light, when signs and tokens would be replaced with the fullness of heaven. In comparison to many, her faith was full and satisfying; she was regularly visited by Christ at the sacrament and in prayer. One "Glorious Morning" after a communion, for example, she "was led as it were to the gate of heaven" and received special assurances of her "Eternal happiness." Another time, just before she partook of the Supper, Christ showed her "the book of life" with her name written in it. In her meditations on Christ's sufferings she often beheld her Savior "upon the accursed Tree" and once, after the eucharist, she was shown, as Thomas had been, Christ's "Bleeding Side" as a help against unbelief. Despite all these comforts, doubts persisted. She had continually to seek renewal, to strengthen herself against the temptations of the world and of the devil. Once when at the Lord's table, Christ had told her that soon "Thou shalt see me as I am," but in the meantime she had to persevere and find contentment in the reflections of a dark glass.[17] For all her longings for heaven and for all the portents of beatific vision, the rhythms and cycles of piety embodied in the sacramental season remained the staple of her spiritual life. Her narrative ends fittingly not in resolution, but in refrain. Cast down by thoughts of sin and the hardness of her heart, Catherine Cameron could console herself, for "The Barrony Sacrament was at hand."[18]

The narratives of Catherine Cameron and Blair's unnamed saint reveal a great deal. They show how complex, rich, and variegated this piety was. The same set of rituals and devotions evoked divergent responses not only from individual to individual but from the same person. The case of Catherine Cameron particularly suggested the range of meanings inhering in these communions, but she hardly exhausted the possibilities. Her experiences changed with each enactment of the Lord's Supper and yet still left a number of facets untouched. Fathoming the complexity of a past mental world—even when we have sources as sterling as those available from Cambuslang—is difficult. As one minister expressed his own difficulties in dealing with this diversity of experience, "Who can utter sentiments suitable to the various conditions of the various souls, at once partaking of this Ordinance?"[19] Variety and nuance in the experience of the evangelical Presbyterians was certainly as notable as commonality and collectivity. It is the understanding of this richness and detail, more than underlying structure or overarching commonality, that inspires this interpretive redescription of a past piety.[20]

SINNERS AND THE SACRAMENT: IMPIETY AND DIVERSION

Many were far less devout in their spiritual travels than Catherine Cameron or Blair's unnamed pilgrim. For the less pious, the sacramental occasions—as well as other devotions and duties—were only haphazardly or even irreverently observed. Pastoral ideals can be too easily taken as the measure of devotional practice; a few saints, set up in the first place as models by ministers, come to embody the sum of a piety. The danger of enshrining these paragons without looking at their less pious, or even impious, counterparts is that we may end up understanding, as Baird Tipson warns, "only the best people at their best moments."[21] The ministers may have been interested primarily in exemplars—as Blair and McCulloch surely were—but historians need to recall not only those who attained unusual sanctity, but also those who fell short, whose wanderings were desultory, fitful, or barely commenced. The sacramental season was a vital, indeed crucial, part of the pilgrimages of these evangelicals, but its power was shared and experienced unevenly. Appreciation of the prevalence of impiety and diversion goes before interpretation of the spiritual disciplines that the saints employed to overcome this worldliness. Indeed, understanding the difficulties of sustained devotion and seeing the alternatives to it make whatever spiritual attainments these pilgrims achieved all the more noteworthy.

Great throngs crowded the sacramental occasions. Many came not to partake of the Lord's Supper at all, but idly to watch and socialize. The communion could be both a solemnity and a fair. To some, as critics charged and defenders reluctantly acknowledged, it was a time to indulge in "drunkenness, lust, and idleness." One detractor reported that the people consider "a sacrament or an *occasion* . . . in the same light in which they do a fair, so they behave at it much in the same manner." This critic further concluded that these communion occasions partook of "an absurd mixture of the serious and comic"; these events, he said, were characterized as much by *"the distraction at Babel"* as "decency and order." For those who came for the occasion's convivial side, for leisure and frivolity, the communion kindled interest in much the same way that harvests, weddings, games, markets, or fairs did. For all, the season was a diversion from the routine and demands of work, a time of sociability and festivity, but for many it stopped with that. These idle, unaffected spectators—always the object of evangelistic concern—had little interest in the deeper mysteries of the occasion. Peopling the edges of the meeting, perhaps drinking, cavorting, flirting, or even mocking, the worldly were only peripherally concerned with what was going on at the table or at the tent.[22]

At times the impieties of sinners and the failings of saints were great. The sacrament could become a time for the indulgence of the flesh, not a time of triumph over it. Church session records and the cases of discipline preserved therein make this altogether clear. As evidenced in such records, drunkenness was among the most common sins at these festal communions. The Cambuslang session in 1744, for example, rebuked in summary terms one Janet Falconer "for being drunk at the time of a Communion," a sin "which she confessed." Some years earlier the session at Stranraer accused one man of being "drunken" on both the Sabbath and the Monday of the communion season, a charge he insisted was overblown: he claimed to have drank only "two or three pints of ale" during the solemnity. Dubious, the session went ahead and rebuked him. Similarly, in 1750 the session at Ayr registered its concern over a tailor, John Smith, who was seen "comeing from Moncktoun Sacrament very Drunk." In 1753 the Barony session cited one of its parishioners, John Murray, for having been "Mortally drunk upon the Sacrament Sabbath." Murray, who "had a long and habitual practice of drunkenness," was prone, the session lamented, to "falling into that particularly Upon the Sacrament Sabbaths." Drunkenness was a perennial problem for the church sessions, and sacramental occasions, despite the great solemnity, were no exceptions. Indeed, in some cases, such as that of John Murray, the communions proved with all their attendant excitement and sociability to be times of particular temptation.[23]

For some the communions also provided an occasion for sexual license. Critics regularly charged as much, and church records suggest that these satiric accusations were not groundless hyperbole. In a number of cases opportunity was found amid the lengthy meetings and large gatherings to perpetuate or even initiate premarital or extramarital affairs. In Ayr, for example, William Ferguson and Isobel Campbell were widely suspected of "scandalous and adulterous behaviour." In particular they were accused of sexual impropriety on "the Monday evening of the last Sacrament," but that turned out to be one in a series of incidents. Witnesses were called; one had seen the couple standing outside Ferguson's back door "in one anothers Arms without anything but their shirts on"; another time they had been seen "laying together" in the fields, both "naked from the belt downwards." For William Ferguson and Isobel Campbell, the communion season, it turned out, was as good as any other time to have illicit sexual relations.[24]

In other cases, however, the sacrament proved a particularly promising occasion for sexual dalliance. An unmarried servant in Carnock, Janet Hutten, when found to be with child in February 1748, said she was guilty of fornication only once, that being during "the Communion in Torryburn last summer." Similarly, in 1712 Andrew Blain and Catherine McBlain were called before the kirk session in Ballantrae on the charge of "uncleanness" at the communion. While "the tables were a serving within the Church and Sermon without," the couple evidently sneaked away to a secluded spot. Despite their care in choosing an isolated place, they were nonetheless espied by one witness who claimed to have seen them "in a very unseamly posture." Sex, more than the sacrament, was clearly on the minds of some who attended these festal occasions.[25]

A final, still more flagrant example of sexual license at a communion comes in the case of Hugh Maxwell, a student, and Isobel Wardrope, a suspected prostitute, in Paisley in 1701. The woman, whom the session execrated for "her notorious wickednesse," "owned her self guilty of uncleannesse with Mr Hugh Maxwell upon the fast, Saturday, Sabbath & munday," in other words, on each of "the communion days." Maxwell, trying desperately to minimize his guilt, admitted that he was alone with her in his chamber "the Door being shutt" and that "he was in the bed with her att thos tymes she alledges but that his cloaths were not off." He even said he was there "to comfort her," she "being sick." But then in a flood of confession he admitted that he did have "carnall Dealling with her upon the munday about midday, that she did frequently Intice him to that act, but that for a tyme he resisted but att [length] yealded, that on the sabbath morning & sabbath night there were mutuall unclean manuell actions besyde the familiar embraces." The session, taken aback by the magnitude of the sin "done att such a solemn tyme," condemned both Maxwell and Wardrope sharply. Wardrope was turned over to the civil magistrates for punishment; Maxwell, after several weeks of public humiliation before the congregation, was finally absolved. The similarly glaring instances of profligacy associated with some of the sacramental occasions in Kentucky at 1800—the "six men & one strumpet" found together under a preaching stand, "a man & woman in the cornfeild" caught "in the act of adultery," or the "waggon load of whiskey" sold at one occasion, so that "many got groggy"—clearly had their parallels across the Atlantic. The efforts of evangelicals to keep in check the passions of all those who attended their festal communions was of long standing, and so was their lack of full success. The communions were obviously never free of sin or sinners, and sometimes indeed these extended, festal gatherings provided occasion for some very bold breaches of evangelical morality.[26]

Besides the common sins associated with sex and drink, there were other ways as well that the sacramental occasion could be profaned. For example, in Barony parish in August 1766 two men were found "guilty of fighting" on the Sabbath evening of a communion season in Rutherglen. More gravely, the kirk session at Govan in 1733 cited a man for "horrid Curseing and swearing" and "being excessively drunk" as he came back from the sacrament at Paisley. With little or no provocation, the offender had called another man a "son of a Damned Buggar" and had laid "violent hands" upon him. His only excuse was that he could not remember what he had done, since "he was Insensible, being so excessively drunk." Similarly, at Culross in 1736 the Monday thanksgiving service was disrupted when a servant, John Norrie, rode through the churchyard in the midst of the tent preaching "cursing swearing and blaspheming the name of God." Likewise, Norrie's only excuse was that he was "so overtaken with Drink as to be quite insensible of his Conduct at that tyme." Perhaps what was more alarming was that Norrie, even when sober, showed "Little or no sense of his Crime." He had profaned the sacramental occasion without any great sense of having desecrated anything; the sacrality with which the event was imbued for the faithful was largely absent in Norrie's view of the gathering.[27]

The great distance of the worldly from the spiritual demands of evangelical devotion can be seen in a rather unlikely figure, Alexander Cunningham, a Presbyterian minister of the 1760s. In 1765 Cunningham was called before the presbytery of Ayr to defend himself against a number of charges. Often accused of drunkenness, he had on one occasion "sat up [a] whole night in Kilmarnock drinking till the morning of the next day being the fast day before the Sacrament of the Lords Supper in that place." Such perverse preparation for the sacrament was matched by other sins. At one point "flusterd with Liquor" in a large company, Cunningham, as the presbytery reported matter-of-factly, "did not only propose a most profane and obscene Question for discussion in Conversation. Viz. Whether fucking or praying was most for the Glory of God; but did yourself support the irreligious and profane side of the Question." Alienated from the evangelical world and the ministerial calling in which he found himself, Cunningham gave clear expression in his actions, words, and coarse wit to his disregard for pious devotion. As he sat up nights drinking, the sacrament and the spiritual disciplines surrounding it, we can be sure, were little on his mind.[28]

That such profound alienation could actually be expressed during and through the sacrament is evident in a highly revealing incident related by the eighteenth-century Scottish pastor (and later American divine) John Witherspoon. "Some young men" in his parish in Paisley on the eve of a communion spent an evening in deriding evangelical preaching and ritual. His account of their "mocking the exercises of piety" reveals a good deal about the alienation of the unconverted from these sacramental solemnities. These young men—whom Witherspoon boldly identified as "Robert Hunter and William Wilson, manufacturers in Paisley, John Snodgrass, writer there, William M'Crotchet, ensign or sergeant in the army, James and David Chalmers, and Robert Cross junior, merchants in Paisley"— were a convivial lot. Though they evidently attended the Saturday preparatory meetings before the sacrament, that evening they gave forceful expression to their contempt for the whole proceedings. Gathering in the room of William Wilson, they began to engage—by the testimony of witnesses in the street who heard them—in "mock preaching, and that not merely imitating the tones or gestures of ministers, but . . . the words of Scripture." And, as if this were not bad enough, they prayed "in mockery" as well and gave vent to "profane swearing."[29]

Merry and sacrilegious, they evidently went on to enact what Witherspoon found "most tremendous of all," what made "the atrociousness of their crime" so clear. They apparently held a mock sacrament. One of them, who Witherspoon said "never was a communicant," had somehow gotten hold of a eucharistic token. Joking that he had received the token from Judas Iscariot, he "offered to play odds or evens" with it to determine who should use it the next day and who would thus have the presumed pleasure, as a "notorious profligate," of desecrating "the table of the Lord." Eventually he sent the token to a young woman, reputedly inviting her not to the Lord's Supper, but to the mock sacrament of his friends. Whether she wound up participating or not, the mirthful company went on with their solemnity. The words of institution were evidently read, and, though Witherspoon did not have all the details or all the evidence, he indeed feared that these "acting mimics" had profanely celebrated the eucharist.[30]

Witherspoon was obviously outraged to have the sacramental occasion mocked in this way and did all he could with his limited evidence to rebuke the offenders. Amazingly enough, the group remained impenitent, refused to submit to censure, and even charged Witherspoon with slander. Their brazen impiety was no doubt exceptional in the form that it took, but the attitudes it revealed were more extensive. Evangelical Presbyterians always complained of the prevalence of the impious and the unbelieving. In their antics these convivial young men vividly expressed such dispositions. For them the sacramental gathering was an occasion not for repentance and meditation, but for fun and scoffing. In deriding "the exercises of piety" they gave clear expression and active performance to the exercises of impiety.[31]

Witherspoon's dramatic story and the various cases from the church records are helpfully complemented by some of the narratives from Cambuslang. As a collection designed to testify to the bounties of God's saving grace, McCulloch's manuscripts would appear an unlikely source for getting at the experiences of the less godly. Yet they contain critical, revealing glimpses. Some of his congregants never received the brilliant illuminations or satisfying comforts of the likes of Catherine Cameron, but were instead mired in unshakable sins that were rarely eradicated by the spiritual devotions surrounding the sacrament.

The narrative of Thomas Foster of Ridley-Wood, "a man of 40 years," reveals with unusual poignancy how bogged down in sin a person could get. Spiritually things went awry for Thomas Foster from an early age. As a child he could not apply himself to learning how to read, so he attained only a cursory knowledge of the shorter catechism and the psalms. Not until years later as an adult did he get to the point where he "could read the Bible tolerably." Prayer little affected him and the Lord's Supper evidently still less. After he married and "began to thrive very fast in the world" he became more dutiful in family devotions and secret prayer—in part at the insistence of his wife. These perfunctory observances did not help solidify his faith. One night when he was at prayer "in the Stable" after having given "my horse his Supper," his doubts openly confronted him in the form of a diabolical apparition. "When I had falln down on my knees there, to pray," Foster told McCulloch, "tho' the place was dark, I thought I saw like a long black man before me, and heard him as it were whisper to me, What art thou going to do? Is there such a thing as a God?" More frightened and confused than ever, he now left off prayer and family devotions altogether and "turnd," he confessed, "very near an Atheist in Opinion."[32]

Foster's outward conduct was in as much, if not more, disarray than his inward faith. "I had been a kind of Atheist in practice almost all along," he admitted, "I livd without God in the world: my life had been a continued Tract of Sin & Folly." Though he said there was hardly a sin he could resist if the temptation arose, excessive drinking was his great failing. Until he was fourteen he had steered clear of alcohol. "I could drink no Ale or other liquor," he insisted, "but would have trembled when any would have put a Cup of Ale into my hand." Corruption, however, was at hand; for "when about that age, two men offered me each a penny, if I would drink one cup full of Ale: I took the two pence & drank it off." This proverbial first glass proved the fatal one. From then on he steadily drank more and more until he made, he said, "a Trade of it."[33]

Some hope of escape from sin and death came for him at Cambuslang in the summer of 1742. A sermon preached by the touring evangelist George Whitefield particularly affected him and put him under "great Terror" of Hell. For a time he refrained from his "Drunken way"—or "at least I did not drink so oft to excess as I usd to do"—and he returned after a six-year hiatus to prayer. But this spiritual concern and discipline gradually eroded, and by 1744 he had again quit his devotions and renewed his old "course of drinking." Soon things were worse than ever; in July 1744 he went on a binge. "Drinking hard" for three days "without intermission," he wandered through the churchyard and collapsed there. He awoke face-to-face with "a Grave-stone" and reflected on the approach of his own death and on his manifold sins. As he looked at the grave of an acquaintance, he was given particular pause for reflection upon his sottishness: "I said within my self, It is a strange thing that I am so enslavd to drink, that I cannot get free of it." He decided at that moment to seek help from his minister. On arriving at the manse he confessed to the minister and a table full of guests that he had recently been "as full as I could hold both of ale & brandy." Instead of finding release in confession, he was suddenly besieged by humiliation and confusion. Quickly he ran out of the manse and into an "Alehouse" and "fell to drinking there, hoping by that means to drink away my trouble of mind: . . . [F]inding no ease by drinking there, I went from that Alehouse to another, & drank a little, & from that to another, & so on till I had gone thro' about half a dozen of them & drank a while in each." Despite all his efforts to relieve the pain, his troubled mind only became more turbid as the night wore on. He felt increasingly the object of God's wrath and figured that he had rebelled against all of God's commands, that his alcoholism in particular had carried him into sin after sin.[34]

Though it was nearing midnight, he finally mustered the courage to go to an elder for help. "I at length," he said, "went to the door and knock'd." His narrative stops here incomplete and open-ended. Whether the elder—or Christ—answered his knock, we are left only to speculate and wonder. Though earlier in his account he noted that he had experienced a "fresh awakening" in the summer of 1744—most likely, as in the summer of 1742, at a sacramental occasion—little would suggest this refreshing solved his problems.[35] Indeed, the open-endedness of his narrative is peculiarly fitting. For Thomas Foster the devotions had never quite worked. Perhaps his fresh awakening—of which he was obviously on the verge when McCulloch's account drops off—was lasting. Most likely it was not. In several cases at Cambuslang, concern wore off almost as fast as it came on. For embattled saints like Thomas Foster the sins more often than not returned. For some the moments of awakening were few and far between.

Like Thomas Foster, others had stories of trial and temptation to tell McCulloch. One old soldier of fifty-one years, for example, sounded the part of a sinner when he reported his early life of degradation—his drinking, gaming, swearing, Sabbath breaking, and atheistic thinking. The last had especially hindered him: "When I was about 22 years of age, I fell under dreadful unbelieving apprehensions . . . relating to the Bible," he confessed. "I heard that the Turks had their Alcoran, the Papists their Traditions, and all Sects pretended to what they received for their Rule to be from God, & yet all was but from man; & I thought, so also might the Bible which I & others I liv'd among, be, for any thing I knew to the contrary. I was much perplex'd about this matter, but kept all within my self, fearing that if I should mention such thoughts to any, I would be taken for an Atheist, and I did not know but the Laws of man might take hold of me & put me to death." As a young man this old soldier sounded as if he were a latter-day Menocchio, the heterodox Italian miller given fame by Carlo Ginzburg, who was plagued by similar doubts arising from the implications of the plural truth claims of the world's religions.[36] Unlike Menocchio, however, this agnostic Scot was soon to resolve his dilemma.

In a short time the old soldier received faith and went on to seal his salvation at the "Lords Table," making on this occasion a "Personal Covenant" to lead a godly life. He reported no dramatic experience at the communion, only a solemn and self-made vow to resist "all filthiness & pollution of the flesh." In the sacrament he had found moral strength and had been guarded against unbelief. After several years of indifference and immorality, he finally hardened his resolve to resist sin and to lead a godly life. The experiences of Catherine Cameron and Blair's zealous pilgrim were always balanced by the failings of other saints, like those of Thomas Foster and this old soldier, or even more starkly by the open impieties of Alexander Cunningham, Hugh Maxwell, Isobel Wardrope, or Witherspoon's mirthful young men.[37]

Even when people were seeking piety and trying to ward off impiety, diversions and distractions from sacramental devotion were legion. Sundry worldly activities regularly competed with otherworldly exercises. These four-day communions demanded time off from work, and often masters and mistresses denied their servants the liberty to attend. The reality of worldly demands could close off the possibility for such extended devotion. "I asked my mistress, if she would allow me to go to that Sacrament-Occasion," one woman reported to McCulloch in a characteristic passage, "no she said." Though she did receive permission to go to the next communion after that, her rebuff by her mistress was typical of the problems faced by these evangelicals in their efforts to retreat from the world for a week of devotions. The requirements of worldly employment could preclude full participation in the sacramental season.[38]

The restraints and concerns of the world were hardly all externally imposed on these would-be saints. Even when wholly at liberty to attend, work could distract them from full participation in the sacramental occasion. "In May 1743, intending to attend the Sacrament-Occasion at Cambuslang; but having at that time considerable Wages coming in to me every day," one industrious saint explained his dilemma, "I followed my Imployment, I began to cast up in my own mind, what might be the Sum I would lose by attending at that Sacrament-Occasion as I proposd, & finding it rise to something considerable, I was tempted to resolve rather to stay away & follow my work." This communicant ultimately overcame his qualms and was helped by God "from thinking of the world when I was there on the several days of that Solemnity." Others no doubt were less successful. Dedication to wages could easily eclipse devotion to the eucharist. Nagging thoughts of how much this cessation of labor cost could readily divert focused prayer and contemplation.[39]

Work was only one of the more obvious impediments to devotion. At the communion itself, people were tempted to religious laxness or inattention in many ways. "When I got there and began to mix among the crowd," one North Carolinian Presbyterian lamented of his distraction at a communion in 1773, "a variety of objects took my attention, and presently I found my [devotional] frame was gone." Another North Carolinian was more specific in complaining of the distractions that accompanied the thronged communions: worshipers, he said, "find their minds distracted by the scenes around them—the new faces, the bustle, the introduction to strangers, the salutations with acquaintances rarely met with." Amid this bustle and excitement the cause of diversion was often quite prosaic; it could be as simple as the clothes of a fellow worshiper that, in catching the eye, turned the mind quickly from God to the goods of the world. "I minded little but looking about me, who was prettiest and who was best drest," one young woman at Cambuslang confessed about her inattentiveness on Sabbath days. Drowsiness could add to the problem of diversion. One woman, for example, who spoke with McCulloch said she was "often guilty of frequently falling asleep" during secret prayer and family devotions. Another woman upon the Sabbath morning of a sacrament found herself "lying & sleeping much longer in my bed than ordinary," so much so that she ended up being "in such a hurry" to get to church that she did not even have "time to retire & say God help me." Drowsiness, distraction, and inattention were problems all too familiar even for the devout.[40]

A nineteenth-century Scottish painting by William Carse of the tent preaching at one of these communions furnishes further insight into the prevalence of distraction and diversion. If somewhat satiric in its intent, the work, like Burns' poem "The Holy Fair," captured a rich and revealing scene.[41] Children play on the walls surrounding the churchyard; babies cry for attention or need to be nursed; dogs wander unrestricted among the crowd; horses clop not far away. Those people who worship and pray—and most do—do so amid a welter of activity. Solemnity and sociability freely intermingle. This same concomitance is evident in David Wilkie's early nineteenth-century sketches of the sacrament and tent preaching at Kilmartin. Taken together, Wilkie's two drawings suggest a similar congruence of communion and conviviality. By turns people talk to neighbors and hear sermons, play with children and weep at receiving the sacrament. These evangelicals, even as their souls were bathed in

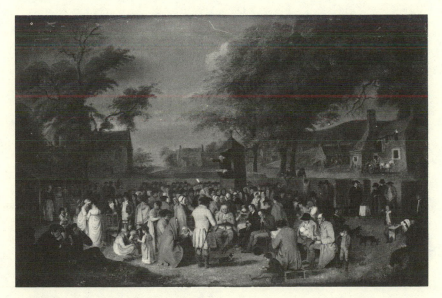

4. William Carse. *On Tent Preaching*.

5. David Wilkie. *Tent Preaching at Kilmartin*.

6. David Wilkie. *Kilmartin Sacrament*.

Christ's blood or illumined by divine love, were never far removed from human frailty or the commonplace.

The common diversions of the world were bad enough. The greatest fomenter of distraction, however, was far more momentous, for that palm was given to Satan. The devil managed to torment almost all of McCulloch's pilgrims at one point or another. Appearing in varying forms from a dog to a cow and even once in the guise of a minister, Satan was as protean as he was powerful. He regularly tempted people to commit suicide or tried to convince them that they were damned or even that they were atheists. Not surprisingly, as part of his machinations, he relished keeping people away from sacramental occasions. "While I was resolving to attend there [the second sacrament at Cambuslang]," a thirty-eight-year-old woman told McCulloch, "Satan suggested that it was to no purpose to go to any more Such Occasions, for that the day of grace was over with me." Once people had arrived at the communion, they might still be unsafe. The devil then might attempt to keep the communicant "back from the Table." "Satan was very active," one woman confided, "in endeavouring to keep me back from communicating" as he troubled her throughout her devotions Saturday night. If failing at this, he might attempt to distract people during the eucharist itself. "When at the Table," a woman reported, "Satan attack'd me . . . hard with his Suggestions & Temptations." Afterward he could continue his assaults on the faithful and might try to undermine their confidence in their experiences during the administration of the Supper. "Satan would have had me to doubt," another saint noted, "if what I had met with at the table, was from the Lord." For all of Satan's tireless activity, he was simply the grandest embodiment of the constant problems of distraction and temptation. Satan subsumed all the many failings to which the faithful were prone in their pilgrimages. As a symbol and as an effective force, Satan suggested all that could go wrong at a sacramental season. He epitomized—at least as far as the communion occasion was concerned—diversion, dullness, and doubt.[42]

Temptations to impiety, unbelief, and distraction everywhere met people as they journeyed in this world. Their pilgrimages to communions were no exceptions; indeed, these extended, crowded meetings were often a particular source of temptation—a time in which worldly and saintly forces were visibly in combat and one in which religion and sociability were inextricably intertwined. While all met such temptations, not all overcame them. Some clearly failed where they wanted to succeed, and still others had no desire to live their lives in pursuit of evangelical ideals. Impiety and diversion were familiar parts of the sacramental season, and this very familiarity gave added urgency to the spiritual disciplines of the saints.

From Diversion to Devotion: Spiritual Disciplines

The best way for the evangelical Presbyterians to bring focus to their spiritual lives and to avoid the distractions of the world and the worldly was through devotional disciplines. For all those saints who sought more in the festal communions than diversion, strenuous preparations were required. From the preparation Sabbath the week before, if not earlier, through the communion Sabbath itself, communicants had various ways of readying themselves for the solemn act of receiving the Lord's body and blood. Much of the preparation was corporate, but much too was private as individual saints retired from the world to examine their souls and to quicken their faith. The saints were to approach this holy mystery with focused, dedicated minds and cleansed, humbled hearts. Punctilious preparation underpinned the whole enterprise.

One young man's account of his preparation offers a place to begin in assessing these devotional disciplines. Dissatisfied with himself for not having "duly prepared" for "the Holy Ordinance of the Lords Supper" in the past, he vowed to engage more fully in such duties. First he studied a sacramental devotional by the Puritan Richard Vines which helped him see what qualifications were necessary to participate in that ordinance as well as to see how far he fell short of them. After that his preparations mounted:

> I essay'd to meditate & examine my self: but found my thoughts confusd & wandring. I then fell to write my thoughts, the better to prevent wandring. And it occurr'd to me first That the Paschal Lamb was separate & brought in & ty'd to a Post for eight days: agreeable to this, I thought I must meditate on Christs death & sufferings before the 2d Sacrament at Camb[uslang] that I had in view. I did so, and while I was doing it felt love to Christ warming my heart. Next, the leaven was to be searchd out with lighted Candles & put away; & I beg'd the Lord might discover to me if there was any leaven of hypocrisy, malice or wickedness lurking in any corner of my heart & help me to put it away; & I essay'd to find it out & have it remov'd. I gave my self Soul body & Spirit to God in way of Covenant, & accepted of God the Father Son & Holy Ghost as my God, Father Redeemer & Sanctifier, & subscribed with my hand to the Lord. I searchd into my Soul wants & plagues, & laboured to have my heart affected with them: & was much & oft in Secret Prayer.

This man's description of his preparations is a revealing condensation of the spiritual disciplines in which these saints engaged. Five devotional exercises are evident in his compact account: self-examination, personal covenanting, secret prayer, meditation, and devotional reading. These were the basic endeavors that helped the saints move from diversion to devotion. These were the primary forms of private devotion in the long process that culminated in the feast with Christ at his table. Unpacking this man's summary of each reveals much about the eucharistic piety of these evangelicals.[43]

Central to this young man's preparation was self-examination, the process of searching his heart with "lighted Candles" for "any leaven of hypocrisy malice or wickedness." This spiritual duty was in a large part predicated on 1 Corinthians 11:28: "But let a man examine himself, and so let him eat of that bread, and drink of that cup." With this scriptural imperative an omnipresent text before the communion, self-scrutiny was made essential for a worthy approach to the Lord's table. In these introspective examinations the saints "took a back-look" at their lives, enumerated their sins—"all the Lusts and Plagues of the Heart," such as "Malice, Passion, Envy, Discontent"—and endeavored to repent of them. The long reach of this "back-look" was evidenced in one pastor's note in his diary; before each communion he examined himself "by revolving in My Mind the whole catalogue of My More remarkable sins from My Being six years of age." Forty-five at the time, he suggested how self-examination before the sacrament was to be rigorous in both its introspection and its retrospection. Communicants were to approach this "most solemn and august Ordinance under Heaven" with careful reflection and painful self-awareness.[44]

The discipline of self-examination required focused, meditative concentration as these interrogations of the soul included extensive self-questioning. Willison in his *Young Communicant's Catechism* enumerated twenty-two questions that would-be communicants should put to their souls, and other catechists and pastors were equally exacting. The inquiry, far-ranging in its scope, probed the spiritual propensities, attainments, and failures of the saints. What evidences did they have of saving grace? Did they long for greater conformity to God's commands? Did they war against lust and backslidings? Did their minds turn regularly to spiritual and heavenly things and away from earthly and sensual ones? Did they express love and affection to their neighbors? Did they have solid doctrinal knowledge, particularly in regard to the Lord's Supper, so that in communing they would show forth Christ's death? And that was only a sparse sampling of the questions the saints aimed inward as they sought to determine their spiritual state and to decide whether they were worthy to come to the feast. In self-examination, this "Free-communing with our own Hearts," the saints sought self-understanding. Sorting and searching, they strove to bring order to their lives and minds, to figure out in exhaustive detail where they stood with God.[45]

After examining himself the young man had related that "I gave my self Soul body & Spirit to God in way of Covenant, . . . & subscribed with my hand to the Lord." Thus he described the discipline of personal covenanting. Others expressed themselves similarly. "At the Sacrament Occasion at Campsie," one young woman noted, for example, "I was inabled in secret to give my self intirely away to God in Covenant." Another young woman reported how on Friday evening before the Lord's Supper "I went apart by my self in the Fields, and aim'd at the duty of Personal Covenanting with God." While the saints might enter into or renew these covenants on various occasions—such as in times of national or personal peril or at the beginning of each new year—the consummate period for covenantal renewal was the Lord's Supper. At no other time was the duty more often enjoined or deemed more appropriate.[46]

Like self-examination, personal covenanting was a complex and detailed devotional discipline. Encapsulating much of the faith, a personal covenant entailed a renunciation of sin, an acceptance of Christ, and a dedication of the whole being—"Heads, Tongues, Eyes, Ears, Hands, Feet"—to God. When initially entered into, especially before approaching the Lord's table for the first time, it represented a renewal of the baptismal covenant that had been made by the parents on behalf of the child. It signalled, as did the first communion, that individuals had "come to Age," that they had closed with Christ on their own and had resolved to live in obedience to God. After having entered into this covenant the saints were expected to renew it throughout their lives and seal it anew each time they came to the Lord's Supper. As was the case with the sacrament itself, the themes that were rung in personal covenanting were not novel, but ones that were sounded repeatedly. They were core truths—about repentance, faith, love, redemption, surrender, and service—that could not be reiterated too often.[47]

What distinguished personal covenanting as a devotional discipline was its potential for external concreteness. While personal covenanting could be accomplished entirely by "outward Words and Expressions of the Mouth" or could even be done silently through inward reflection, the prescribed technique was to compose the personal covenant "in Writing" and then to subscribe to it "with the Hand." Thus people not only reflected on the various aspects of their covenantal relationship with God, but often externalized them in written form. The act of drawing up a covenant and subscribing to it, undertaken with great solemnity, was a way of embodying readiness to partake of the sacrament. On bended knees in a posture of reverence and humility, the saints took up their pens in the sight of God and bound themselves (and often their families as well) to the Lord. Far more tangible and durable than spoken words or silent thoughts, these documents helped assure the saints of their worthiness and helped them give focus to the difficult, sometimes nebulous task of self-examination. If people with their dim candles searching the dark recesses of their hearts were ever in danger of getting lost, the discipline of personal covenanting provided specificity and concreteness in a vast realm of introspection. Like a stone pillar, a personal covenant was set up as a monument that attested to the solemn transaction that had passed between God and the pilgrim soul—a transaction that was then sealed in the Lord's Supper.[48]

Self-examination and personal covenanting as preparations would have meant little without prayer; for prayer was a sine qua non in the devotional lives of these evangelicals. As the young man related of his preparations for the sacrament, almost as an afterthought because it was such a given, "I . . . was much & oft in Secret Prayer." Or, similarly, one pastor observed in his diary after detailing his extensive preparations for the eucharist in self-examination, personal covenanting, and meditation that "in all this I begin with prayer, intermingle prayer, and conclude with it." A few, like Thomas Foster, may have been lax or dull in their observance of this duty, but most prayed daily both with the family and in private. "I was almost always praying," one saint exuded, "when I walked on the streets and Every Where."[49]

An incessant, day-in, day-out activity, prayer was even more "*Fervent and importunate*" during the week leading up to the sacrament than at other times. The routine moments of prayer before bed or after waking were extended in these seasons to lengthy vigils often lasting all night. Whether conducted in a home, a barn, or the fields, the saints sought an isolated, private place to pour out their hearts to God. Again and again in the Cambuslang materials, Friday and Saturday nights in particular became the occasion for long hours of preparatory prayer in anticipation of the eucharist. Sometimes these vigils, out in the darkness of a barn or the fields, yielded religious experiences as intense and satisfying as any gained at the table or during sermons. "I went out by my self, and . . . stayed in the fields all night," one woman reported of a Saturday evening before the eucharist, "Enjoying sweet Communion and fellowship with God; and had as sweet a time as ever I had in my life, and thought I could not have a sweeter time in this world. I continued in that frame all the next day . . . and was much refreshed and delighted with what I heard and found in sermons and at the Lords Table."[50]

Usually, however, such secret prayer was more preparation than culmination. During the communion season people went out to the fields or retired to their closets for secret prayer primarily to ready themselves for the sacrament rather than to receive startling assurances from God. As the communion drew closer, confessions of unworthiness and fervent entreaties for blessings during the sacrament were the staples of secret prayer. One young communicant in Cumberland County, Pennsylvania, suggested the import of those prayers in a simple diary entry in September 1799: "Lord's day, arose in the morning . . . went to prayer, prayd for the grace of God to enable me to the worthy receiving of the Lord's Supper, was much engaged in prayer this morning & shed tears, . . . before going to church I again implored the assistance of God that he would be present with me in a gracious manner, . . . was much engaged while sitting at the Lords table." Having already been in secret prayer on the fast day before the communion, endeavoring then as well that "I might be prepared for sitting at his table," this young man, in his compact relation, suggested the ardor and constancy of these prayers, the tearful yearning for worthiness and blessing. Only after the eucharist, when the saints again retired to secret prayer, did their petitions regularly turn to joy, praise, and thanksgiving. Before the communion the focus remained on repentance and longing, on the preparation of the soul for this "Awful Solemnity." Long, fervent prayers, uttered in humility before God, were a critical part of this preparatory process as the saints sought the strength, the "supplies of grace," needed for so near an approach to God.[51]

Often in these prayers for pardon or for blessing the saints passed from supplication to meditation. One woman at Cambuslang revealed this transition clearly in her narrative:

I went out to the Fields by my self for Prayer, & there falling down, While I was earnestly pleading, That the Lord might give me a clearer sight & more affecting Sense of the Evil of my Sins as dishonoring to him, and as the procuring Cause of Christs Sufferings, than ever I had yet got: the Lord was pleased accordingly to give me the desire of my heart in that matter, & more than I ask'd or could think of. For I then got a most humbling sight & sense of the exceeding sinfulness & hatefulness of Sin; and I was made to see my Sins especially my Unbelief as the Nails & Spear that pierced his hands feet & side, & was made spiritually & in the most evident manner by faith to look as it were thro' his pierced side into his heart, & see it filled with Love to me, & his Love engaging him to undergo all these his bitter Sufferings for me.

Though closely connected with the other spiritual disciplines, meditation on Christ's sufferings was the one perhaps most closely associated with the sacrament. Like prayer and self-examination, meditation as a devotional technique was a regular part of the spiritual lives of the saints, proper indeed as a preparation for each Sabbath. But meditation intensively and almost exclusively on Christ's sufferings was characteristic of preparation for the eucharist alone. When the sacrament drew nigh, it was then, above all, that these evangelicals focused their minds on the sufferings of Christ.[52]

The consummate catechist, John Willison, described this preparatory duty of "*solemn and retired Meditation*" as "the Soul's abstracting and retiring itself from the World, and setting itself seriously to contemplate . . . spiritual Objects." "Let us meditate upon one Thing at once," Willison instructed, "and labour to keep the Mind and Thoughts fixed upon the Object that we think on, for some Time together, till once our Hearts be affected with it." "The principal subject of our Meditations," Willison specified, was to be "the *Sufferings* of Christ," which were to be envisioned in sanguinary detail and viewed "as in a bright Looking-glass." With Christ's Passion in fixed view, the saints meditated upon the nature of sin and atonement and marvelled at the sights that contained their redemption. They prepared themselves for the re-presentation of those scenes of suffering and salvation that was to come in the Lord's Supper. These evangelicals in their retreats during the week leading up to the sacramental occasion made their barns, fields, or closets the setting for retired, intensive meditation and reflection.[53]

The difficulties in this discipline, as in the others, were many. Various problems of impiety and diversion pursued the saints in their meditative retreats from the world. The minds of these saints were regularly, as one said, "busy wandring after Sinful & vain Objects" instead of spiritual ones. Or, as the young man cited at the outset of this section observed, "I essay'd to meditate . . . but found my thoughts confusd & wandring." Willison was certain that these devotions were much hampered by the dullness of the mind—its inattentive, digressive wanderings and its carnal, obsessive concern with "worldly Business." The mind too often was unfixed and drowsy, crowded with "impertinent thoughts" and cursed by "a bad memory." One man, in lamenting his lack of focused devotion, said that sometimes his thoughts were "in such ane Extravagant and disorderly confusion and Number as resembles to me a Multitude of Midges confusedly dancing." These evangelicals had to struggle continually in their devotions to overcome the limitations of the mind, to bring concentration out of confusion and focus out of blurred reflection. This quest to achieve "Stayedness and Fixedness of Thought" was an ongoing struggle for these pilgrims as they undertook these devotional disciplines.[54]

Amid these struggles the saints often turned to devotional reading as a help against wandering minds, especially as a way to bring focus to meditation. In turning to such manuals these evangelicals hardly assured themselves of success. The same problems of failing concentration and blurred reflection often dogged them still. "After breakfast I took Willison's Sacramental Catechism in my hand, and went out," one North Carolinian Presbyterian related of his efforts to bring order to his restless mind in 1773. "I sat down to read, but found I could not keep my eye upon the book, and far less fix my attention to anything in it." John Chestnut of Northumberland County, Pennsylvania, must have found it similarly hard to concentrate when reading Thomas Vincent's *Explicatory Catechism*; for his copy includes several lines of doggerel unrelated to his spiritual exercises as well as a number of hastily drawn birds and other doodles—clear signs of an unstayed mind.[55] In their efforts to prepare themselves for the great solemnity at hand and to bring order to their unfixed minds, these evangelicals sought assistance from devotional reading, but this discipline was obviously subject at times to the very shortcomings it was supposed to help the saints overcome.

If not foolproof, devotional reading was certainly a help. Foremost assistance in this regard came in the Bible. Reading and reflecting on Scripture was a given in the spiritual lives of the evangelicals, but it was particularly helpful before the communion. For example, looking into the Bible might facilitate the process of self-examination as the saints used scriptural texts to try their own souls. Thomas Boston for one did this, once closely applying at least eight specific scriptural verses to his case in his efforts to examine himself before coming to the Lord's table.[56] Reading Scripture also might facilitate meditation as few aspects of the Bible excited more reflection and devotion than did those chapters dealing with the sufferings of the Messiah. These chapters—notably Matthew 26–27, Mark 14–15, Luke 22–23, and John 18–19 as well as Isaiah 53—were fit reading throughout the year, but were particularly dwelled on as the sacrament approached. "When the Next Communion occasion at Glasgow drew on," one saint averred, "Some days before it . . . I . . . began to read the Sufferings of Christ in the gospels and was made to see that our sins were the procureing cause of Christ's Sufferings." In particular, pilgrims were encouraged to set aside the Friday before the eucharist—fittingly mirroring the day of crucifixion in this re-presentation of the Passion—as a day for reflection on Christ's sufferings as revealed in Scripture.[57] Whether meditation was on Friday or another time, these scriptural texts were nearly always in evidence. Repeatedly these passages on Christ's Passion inspired heart-piercing, heart-warming tears of grief and love. One woman at Cambuslang had been so enthralled by what Scripture had revealed to her that she had kissed her Bible.[58] The Bible was indeed precious to these saints, and it often proved especially dear as they readied themselves for the eucharist.

For some the Scriptures were all the devotional reading they needed to prepare themselves for the sacrament. Many, however, wanted additional reading as did our twenty-three-year-old contemplative who delved into Richard Vines' volume on the Lord's Supper. Others turned to works on the sacrament or the spiritual life by such popular authors as John Willison, William Guthrie, Thomas Vincent, Isaac Ambrose, or Elisabeth West. "I have found my heart much affected in reading some little Books of Devotion," one saint averred, "such as Mr Willisons book on the Sacrament, Eliz. West's account of her life, one of Isaac Ambrose's books &c."[59] Just how much these devotionals, particularly those concerned with eucharistic practice and piety, were read by the evangelicals at Cambuslang or by their counterparts in the colonies is difficult to determine, but a good deal of evidence suggests that usage was considerable. Not only were these books written for the laity, for "the perusal of all private Christians, . . . being easy and plain to common capacities," but they often ran through edition after edition. Ministers believed that such books had been "blessed to the edification of many thousands," and the numerous references among the saints at Cambuslang to the "good Books" that they had read suggests that ministerial hopes were not vain fancies.[60]

Further evidence that these devotionals were in the hands of the laity comes in two rare subscription lists, one to John Spalding's eucharistic collection *Synaxis Sacra* and the other to a volume of James Robe's sacramental sermons. The list in Spalding's work included over 1100 names, only four of which were identified as ministers. Thus the overwhelming majority of the subscribers were laypeople who came from various occupations and included, for example, 118 merchants, 94 weavers, 52 farmers, 42 wrights, 39 tailors, 33 shoemakers, and 31 smiths as well as 7 surgeons, 5 wigmakers, 4 butchers, and 1 musician. In Robe's work the numbers were nearly as disproportionate. Of 372 people listed, only twenty were ministers. The clerics found themselves outnumbered by both weavers and merchants and shared company alongside servants, coal-hewers, maltmen, farmers, vintners, a tobacconist, a brewer, a chapman, a bonnetmaker, a distiller, a writer, and other laypeople.[61] Such lists clearly suggest the popular base of support for these sacramental manuals. Also some sense of lay access to these books comes from those copies of the devotionals that do survive. Often they are inscribed with the names of laypeople, sometimes more than one as the book was passed from one saint to another.[62]

Visual evidences give yet another indication of the prevalence of devotional reading. Alexander Carse's *Sunday Morning* suggests this as the family is gathered reading Bibles, catechisms, or other religious books. The young child demanding her mother's attention reminds us again of the problem of sustained engagement. Reading may often have been episodic and broken, a page here and a page there. This is even clearer in William Carse's *On Tent Preaching* in which devotional reading goes on amid the face-to-face bustle of the sacramental occasion. People peer over each other's shoulders, point out passages, or listen to others read. For some their exposure to devotional texts may have been as much oral as printed; books, whether the Bible or religious manuals, were read and they were read from. If rarely pored over with unbroken concentration— in reading, as in meditation, "Stayedness and Fixedness of Thought" remained elusive—the sacramental manuals were important to the process of preparation. A vital part of the religious literature of early modern

7. Alexander Carse. *Sunday Morning.*

Scotland and America, such works regularly played a significant role in the spiritual lives of the laity.

While devotional reading was useful in various religious contexts—for example, in catechetical instruction, doctrinal understanding, or biblical study—the saints had particular occasion to search out these manuals as they prepared for the sacrament. In them, as in sermons, they learned about the nature of the eucharist, about its symbols and actions, about the qualifications for it, about the dangers of approaching unworthily, and about preparatory duties. The devotionals clearly supplemented and supported the spiritual disciplines of self-examination, personal covenanting, and secret prayer, but they especially reenforced the tradition of retired meditation upon the sufferings of Christ. This was wholly evident in the work of one of the more popular spiritual guides, Daniel Campbell. His *Sacramental Meditations on the Sufferings and Death of Christ*, a favorite eucharistic devotional among the Presbyterians from its publication in 1698, was the first to be reprinted in America. Campbell's "little

Book on the Sacrament," popular on both sides of the Atlantic, can be taken as one exemplar of this rich devotional tradition.[63]

Campbell designed his book to be read "the Week before the Communion" and to that end conveniently divided his manual into seven chapters, presumably one for each day leading up to the eucharist. He hoped that his devotional would be read again before every sacramental occasion and that the images would become fixed in the reader's mind. All of Jesus' life was filled with suffering, Campbell attested, as he moved through Christ's tribulations step by step. Abased from his conception in Mary's womb, Jesus lived, as Campbell described it, in constant humiliation and sorrow. "His whole Life," Campbell summarily related, "was full of Temptations, Persecution, Toil, Poverty, Sorrows, Reproaches, Hunger, Thirst, Weariness, Danger." As Campbell neared Christ's death, his meditations grew more vivid. He detailed "Christ's Bloody Sweat and Agony in the Garden" and then moved from there to his betrayal and apprehension. The moment of arrest was envisioned as violent and debasing. Christ is pulled by the hair, taunted, spat upon, and beaten; around his neck, Campbell suggests, is "a chain of iron." In the inquisition that followed, Christ at one point, as the Gospel of John records, was struck by an officer who was angered by Jesus' answers to the high priest. Such a detail provided Campbell with ample room for a sanguinary excursion. Working with an image he borrowed from Bernard of Clairvaux, Campbell saw Christ's face as "swelled and wan-coloured, by the Blow of an Iron Glove." Christ's visage grew more grisly as Campbell compounded one image of suffering upon another with relentless force. Soon his divine countenance was covered with "the *froathy Spittles and nasty Bubbles, and filthy Phlegm*" of his enemies; his mouth and nose were bleeding, and his whole head was swollen from blows. "It was a nauseous sight," Campbell observed, "and enough to make one spue."[64]

The grotesque, overwhelming images continued to mount as Campbell inched toward Golgotha. Christ is stripped, scourged, and derided. The gashes made by the scourging were so wide that "his Ribs, and Bones, and very Inwards" were visible. Jesus, already "*a Purple Gore of Blood, from top to toe,*" then had the crown with "the sharp Prickles" that pierced to the skull placed upon his head. The visions pounded harder and harder as Campbell's refrain of "behold . . . behold . . . behold" and "see . . . see . . . see" became more insistent. Devout readers were to relive these events, to imagine themselves there in the streets of Jerusalem as Christ, shouldering his cross, came by. They were to situate themselves on Mount Calvary in order to bathe their polluted souls in the blood that poured from Christ's wounds. There on Golgotha, under cleansing streams, they saw Christ stretched upon the cross; his flesh torn; his whole body distorted. One of McCulloch's saints indeed feared, as some had told him, that "the Cross on which Christ suffered, was made with a bow in it, and that it was streighted when he was nailed to it, and his sacred body was thereby Rackt." Images of extreme suffering on the cross, popularized in manuals such as Campbell's, passed readily into the piety of the laity where they were given further elaboration. Campbell's devotional and others like it provided detailed visions that helped transport those employing them back to the Passion.[65]

The physical sufferings Campbell described were seemingly without end. To these he added the "Soul-sufferings of Jesus," his endurance of God's consuming wrath in the sinner's stead and his desertion by his Father. These torments of the soul, Campbell assured, far exceeded any physical pains Christ had to suffer. Even that, however, was not the end of the sufferings, for the agony continued in death; the spear is thrust into his side, the nails jerked from his flesh, his body entombed in "the Prison of the Grave." Coming at last to the moment of triumph, Campbell drops off his narration. "I will not meddle here with Christ's Resurrection, Ascension,—I confine myself to his Sufferings and Humiliation, *Synecdochially* included in these Words, *This is my Body which is Broken for you*; For his Death, Humiliation, and Sufferings, are the proper Objects of *Sacramental Meditations*." He went on to close with some "*Practical Inferences*," drawn from Christ's torments, that would be helpful for communicants as they approached the sacrament. But the marrow of his meditations remained the sufferings. The images, carrying their own inferences about the cost of sin and about human redemption made possible through divine-human sacrifice, were the substance of contemplation.[66]

The focus of Campbell's devotional was clearly on penitential preparation, not on joyful rebirth. His work was aimed at humbling the would-be communicant through highlighting Christ's incomprehensible love in suffering such a death for the redemption of humankind. He hoped his meditations, riveting the contemplative's attention on the Passion, would intensify preparations for the sacrament and make participation in it more meaningful. Having for a week meditated on Christ's sufferings "with the greatest Attention and Devotion," the saint, Campbell believed, would have a livelier understanding of "the Sacramental Actions and Elements." "So shall broken Bread, and poured Wine," Campbell instructed, "clearly point out to you *a broken Jesus*, his torn Body, and shed Blood." In all his reflections Campbell kept this end constantly in mind. He returned time and again to the theme of preparation for the Lord's Supper. His meditations were aimed as arrows at the "flinty, rocky, adamantine Hearts" of these sinner-saints who he hoped would "dissolve in Tears of Repentance" at the thoughts of such scenes. Humbled and penitent, they would be ready to meet with Christ in sorrow and in joy at the Lord's table.[67]

This meditative focus on the suffering Christ in the sacramental devotionals profoundly affected lay piety; few other images were seen with such starkness or such frequency as Christ on the cross. Not many evangelicals probably took this emphasis as far as "the Presbyterian silly woman" who, the Reverend Thomas Boston noted with indignation, had "a picture of Christ on the cross, hanging on the wall" of her house.[68] But these meditative images were nonetheless at the core of eucharistic experience. A young man of nineteen made this centrality quite evident: "When I came to The Lords table, as I was pleading with him, for a broken heart to mourn for Sin as dishonouring to himself, and when I received the first Element," he told McCulloch, "I had a most lively & affecting representation made to my Mind, of the Sufferings of Christ: I thought I saw Jesus Christ evidently set forth before my Eyes as Crucifyed, Hanging & bleeding & dying on the Cross, and that it was my Sins [that] had procured his Sufferings, . . . I found the tears rushing down my Cheeks I could have even wished they had been tears of blood, and all too little for such heinous guilt."[69] The preparatory disciplines often gave way to more direct encounters with Christ in the Lord's Supper, encounters that suggested such preparation might yield at times to visionary experience.

POPULAR VISIONS AND MINISTERIAL REVISIONS

The spiritual discipline of meditating upon Christ's redemptive sufferings suggests in itself that this evangelical piety was often intensely visual. While devotionals such as Campbell's attest to a spirituality charged with images, the frequent visions of Catherine Cameron and the above young man's sight of Christ "Hanging & bleeding & dying on the Cross" point to a piety that often passed from the meditative to the visionary. Though visionary experiences were reported in a variety of contexts from private prayer to ordinary Sabbath worship, the communion season as the most concentrated period of devotion in the year was especially the occasion for such spiritual attainments. After extensive preparation and longing— in fasting, vigilant prayer, and contemplation—the saints often received blessings that carried them over into the ecstatic. Lapsing into trance, fainting or falling down as if dead, hearing voices, dreaming dreams, and seeing visions—all were possibilities within this piety. If not ordinary aspects of evangelical Presbyterian experience, as were the practices of prayer, self-examination, personal covenanting, meditation, and devotional reading, these extraordinary revelations were not isolated eccentricities either. From Shotts to Cambuslang to Booth Bay to Gaspar River, ecstatic religious experience was part of the communion occasion. During these festal events laypeople often had very direct and overwhelming encounters with the divine.

Yet ministers were usually very wary of such experience. Like most evangelical leaders, those who edited the Cambuslang manuscripts were especially concerned to minimize this aspect of the saints' piety in order to save revival supporters from charges of enthusiasm and disorder and to reaffirm the rational and scriptural soundness of evangelical spirituality. They thus cut out almost all mention of ecstatic religious experience, such as visions, voices, and trances—all of which potentially threatened the authority of Scripture as well as the authority of those who were the superintendents of that Word. Some of the evangelicals at Cambuslang were well aware of ministerial suspicion of such experiences: a common disavowal was, "I never swarfd nor faintd any Nor had I ever any visions."[70] In fact, this sort of statement occurred enough times in these narratives that one suspects McCulloch solicited such testimony with a point blank question or simply supplied this formulaic answer on his own. Despite these standardized disavowals, most of the laity disappointed McCulloch and his co-adjutors in one way or another. The number of visionary experiences was a particular source of disappointment for the ministerial editors. Their troubles were evident in their summary reaction to one man's relations: "There is something Visionary in this mans experiences"; they "doubt[ed] if it be proper to publish them."[71] Perhaps at no point was the gap between the mind of the ministers and the piety of the laity more profound. Yet the division between pastor and congregant on this point proves on close examination not clear and decisive, but blurred and problematic. Eucharistic visions, voices, and trances provide perhaps the clearest opportunity to assess the relationship between ministerial expectations and lay experiences at these festal communions.

Visions or voices at the Lord's table or elsewhere during these solemnities were common, indeed much more common than any disavowal of such experiences. One man, for example, related in a passage expunged by the ministerial editors that when he was at the Lord's table "earnestly pleading & looking to The Lord for some tokens of his Love and favour" that he suddenly fell into "a trance, being just as if I had been in a sleep with my eyes shut." "I . . . saw Divine justice stretching out its hand to take hold of Me," he recalled, "and Christ, as it were, stepping in betwixt justice & Me, shewing his wounds, and what he had suffered for me, in satisfying Justice; And saying, I have satisfy'd you for his sins: Upon which the hand of Justice could not touch me. And recovering out of that trance I felt my soul filled with great joy and comfort & thankfulness to God." Here both voices heard and visions seen in trance at the Lord's table offered this man assurances of pardon and salvation, but they were comforts that the ministers would have left out entirely. Similarly, a woman who at the table heard a voice, presumably Christ's, saying "Ye are all my mourning Doves" had her religious experience recast with this divine assurance expunged. That such corrections were proposed shows that ministers had failed to mold lay piety as fully as they would have liked. They might enjoin certain preparations for the Lord's Supper and might delineate certain suitable thoughts to have while at the table and afterward, but they could not fully control popular piety. The eucharistic experiences of the laity often diverged from ministerial expectations.[72]

The experiences of another saint, a married man of forty-seven, makes this divergence even clearer and suggests the richness of the visionary strand in this piety more dramatically. "On the preparation Sabbath and all the days at the Communion in Glasgow in October this year 1743," he began his relation of this juncture in his narrative, "I had a comforting and reviving time, particularly at the Lords Table, and on Munday." On Monday night, having been absorbed in the devotions of the sacramental occasion for more than a week, he "fell very low in my body, and frail, my strength being very much exhausted." Yet his "senses and soul faculties were as vigorous as ever," and he "fell a meditating." While "thus exercised," drained but contemplative, he reported:

> I saw as it were, before Me, a great multitude of dead Mens bones, first their sculls, and then the bones of their bodies, dry and without flesh, just as if they had ascended out of the grave, before me. At which sight I began to be alittle affrighted, and turn'd my thoughts off from them to Jesus Christ. After I got my heart fix'd on the Redeemer, I saw these dead Bones, as it were a great Multitude of living Men, walking about Me and some of them appeared as strong Country Men with staves in their hands, runing to Churches, & a great dale of them rushed in towards some Churches that I knew. . . . After which I thought there was a sweet and thick white and soft & refreshing shower, falling about me; And when I saw it, that Word came in with power to my soul, "Manna": And then I prayed, O That this may be Manna from Christ, who is the bread & water of life to fill hungry souls.[73]

After days of eucharistic preparation and thanksgiving, this reverielike vision came. Though there were other sights for him, this was perhaps the most dramatic. The ministers wanted nothing to do with it and registered a strong word of caution against viewing such impressions as being from the Lord's Spirit.

The images he saw were suggestive of both revival and eucharist and were a fitting culmination to the renewal he experienced through the communion. Those who were spiritually dead were resuscitated and brought to the church in droves. After which appeared the manna, a common emblem of the sacramental bread, and the prayer that hungry souls receive Christ, "the bread & water of life"—a passage that actually echoed his description of an experience he had earlier at the Lord's table. Evangelistic and sacramental, this man's meditative sights reflected an elaboration of themes that were at the very foundation of the communion season. Yet the way in which these basic truths were experienced diverged from ministerial prescription. The sacramental occasions often issued in visionary experiences that went beyond ministerial formulations of what constituted fitting communion frames.

While ostensibly clear-cut, the issue of visionary experience was actually not so easily decided. If these views of Christ or heaven were presented in certain ways, the ministers occasionally let them stand. For example, one woman told McCulloch that at a communion occasion in Glasgow, when "in a low condition, I saw with the eyes of my mind, The Redeemer bleeding upon The Cross, as it were, for my Sins, and my whole soul was filled with deep wonder and amazement, at his dying love for me." Though the ministers retained this passage, when another woman said that "I thought I saw Jesus Christ in his bloody Sweat in the garden, and Suffering on the Cross, and apprehended that all these Sufferings were for me and my Sins," it met with censure. It was not simply a matter of ministerial oversight that the first woman's view of the suffering Christ slipped through and that the latter's was expunged (though the ministers were not wholly consistent in their editing). The ministers, working with a distinction between the eyes of faith and the eyes of the body, were able to circumscribe the visual aspects of this faith without completely destroying them. What they opposed most were visions seen with the "bodily eyes" and wanted all sights attributed explicitly to the eyes of the mind, to disciplined meditation, to what they called again and again "the Eye of faith." For example, when Catherine Cameron reported having seen Christ reaching down his hand to draw her to himself during the serving of the tables, one editor marked it outright for deletion, but another tried to save the passage through adding the phrase *by the eye of faith* to her description of how she "saw him." To the ministers, though not the laity, the distinction was clearly critical. As a minister scribbled in the margins of one account, "I think always these sights should be mentioned by the Eye of faith."[74]

With this distinction in place, the ministers were in a position to encourage an intensely visual faith without sanctioning ecstatic religious experience. For example, John Willison, who was involved in the revivals at Cambuslang and who may have helped edit the manuscripts, composed meditations as provocatively imagistic as those drawn by Campbell. While Campbell had generally used the second and third person, Willison often cast his prayers in the intimacy of the first person. "I am now to ascend Mount *Calvary*," he wrote in one preparatory meditation, "and to go to the Place where Christ is to be set forth as crucified before mine Eyes; O that there I may look on him whom I have pierced, and mourn for Sin that made the Nails, and drove them in to my Redeemer!" Elsewhere, in a speech as he dispensed the cup at the table, Willison wrote in the second person, but with the same emphasis on re-presenting the sufferings of Christ. "Will you see his Blood shed?" Willison asked. "You are now upon Mount *Calvary*, at the Foot of the Cross, near the Wounds: He is saying, Pray, believing Soul, reach hither thy Hand, feel the Prints of the Nails; yea, thrust into my pierced Side, and feel my warm bleeding Heart." In passage after passage in his meditations, catechisms, songs, and sermons, Willison sounded as visionary as any saint at Cambuslang: Christ was not only seen anew, but he was heard and felt as well. Yet with the underlying distinction between the eyes of faith and the eyes of the body operative, Willison and other ministers could advocate disciplined, if extremely vivid, meditation without accepting visionary experience.[75]

Given diction like Willison's and Campbell's that was as startlingly imagistic as it was pervasive, it is not surprising that the limits placed on how to see the suffering Christ were often obscured. An illustration of this comes in the sermons of the American revivalist James McGready who, like his counterparts abroad, held visionary experiences among his congregants suspect, but who nonetheless promoted stark visualization, especially of Christ's sufferings. In one sermon, for example, McGready openly condemned those who had seen "something in the form of a man bleeding and dying on a cross." Seeking to reestablish the limits to the visual, McGready retraced what in effect amounted to an official position that was set against popular experience: "They have seen his bloody robe—the wound in his side—and the blood running in streams," he preached. "This is no view of Christ, but a deception of the Devil; for in a saving view of Christ, the object discovered is nothing which can be seen by the bodily eye, heard by the ear, or comprehended by the organs of sense; nor yet any ideal image formed in the imagination. The object is infinite and incomprehensible—only to be seen by the eye of understanding when enlightened by the Spirit of God." The visions and strong imaginations of McGready's congregants spawned this uncompromising attack on the senses. Ministerial problems with reining in lay propensities to cultivate a sensual, visual eucharistic piety were widespread and spanned the Atlantic.[76]

Even after taking such an unequivocal stand on the visionary, McGready quickly revealed how hard it was to keep the lines in clear focus. In sacramental meditations (and in this case in this very sermon) he talked about times when Christ meets with his people "in the lonely wood" or "at his table," where he "appears to their view," "shows them his pierced hands and feet, and permits them to look into his bleeding side." "He shows all the scarlet streams of divine blood flowing from all his open veins," McGready conjured, "until their hearts are broken with deep contrition and penitential sorrow for sin." Like Campbell, McGready employed incantations of see, see, see. Even if McGready intended only to encourage "a faith's view" of these things, it is clear his words begged a more literal reading, that he was to some degree responsible for the very visions and vivid imaginings he censured. That a sharp distinction between the eyes of faith and the eyes of the body failed to be maintained at the level of popular piety was evident; that the ministers were often partners in this blurring of lines is also clear. Their own diction, especially their vivid re-creation of the Passion at these communions, suggested a highly visual faith. Important distinctions were pushed aside—or simply forgotten—as the people kept enough ground clear to cultivate a eucharistic piety fraught with the imagistic and the visionary.[77]

The problem of defining the proper scope of visionary experience was further illustrated in religious dreams and the interpretation of them. With the extended devotions and night vigils connected with the sacrament, it was perhaps to be expected that people would have very powerful dreams during these events, dramatic spiritual experiences that came in sleep. These "night frames" or "Nocturnal frames in sleep," as one minister called them, presented another dimension of visionary experience with which ministers and laity concerned themselves. McCulloch and his co-adjutants faced a number of dreams in the Cambuslang manuscripts that were often of profound significance in the spiritual lives of those who dreamt them. Sometimes the ministers were quick to revise the interpretation given them as was the case with one man who had dreamt of his being "led thro' the World, and then taken up to heaven." He said that he had found great assurance in this night frame, but the ministers were quick to question whether this dream was "a rational Scriptural ground for removing his fears." They bracketed this dream, like other visionary experiences, for deletion. For the layman his sights of heaven in sleep were indeed good grounds for assurance; for the ministers such dreams were not.[78]

Presbyterian ministers in America confronted religious dreams as well. At one sacramental season in Kentucky, for example, pastor John Lyle talked with a man who, when "slumbering" on Monday night of the occasion, dreamt that "his spirit went out . . . into the earth & saw strange curious caverns &c." As he slept, he also "saw a mountain clothed with beautiful trees silver top'd or leafs tip'd with silver, he thought this mountain led to God & heaven[.] [T]hen above he saw a great light & he pray'd to see a little further & a little to the right[.] [H]e saw still more dazzling light & he sigh'd & sunk before it as the great all in all." Lyle's simple comment on this extraordinary dream was: "I try'd long to state the evidence of true grace to his mind," probably without much success. The dreams of the laity challenged ministers in yet another area to define the limits of visionary experience. And though pastors were often at great pains to state what were acceptable meanings to give these night frames, they could never be certain that the laity would not accord such dreams different or greater significance.[79]

Again, however, it would be precipitous to draw a sharp line between pastors and people. One eighteenth-century Scottish minister, Henry Duncan, made this clear in his memoirs and diary. An ardent evangelical and fervent Presbyterian, Duncan saw dreams as among the most important aspects of his spiritual life. "I was wont in my Sleep," he said, "to be wonderfully transported with a Celestial and heavenly joy in God and about spiritual things." One night, for example, he "was sweetly seasoned with joy all over," when he dreamt he "was communicating and it was very like communicating in Heaven but I cannot Make words of it." Another time on the Sabbath morning of the sacrament he experienced "the Most spiritual frame that ever I had." "My Frame began in My Sleep," he noted, "in time of which I was sweetly and ravishingly exercised in My spirit about My Saviour's resurrection and Peter and John's Emulous running to his grave and about all the rest of the Circumstances of this according to the gospel History." These "representations of Christ" in sleep were overwhelmingly real; it was as if "Mine Eyes had seen and My hands handled." For Duncan such religious dreams were so important and powerful that "Sometimes I have quickly got out of Bed and upon my Knees Naked as I was" wrote them down. Though he worried at times that such dreams "might be satannical designs to put me in Love with immediate inspirations, and to carry me off the ordinary and plain way of Gods manifesting himself," he did not allow this characteristic ministerial reservation to ruin his "sweet night frame[s]." Instead he savored these "pleasant vision[s]" again and again.[80]

If ministers were more careful and circumspect about the meanings attached to these "Nocturnal impressions," they were never wholly unreceptive to religious dreams. They were not always as wary as McCulloch, his co-editors, and Lyle were. Like Duncan, pastors too could find "delight unspeakable" in dramatic dreams. Care and caution were obviously exercised, especially on the part of ministers, but never so much as to discredit such experience. Night frames added to the visionary component of this piety as evangelical experience could engulf both sleeping and waking hours.[81]

Dreams and visions were not the only aspects of lay relations of their experiences at these communions that the editors of the Cambuslang manuscripts sought to qualify or revise. Ministers also worried, for example, about how their sermons were understood by the laity and what was remembered about them. Sometimes the laity recalled colorful expressions from sacramental sermons—such as one about Peter's "dirty stinking feet"—that the ministers thought better forgotten and thus marked them accordingly for deletion. The editors took care to guard themselves and their colleagues from any objectionable recollections, bracketing, for example, a passage describing a cleric as preaching in a legal and deadening strain at one of these solemnities and editing another section that suggested a pastor was lax in carrying out examinations before the Lord's Supper. Ministerial concern over how the laity perceived them or how their sermons were misunderstood was evident. Safeguarding ministerial authority, whether from lay criticism or from the subversive potentialities of visionary experience, was a primary part of the editorial task.[82]

Sometimes, however, the ministers actually had to be watchful for the opposite tendency, the according of too much power and importance to the cleric. One woman who talked with McCulloch reported, for example: "When I was at the Table, I sate Next [to] the Min[iste]r, . . . seeking the Upper most seat; & getting the Cup out of the Minister[']s hand." Instead of receiving the elements from one of her fellows, she had sought in effect clerical distribution. In the seventeenth century David Calderwood came across an "ignorant woman" who, presuming that it would make the rite more effective, had likewise striven "to be neerest" the minister at the table in order to receive the elements out of the pastor's hands. Calderwood condemned her efforts in no uncertain terms as evidence that popish superstition still lingered in Scotland. Official prescription and lay practice at communions could potentially diverge in not so subtle ways.[83]

Perhaps the least subtle, most glaring divergence came in ministerial accusations that some laypeople viewed the Lord's Supper, and the sacramental elements in particular, as charms. One eighteenth-century Scottish pastor complained that his parishioners viewed the sacrament as "a charm to save them," and that no matter what he said or did he could not "beat this delusion out of their heads."[84] Popular beliefs in the efficacious power of the sacrament were particularly notable in "the old superstitious custom of some," as pastor John Spalding complained, to take "a bit of this Bread" away from the table, secreting it in a handkerchief or pocket.[85] Church session records added substance to Spalding's complaint. In 1703 in Galston James Richmount was called before the kirk session "for his scandalous & offencive cariage at ye lords table . . . in putting up part of the bread in his pocket"; similarly, in 1711 in Dundonald John Dick was seen at the table placing "some of the elements in his pocket." Both men confessed to having done so, and both were publicly rebuked before the congregation.[86]

Perhaps such cases were exceptional, and no doubt the vigilance of church sessions and the spectacle of rebuke were increasingly effective in curbing such "superstitions." Still Reformed eucharistic ritual in which the bread was put into the hands of the people, instead of directly into the communicant's mouth, made it easier for such practices to persist than otherwise would have been the case. Whatever the level of incidence, accounts such as those of James Richmount and John Dick, coupled with ministerial warnings, suggest a lingering gap between pastors and some of their people. To take the consecrated bread away from the table, to reserve it for personal use later—whether in matters of health, courtship, crops, or salvation—was simply unacceptable to Reformed orthodoxy. Unlike issues of visionary experience, the lines drawn here were unblurred and unbroken.[87]

The mental worlds of pastors and people at these communions were not coterminous or in complete harmony. Sometimes laypeople misconstrued sermons; sometimes they dreamed dreams that their pastors found suspect. On occasion they even held to folk beliefs about the sacramental elements that were wholly proscribed by their ministers. Still the problem that pastors had to confront most often was the tendency of eucharistic devotion to spill over into the visionary. Many laypeople enjoyed sights and sounds at these communions that the ministers did not see and hear— or at least did not see and hear in the same way. Ministers relied on distinctions that simply were not interiorized by a large number of their communicants. Even so the gap between pastors and people on this point was hardly unbridgeable. Ministerial expression often blurred the distinctions, and lay experience elaborated upon, as much as controverted, pastoral diction and devotion. All along evangelical clerics and congregants alike yearned for "an Eye of immediate Vision," for the day when they would see Christ "as he is." In the interim both were sustained by sights seen not dimly, but clearly in acts of eucharistic ritual and in that "bright Looking-glass" of meditation. Popular visions were revised, criticized, clarified, and even suppressed, but vision—seeing and visualizing—remained central to the evangelical faith of pastors and people alike.[88]

THE RHYTHMS OF PIETY

Though eucharistic experience was often ecstatic and visionary, it was not always so. Sights faded or were never seen at all. Overwhelming experiences of assurance lost their immediacy or eluded attainment. Sacramental preparation and participation led the communicant not so much to resolution or transcendence in a lasting way, but through a cycle of penitence and thanksgiving, humiliation and joy. The spiritual rhythms of the sacramental occasion thus were interwoven with a larger pattern of piety in which spiritual deadness was followed by agonizing repentance which in turn was prelude to joyous release. The sacramental season clearly embodied this spiritual cycle. From the penitential confessions on the fast day to the thankful praises on Monday, this larger pattern inhering in Reformed piety was reenacted in miniature. The sacramental season was constructed in such a way that the pilgrim was enabled to move through the essential stages of the Reformed faith in a concentrated period. Distilled into few days of devotion, the cycle of Reformed piety with its "Up & Downs"—with its rhythm of repentance and renewal—was epitomized in the sacramental season. In the incessant struggle for spiritual invigoration, for assurance and confirmation, the communion occasion was an essential part of the quest.[89]

These evangelicals looked forward to the sacramental occasion as a period of awakening and renewal. During a long period of spiritual disconsolation, one saint sought light in "this dark night" from the communion season, almost as if it alone could provide rejuvenation. "For a considerable time," she related, "I fell under damps & long'd for a Sacrament Occasion to get a revival." Another attested that she "had such a longing for that ordinance" that in waiting for it "every day seemed to be a week long." Similarly, one saint, on leaving one of these solemnities greatly refreshed, "went home with much love & joy longing for another Communion occasion." Time and again these evangelicals averred that the sacramental season was the time they looked to for revivification, that this event, above all, could lift them out of spiritual deadness.[90]

The sacramental occasion was not only a source of renewal for those whose spiritual concern had declined since the last communion, but also a means of resolving the doubts of those who were downcast and despaired of their salvation. These pilgrims, who "climb[ed] to heaven, between the two sharp rocks of presumption & despair," searched for ways to overcome the impediment of despair without falling upon the pinnacle of presumption. The festal communions provided considerable assistance in this trek. In prompting repentance for sin as well as effecting reconciliation with God, the sacramental occasion provided an opportunity for release from spiritual uncertainty. One woman at Cambuslang in particular attested to the painfulness of her recurring distress and the effectiveness of the communion season in assuaging these pains. "I have been many a time when under convictions & distress for Sin, in great bodily pains and distress: I have born several Children, but have been in as great bodily pains under my Convictions, as at bearing any of my Children," she reported in an unusually poignant passage. "These pains usd to begin at my left side, when I fell under distress of Spirit for Sin: & if I had not got my Cloaths loosd when I found my Side rising, I had been in hazard of my Life: And the Pains would have proceeded from my Side to all the other parts of my Body. My Bones especially would have been all sore and pain'd, as if they had been bruis'd by beating." Relief from such horrible distress came, when it came at all, in the communion occasion. "At Eastwood Sacrament," she related, "I got my longing Soul satisfied, by the sensible presence of Christ and the Refreshings of his Grace: and much of this frame continued with me for a good while after." While the spiritual cycle of most saints was not subject to such dramatic despair or such physical pain, nearly all found in the sacramental season at one point or another welcome release from spiritual doubts and discomforts. Through it, they might be raised out of the doldrums of spiritual deadness or relieved of the distress of salvific uncertainty.[91]

For many the refreshening lasted a great while, perhaps carrying the pilgrim through until the next sacramental occasion. One forty-year-old man noted, for example, that the "sweet frame" he had obtained at a "Solemnity" lasted "with me in a good measure, for about a half a year thereafter." Another reported that at the table "my heart was even almost overwhelmed under the sensible out-lettings & manifestations of the love of Christ to my Soul." After that experience this young woman continued for several months to receive similar evidences of God's love to her almost every day. Others related similarly durable experiences at the sacrament—ones that kept them invigorated for weeks, if not months, at a time. For some the blessings of the sacramental season were enduring, providing lasting assurance of salvation amidst the troubles and turmoil of the world long after the communion was over.[92]

Yet even in the best cases the peaks eventually levelled off or worse dropped precipitously into a valley. The infusion of grace that the sacramental season offered was far from inexhaustible. One wry critic, in penning a letter to the ministers and elders of the Church of Scotland, stressed how ephemeral the benefits of the sacramental occasion were: "These *occasions* . . . serve nearly the same ends in our church, that confession and absolution do among the papists," he bantered. "But in both countries, the professed repentance proves only a flash of devotion, and, as if matters were made up with the Deity, and all former accounts cleared, the papist soon puts off his penitential countenance, and the presbyterian lays by his sacramental face, and they and we, in a little time, are the same men that we were before." Though polemical, this observation underscores the cyclical quality of this sacramental piety as well as the limits placed upon it by human weakness, if not depravity.[93]

The evidence from Cambuslang to some degree confirms this critic's observation. The effect of the sacramental season on these evangelicals, even when intense and satisfying, often wore off quickly. "I seem'd at times, particularly about Sacrament-Occasions," one woman confessed of her past, "to have some desire after [God], & some concern to be good, but after such Occasions were over, I return'd again to my former carnal

security & worldliness." These sorts of confessions are strewn throughout the pages of the Cambuslang narratives. A young woman of sixteen
years admitted, for example, that despite the stirring power she experienced at her first communion, the concern soon faded: "When I lookt to
the Elements at the first Sacrament Occasion ever I was at, the tears came
running down my cheeks, but I scarce could tell for what, only I then
thought I was a great Sinner: but this wore quickly away." In a similar
vein, another young communicant, when at the Lord's table, made a
promise to God that "wherein I had done iniquity I would do so no more.
But soon after this Sacrament Occasion was over, I broke all these prom-
ises. . . . I soon turn'd carnal & secure, again, & took great pleasure in
carnal mirth jesting & sporting." For many, if not most, the cycle of renewal and decline, rededication and relapse went on and on.[94]

If at times the moral energy generated by these communions dissipated
quickly, the spiritual assurances gained there were subject to the same
entropic decline. For some the fears and doubts returned immediately or
were only partially resolved. Damps and sweetnesses alternated in rapid
succession or were even experienced simultaneously; joy and grief, after
all, merged in the sacrament. Monday might well have been a day of release, but often it was not. Even when it was, there was no telling how
long the comforts would last. One saint reported that in the thanksgiving
service on Monday "I found all the present want of my heart supply'd, &
my soul filled with inexpressible love to Christ and joy in him; and that
frame continued with me, as I went home and that night, and I felt my
face just glowing with that heat of love and joy I felt with in me." The
next sentence in her narrative, however, confirms just how fleeting these
joys could be: "But on twesday, I fell under a terror of Satan; and it was
suggested to me, That all was but delusion I had met with, & [this] filled
me with great distress." Dullness or distress could return all too rapidly.
One young woman, after receiving great benefits and blessings at the
Lord's Supper, added her testimony to what amounts almost to a refrain
in these narratives. "Alittle after that Sacrament," she related, "I was
seized with affliction, & the Lively impressions I had got at that Occasion,
wore much off, so that I became more dull & lifeless, as to spiritual
things." Peace followed by turmoil, alertness by torpor, this spiritual cycle
was well-nigh inescapable.[95]

Within this rhythm of renewal and decline, the outlines of a larger pattern can be discerned. Communion occasions were predominantly seasonal events, confined almost entirely to the summer and early fall, interwoven particularly around the agricultural events of planting and
harvest. Between May and October sacramental solemnities would be
held from one parish to another almost without interruption; indeed, for
the pious, these months constituted something of a sacramental *season*—

a temporal ordering apart from spring, summer, fall, and winter. These months, as one North Carolinian said, "may be considered our holy season." With the more zealous saints often attending several sacraments during the course of these months, this period was uniquely a time of renewal, the high days in a faith otherwise unguided by calendrical feasts and festivals. Even amid years of unusual awakening, this pattern tended to hold. As John Lyle noted at the height of the Great Revival in Kentucky, "Through the winter we held no sacraments. . . . [I]n most places there have been but few comparatively who have profess'd to be convicted & converted." With these annual rituals the focus of much of their devotion, the saints came to expect that the summer and early fall would be a period of special renewal for them—an expectation that was regularly met. "Thro' the Summer & Harvest," one woman told McCulloch, "the World & all things in it, sank into nothing in my esteem; I was made to sit down under Christs shadow with great delight; and his fruit was sweet to my taste: But when Winter came on, I turn'd more dead." A part of a calendrical rhythm, the communion season of summer and early fall constituted the high days of the year.[96]

As the above woman's testimony suggested, not only were summer and early fall high points in the year, but conversely the other seasons—winters particularly—were often associated with spiritual deadness or at least lukewarmness. "Last winter," another saint observed, "I found it to be a time of much deadness, doubts and unbelief with me." This contrast between summer and winter was suggested, too, in ministerial writings. Winter was often associated with "Affliction and Desertion," summer with spiritual renewal, growth, and light; "the winter of sickness and old age" was juxtaposed with "the summer-days of grace." In this context of summer over winter, the text of Jeremiah 8:20 often took on special relevance and meaning: "The harvest is past, the summer is ended, and we are not saved." Exceptions to this seasonal pattern in the Cambuslang narratives and in other sources were, of course, numerous; winter might be a time of spiritual vitality, summer and early fall a period of deadness. Obviously no temporal rhythm fully subsumes the year-to-year flux of religious experience related by these evangelicals. All the same, this distinctive calendrical pattern was evident. The sacramental occasions marked the high days of the spiritual life of the evangelical Presbyterians; stretching roughly from May to October, the festal communions constituted a "holy season" of their own.[97]

The spirituality of these evangelicals with its cycles and seasons was focused on renewal and refreshment as much as on conversion. As a revival form, the sacramental occasion was designed to rejuvenate those who were already God's people as much as to convert the unregenerate. In tabulating the success of a sacramental occasion, often these evangelicals kept track not only of the number in attendance and the number awakened, but also of the number communing, those who reaffirmed their covenant with God in the Lord's Supper. Within the longer view of the Christian life, the new birth was only a small part. Since any sustained certainty of salvation was by and large a forlorn hope, the essence of this piety was not a singular conversion experience, but a life-long struggle for confirmation. Rhythmic and seasonal, evangelical Presbyterian piety was not characterized by a narrow focus on the new birth, but instead by a broad emphasis on the arduous, life-long trek toward heaven. Pilgrimage and preparation, as Charles Hambrick-Stowe has detailed for Puritan piety in New England, characterized Reformed spirituality. One saint, Elisabeth West, gave this larger Reformed truth a fittingly Scottish timbre: "There is one thing I have to observe from the Lord's way with me, in my journey heavenward," she said, "it is up the brae, and down the brae." At communions she was "upon the top of the brae," but afterward she invariably had to go "down the brae, and enter a new combat." Though remaining ardently conversionist—Elisabeth West spoke not only of braes, but also of "the new birth"—the Reformed piety of the evangelical Presbyterians was nonetheless far more complex than that, more Puritan and Catholic. And the sacramental revivals were not so much soul-winning crusades, but part of a circle, spiraling upwards, that all of God's people wound their way around again and again.[98]

COMMUNION AND CONSUMMATION

If the sacramental season was the whole Christian life writ small, the Lord's Supper itself was "the Compend" of this miniature. The partaking of the bread and wine was at the center of the occasion and was, in turn, at the heart of the piety of these saints. In this ritual the full range of this piety was displayed. All of the complex emotions, attitudes, and thoughts of evangelical Presbyterian devotion were encapsulated in the eucharist. In it was contained repentance in all its stages, no matter how enumerated—conviction of sin, humiliation, and confession. At the table "true Penitents" experienced "a holy Shame and Blushing of Soul" for the sins that had caused Christ's death. Mourning and weeping, they came to receive the "broken Christ" with a heart rent at the sight of the elements, mystical symbols of the Savior's body and blood. Fearful and uncertain over their worthiness for so near an approach to God, the saints agonized over their salvation and prayed for some token of blessing and assurance. Repentant and anxious, the communicants melted into tears at the thought of Christ suffering and dying for them. Love, too, overboiled as the saints experienced union with Christ at his table. If caught up in a "suitable Communion-frame," they revelled in powerful and contradictory emotions—"a mixture of holy *Mourning* and *Rejoicing*." In this paradox of simultaneous grief and joy lay much of the spiritual power of the Lord's Supper. The sacrament gathered the various refractions of this piety and focused them into a single, exceptionally bright shaft of light. Often the communion became the consummation of the spiritual life of the saints.[99]

If the communion was to be the consummation of faith, the old problems of wandering minds, worldly distractions, and unprepared hearts all had to be overcome. And this, it is clear, was no given. Impiety and diversion always threatened to intervene and deflect this powerful light. To the old problems, new ones were added. Sometimes, for example, the Lord's Supper simply did not have the desired effect. All the preparations might be conducted with scrupulous care, and still Christ might hide his face from the longing communicant. "At the first Sacrament at Camb. in July 1742," one disappointed saint averred, "I expected great things; but found my self very dead & lifeless: . . . I got nothing sensibly at the Table." After all the hours of preparation—in self-examination, personal covenanting, prayer, fasting, meditation, and hearing sermons—the Lord's Supper itself could be a letdown. "On Sabbath I communicated," one evangelical reported after a series of strenuous efforts, "but did not get all that I thought to have got." The infusions offered by the eucharist were dispensed unevenly; for all its power many saints went from the table at one communion or another "empty away."[100]

In addition to these vicissitudes, the saints also confronted great anxieties in their approach to the table that could distract them from the blessings of the occasion. Though doubts were usually a healthy prelude to joy, sometimes they became overwhelming. The fears of communicating unworthily might torment these evangelicals to the point of ruining the communion season for them. The severe admonition of Paul in 1 Corinthians 11:29–30 loomed as a fearful, stark specter over the sacrament: "For he that eateth and drinketh unworthily, eateth and drinketh damnation to himself, not discerning the Lord[']s body. For this cause many are weak and sickly among you, and many sleep." This threatening warning of spiritual woes and temporal harms, invoked again and again in sermons and exhortations, was taken with the utmost seriousness. "Plagues spiritual and temporall" were said to have resulted from unworthy reception of the sacrament, even to the point of death and damnation. As one minister noted matter-of-factly in his diary in 1755, "God struck a healthy young man suddenly dead, who presumed to come to the Lord's table while living in whoredom." Others, such as Robert Wodrow and John Spalding, added similarly sobering and frightening stories. Endangering themselves and perhaps even their family (Spalding called this "a Relation-murthering sin"), unworthy communicants were under "the greatest hazard both of Body and Soul." Powerful and dangerous, the Lord's Supper was to be approached with great care and trepidation.[101]

Such warnings and dangers served to inspire fears of profaning the eucharist that often ran to great heights. "When I came to the Table, . . . I was seiz'd with great tremblings," one communicant reported, "so that my body was like to shake in pieces. . . . [T]his Trembling now at the Table, exceeded any thing of that kind I had been under before or since; and yet to this day I cannot say what was the cause of it. Only I had been under great fears to come there, & fears of unworthily communicating when there: & I found my mind very confusd & got nothing sensibly." Though this troubled saint resolved his confusion later that night, his "fears of an unsuitable approach" had rendered his experiences at the table painful and unfulfilling. Thus could anxieties prevent saints from consummating their faith through communion.[102]

In approaching the Lord's table, these evangelicals were caught in a double bind: they believed that it was a sin not to come to the Lord's table, but also that it was a sin to commune rashly or unworthily. "If I stay here, I perish, and if I go forward I'll but perish," one evangelical said in describing her dilemma, "and so I came to the Table: but meeting with nothing sensibly at it, as I was going away I thought I had now committed the greatest sin of all, and that there was no help for me." Convinced she had eaten and drank damnation unto herself, she despaired of her salvation. Again fears predominated over love and joy. Such unnerving anxieties had to be combatted again and again. The sacrament never fostered easy contentment or simple satisfaction; indeed, at times the communion only redoubled confusion, anxiety, and fear.[103]

In a paradoxical way, however, this very anxiety was critical to the consummation of faith through communion. Heightening the care and awe with which the Lord's Supper was approached, the pressing question of worthiness demanded resolution. Willison made this plain when he put the dilemma this way: "I am in a Strait betwixt two. If I decline to come to this Table, then I disobey my dying Saviour, who commands me to shew forth his Death in this Manner. If I come unworthily, then I fear, lest I contract the Guilt of his Blood, and eat and drink my own Damnation. Alas, my Unworthiness makes me tremble to come; and yet my Need pinches me, so that I cannot stay away." A source of great spiritual tension, it was a conflict that often issued in powerful resolution. Played upon and accentuated, such fears and uncertainties, such tensive ambiguities, served to enhance the solemnity and power of the sacrament. Overwhelming anxiety dissolved in overwhelming love as communicants found Christ—perhaps even mystical union with him—through the communion.[104]

Dramatic eucharistic experience, more than being built upon anxiety,

was founded ultimately upon Christ's presence in the sacrament. In catechisms, devotionals, and sermons, people were instructed about the way
in which Christ was "spiritually, and yet really present" in the eucharist.
At the same time they were told about the ways in which the Lord was
not present, notably through transubstantiation and consubstantiation.
Yet issues of *how* Christ was present in the eucharist were of far less importance to these evangelicals than the bold reality of that presence. Presbyterian divines from Robert Bruce to John Willison worked their way
through the intricacies of Reformed eucharistic doctrine, but most of the
laity, at least in the Cambuslang narratives and other memoirs, did not
buttress their spiritual relations with theological rigor on such points.
Catechetical and doctrinal knowledge were important, but eucharistic devotion nevertheless remained only peripherally concerned with questions
about the nature of Christ's presence in the sacred symbols of bread and
wine. Most, if pressed, probably would have averred with pastor Thomas
Boston that "the mystical union" between "the signs and the thing signi-
fied," between the elements and Christ's body and blood, was a "glorious
mystery" not to be solved. As Boston said simply, "I see it, and believe
it."[105]

The mystery of Christ's presence in the eucharist did not make that
presence amorphous or distantly ethereal. If spiritual and noncorporeal,
this presence at an experiential level often remained startlingly real and
concrete. This is evident in the sweet, scriptural words that came to one
woman as she communed: " 'It is I myself, handle me and see, for a spirit
hath not flesh and bones as ye see me have.' "[106] If few had as disconcert-
ing an experience as the man who, when at the table, sensed "a singular
smell in the bread and wine of flesh and blood," many indeed saw and
felt the reality of Christ's presence in this rite.[107] Awed by that spiritual
reality, people often had their most profound encounters with Christ
through the eucharist.

With Christ present at his table, these evangelicals regularly experienced his redemptive love there. One individual at Cambuslang evidenced
this in a passage that reveals the potential richness of eucharistic experience: "When I came to the Table, I could for some time do nothing but
wonder, crying out in my heart, Redeeming Love! Redeeming Love!" this
saint celebrated. "When I received the Element of Bread, I saw my sins as
piercing Christ & was made to melt & mourn at the sight: at receiving
the Cup, I was made to apply by faith to the blood of Jesus for cleansing
from all my sins, & immediatly after to say with joy in my heart Now am
I clean, Now am I sealed to the day of Redemption." Those longing for
signs of their salvation often discovered such comforts at the table. During the eucharist many gained a near ecstatic surety of their redemption.
"At The Table I cannot express what I met with there," one communicant

exulted, "I can only say, my soul was filled with Rays of Divine light & love and I was so full of The Gracious Presence of God, That I could hold no more." The great, concentrated light of the sacrament permeated this young woman's soul and luminously confirmed her salvation.[108]

In her joyful communion this eighteen-year-old saint was helped to express the love she experienced by invoking the Song of Songs 5:16: "His mouth is most sweet yea He is altogether lovely." "I thought I could speak of Christ in the Words of the Spouse," she explained, "and my heart was greatly inflam'd with love to him and made to rejoice & delight in him." As was the spirituality of Catherine Cameron, the piety of this young saint was warmed by the Canticles. Time and again the most joyous and fulfilling experiences that these evangelicals had during the sacrament were cast in the diction of the Song of Songs. One communicant, when bathed in tears of repentance at the table, then had these words come into his heart that echoed Song 5:1 and 5:10: "Eat, O Friends, drink, yea drink abundantly, O Beloved: My Beloved is white and ruddy, the Chief among ten thousand: And I found my heart just ravished with the love of Christ." Another saint, a young woman of seventeen, expressed a similar experience, but this time the words echoed Song 2:16: "When I was at the Communion Table, I asked of the Lord that He might give me some token for good, for it was the first time I had ever been there, & that word came into my heart, My Beloved is Mine & I am his, he feedeth among the Lillies: this came with great power & Joy." Or perhaps the experience would be cast in terms of 2:4: "When I came to the Lords Table, he was pleased to give me much of his gracious presence; & I may say, He took me into his banqueting-house, and his banner over me was love." Regularly these evangelicals turned to the Song of Solomon to express their deepest experiences of union with their beloved in the Lord's Supper. Invited by Christ to his table—again in the cadences of the Canticles, "Arise my love, my fair one and come away"—they were often overwhelmed by the love he showed them while there. In such moments they were betrothed to the Bridegroom; "the Marriage Knot" was tied; Christ in this "Marriage-feast" became their beloved husband.[109]

The evangelical Presbyterians were led, through the Lord's Supper, to an experience of consummation, of marriage between Christ and the soul. Christ was thus cast as husband and lover in terms both ecstatic and passionate. One communicant, having been called by her beloved to arise and come to his table, found "that I could scarce walk, I was swallowed up in love & Enflamed affection to the Redeemer." Another saint, a girl of thirteen, when at the table "could say with the Spouse that I was sick of Love to Christ." The imagery, though understood in wholly spiritual ways, bordered at times on the erotic. One woman, for example, confessed she had "earnest longing desires immediatly to be Uncloathed and to be with Christ." Though, she said, "I did not get presently what I was wanting," she continued patiently waiting "for that happy time" when she would be united with her beloved. Such images, even when this provocative, should not be misread; veiled, repressed, sublimated, or projected sexuality was hardly the issue. To translate these experiences into terms understandable to our therapeutic culture would only distance us further from the mental world of these saints. Immersed in such sensual metaphors and symbols, the saints used such biblical—and sexual—images to express a divine love that was for them little related to, and far greater than, earthly love.[110]

Christ's love lifted the saint, at least for a time, into another realm where worldly affections were put aside. One woman noted that she was filled "with such a love to Christ, that I could have been content . . . never to have seen my husband or nearest Relations or any body in the World, but to have been just swallowed up of that Love to Christ." Similarly, another woman revealed how love to Christ was conceived as pure and transcendent of mundane sexuality. Overcome by the vileness of sin and the loathsomeness of her body, she could not even endure to look at herself in the mirror; she felt herself "all crawling with Toads of Corruptions." Disgusted by her own carnality, she was repulsed by thoughts that "my Husband should come near to me," but at the same time found her heart "leaping out of love to Christ." Her Savior's love was cleansing, that of her husband polluting. Agapé took the place of eros.[111]

The ministers themselves encouraged such expressions of divine love. When the clerical editors confronted passages describing this ravishing love, they rarely expunged or corrected them. There were exceptions, of course. For example, Catherine Cameron, in her passionate search for the Bridegroom, related that "I had great delight in prayer, when I would sometimes have gone to Bed, I thought I would have had Christ between my Arms: He was a Bundle of Myrrh to me & sweet to my soul." The ministerial editors—somewhat inexplicably—marked this passage for deletion, despite its simple and clear echoing of Song of Songs 1:13: "A bundle of myrrh is my well-beloved unto me; he shall lie all night betwixt my breasts." In a similar instance, she reported that after a communion "I came home from that Sacrament with Christ in my Arms." One of the ministerial editors hastily added "of faith and love" to the end of this sentence in order to underscore the metaphoric quality of this language— an addition that no doubt diluted the directness and passion of Catherine Cameron's experience. But these examples remain exceptions. The ministerial editors usually left such expressions unadulterated; for they themselves understood their eucharistic experiences in much the same terms. In sermon after sermon and meditation after meditation, they too recalled the intimate love between Christ and his fair one. "Let him there kiss me with the Kisses of his Lips," Willison prayed in one of his sacramental meditations, "and enable me to embrace him in the Arms of my Faith, saying, *This is my Beloved, and this is my Friend.*" Pastors and people shared passionate longings for the Bridegroom.[112]

Though consonance between pastors and people was notable in the diction used to describe the rapturous love that both experienced in the sacrament, all was not necessarily harmony on this point. The very diction of Christ as Bridegroom or Christ as husband suggested that issues of gender were interwoven with eucharistic piety. Was this consummation of faith, of being married to Christ in the eucharist, more characteristic of female piety than male? More than that, even when pastors or laymen referred to Christ as their husband or their beloved, would this relationship be the same for them as it would be for women? Or, to put this question in still broader terms, did social experiences of gender affect the way people understood their relationship to Christ?[113]

Even though ministers spoke of nuptial intimacy with Christ as a relationship available to men as much as women, it is fairly clear from McCulloch's examinations and other sources that more women than men ended up experiencing their relationship with Christ in such terms.[114] To receive Christ as Bridegroom and to embrace him with a passion reminiscent of the Canticles was, as Catherine Cameron's experiences and those of various others have suggested, a prominent feature of female piety. Other spiritual narratives and memoirs of the period bear this out as well. One woman, Elizabeth Cairns, who, her biographer noted, in never marrying "lived and died a *Virgin*, . . . a *Chast Virgin to Christ* her *everlasting Husband*," found herself at "Communion-times" regularly "swallowed up with . . . sensible Enjoyments of Divine Love." Another woman, Mary Somervel, said of one sacrament—which she described as a "trysting place" for Christ and her soul—that "on this occasion I found him whom my soul loveth, I held him and would not let him go." Also Elisabeth West gave forceful expression to this nuptial piety when she described her sacramental experience in the diction of a wedding vow: "I this day take thee to be my husband and Lord, and I to be thy married spouse, and will not be for another." Women, as suggested in the last chapter, at times dominated the sacrament numerically, but more than that, they seem to have shared disproportionately in its greatest blessings. When Christ took brides at his table, he apparently took women more often than men.[115]

To unite with Christ as husband or Bridegroom through the eucharist was for women a relationship that was continuous with their experiences and identities as wives and lovers, as women. When "a widow woman" of twenty-six at Cambuslang responded to the exhortation of "come and be married to Christ, and you'll have a Dear Husband," the words made sense and were given power within the context of her social experience.

Or, as a woman of twenty-nine observed during one of these solemnities, "I found My self just sick of love to Christ: and was made to believe that my Maker was my Husband; and instead of all Relations." Even as this woman was lifted out of her old relationships, her new relationship with God reaffirmed her understanding of herself as female. Similarly, another woman, who often rejoiced in having "Christ as my Souls Husband," described her eucharistic experience in nuptial terms: "At the close of the service of the Second Table, these words were pressed upon my heart with great Power, At mid-night there was a cry, Behold the Bridegroom cometh go ye forth to meet him: at which my heart was filld with joy at the thoughts of Christs coming to me as the Bridegroom of my Soul: & immediatly upon that I got to the Table; and when there felt my heart burning with love to Christ." For women the consummate experience in the sacrament, that of union with the Bridegroom or marriage to Christ, was indeed powerfully transformative, yet at the same time essentially continuous with their identity as women.[116]

For men this nuptial relationship was more problematic. It demanded, as Caroline Walker Bynum has noted in her studies of medieval piety, that men "use symbols of reversal and inversion," that they transform their sexual identity and subvert their status as men.[117] In the case of many men, more so than women, such diction was simply not employed. Less often were men ravished or embraced by Christ; rarely, if ever, did a man go to bed with Christ in his arms. Though some men obviously followed Willison in ardently embracing Christ the Bridegroom, hesitancy and half-heartedness were notable in others. One man, for example, having heard a call at a communion to take Christ as his husband, avoided the language and established instead a "Covenant relation with Christ as Prophet, Priest, and King." Maybe he found it simpler to conceive his relationship with Christ in legal rather than nuptial terms. Or another man who spoke with McCulloch solved these problems by turning the language of the Canticles around, speaking at one point of Christ's love as female: "Thou hast ravished my heart my Sister my Spouse, with one of thine Eyes, with one chain of thy Neck." Perhaps it was easier for some men, at least in rare moments, to change the way they thought about the gender of God than to invert their own sexual identities.[118]

A young man of twenty-one revealed quite well the difficulties and ambiguities that some men experienced in relating to Christ as a husband. During a sermon on the Sabbath evening of a sacramental occasion on the text "Thy Maker is thy husband," he recalled: "I felt love to Christ in my soul, & so much joy at the sweet offers of Christ as a husband to my Soul, that the joy of my heart had almost made me to cry out among the people, that I was ready to strike hands on the Bargain." Offered Christ as a husband, this young man described not an experience of himself as a bride but instead employed the distinctly male image of striking hands on a bargain. Thus could gender influence the way people understood and experienced their relationship with Christ. The sacramental occasion always held the power to marry souls—male and female—to the Bridegroom, but it would appear that women responded to Christ's nuptial offers more often, more comfortably, and more fully than did men.[119]

Sacramental piety, as it shifted from recollecting the suffering Christ to awaiting the mystical marriage to the Bridegroom, began to look more forward than backward. The eucharist not only re-presented the Last Supper and the Passion, but also anticipated the great feast with Christ in heaven as well as his triumphal return. Eschatology was the final grand theme of the sacramental occasion. The saints, no matter how wrapped up in Christ's love, were still waiting for something more. The Song of Songs itself had suggested longing as much as fulfillment. Their souls might be married to Christ in the sacrament, but final union eluded them. Their sacramental piety recognized that lack, affirmed the need to wait, and offered foretastes of the glories to come. Whatever consummation of faith they experienced in this world was but prelude to a grander fulfillment in heaven.

One forty-four-year-old woman at Cambuslang suggested how the focus of this sacramental piety could shift from Christ's redemptive sufferings to loving union with him in heaven. "I lov'd him for a while," she said, "mainly because he has done and suffered so much for me, but now I love him for himself, and because of his own Excellency & loveliness, which he hath discovered to me." These discoveries had come primarily "at several Sacrament-Occasions" at which "my joys have . . . overflow'd . . . [and] my Body has been made to shake & tremble." At such times Christ had made "it known to me, that he has taken me (poor deform'd hell-deserving me) for his Spouse, that he hath betrothed me to himself: and I now consider Death as a messenger to come & call me home to my Lord and Husband to be where he is: And . . . the thoughts of Death are as pleasant & delightful to me, as a message would be to a Loving wife to come away home to her Husband. Until the day break and the shadows fly away: make haste my Beloved & be thou as a roe or a young hart upon the mountains of Bether, Even so come Lord Jesus."[120] This sacramental spirituality, again laden with the diction of the Canticles, opened outward and upward. The beauties of heaven and the triumphs of the second coming brought the piety full circle.

The sacramental occasion took on such eschatological significance in a variety of ways. The solemn celebration of the Lord's Supper—with the saintly sheep gathered around the table and with the sinful goats carefully excluded—suggested in itself the last judgment in miniature. "O poor Sinners!" Gilbert Tennent preached at "a *Sacrament* Season" in New Brunswick, "when you see others admitted to the Table of the Lord, and your selves shut out, it may justly make you think with bleeding Hearts, upon the great Decision Day, when the Sheep shall be separated from the Goats." One woman at Cambuslang, when at a communion at Calder, testified persuasively to the apocalyptic dimension of the occasion. When listening inattentively to a sermon on Saturday, she all of a sudden "thought I heard a great number of Bells ringing & Drums beating just at hand and such a terrible noise that I thought the day of Judgment was come." Thrown into "the greatest Confusion & consternation that could be imagined," she was struck by her unpreparedness to meet the Bridegroom. When the alarm she thought she had heard proved false, she retired quickly to secret prayer. Joining others in their vigils, she received along about midnight "a ravishing discovery" of her beloved and closed with him. The eschatological underpinning of the sacramental occasion prompted her to new concern over whether she would be prepared for "the great Decision Day." Now she was ready to meet the Bridegroom; she had been delivered from the wrath to come.[121]

Thoughts of Christ's return might inspire fear in the hearts of sinners, but it enkindled expectation in the souls of the saints. Over the whole communion was Paul's reminder in 1 Corinthians 11:26: "For as often as ye eat this bread, and drink this cup, ye do shew the Lord[']s death till he come." In the eucharist the saints looked in hope and longing to Christ's second coming. "That will be a glorious Day," Willison clarioned in his sacramental meditations, "when he will rend the Clouds, come down and set Tryst with me in the Air; and send his Angels to carry me up to meet with him there." Though these evangelicals were dedicated in the eucharist to "*Shewing forth the Lord's Death* till he come," they ultimately looked beyond his return to the pleasures of communion with Christ in heaven. The Lord's Supper was understood as "an Emblem of the *Marriage Supper of the Lamb* hereafter"—"a Representation of that heavenly Communion above, which the Saints for ever will partake of with the *Lord Jesus*." One Cambuslang evangelical, who experienced "great joy" in thoughts of this heavenly banquet, stated his hope thus: "That as sure as I was sitting at his Table below, I should sit down at his Table above." Or, as another Cambuslang saint, Margaret Bruce, said, "When I was to rise from the table, my heart was made to long for that time when I should be set down at his table above, never to be drawn." The sacramental piety of these saints was thus cast not only in remembrance, but also in anticipation of "that glorious eternal Feast above."[122]

At the sacramental occasion these evangelicals received foretastes of that feast and anticipated the day when such inklings gave way to fullness. Catherine Cameron had reported during a communion season that she "longed to be out of the Body and to be with Christ. When a meeting with him here was so ravishing to my soul, I desired to meet with him never to part." Once transported to such heights, these saints were reluctant to return to the world. "O must I go back to the World again!" one woman cried, "O all in it is but dross & dung compared to Christ." The sacramental occasion and the devotions surrounding it lifted the saints out of the world—"a strange Country, a Place of their Pilgrimage"—and gave them glimpses of "*the other World above*"—"their Country and their Home." Strengthened and renewed, the saints could persevere until that day when all earthly toils would be wrapped up, when the shadows would fly away.[123]

The Lord's Supper ultimately pointed beyond itself to an empyrean realm where shadows would give way to light, where "the Saints see Christ as he is, and feed on him eternally, without Signs or Symbols," where there was finally "no Need of Sacraments." In this world the saints were united with their Savior through the symbols of bread and wine. In that world symbols and rituals would dissolve in "immediate Vision." The mystical presence of Christ would give way to the bodily presence; the distractions and the disjointedness of spiritual experience in this "strange Country" would yield to "full, satisfying, and everlasting" communion in heaven. When the saints finally moved from "the *lower* Table" to "the *higher* Table," they had completed their transit.[124] The pilgrimage was over; the rhythm stilled. Heaven was the sacramental season perfected.

CHAPTER 4

The Autumn of the Sacramental Season:
The Decline of a Popular Festival

As A YOUNG and diligent Presbyterian pilgrim in Kentucky around 1800, Thomas Cleland regularly attended sacramental occasions. At the Cane Ridge sacrament in 1801 Cleland was particularly caught up in the power of the occasion. Enthralled by an action sermon on a familiar text from the Song of Songs—"Rise up my love, my fair one, and come away"—he was suddenly overwhelmed. "My heart was melted! my bosom heaved! my eyes, for the first time, were a fountain of tears," he exclaimed. "I wept till my handkerchief was saturated with my tears." This "weeping, dissolved, humbled situation" lasted, Cleland said, through the rest of the sermon and through "seven courses of [the] sacramental service." This powerful experience at the Cane Ridge communion marked a high point in young Cleland's spiritual life.

A little more than two decades after this communion, Cleland—unlettered layman turned educated cleric—began dismantling within his church the eucharistic rituals in which he had earlier participated with such fervor. The long tables and old benches were removed; communicants were now to remain in their pews and receive the elements there. Tokens too were "dispensed with" and the rituals that went with them—for the sake of "convenience." The "old plan" for the communions was unwieldy and inefficient; it simply consumed too much time. Streamlined quarterly communions replaced the annual festivities of the summer and early fall gatherings. Cleland, having become a doctor of divinity, was in retrospect almost embarrassed by his earlier devotional zeal during the communion seasons—particularly by his weeping response at Cane Ridge and by his "extravagant notions" about the power of the sacramental elements and the dangers of an unworthy approach. All this, he suggested, was evidence of his erstwhile ignorance and "want of religious training." The difference between Cleland's youthful devotion in the 1790s and his calm revisions of worship in the 1820s suggests in miniature the fate of the sacramental season. Somehow the traditional rituals lost their hold on Presbyterian culture.[1]

In the 1820s the autumnal retreat of the communion season was far from complete. Cleland himself still associated the refreshings within his church with the quarterly sacramental meetings and remained devoted to much of the old way. Others would preserve the traditional eucharistic practices for another decade or two, and some, especially in parts of Scotland, would hold out even longer. Yet Cleland's reorientation between 1800 and 1825 was indicative of the much larger and longer process of change that ultimately ended in the demise of the sacramental season. In abandoning the traditional forms, he joined in a wider stream of change that had gone far to running its course by mid-century. What encouraged the likes of Cleland to begin forsaking traditions of such long continuance? How was it that this once popular festival became unpopular? This chapter attempts to suggest the changing context in which the lengthy, crowded communions no longer made sense and to see how it was that these sacramental festivals were gradually reformed and abandoned.

BURNS AND THE BLACKSMITH: ENLIGHTENED SATIRE

The sacramental festival that developed in post-Reformation Scotland always had its detractors. Seventeenth- and early eighteenth-century critics, whether Episcopalians or moderate Presbyterians, complained that the evangelicals had "turned the holy Supper . . . into a Theatrical Pomp" and had made "a *Prodigie* of this *Divine Mystery*." They criticized the excessive length of the services, the lack of a set liturgy, the infrequency of communion, the perfervid outdoor preaching, and the unseemliness of the great multitudes that convened. They made known their disgust for all that contributed to the "*vain shew*" and "*needless ostentation*" of this elaborate solemnity. "The *Presbyterian* Communion . . . has more of the Confusion of a Fair, than of the Order and Decency of a religious Assembly," one Episcopalian, Thomas Rhind, charged in 1712. "And how can it otherwise be, when they not only allow, but encourage, on these Occasions, such Rendevouzes of the promiscuous Rabble." In tones worthy of Burns several decades later, Rhind wondered at "the religious Freaks of the *Presbyterian Converts*," their "Illuminations and Raptures," their "pious Grimaces," their "*Animal* Agitations, luscious Fervours, and amourous Recumbencies." Like other critics, Rhind scorned "the religious *Parade*" and the "empty Pageantry" of the sacramental occasions. He pled for the decency of "the *Liturgick* way."[2]

Though these charges, as levelled by Rhind and others, were forceful, rarely were they accepted. Early opponents were almost entirely unsuccessful in discrediting or restraining the popular festival that they attacked. Not until the latter half of the eighteenth century were such critical views widely heralded and somewhat heeded. They were to find consummate expression and widest circulation in Robert Burns' satiric poem, "The Holy Fair," and in one of the most popular works on worship in the eighteenth century, *A Letter from a Blacksmith to the Ministers and Elders of the Church of Scotland*. Frequently published in Scotland and England, both texts were often reprinted in America and Ireland as well.[3] Throughout the nineteenth century and into the twentieth, church leaders canonized both texts for having laid bare the evils of the sacramental season. Burns and the Blacksmith were taken as the great beacons of enlightened reform.

The satires of Burns and the Blacksmith were rivulets within a much larger flow of change that historians have come to denominate the Scottish Enlightenment. Representing a complex cultural shift, the Enlightenment transformed much of Scottish life and thought. Affecting theology, philosophy, literature, and art as well as education, politics, agriculture, and commerce, the cultural transformation of late eighteenth-century Scotland was truly momentous. Undermining the foundations of orthodoxy, the Enlightenment would severely challenge Reformed truths—for example, the doctrines of original sin, limited atonement, total depravity, and justification by faith alone. Enlightened rationalism would also threaten traditional Reformed views of the eucharist; Christ's real spiritual presence in the sacrament, for example, would be increasingly challenged as memorialistic doctrines or even more skeptical ones gained ascendancy. Not only the doctrines of the evangelical Presbyterians, but also their rituals were challenged by the incoming tide of the Enlightenment. To those who shared in this cultural reorientation, few aspects of the popular religious culture would look more glaringly unenlightened than the festal communions. Both Burns and the Blacksmith suggested the profound effect the Enlightenment would have on the way such popular traditions were perceived. Both lead us into one of the primary currents responsible for floating the sacramental festivals into the past.[4]

Robert Burns was in many ways an unlikely compatriot of the enlightened. Raised in the traditional agrarian culture of Ayrshire, he was a self-described *"rustic Bard"* who wrote not simply to regale the refined but "to please my Compeers, the rustic Inmates of the Hamlet." His muse bid him "sing the loves, the joys, and rural scenes and rural pleasures of my natal Soil, in my native tongue." He posed as a simple, but inspired plowman whose poems owed their merit to "honest Rusticity," not "prostituted Learning." His poems, laden with what the well-bred considered an unrefined Scots dialect, emerged out of the culture he shared with the folk of the countryside. The traditional agrarian world of the southwest was his world, and his fondness for much of it never left him, even after he curried favor with the literati of Edinburgh.[5]

If in social and economic background Burns was a rustic, in intellectual aspiration and religious orientation he identified with that "candid lib'ral band" of men who were the vanguard of the Enlightenment in Scotland.

Though in his childhood he had been immersed in the evangelical Calvinism that dominated rural Ayrshire, he gradually moved away from the "enthusiastic, idiot piety" of his boyhood. He spurned the traditional Presbyterian faith of his rustic compeers in the southwest and turned to the Enlightenment, to its skepticism, anticlericalism, humanism, and secularism. He declared himself to be "in perpetual warfare" with the doctrines of "our Reverend Priesthood" and set himself upon overthrowing the superstitions of the old faith. "Auld Orthodoxy" or "Poor gapin, glowrin Superstition" was in Burns' mind "past redemption." In caustic lines Burns captured his disdain for the pious:

> But I gae mad at their grimaces,
> Their sighan, cantan, grace-prood faces,
> Their three-mile prayers, an' hauf-mile graces,
>   Their raxan conscience,
> Whase greed, revenge, an' pride disgraces
>   Waur nor their nonsense.

In such verses Burns gave poetic expression to the anti-Calvinistic, anti-evangelical thrust of the Scottish Enlightenment. In this enlightened, spiritually rebellious plowman the literati discovered an ally who exposed from within "the ignorance and fanaticism of the lower class of people" of rural Scotland.[6]

Burns' disdain for traditional Presbyterianism found keen expression in "The Holy Fair," one of his greatest works and perhaps his most penetrating satire of the evangelicals. Burns prefaces his poem, which apparently was composed shortly after his attendance at a large communion gathering at Mauchline in August 1785, with an epigraph on religious hypocrisy that sets a harsh tone for his observations on the sacramental festival. After an idyllic opening stanza on the fairness of this *"Sunday morn,"* the poet introduces three women—personifications of Fun, Superstition, and Hypocrisy—who embody the different spiritual dispositions of those peopling the occasion. The clothes and visages of the threesome first suggest their distinctive characters:

> As lightsomely I glowr'd abroad,
> To see a scene sae gay,
> Three *hizzies*, early at the road,
>   Cam skelpan up the way.
> *Twa* had manteeles o' dolefu' black,
>   But ane wi' lyart lining;[7]
> The *third*, that gaed a wee aback,
>   Was in the fashion shining
>   Fu' gay that day.

The *twa* appear'd like sisters twin,
In feature, form an' claes;
Their visage—wither'd, lang an' thin,
    An' sour as onie slaes:[8]
The *third* cam up, hap-step-an'-loup,
    As light as onie lambie,—
An' wi' a curchie low did stoop,
    As soon as e'er she saw me,
                Fu' kind that day.

From the first Burns makes clear his affinity with the lithesome beauty, Fun, and his disregard for the "runkl'd pair," Superstition and Hypocrisy, the dour embodiments of the faithful. With Fun, Burns is ready to "get famous laughin" at the pious. The dark, gloomy figures of Superstition and Hypocrisy, which Burns' various illustrators were quick to latch onto, were forceful caricatures. Wizened in countenance and spirit, the devout were the stark antithesis of Burns' own goddess, Fun.[9]

With Fun, Superstition, and Hypocrisy in place as the leading personae, Burns shifts his poetic observation to the "droves" crowding the roads "frae side to side" that lead to "the holy spot." Farmers, cotters, swankies, and lasses are all dressed in their best and thronging to the meeting.

8. J. M. Wright and J. Rogers. *The Holy Fair.*

Once at the churchyard, the various pilgrims appease with some "tip-pence" an elder, "a greedy glowr *Black-bonnet*," who holds a collection plate seemingly demanding money for himself as much as for the poor. This admission paid, they get in "to see the show." Besides the scowling, austere elder, Burns recalls other less saintly characters, including two or three whores as well as a number of roistering youths from Kilmarnock who have come "for *fun* this day." The salacious and the sacred become still more intertwined as Burns proceeds:

> O happy is that man, an' blest!
>   Nae wonder that it pride him!
> Whase ain dear lass, that he likes best,
>   Comes clinkan down beside him!
> Wi' arm repos'd on the *chair back*,
>   He sweetly does compose him;
> Which, by degrees, slips round her *neck*,
>   An's loof upon her *bosom*
>   Unkend that day.

The wild preaching of hell-fire, the "tidings o' d-mn-t—n," little disturbs the complacence and carnality of the impious and the hypocritical. And the "cauld harangues" of those who preach "on *practice* and on *morals*," but "ne'er a word o' *faith*" are deserted by the godly and ungodly alike. With the gospel of the moderates evoking only popular disgust, all that is left are the "auld wives' fables" of orthodoxy.

Many are happy to escape these fables and these harangues through various amusements—eating, drinking, arguing, and courting. Con-cerned mostly with those who have come solely for fun and far less with those who are interested in the religious engagements of the communion, Burns turns his eye to the mock sacramental activities on the edges of the meeting. He depicts, for example:

> The lads an' lasses, blythely bent
>   To mind baith *saul* an' *body*,
> Sit round the table, weel content,
>   An' steer about the *Toddy*.
> On this ane's dress, an' that ane's leuk,
>   They're makin observations;
> While some are cozie i' the neuk,
>   An' forming *assignations*
>   To meet some day.

One of Burns' illustrators aptly captured this mock sacramental scene: a jovial celebrant acts as priest, providing a woman with drink; empty flag-ons and plates litter the floor.[10] In the poem, as in the engraving, the tables, cups, liquor, and bread in the ale-house take the place of the eucharist. Sacramental devotion, presumably left to Superstition and Hypocrisy, goes unnoticed amid the sociability.

Ultimately, Burns points beyond the jarring mixture of religion and sociability at the communion to the triumph of sexuality over spirituality. "Wi' *faith* an' *hope*, an' *love* an' *drink*," the people "swagger home," gossiping and flirting. Burns thus summarizes the results of the day:

> How monie hearts this day converts,
>   O' Sinners and o' Lasses!
> Their hearts o' stane, gin night are gane
>   As saft as ony flesh is.
> There's some are fou o' *love divine*;
>   There's some are fou o' *brandy*;
> An' monie jobs that day begin,
>   May end in *Houghmagandie*
>   Some ither day.

To Burns, these gatherings for the sacrament find their consummation not in conversion but in "*Houghmagandie*," that is, in fornication.

Students of Scottish literature and culture have nearly always accepted "The Holy Fair" as an apt description of the sacramental occasion in the late eighteenth century, that such events had indeed become "jostling promiscuous carnivals," that those who proclaimed "the sacred holiness of the day" were "blind" to what was "in front of their eyes." Following Burns in his estimation of the sacramental occasion, historians and literary critics have almost invariably assumed that the poet saw this "traditional religious festival" for what it was—"a decadent survival." The poet's brother Gilbert, after all, had attested that "the farcical scene" of the communion season was "often a favourite field of [Robert's] observation" and that "most of the incidents" he described in "The Holy Fair" had "actually passed before his eyes." Thus the poem is viewed as a judicious depiction of the frivolity and hypocrisy of these meetings by one in the know and is celebrated for "the truth of the whole picture" that it presents. What such perspectives reveal, however, is not so much insight into Burns' poem or into the sacramental occasions, but instead a shared attitude between Burns and his interpreters toward popular religion. Clearly the saints were not alone in their limitations of perspective.[11]

That Burns in this poem had as large a blind spot as any of the saints is clear enough. He evoked the scene of the Mauchline communion through the lens of an idle spectator—a lens that colored his depiction as surely as the orthodox were constrained by their own angle of vision. Indicative of this, Burns forbears allusion to the central solemnity of the Lord's Supper, and yet in these years the communion at Mauchline drew between 1240

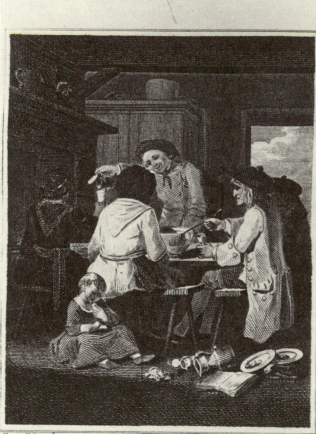

Burnett Pinx.   *T. Clerk Sculp.*

The lads an' lasses, blythely bent
To mind baith saul and body,
Sit round the table, weel content,
And steer about the toddy.

Engraved for Morison's Edition of Burns

9. J. Burnett and T. Clerk. *Holy Fair.*

and 1400 people annually to the Lord's table.[12] Given such numbers, the successive table servings and solemn sacramental meditations would have gone on all day. Burns, in neglecting these activities in his poem, revealed the selective vision of a disengaged, sardonic spectator. Obviously this vantage point was not the only one at these communions; instead it was an angle of vision with its own peculiarities and limitations. As Kenneth Burke has aptly said, "A way of seeing is always a way of not seeing."[13]

In this poem—and often in life—Burns presented the figure of an enlightened scoffer, a convivial companion of Fun, diverted from devotion by clothes, gossip, food, drink, and young women "wi' heaving breasts an' bare neck"—the sort of person over whom the devout had always worried. His poem, in effect, highlighted the experiences of unrepentant, unaffected sinners—experiences that were in direct tension with the spiritual relations of the pious and ones that made any devotion at these occasions look suspect. Seeing only superstition, hypocrisy, and frivolity among the faithful, Burns saw only absurdity among the evangelical preachers—their histrionic gestures, strange tones, nonsensical doctrines, and hell-fire images. To say the very least, Burns depicted the occasion from outside the circle of pious communicants and devout hearers. In this poem he looked at the event not from the table or the tent, but from the periphery of the meeting. Sharp, witty, polemical, the poem gave expression to Burns' distance from the religious activities of the saints.[14]

Burns' distance from the religious dimensions of the holy fair is a critical and revealing aspect of the poem. While he fondly describes those who were spiritually unaffected by the communion Sabbath, he remained at arms-length from the evangelicals and was often overtly contemptuous of them. The very form that the poem takes points to Burns' sardonic disengagement from this sacramental festival. Following a particular Scottish poetic genre—often denominated the Christis Kirk tradition from a fifteenth-century exemplar employing this stanzaic form—"The Holy Fair," by the very conventions governing this genre, aimed at satire of "peasant customs and peasant character." Distance between the poetic observer—"an amused and superior onlooker"—and the observed rustics was built into the tradition. Burns in choosing this form marked out the gap between his religious and intellectual world and that of the evangelicals. Though the poet displayed a certain empathetic fondness for those who profaned the event, this only added to the satiric distance between the poet and those who superstitiously sacralized the occasion. "Theme and form" thus converged in the poem to express Burns' enlightened view of the sacramental season and his distance from those who worshiped through it.[15]

Burns' enlightened view of the sacramental occasion, presented as brazenly as it was, elicited a considerable response. Those who shared his perspective hailed "The Holy Fair" as an incisive and welcome satire. Viewing the poet as "a friend of true religion," they congratulated him for "exposing" the "absurdity" of the communion season, for debunking its "enthusiasm, fanaticism, mysticism, hypocrisy and cant." Some reformers saw in the poem an inducement to change and called pastors and people "to put an end to *holy fairs* in every church." Though frustrated that these festal communions had endured so long, such reformers took heart that these events were "discountenanced by the most enlightened clergymen of the present day" and hoped that "in less than twenty years hence there will be nothing in Scotland at all resembling the *Holy Fair*." The poem, embraced as a forceful party piece, helped the moderates and the literati to distinguish further "the reasonable from the absurd" in Christianity. That "The Holy Fair" as well as Burns' other satires found widespread acceptance and defense in Presbyterian Scotland was indicative of the growing impact the Enlightenment had on the way popular evangelicalism was perceived. Many, it was clear, shared Burns' way of seeing the rituals and beliefs of evangelical Presbyterianism.[16]

Response to Burns' poem was far from univocal; the pious indeed moved to counter the derision of detractors. Though rarely adduced by latter-day commentators except to corroborate Burns' view of the orthodox, evangelical Calvinist rejoinders suggested the deep anger the poem aroused and the significance of the event being caricatured.[17] In blasting Burns' poetry and character, the popular evangelicals did not receive a particularly sympathetic hearing from their enlightened contemporaries nor would they from historians and literary critics. Yet their views of "The Holy Fair" are highly instructive, for they confirm the growing gap between popular and enlightened ways of seeing this sacramental festival.

To the faithful, Burns was an ally of David Hume and Tom Paine and other "heroes of infidelity," noteworthy mostly for his irreligion and immorality, not for the artistry of his poetry. One pastor indicated the evangelical view of Burns in verse:

> So! zealous Robin, stout an' fell,
> True Champion for the cause o' Hell
> Thou beats the Righteous down pell mell
>   Sae frank an' frothy

Or, as another versified:

> A champion for Satan, none like him before,
> And his equal, pray God, we may never see more.

They feared Burns' anticlericalism, his making the ministers "the butts of his contempt and displeasure." They despised his morality, particularly his drunkenness and his various amours. They lamented his impiety, his open disdain for Reformed doctrine, his Sabbath breaking, and his espousal of the religion of the Enlightenment—its rationalism and skepticism. They worried, too, about the anthropocentrism that Burns brought out in others, "the worship of mere intellect," the humanistic "adoration of genius," the Promethean aspirations that he inspired. For the evangelicals, there was so much about Burns not to like.[18]

Among the things not to like was the way he had described their communions. Reverend William Peebles, one of the evangelical preachers "gibbeted" by Burns in "The Holy Fair," was particularly aggrieved by the poet's unhallowed depiction of the sacramental occasion. Though Burns had scoffed that when Peebles "ascends the *holy rostrum* . . . COMMON-SENSE has ta[k]en the road," the latter was lucid enough when he stood by the communion season:

> In the house of God, and in the most select societies there may be some deficiency, some thing to be regretted in the disposition and views and seriousness of the assembly: it is less wonderful, that when thousands assemble, and when blackguards go, as Burns professedly went, for fun, some improprieties may have been discovered. But my firm persuasion is, that besides hypocrisy and superstition, and the merry goddess Fun, true religion, true devotion, have often assembled on such occasions; that on such occasions the interests of piety have been promoted.

Peebles questioned the truthfulness of Burns' description and suggested that the sacramental occasions should continue to be seen as the pious had seen them all along—as hallowed, solemn events. Though confessing there were some transgressions at these meetings—since idle spectators like Burns were among the multitudes—Peebles and other popular preachers were unbowed. They held to the communion season not because they were blind to hypocrisy, but because they saw in the spectacle of the sacrament and the Word their own salvation and the salvation of others. The counterweight of Peebles and other defenders attested that Burns' understanding of the sacramental occasion had yet to gain the dominion it would eventually enjoy, that traditional perspectives, despite the advances of the Enlightenment, remained formidable.[19]

Burns' poetical satire of the sacramental occasion cast in verse what the Blacksmith put in a letter. This anonymous epistle, urging the reform of public worship in the Church of Scotland, has sometimes been attributed to John Witherspoon, who eventually attained renown as president of the College of New Jersey, but who before leaving Scotland gained considerable notoriety for his satires of the moderates. Though Witherspoon was a noted satirist, his sardonic wit was employed in service of the popular evangelical party. An arch-Presbyterian of the southwest, he is an unlikely candidate to author a letter that advocated the development of a liturgy, criticized the Scottish Reformation, and dealt glibly with Presbyterian eucharistic practice and doctrine.[20] More likely candidates would come from the ranks of the Edinburgh literati, the moderate Presbyterians, and the Scottish Episcopalians. The issue of authorship aside, the Blacksmith's *Letter* was an important text in the increasingly hostile evaluation of traditional Presbyterian worship in the eighteenth century. Its bitter critique of the communion season revealed again that from the perspective of the enlightened this sacramental festival was subject to a range of censures.

The Blacksmith based his letter on the conviction that religious practice in Scotland was in desperate need of reform, that "low superstition," ignorance, and enthusiasm continued to sully "our worship." With a refined understanding of what constituted "decency," the Blacksmith set out to purge Scottish worship of its many "indecencies and follies" that came from indulging "the perverseness of the people." Among the greatest indiscretions were the superstitions of the communion season. As Burns did, the Blacksmith saw the communions as occasions for immorality as much as for devotion. He pointed to the "ale-barrel[s]" and the "assignations" as indicative of the improprieties of these events. "Whatever others may think," he asserted, "I would not chose a wife that often frequented them, nor trust a daughter too much among those rambling saints." What spirituality he saw amid the sensuality hardly redeemed these occasions. To the Blacksmith, "these religious farces" too often ended in "popular frenzy" as preachers worked up "the mob to the highest pitch of enthusiasm," bringing "the weak and ignorant to the very brink of downright madness." "I have seen scenes," he said, "that had much more of the fury of the bacchanalia, than the calm, serious, sincere devotion of a christian sacrament."[21]

As did Burns in "The Holy Fair," the Blacksmith saw the sacramental occasion from a different perspective than did the pious. The Blacksmith himself said that he viewed the communion not from within "the inner circle" of evangelicals, but from a distance where he was able "to see the indecency and absurdity of the whole scene." Indeed, he suggested that from his vantage point he could "describe it, as it really is." Evangelical Presbyterians, though historians have failed to take notice, were quick to dispute the Blacksmith's claim to have a corner on interpretation. As one champion countered, the Blacksmith's description was "general and indiscriminate"—a result of his being among "the careless and profane" rather than among the devout. What the Blacksmith had produced, according to this critic, was "a picture whose true original was never realized by any spectator at the sacrament in Scotland, besides himself. Thousands, if not hundreds of thousands, throughout that nation, are witnesses every year" to sacraments that proved this pamphlet to be full of "impudent and bare-faced falsehoods." Though, like Peebles, this defender was willing to grant that some "hardened wretches" abused the occasion, he did not see such "instances of folly and impiety" as discrediting solemnities that were peopled mostly by "sober and serious" Christians. In contrast to the Blacksmith, who this opponent thought would be pleased "to make bolts and fetters to bind at home the irregular rabble," this traditionalist saw the idle spectators not as hindrances to polite piety, but as spurs to greater devotion; for during the festal communions the saints vividly displayed their sanctity to the worldly. Disputing the Blacksmith's angle of vision and upholding the traditional communions, this vindicator of evangelical Presbyterian worship made clear that the enlightened way of seeing this sacramental festival was a profound departure from the way the faithful saw it.[22]

Behind the Blacksmith's way of seeing the sacramental occasions was an impelling spirit of reform that extended to other facets of worship. He wanted to save pure, refined religion from the various deformities of popular evangelicalism. Distinguishing between "the common people" and "the rational people," the Blacksmith made clear that his proposed liturgical reforms catered to the latter, not the former, whom he also referred to as "the silly, ignorant vulgar." His arguments for reform were propelled by his desires to control the unruly, mobbish people and the preachers who aroused them. Nowhere was this clearer than in his extended condemnation of "our present extemporary way of worship" and his advocacy of "the composition and establishment of some devout liturgy." The aim was to take the formation of prayer out of the hands of "every private parson" and put this task into the hands of "a number of the most learned and judicious men of the age" who would produce "a rational, well-composed liturgy." Though the Blacksmith noted that this would place a curb not only on popular preachers, but also on irreligious, skeptical divines, his clear enemy remained the evangelical enthusiasts who spoke of inspired prayer and valued Spirit-filled effusions over set forms. His vision of reform even extended to how prayer was performed in public worship. He condemned "the unnatural cant, the frantic gestures, and fearful distortions of the face" that went along with the fervent prayer of the evangelicals. Seeking control over various aspects of evangelical Presbyterian worship, the Blacksmith would thus use liturgical forms to calm evangelical fervor and to forward elite dominance of popular religion.[23]

The Blacksmith's vision of bringing popular evangelicalism into line with the aesthetic values of the elite embraced as well the way people sang. "As to Praise," he said, "we seem to study to give this part of our worship as much the air of rusticity, and contempt of God, as possible; . . . Many of the words we use are obsolete and low: the versification is mean and barbarous; and the music harsh and ill performed." The rustic timbre of untrained lay voices had come to offend the ears of the refined. Where John Willison and other evangelicals had charged all to sing heartily no matter the quality of their voice, the Blacksmith and fellow reformers sought—in the apt words of one historian of Scottish psalmody—"to tone down and subdue the singing of the people." James Beattie, one of the Blacksmith's colleagues, even thought that it would be best for "those, who sing very ill, not to sing at all, at least in the church." For subsequent reformers, choirs—or, as one traditionalist said, "praising God by a committee"—would be the answer to the cacophony produced by congregational singing. To the Blacksmith and to those who followed him, refinement of the traditional psalmody and its performance was an aesthetic imperative. Lay voices needed to be trained; they needed to be refined.[24]

The Blacksmith's desire to subdue popular evangelicalism involved not only public devotions—such as the sacrament, extemporaneous prayer, and psalmody—but also extended to family worship. Offended by the "miserable mixture of nonsense, errour and blasphemy" that he discerned even in family devotions, the Blacksmith advocated forms for these prayers as well. "What rude and shocking expressions! what blasphemous petitions have I heard! how often have I trembled, when the ignorant and proud *enthusiast* kneeled down with his family to his extemporary worship!" the Blacksmith hammered. Defenders of evangelical worship were quick to question such "*genteel*" assumptions and to insist that all "the beauties of rhetoric" could not match the simple, heartfelt prayers of "weak and illiterate *Christians*." Even if the language sounded "uncouth" to the Blacksmith, extemporaneous prayers were nonetheless fundamental to true Christianity; they were essential to "the liberty of christians." Such debates clearly revealed a growing division between popular evangelicalism and the religion of the enlightened. They revealed, too, a compulsion for control, order, and reform on the part of those who held to the latter. Indeed, the Blacksmith aimed to place control of the religious speech of the common people and their preachers in the hands of the church's hierarchy.[25]

The sacramental season was caught up in the widening divide between the popular religious culture of the Calvinistic evangelicals and the elite religious culture of the rationalistic moderates. As a central event within the traditional Presbyterian culture, the communion occasion was viewed with particular acerbity by the enlightened who were distancing themselves from what they saw as the superstitions of popular religion. In this process of moving away from the old religion, the enlightened shifted fundamentally the perception of the sacramental season. Seeing the festival in a new light—as superstitious, enthusiastic, and licentious—they invited others to see it that way too and rendered suspect those who continued to see it in the old light—as awesome, powerful, and transformative. In other words, the sacramental occasions themselves did not change as much as the lens through which they were viewed. The Enlightenment provided a context in which such popular religious events as the communion season came to be seen, more and more, as degenerate and contemptible.[26]

In forwarding this changed perspective, bearers of the Scottish Enlightenment made way for the nineteenth-century bourgeois understanding of this festival as an undisciplined and uncouth event. Victorians, inheriting the views of Burns and the Blacksmith, rejoiced that the "immense gatherings of people" for the sacrament had finally succumbed to reason. The sacramental occasions, they confirmed, had been brought into "justly deserved ridicule and contempt." One Victorian, inspired by Burns' poem, even went so far as to conclude that the communion season had been but "a sacrament in masquerade, a grotesque pagan remnant unbecoming to a Christian people." Looked to as prophets of religious reform, Burns and the Blacksmith helped set the tone for subsequent views of these sacramental festivals. As canonical texts, Burns' poem and the Blacksmith's *Letter* suggested the lasting impact that the Enlightenment had on the way such popular festivals were perceived. Deeply permeating Scottish and American culture, the Enlightenment in its various valencies contributed substantially to the demise of the festal communions.[27]

FREQUENCY VERSUS FESTIVITY

In order to prevent much of the "disorder and irregularity" that attended the festal communions, the Blacksmith proposed that "the assembly be graciously pleased to appoint some particular Sundays in the four seasons, for the administration of this sacrament, over all the kingdom." This would return Scotland to the ideal of the early reformers who had advocated quarterly, or even more frequent, communion. It would also help bring the sacramental occasions under control, limiting the crowds and lessening "the great noise that we make about these *occasions*" each summer. What the Blacksmith put forth in brief, others propounded at length. The debate over the frequency of communion, a perennial issue throughout the history of the church, took on special importance among Presbyterians in the late eighteenth and early nineteenth centuries. A critical liturgical question, the frequency debate carried immense cultural significance as well. Among the Presbyterians, the issue would decide the future of the sacramental season. It would be essential in determining whether the traditional pattern of popular festivity would finally succumb to the levelling influences of reform.[28]

The issue of how frequently Christians should partake of the Lord's

Supper was a problem that through the centuries had caused considerable debate. In the apostolic church the eucharistic act of breaking bread together was seen as a regular feature of Christian fellowship, even a daily activity. Though frequent, usually weekly, communion predominated in the first centuries of the church, this pattern gradually yielded to greater infrequency. By the twelfth and thirteenth centuries the laity generally received communion only once a year—a pattern that found formal acceptance in 1215 at the Fourth Lateran Council. The triumph of infrequency, however, did not mean a decline in eucharistic piety; indeed, quite the opposite was the case. The eucharist—awesome and mysterious—was at the center of popular piety and festivity in the late medieval church. This was true particularly at Easter, but was also evident in the importance of the Host in the celebration of the great medieval feast of Corpus Christi. As the implications of the doctrines of the real presence and transubstantiation became more apparent and as the processions of Corpus Christi became more elaborate, sacramental devotion and veneration of the Host reached an apex. In this context, infrequent reception of the sacrament on the part of the laity only underscored the unusual solemnity and unique power of the eucharist.[29]

On the eve of the Reformation, eucharistic devotion was extensive, variegated, and intense. The reformers in Scotland, as elsewhere, thus confronted a situation in which eucharistic piety was at the core of popular spirituality and thoroughly intertwined with popular festivity. The reformers also confronted a situation in which people were accustomed to annual communion and to penitential preparation for it. To propose more frequent, less festal communions was to assault a calendrical rhythm of devotion that people had found meaningful for hundreds of years.

Still the Scottish reformers were convinced that apostolic example and scriptural warrant compelled them to seek more frequent communions and to abandon the corrupt medieval system. They initially sought monthly administration of the sacrament, but soon because of a variety of impediments—not the least of which was said to be popular intransigence—they settled for quarterly and even semiannual communions. By the early seventeenth century, quarterly celebrations were rare, and semiannual and annual eucharists common. This return to the older pattern of infrequent communion did not result in indifference to the sacrament—at least among the evangelical Presbyterians. Instead, as had happened in the medieval church, infrequency made possible sacramental festivity. Slowly the older festal pattern reemerged under the new guise of the sacramental season and under the new guidance of the most zealous Presbyterians. In the ongoing battle between frequency and festivity among Presbyterians, the latter proved to have a tenacious hold on evangelical pastors and their people. Reform-minded advocates of frequency would have a long, tough fight before they prevailed in the nineteenth century.

This failure of frequency to triumph over festivity before the nineteenth century was not for lack of effort on the part of the reform-minded. From Knox onward, the Reformed tradition in Scotland often yielded ministers who made frequent communion a touchstone of the purity of Presbyterian worship. The First Book of Discipline had codified this wisdom, and the Westminster Directory, too, had reaffirmed frequency as an ideal of Reformed worship and left little room for sacramental festivity.[30] Advocates of frequency would often recall the eucharistic principles of both the Reformation and Westminster as evidence that Scottish sacramental practice had gone astray. This disparity between confessional ideal and actual practice would long fuel the frequency debate as well as the zeal of various reformers.

After the Glorious Revolution, efforts to insure that the Lord's Supper was duly and regularly administered were stepped up. In the Clydesdale Synod in the southwest, for example, attempts from 1692 to 1725 to bring order to the "great confluences of people" at communions centered on increasing the frequency of the Lord's Supper. Celebrating the sacrament at set times in each parish during "the severall Seasons of the year" was deemed "the best expedient" for "preventing disorders occasioned by exorbitant crowds of people that flock to communions." The vision of the church hierarchy was to put a damper on these popular sacramental festivals through frequency. "Winter Communions," in particular, were advocated, since it was supposed that the weather would discourage many people from attending and would most likely keep the communions out of "the fields" and "in the Church." But the Clydesdale Synod and the various presbyteries that composed it were hard pressed to get the local church sessions to comply with their designs for greater frequency or for winter communions. In Irvine Presbytery, for example, only two out of twenty parishes in 1724 scheduled winter communions; the rest crowded their sacraments into the usual months of June to October, and none of the parishes had more than an annual communion. With compliance like that, it is no wonder that notes of failure were often registered in the synodical records, as was the case in 1709, 1711, 1713, and again in 1725. For the most part, the synod's proposals had been deemed "Impracticable." Still in 1748, the synod was trying without much success to reconcile "the Minds of the People" to new proposals to have the sacrament—minus all the extra services, sermons, and sociability—celebrated "at least four times a year in every Parish." Like previous plans, this latest overture proved unpopular and unenforceable. In their early efforts to promote frequency, the reform-minded in Clydesdale failed to dislodge the entrenched, popular traditions of sacramental festivity.[31]

The experience of this synod in the southwest was indicative of the failure on the part of the General Assembly as well. The highest governing body of the church regularly issued acts urging more frequent communion in hopes of promoting "the glory of God, and edification of souls" as well as in hopes of taming the "disorders" of the summer and early fall communions. In 1701, 1711, 1712, and 1724 the General Assembly encouraged more frequent communions and particularly wanted to see the sacrament celebrated "throughout the several months of the year." Each time the assembly also enjoined all presbyteries and synods to enforce "the punctual observance" of these acts. Yet by 1751 the General Assembly, while still urging "more frequent celebration," nonetheless settled for insuring that the sacrament was administered annually in each parish. "Yearly Sacraments," a supporter of official efforts at reform lamented in 1749, remained "universal." Even as late as 1795, an advocate of frequency said he knew of only one Presbyterian church in Scotland that had succeeded in going to quarterly communions.[32]

In America similar efforts by some clerical leaders in the Synod of New York and Philadelphia to enjoin more frequent communion met with rebuff from the churches. In 1787, in a draft of the directory that would establish the form of worship for the Presbyterian Church in the new United States, an urban, highly anglicized committee proposed moving away from the sacramental season to streamlined quarterly communions. Deeming that the sacrament should be celebrated in each congregation at least "once in every quarter of the year," the committee suggested that the fast, Saturday, and Monday services were dispensable and that gathering large numbers of people and their ministers together from over a wide area for the communion was inexpedient. But the next year, when the final constitution of the church was issued, the synod had been forced to drop these recommendations and to accept the continuance of the traditional practices. The proposal for quarterly communions, prominent in the draft, was kept out of the church's constitution entirely. In America, as in Scotland, the church's hierarchy failed in the eighteenth century to eliminate the immense sacramental gatherings and to enforce frequency. At 1800 the festal communions continued to endure and, in many cases, to flourish despite long, persistent calls for reform through frequency.[33]

Official efforts to reform popular practice in the eighteenth century were not simple failures, however. These endeavors clearly laid the groundwork for change. If through much of the eighteenth century the reforms consistently foundered upon "the prejudices of the people," inroads were nonetheless being made. In 1750, when the presbytery of Ayr despaired of "Bringing about a reformation" of the sacramental occasions and of enforcing streamlined, semiannual communions in each parish, instead of giving up, the presbytery dug in for the long haul. The presbytery recommended "that Every Minister should be Appointed in his publick sermons, Catechizing, and Visitations of families to endavour to remove from the peoples minds all Mistaken notions with regarde" to the frequency and lengthiness of communions. Strict diligence in this educative program was enjoined upon each minister until "the Effect" of this policy became "visible." It would be through such yeomanly means, rather than official pronouncements, that reform ultimately succeeded. If this process of reforming lay belief and practice was slow, at times almost insidious, this sort of instruction and reeducation—whether through sermons, tracts, or catechizing—was nonetheless a winning technique. Popular practice would be transformed; "the prejudices of the people" for sacramental festivity and against frequent, streamlined communions would ultimately be removed.[34]

Though the church hierarchy involved itself from the outset in the frequency debate, the most revealing discussion of the issue is to be found not in ecclesiastical records, but in ministerial treatises. Two of the earliest and most influential advocates of frequency, John Erskine and Thomas Randall, both penned tracts in 1749 in defense of official efforts at reform. At mid-century their works ran up against the same popular "Prejudices" that thwarted official plans and pronouncements, but by the close of the century their texts had emerged as bellwethers for the cause of reform.[35] By the 1790s the debate had widened, and the forlorn tone of the frequency advocates had turned more hopeful and insistent. Engaging many, the controversy produced a variety of different arguments from Scripture and tradition. If the interlocutors were numerous, the fundamental issues and stances can nonetheless be seen clearly in one particularly perspicacious exchange, that between John Mitchell Mason of New York and John Thomson of Glasgow in the late 1790s. Mason, born in America the son of a Scottish Presbyterian minister and educated at Edinburgh University, wrote his *Letters on Frequent Communion* in 1798. Thomson, an adamant traditionalist, responded shortly with his *Letters Addressed to the Rev. John Mason, A.M. of New-York.* Together they made clear the significance of a debate that disturbed Presbyterians on both sides of the Atlantic.

John Mitchell Mason was driven, he was certain, by the purest of Protestant principles. He wanted to restore Presbyterian worship to its scriptural foundation and to foster "a sound and evangelical piety." For him the "pompous ceremonial" of the sacramental season was a clear "deviation from the simplicity of evangelical worship." He advocated the elimination of fast and thanksgiving days and strove to "reduce the supper of the Lord" to what it should be—"a very simple thing," a compact weekly celebration. In proposing this drastic reform, he was hopeful that this plan for simple, frequent communions would *"usher in a time of refreshing,"* that this reformation in worship would be prelude to revival. Like earlier reformers, such as Erskine and Randall, Mason believed that frequency would enhance eucharistic devotion and invigorate Christian communities. His was an honest zeal for the "fundamental principles" of evangelical Protestantism.[36]

Through frequency, Mason hoped to transform the devotional rhythm of evangelical Presbyterianism. He wanted to create a steady piety that exalted all spiritual activities equally. "Is God more holy on sacramental than on other occasions?" he asked. "Does communicating possess either more inherent or more accidental sanctity than any other act of spiritual worship?" Pounding out his negative answer to these questions, Mason attacked the traditional proposition that in the Lord's Supper the saints made their nearest approach to God this side of heaven. *"Every act* of worship" was of the same "degree of sacredness"; God never intended, Mason insisted, to have "one divine institution" exalted "at the expense of the rest." "Were we rightly affected, as deep solemnity would rest on our spirits in asking a blessing at our meals, as in breaking the sacramental bread," Mason concluded; "And it betrays either much ignorance, or much carnality, if a communion-season fills us with awe, while the other offices of piety find us and leave us cold or unconcerned." Disillusioned with the traditional cycle of piety, he wondered why people were so enthralled by the old way and whether they gained any lasting benefit from the festal communions at all: "What means this religious parade, when that blessed exercise draws near? Whence this unusual sternness? these sudden austerities? Whence that mortified air which vanishes like a phantom, and never returns but with a returning communion?" He wanted to eliminate the spiritual sloth of the old way, to impress saints with the need to strive for perpetual devotion. God was as accessible through daily prayer as through the annual sacrament, Mason insisted. To expect special blessings from the Lord's Supper above other duties smacked of idolatry and superstition. In Mason's understanding Christianity permitted no high days, no festivals, except the Sabbath itself. Continual vitality and sustained discipline were the hallmarks of genuine Christian piety, and frequent communion would nurture such a spirituality. At the same time frequency would help dissipate that "air of superior sacredness and awe" that had come to surround the Scottish sacrament—an air that suggested excessive, even papistic veneration. It would put an end to the corrupt, undisciplined festivity of the communion season.[37]

John Thomson failed to see the benefits of Mason's "reforming zeal." He wondered why his opponent wanted to lessen the solemnity of the Lord's Supper and saw the consequences of this effort as inimical to eucharistic devotion. "I indeed think, Sir, that your self-devised plan of FREQUENCY, has a native tendency to weaken and even to obliterate that exalted reverence, which becomes communicants, when they DRAW NIGH to God, in this solemn ordinance." Thomson affirmed the long-standing conviction that the Lord's Supper was imbued with unique power and that participation in it demanded extensive, formal preparation. Adducing Old Testament feasts, especially Passover, as warrants for this gospel feast, Thomson went on to make a case for preserving sacramental festivity:

> The sacrament of the supper, Sir, is a divinely instituted feast; yea, the only instituted feast under the gospel. This character is diametrically opposite to that frequency which you would impose upon us, as the positive command of our dying Saviour. A feast, Sir, is a character which distinguishes the day wherein it is made, from other or common days; and distinguishes the entertainment from common meals. To extend the frequency of a feast to the extent of our common meals, is contrary to its nature and destructive of its specific idea.

Thomson discerned the fundamental hostility between frequency and festivity. "Our most distinguished Sabbath, or feast days" would be levelled, he charged Mason, by "your extravagant frequency, and ridicule of preparation." Frequency, far from issuing in renewal, would end in "that solemn ordinance" being "divest[ed] of every idea of solemnity, and degrade[d] to the level of a common meal."[38]

Thomson saw frequency as having an adverse effect not only on the solemnity of the Lord's Supper, but also on the spirituality of the saints. Where Mason thought he was jarring the faithful out of complacence, Thomson saw a misreading of the temporal predicaments of the pious. "Your plan in this matter, Sir, is most unsuitable to the condition of the saints of God in this their imperfect state; they are," he recalled, "constantly engaged in a spiritual war within, and exposed to temptations without. Besides, Sir, they are immersed in the toils and cares of human life, and their minds often embarrassed and distracted from spiritual things; and therefore we who are in the bodily tabernacle, do groan, being burdened." To Thomson and to all those who had come to pattern their piety around the festal communions, the advocates of frequency were unrealistic to expect that people week-in, week-out could be ready to partake of the sacrament. Thomson showed greater sympathy—or softness—than did Mason toward the "infirmities" of people as they struggled and faltered in their pilgrimages. On behalf of the heavy-laden, Thomson countered his opponent's recommendations. "Perhaps, Sir, you and some of your consociates, may have attained such eminent degree of spiritual perfection, in the Christian life, as to feel little need of preparation for the most solemn exercises of religion," he taunted. "But, methinks, you should have some more sympathy with, and compassion of your poor suffering brethren, who come so far short of your great attainments." For Thomson sacramental festivity was a balm for the human weakness that frequency would not heal.[39]

Though at 1800 the reforms that Mason and others like him advocated had still only begun to take hold, backers of sacramental festivity such as Thomson were clearly losing ground. Mason's book in itself, though indebted to earlier formulations, marked something of a turning-point: it was among the fullest, most influential treatises on the subject, a text that was said to have "made a great sensation among Scottish people everywhere" and one that helped further solidify the official line of thought on the issue.[40] But more important than Mason's specific tract was the weight of opposition to the traditional practices: the number of works for frequency simply dwarfed the number for festivity. The call to pay "homage to truth" by purging this corrupt tradition grew ever louder, more insistent, and univocal.[41] If after 1800 the process of moving from festivity to frequency still often remained slow, it was nonetheless all but inexorable. Parish by parish, congregation by congregation, pastors like Thomas Cleland moved away from the traditional forms and conducted more limited, parochial communions. As the logic of frequency triumphed, semiannual and quarterly communions gradually came to supplant the annual festivities of the summer season. Fast and thanksgiving days diminished in importance or, as Mason had advocated, were dropped entirely. In many churches people remained in their pews to receive the elements, and the long tables, careful fencing, and communion tokens began to pass from the scene. All those "incumbrances" and "customary appendages" about which Mason and others complained were slowly pared away as Presbyterians strove to fulfill the complementary principles of frequency and simplicity. Successful in reforming the traditional communion season, proponents of the new scheme awaited a eucharistic revival that never came. As Thomson had feared and Mason had hoped, the profound—or superstitious—awe and mystery that the old way had evoked were gradually lost. Significantly lessening the solemnity of the Lord's Supper, the acceptance of frequency put an end to sacramental festivity.

The triumph of frequency over festivity was fraught with irony. For one thing, the form that frequency tended to take—set quarterly communions within each parish—may have actually ended up reducing the opportunities for people to partake of the Lord's Supper. Under "the good old way," the sacrament was usually administered only once in any given parish in any given year. But since neighboring congregations also administered the eucharist annually, several other sacramental occasions could be attended. Willison, for instance, spoke of "many serious exercised christians who communicate almost every Sabbath during the summer season" as they traveled from place to place to participate in the festal communions. Thomson also noted that people happily journeyed as much, if not "more than forty miles distance" to share in the Lord's Supper with those from the surrounding region and that this practice encouraged participation in several communions. "Christians in Scotland," he said, have "opportunity of approaching the Lord's table many times, I may say eight, ten, or twelve times in a year." McGready's toils in Kentucky similarly attest to the abundant opportunities that the evangelical Presbyterians had of participating in the sacrament; week after week, in the summer and early autumn, McGready would assist at communion seasons in one congregation or another, where pilgrims then trekked from over a wide area. John Livingston explained early on that requiring more frequent communions within each parish was unnecessary, since "the Religious People" within "the bounds of twenty Miles or little more" were accustomed "to resort[ing] to the Communions of the rest of the Parishes." Given these traditions of pilgrimage, quarterly communions did not necessarily increase the number of eucharists people participated in each year and at times probably even acted to decrease the number. Narrow and parochial events, quarterly communions curtailed the regional festivities of the summer and early fall sacraments without substantially augmenting the opportunities for partaking of the eucharist.[42]

The irony that the eventual triumph of frequency may have actually decreased the number of opportunities to participate in the eucharist is a profound one. But given the motives of some of the reformers, this result was not that surprising. What some of them—the Blacksmith or members of the Clydesdale Synod, for example—had been after all along was not so much more frequent communions as less festal ones. They wanted circumscribed, controlled, convenient sacraments, essentially parochial events instead of regional festivals. And frequency was a means to that end, not necessarily an end in itself. This gave the defeat of festivity through frequency another irony: what had been trumpeted as a genuine evangelical reform was also a suppressive stratagem and what had been put forward as a means to revival was also a way of marginalizing popular evangelical traditions within Presbyterianism. Reform and suppression were joined in the promulgation of frequent communion as a liturgical ideal.[43]

A final irony in frequency was the way in which its advocates became allies, in spite of themselves, in the diminution of community. Many of the reformers, like Erskine or Mason, were fervent evangelicals with a vision of renewing Christian community through eucharistic revival, and yet frequency ended up undermining one of the primary bases of Presbyterian community. Thomson recognized this when he complained to Mason that "your novel plan" will result in "confining, or restricting our sacramental communion of saints, to a particular congregation; whereas our established custom extends this communion very widely, even to an indefinite extent, and introduces a reciprocal knowledge of the saints to each other, and a mutual intercourse with each other, by which spiritual intimacy and friendship does often commence, and is promoted, to their mutual comfort and advantage." Frequency, in other words, was at cross-purposes with the community, sociability, and mutuality that came in the communion season. Frequency, according at least to its more far-seeing critics, was a handmaiden in the decline of traditional forms of community.[44]

Through frequency, reformers tried to divorce the Lord's Supper at long last from festivity. Seeking order and discipline, they called people back to a Protestant vision of steady devotion Sabbath after Sabbath. Increasingly successful in their campaign to bring popular practice into line with Reformed principles of worship, they gradually levelled a distinctive evangelical festival. As one Presbyterian observer in America revealingly commented at mid-century, "Now Sacramental occasions come and pass away very much like an ordinary Sabbath exercise." The vision of the reformers that "all Sabbath days" be "upon a level" had largely come to pass. Religious festivity, long under assault from various reformers of popular culture, lost further ground with the demise of the sacramental season.[45]

The Reform of the Holy Fair

To the reform-minded, the sacramental occasion was an unholy fair that encouraged idleness, intemperance, immorality, and enthusiasm. It stirred up the people and distracted them from their work for days on end. If people were to become truly disciplined, sober, industrious Christians, these holy fairs would have to be chastened. That was the conviction of enlightened detractors and evangelical reformers alike. Yet as long as the people continued to find meaning in the old way, curtailing these sacramental gatherings would be difficult, if not impossible. Charles II had found this out all too clearly in the seventeenth century as had the General Assembly in the eighteenth. As long as the communion occasions moved the people and as long as there were popular preachers to lead the meetings, the Lord's Supper would remain cloaked in festivity. But by the early nineteenth century ever increasing numbers of Presbyterians were becoming alienated from these popular traditions. This disaffection gave a tremendous boost to the reformers and critics of the sacramental season. In the context of nineteenth-century America and Scotland, the festal communions hardly needed to be suppressed; they would expire through obsolescence. Reforms would less often have to be imposed; instead, they would increasingly be embraced. With the ascendancy of bourgeois culture—and its ethic of disciplined self-control and diligent economic advancement—the traditional sacramental occasion simply no longer made sense to most Presbyterians.[46]

One of the great sins of the sacramental season was that it consumed too much time—as much as a week once travel to and from the occasion was figured in. The Blacksmith for one had been adamant in his criticism of the communions on this score. Through these holy days—or "idle days," as he called them—the Presbyterians squandered several days of work, all for the sake of "miraculous conversions, by which the converts' morals" were "rarely mended" in any case. "Our idle days," he complained, "whatever miracles they may produce, do hurt to true religion: the people lose many labouring days by them, and the country is deprived of the fruit of their industry." He worried that people who frequented these occasions would "contract an idle disposition of mind" and "get into a *bad habit of body*." Considered in this social and economic light, the sacramental season was backward and debilitating. Displaying his commitment to improving Scottish commerce, the Blacksmith went on to calculate the cost of this idle piety:

> I have seen above three thousand people at one of these *occasions*. But supposing that one with another, there are only fifteen hundred, and that each of them, one with another, might earn 6d. a day. Every sacrament, by its three idle days, will cost the country much about 112l. 10s. sterling, not including the days that they who live at a great distance must lose in coming and going, nor the losses the farmer must sustain when *occasions* happen in the hay, harvest or seed times; the man of business, when they chance to fall upon market days; or the tradesman, when any particular piece of work is in hand that requires dispatch. Now, supposing the sacrament should be administered only twice a year in all our churches, which, if it be not, it ought to be, these *occasions*, as they are managed at present, will cost Scotland at least 235,000l. sterling; an immense sum for sermons!

For those who would forsake the holy fairs, issues of idleness and discipline, of labor and commerce, were central to their abandonment of this sacramental festival.[47]

The Blacksmith's figures were calculated to make people value the diligent pursuit of worldly business more than the cultivation of idle piety. Expanded farming, commerce, and trade should supersede the needless festivities of the communion season. Thus, in what amounts to an ironic inversion of the Protestant ethic, the Reformed piety of the evangelical Presbyterians was seen not as encouraging discipline, but as fostering sloth. A late Victorian commentator on the sacramental occasions went so far as to conclude that these events had severely impeded agricultural and commercial progress, leaving "the people much poorer, if more pious." From this critic's vantage point, the traditional piety had tended "to consecrate laziness." To those holding to this bourgeois perspective, these sacramental festivals were not fair-days of the gospel or "Jubilee feasts," but instead "great nuisances" unacceptable because of "the pecuniary loss they occasion[ed] to the community by the suspension of trade and labour." The communions were thus seen as the enemies of vigorous commerce and inimical to the ethic that would propel a capitalistic economy forward. "The claims of secular industry" were at odds, the American Samuel Miller concluded summarily, with all forms of popular festivity— and the latter had to give way to the former.[48]

The gradual triumph in Scotland and in America of a capitalistic economy with its accompanying bourgeois ethic contributed heavily to the slow decline of the communion season. The economic critique of the sacramental occasion that the Blacksmith had offered somewhat forlornly in the 1750s became accepted wisdom among his Victorian heirs. As one Scottish layman put the matter in 1830, "This . . . has become a great commercial country altogether different from what it was, and people engaged in the business of life cannot now go about to sacraments, with conveniency; and in all ages man's observances have given way to existing circumstances." It would have been hard to spell out a social and economic determinism more absolute than this. Religion was subject to these socioeconomic changes, and there was, to this layman at least, no fighting it. And in many ways he proved right. Both middle-class businessmen, such as "*shop-keepers* or *manufacturers*," who did not want to lose "the week's sale and profits," and workers, such as "artizans and labourers," who depended on daily wages, increasingly saw the traditional communions as "causes of grievance," not celebration. The economic realities of nineteenth-century society made this evangelical festival with its "long train of week day services" impractical and objectionable. In such a context the festal communions would indeed yield to "the dictate[s] of a secularizing spirit."[49]

By bourgeois standards, the sinfulness of the sacramental season consisted not only in its promotion of idleness, but also in its encouragement of excessive conviviality. Sociability came with the crowds that thronged the communions, and keeping it within the bounds of evangelical morality was always a difficult task. Keeping sociability within the bounds of a increasingly stringent ethic of self-control and discipline proved more difficult still. Much of the conviviality long tolerated by the evangelicals became intolerable when subjected to the scrutiny of the bourgeois. Changing understandings of alcohol and sexuality in particular undermined the legitimacy of the sacramental season through discrediting the forms of conviviality—and piety—that had long accompanied it.

Traditional Presbyterians of the early modern period accepted, within limits, the congruence of drink and religious fellowship. All along, of course, the evangelicals showed little patience with those who openly profaned their meetings through drunkenness. They obviously deplored the "low, vulgar drunkards, buffoons and debauchees" who occasionally peopled the edges of their sacramental gatherings and sought, through the church session, to discipline such offenders. If pious Presbyterians did not celebrate alcohol in the way that waggish scoffers like Burns did—"Leeze me on Drink! it gies us mair / Than either School or Colledge"—they nonetheless were comfortable combining religion and drink. To the exasperation of many of their Victorian heirs, early modern pastors and people had considered "the moderate use of ardent spirits as highly salutary" and allowed liquor to be "freely used at all meetings of every kind." Sacramental occasions hardly constituted exceptions, and indeed the congruence of religion and drink was often particularly marked at these events. The Blacksmith, while obviously exaggerating this concomitance for satiric effect, nonetheless suggested how drink and religion might intertwine during the sacramental gatherings:

> In another place you see a pious circle sitting round an ale-barrel, many of which stand ready upon carts, for the refreshment of the saints. The heat of the summer season, the fatigue of travelling, and the greatness of the crowd, naturally dispose them to drink; which inclines some of them to sleep, works up the enthusiasm of others, and contributes not a little to produce those miraculous conversions that sometimes happen at these *occasions*.

During the communion seasons—at least at the larger, more festal occasions—sociability, drink, and religion were all interconnected: Christian fellowship and communal festivity went hand-in-hand.[50]

If always vigilant against excesses, the evangelicals nonetheless generally accepted the sociability and conviviality connected with these occasions. Rather than "seclude" this gospel feast from the multitudes, it was best, as one Scottish pastor said, to accept even ale-barrels and "ale tents" as necessary forms of refreshment for such large auditories. Any harm that resulted from this indulgence was outweighed by the benefits of having the sacrament held "up to the world," a spectacle of Christ's redemptive sufferings. A concrete example of the moderation church leaders often exercised toward those indulging in such "refreshment" at the communions comes in the Kilsyth session records for 1741, a notably evangelical parish on the verge of renewed awakening. In August the session summoned two members, Janet Smith and Alexander Nimmo, for "drinking" during the tent preaching on the communion Sabbath; in-

deed, they suspected Nimmo of being "drunk." But in his defense Nimmo
said that there had been "twelve of them in Company" and "that they
had only five pints of ale in Mary Browns." For her part Janet Smith admitted that she had also been in "the forsaid Company" and that she had
"Smoaked a Pipe of Tobacco with her husband and Sister." Deciding that
neither were in fact drunk, the session simply suggested that they "be
more Cautious of their Behaviour in Time Coming." Conviviality in various forms—in this case, in drinking and smoking with friends and rela-
tives—was a widely accepted part of these communions. If always monitored for excess, such sociability was nonetheless a familiar feature of
these festal gatherings.[51]

More sober evangelicals as well as enlightened critics increasingly condemned this coincidence of *convivium* and conviviality. They saw the ale-
barrels and other forms of refreshment differently—as gross abuses, as
outright evils. Reformers, such as the Blacksmith, drew clear lines between religion and sociability, between faith and festivity. Alarmed by
what came to be seen as the "immorality and dissipation" of "the peasantry" on these occasions, reformers increasingly drove a wedge between
drink and religion. Where once there was congruence, they saw irrecon-
cilable conflict. "Unfortunately the carnal things and the devotional were
in too close proximity," one late nineteenth-century churchman said of
the bygone communion seasons in his parish, "for the baps of bread and
barrels of ale were planted around the churchyard dyke. All day long
there was an oscillation between the one and the other. . . . There was an
unceasing contest between the spiritual and the spirituous—the holy day
was turned into a holiday." Reformers of the festal communions from the
Blacksmith on would see an increasingly sharp divide between holy day
and holiday, between shared drinking and Christian fellowship. This fundamental shift in perspective further eroded the credibility of popular religion as embodied in the sacramental season.[52]

Victorian designs to separate religion and drink would reach their log-
ical conclusion in the move to replace the communion wine with an un-
fermented equivalent—an effort that received growing support and
caused increasing controversy from the 1830s on. During the traditional
sacrament considerable evidence suggests that communicants often im-
bibed heartily at this eucharistic feast. The seventeenth-century Presbyterian patriarch David Calderwood suggested this when he eschewed the
"pinched tasting" of the prelatical party and noted how Presbyterian
communicants "eate and drink in such measure, as they may find themselves refreshed sensibly." For the communions at Cambuslang in 1742 a
minute in the kirk records suggests that at least 112 bottles of wine were
required, and in other places wine was supplied by the gallon or even by
the barrel. An eighteenth-century pastor on the Pennsylvania frontier,

John Cuthbertson, provided unusual specificity on this point. In a terse, but revealing diary entry in 1753, he noted that two hundred people had communed, requiring six gallons of wine and four bushels of wheat. This meant that about four ounces of wine were provided for each communicant—enough certainly for each to be "refreshed sensibly." Sermonic meditations that spoke of Christ's love warming the heart as the wine warmed the stomach further suggested how this symbol of Christ's blood was sensibly experienced.[53]

To the absolutists among the reformers, the use of fermented wine at all in the communion was wrong, let alone in such large quantities. That the movement to eliminate wine from the Lord's Supper could attract extensive backing from the 1830s into the 1880s and beyond is a fair indication of the changing context in which the traditional sacrament no longer made sense. As one minister appealed, "the demand of the times, the spirit of the age, the more enlightened Christian conscience and the necessity laid upon our Church in witnessing against intemperance in every possible form" compelled removal of wine from the eucharist. "The very taste and even the smell of intoxicating liquors" presented "a great temptation," and such a danger had to be removed from the center of the Lord's Supper. Stories were regularly told of people who were led to drunkenness through participation in the eucharist or who lost "all control" after their "dormant appetites" had been aroused through the communion wine. To "converts from intemperance" especially, the Lord's Supper was not an uplifting rite, but "a fiery ordeal" through which they passed in anguish and temptation, always in danger of falling anew into drunkenness. In Scotland and in America the pressures were great to make certain that the eucharist was not so much exhilarating or enlivening as it was safe and sobering. Victorian Presbyterians, adjusting their communions to "the spirit of the age," distanced themselves from the eucharistic practices of their forebears. From their perspective, what had gone on during the old sacramental season came to look more like boisterous peasants at their cups than devout Christians at a communion.[54]

If drink and religion did not mix, certainly sexuality and religion did not either. The Blacksmith spoke of the "odd mixture of religion, sleep, drinking, [and] courtship" at these occasions and observed disdainfully the "knot[s] of young fellows and girls making assignations to go home together in the evenings." "What must the consequence be," he asked, "when a whole countryside is thrown loose, and young fellows and girls are going home together by night in the gayest season of the year, when everything naturally inspires warm desires, and silence, secrecy and darkness encourage them?" The evangelicals obviously opposed this sort of lustful sexuality as much as the Blacksmith and tried to insure that such profligacy did not sully the proceedings. Yet at the same time the evangelicals recognized the importance of these meetings as occasions for courtship. The seventeenth-century preacher John Livingston, for example, said of his wife that he had seen "her frequently at Communions" before their marriage. Even the Blacksmith acknowledged that courtship as much as licentiousness was often at issue; for, as he scoffed, those "who are in pain to be provided with husbands, may possibly find their account in frequenting those *sacred* assemblies." In 1854 a minister in western Pennsylvania, recalling the "high days" the Presbyterians had lost, extolled the communion seasons for having "paved the way for many happy marriages and many auspicious nuptials." The evangelical Presbyterians accepted, at times even praised, the proposition that their festal communions would also be times of courtship. Reformers, by contrast, increasingly put asunder courtship and communion.[55]

Victorian reformers were offended not only by the undercurrent of sexuality that characterized these events, but also by the warm, sensual piety of "those rambling saints." Drawing especially upon the rich, erotic metaphors of the Song of Songs, the early evangelicals, as we saw in the last chapter, cultivated a spirituality that regularly employed carnal images to express divine love. The Canticles, many passages of which were given eucharistic readings, were integral to the passionate piety of the saints. The sacramental spirituality of the evangelical Presbyterians was indeed infused with metaphors of sexual ardency and longing.[56]

By the nineteenth century this spirituality was under suspicion, even attack. Commentators on the Song of Songs worried more and more about how to salvage the book from its apparent "indelicacy" and "licentiousness." Certain hymnists, uncomfortable with images of Christ as lover, began to drop them from their own works and to refine older compositions. Even an evangelical Presbyterian classic, Samuel Rutherford's collection of letters, *Joshua Redivivus*, had to be guarded from objection; its "sometimes coarse and indelicate" language and its "graphic imagery" of Christ as amorous Bridegroom and the soul as equally passionate bride had to be explained and defended, not assumed as a commonplace. The trend toward a desexualized piety was epitomized by a mid-nineteenth-century American commentator on the Canticles, Moses Stuart, when he remarked: "We shrink instinctively from connecting amatory ideas and feelings with a devotional frame of mind. We find the temptation to dwell on carnal imagery sometimes, perhaps often, leading us away from pure and spiritual devotion. This I believe to be the general—the all but universal feeling among us. . . . I commend it. It shows what progress Christianity has made, in inspiring the mind with quick and powerful sensitiveness, in regard to a matter which is always fraught with danger." The distance between this particular Victorian view of piety and the spiritual narratives at Cambuslang or the letters of Rutherford is tremendous. The ascendancy of a more circumspect Protestantism rendered the old spirituality increasingly anachronistic and discordant and further encouraged the discontinuance of sacramental occasions that enkindled such passionate piety.[57]

To the reformers who abandoned it, the holy fair encouraged idleness, intemperance, and immorality—and it encouraged enthusiasm. The sacramental occasions were renowned for the great public displays of piety that occurred during them—the weeping, fainting, groaning, trembling, and rejoicing of the newly converted and the freshly revived. From the early seventeenth century into the nineteenth, intense, often ecstatic religious devotion was associated with the festal communions. To eliminate "the popular frenzy" produced by these occasions was one of the great ambitions of the reformers. Middle-class respectability, decorum, and self-control were incompatible with the fervor of these traditional sacraments. Reformers sought to bring under control those elements of the sacramental season that they believed were most responsible for inciting enthusiasm.[58]

Proposals for reform often centered on gaining control over the outdoor meetings, particularly the tent preaching. The emotional, extemporaneous preaching to hundreds, often thousands, of spectators was of great significance in arousing the fervor of the people. Situated outdoors since the churches were usually too small to accommodate the crowds, the preaching from the tent encouraged the formation of immense public assemblies that throbbed with religious excitement. Critics found this preaching, which whipped up the enthusiasm of the thronged gathering, particularly disturbing and dangerous. "I defy Italy, in spite of all its superstition," the Blacksmith challenged, "to produce a scene better fitted to raise pity and regret in a religious, humane and understanding heart, or to afford an ampler field for ridicule, to the careless and profane, than what they call a field preaching upon one of those *occasions*." Another critic, equally put off by this tent preaching, suggested the church should not on this point yield to the inclinations of the people. "As to the Sermons in the Church-Yard, or without Doors," he said, "there can be no solid Argument for the same, except to please the Populace." This critic feared that if the church could not control the activities of these outdoor sacraments—the heated sermons in particular—they would lose control of the people. "All government," he warned, would end up being turned over to "the Independent Lay"—an eventuality that he believed would end in "anarchy and Confusion." To put limits on the outdoor preaching was to place constraints on popular religion, to rein in evangelical enthusiasm, and to assert the hierarchical authority of the church. The gradual elimination of outdoor preaching was indeed among the most important and encumbering constraints placed upon evangelical Presbyterianism.[59]

At many of the communions not only was there preaching in the fields or groves, but the sacrament as well was celebrated outdoors. Though in some places the sacrament was administered inside the church while the tent preaching went on outside, often all the rituals were conducted in the open air. Outdoor services, as one observer said, often attained "a solemnity and sublimity not realized within the church" as the elements of festivity and spectacle were heightened in these great, open-air gatherings. Wary of these festal communions in field or forest, opponents strove to bring the Lord's Supper within doors where they insisted it belonged. One kirk session, refusing to accept the designs of a new minister who thought the sacrament should only be performed inside the church, declared it "most unseemly that the holy communion should be celebrated in a hole-and-corner way like that." Adamant in their resistance, the elders nonetheless lost the battle. The Lord's Supper was brought indoors.[60]

As reformers struggled to reduce the spectacle of the Scottish sacrament, the eucharist indeed was celebrated in what by comparison was "a hole-and-corner way." In withdrawing from the fields, groves, and churchyards, the Presbyterians retreated from open, public spaces into the more private and closed spaces of their churches. Fearing the enthusiasm, spectacle, and festivity of the outdoor meetings, they sought refuge in what a later churchman praised as "more seemly private celebrations" of the sacrament. The Reformation had appeared to pledge the privatization of religion through its levelling of the public festivals and processions of the medieval church. In the successful reform of the holy fair in the nineteenth century, this pledge was renewed and extended. The slow destruction of "[the people's] old Church in the Fields" was one of the most telling signs of the ascendancy of middle-class Protestantism and the reform of popular religion.[61]

To the reformers of the holy fair, this privatization of religion was essential for safeguarding public order. The indulgence of crowds, within a religious context as well as others, had come to be seen as fraught with social risk, especially as the changing economic order made control of an increasingly distinct working class ever more difficult. Disorder, drunkenness, immorality, even violence, were rightfully viewed as potential concomitants of such religious spectacles. As one North Carolinian explained the decline of such meetings in 1882, "The promiscuous huddling together of neighbors and strangers without police regulations at length became a source of disorder and immorality." Thus, this commentator observed, the Presbyterians had wisely abandoned both the sacramental occasions and their offspring, the camp meetings. Reformers of the thronged communions—and the camp meetings for that matter—saw a more private and domestic religion as the answer to such social dangers.[62]

The private, domestic course of the reformers is perhaps best illustrated by returning to Robert Burns. To his heirs, not only had he managed to expose all that was wrong with religious festivity in "The Holy Fair," but in another poem, "The Cotter's Saturday Night," he had succeeded in capturing the admirable abode of true religion, the home. Among the most beloved of Burns' poems in the nineteenth century, on both sides of the Atlantic, "The Cotter's Saturday Night" paints a warm, touching scene of family worship:

> The chearfu' Supper done, wi' serious face,
>   They, round the ingle, form a circle wide;
> The Sire turns o'er, with patriarchal grace,
>   The big *ha'-Bible*, ance his *Father*'s pride:
> His bonnet rev'rently is laid aside,
>   His *lyart haffets* wearing thin and bare;
> Those strains that once did sweet in ZION glide,
>   He wales a portion with judicious care;
> '*And let us worship GOD!*' he says with solemn air.

True religion consisted in such simple acts of family devotion, not in festivity, pageantry, and pomp:

> Compar'd with this, how poor Religion's pride,
>   In all the pomp of *method*, and of *art*,
> When men display to congregations wide,
>   Devotion's ev'ry grace, except the *heart*!
> The POWER, incens'd, the Pageant will desert,
>   The pompous strain, the sacredotal stole;
> But haply, in some *Cottage* far apart,
>   May hear, well pleas'd, the language of the *Soul*;
> And in His *Book of Life* the Inmates poor enroll.

To Burns' Victorian interpreters, the "sanctimonious sensuality" of the festal communions paled before "the sacrament of domestic reunion." Worship within "the Paradise of Home" put to shame such great religious meetings as the "motley gathering" for the eucharist.[63]

The growing contrast between "the world of happy homes" and the world of open-air sacraments can be seen as well in two nineteenth-century illustrations of outdoor tent preaching versus two typical depictions of domestic religion. Both the engraving *The Holy Fair* and James Howe's *Tent Preaching at Bothwell* display little affection for the proceedings that they depict. The engraving's crowded scene suggests disorder and confusion; people quaff in an ale-house across the street from where the minister harangues a mixed and bustling auditory. Similarly, Howe's drawing suggests a deformed piety through deformed figures: the minister is rotund and gluttonous; the features of several people are distorted; a

Hear how he clears the points o'Faith
Wi' rattlin an' Wi' thumpin'.

10. A. Carse and R. Scott. *The Holy Fair.*

11. James Howe. *Tent Preaching at Bothwell.*

horse's backside occupies the center of the work. By contrast, depictions of family worship were fond and sentimental. This was true in the engraving and the drawing shown here (illustrations 12 and 13), both of which took their inspiration, like dozens of similar depictions, from "The Cotter's Saturday Night." In the home, safely away from the hubbub of tent preaching, people were now able to be devout and serious. Bathed in the glowing light of the hearth, the family in reverential postures displayed genuine piety. (Here, around the fire, even the quiet, domesticated dog cooperates in contrast to those that roam in William Carse's *On Tent Preaching.*) As the home emerged as "the major center of Victorian piety"—to use Colleen McDannell's words—the former balance between the private and public in evangelical Presbyterianism was increasingly tipped to the domestic. In the process, large outdoor religious events, like the festal communions, fell into growing disrepute.[64]

This privatizing thrust can also be seen in changes in the eucharistic rituals themselves. For example, communicants increasingly stayed in their pews when receiving the elements; the long tables began to disappear. John Bossy has suggested that the placing of pews in English parish churches in the seventeenth century reified "the conception of public worship as an assembly of segregated households" and severely impeded "Christian integration." The Presbyterian move from table to pew for the sacrament might be interpreted in a similar way, for it suggested growing boundaries between Christians that were preserved in the eucharist, rather than dissolved. Instead of displaying a community feasting together, the Victorian sacrament suggested a collection of independent, hierarchically ordered families partaking of the elements in relative isolation from one another. That hierarchy replaced commensality as a guiding principle is quite evident: unlike the generally open seating at the long tables, pew assignments were often explicitly tied to social and economic standing. The move from table to pew also suggested lessening distinctions between the saints and the world, for with the removal of the tables came the gradual decline of fencing. No longer would there be a grand display of evangelical morality, eschatology, and membership through the fenced table. No longer would communicants be expected to separate themselves from the rest of the congregation. Increasingly communing in their pews rather than at a table for all to see, Victorian Presbyterians, comfortable in the closed space of their churches, were still more at home in the private, familial space of their pews. Far removed from the crowded, face-to-face bustle of the communion season, modern Presbyterian worship was more refined, ordered, and controlled than the early modern traditions it replaced.[65]

A final indication of how far the nineteenth-century reforms in worship would carry Presbyterians from the communal festivity of the early mod-

12. Alexander Carse. *The Cotter's Saturday Night*.

The priest-like father reads the sacred page.

13. F. A. Chapman and J. Filmer. *The Cotter's Saturday Night*.

ern sacrament came in the small, individual communion glasses that often replaced the common eucharistic cups. In the late nineteenth century, especially among American Presbyterians, individual glasses often supplanted—for mostly hygienic reasons—shared communion cups. At the sacramental occasions hundreds, if not thousands, had drunk heartily from the same vessels, as the communicants passed the large, weighty chalices from one to another. To many nineteenth-century reformers, this practice of drinking from common cups seemed dangerously polluting. More and more people came to fear that disease, as much as Christ's blessing, was communicable through the traditional sacramental practices. Though this change in eucharistic vessels by no means affected all churches and though it only came after the sacramental season had been largely reformed, it nonetheless remains profoundly suggestive. Not only does this change point to transmuted liturgical arrangements, but also to transformed social relationships among Christians. Where Victorians discerned contagion, their forebears had discovered community; where modern Christians wanted safe distance, their early modern predecessors had sought intimate sharing. The small, individual glasses were ready symbols of the diminished communal power of the sacrament.[66]

By the latter half of the nineteenth century the festal communions, for better or worse, had been thoroughly reformed. The ascendancy of a bourgeois, Victorian culture in Scotland and America had pushed the reforms forward at an accelerated pace. Rituals, once at the center of evangelical Presbyterian culture, became anachronistic—hindrances to commerce, inducements to undiscipline, and encumbrances to genuine worship. The popular or traditional Christianity embodied in the sacramental season thus yielded to a bourgeois or Victorian Christianity that was more privatized and domesticated, more dignified and decorous than the faith it replaced. In smoothing out the roughness of the old way and in forging a new liturgical aesthetic, nineteenth-century Presbyterians put the "irrational, unedifying, and preposterous" traditions of their forebears behind them. Wondering at their "forefathers' superstitions," they squared their worship with their own culture. "Our circumstances are different;" they proclaimed, "our experience is incomparably wider, and our lights are far greater." With such confidence did leaders of the nineteenth-century church move beyond the "great evils" of the old system and "introduce a more excellent way."[67]

LEGACIES AND LAMENTS

By the 1840s the demise of the festal communions, if not complete, was assured. In some rural congregations in America, particularly in the South and West, these occasions persisted with some semblance of their former power for another decade or more. "In our own day," James W. Alexander noted in 1846, "there are portions of the country, where the ancient zeal in regard to sacramental means is fully maintained, and where they still are festivals of gracious communication." In Scotland vestiges of the old traditions would be evident in certain areas—notably portions of the southwest, the Highlands, and the Hebrides—into the twentieth century. Pockets of traditionalism notwithstanding, by 1850 the old sacramental festivals had been largely reformed and abandoned. Saturday and Monday services were increasingly "omitted," and fast day services were often neglected, being casually profaned or even formally rejected. The traditional "forms and extra services" had been "in a great degree laid aside." The rituals of the old way were expiring, and the new eucharistic rituals—streamlined and efficient—were geared to frequency and to celebration by local, closely circumscribed churches, not by multitudes from all over the surrounding area. The immense festal communions of Shotts, Cambuslang, or Cane Ridge or their smaller counterparts—at Booth Bay or Cross Creek—were essentially things of the Presbyterian past.[68]

The old festal communions, though lost, left legacies. For example, the sacramental piety occasioned by these lengthy communions, though disembodied from the extended meetings, lingered on amid the shortened eucharistic events. The theologian John Williamson Nevin, amid his despair over the declining mystery and power associated with the Lord's Supper, found some solace in the persisting influence of "the devotional books of the Scottish Church." "The piety of the old Scotch divines," he consoled himself, was "still *felt*" by many, even though Reformed eucharistic theology had been undermined by the rationalism of the Enlightenment and the subjectivism of radical Protestantism. The traditional sacramental piety, as Nevin suggested, did survive to some degree the passing of the rituals that had elevated it to the height of the Scottish Presbyterian faith. The old eucharistic devotionals and catechisms continued to be reprinted, and new ones were devised that breathed much of the traditional spirit.[69]

Despite efforts to preserve this devotional legacy, it was difficult to hold onto a piety that had found reification in the festal communions. Without these high days to serve as a focus for this practice of piety, the traditional forms of sacramental preparation were increasingly marginalized. As the reformers pressed for simplicity in worship, they failed to see how the rich piety and the intricate rituals were interdependent. In loosing themselves of the rituals, the Presbyterians gradually loosed themselves of much of the piety as well. The shortened communions simply did not produce, as one American Presbyterian lamented, "the same intensity of enjoyment—the same ardor of love—the same sweet sense of the divine presence, which were the accompaniments of the celebration in former days."[70]

Separated from the extended rituals that had heightened the significance of the Lord's Supper, the traditional sacramental piety of Scottish Presbyterianism became increasingly attenuated. The eucharistic spirituality long at the center of the evangelical Presbyterian faith was often edged among Victorian churchgoers to the periphery.

As an early modern form of Protestant renewal, the sacramental occasion also left a legacy of revivalism. The Presbyterian communions were tributaries to a wide stream of evangelical revivalism—a current that flowed with great force in the nineteenth century. The older traditions of renewal provided a foundation for new forms of evangelism, most notably in the case of the camp meetings which had first emerged out of the sacramental occasions of the Great Revival. The very persistence of such festal religious gatherings, if under new guise, nonetheless suggested the continuing strength of traditional forms of popular evangelicalism. Besides their foundational importance for the camp meetings, the communion seasons also offered an initial context in which to test new revivalistic techniques. For example, anxious benches—pews at the front of the church to which would-be converts were called in order to facilitate their passage into the evangelical faith—were at times in their early development among the Presbyterians grafted onto the sacramental occasion. The extended communions, by way of historical precedent, also offered validation of another new measure, the protracted meeting. The consummate Presbyterian revivalist, Charles Grandison Finney, would adduce the lengthy Scottish sacraments in defense of protracted meetings—many of which, as four-day meetings, actually grew directly out of the traditional communion seasons. The modern revivalism of Finney, his lieutenants, and his successors was founded, at least in part, upon the evangelical Presbyterian heritage of the seventeenth and eighteenth centuries.[71]

The new revivalism, however, was a poor conservator of tradition. While it no doubt built on the evangelical traditions of seventeenth- and eighteenth-century Presbyterianism, it also helped bury them. Often brashly innovative, the leaders of the new revivalism little regarded tradition. "The object of our measures is to gain attention," Finney said, and for that "you must have something new." Or, as Dwight Moody would put the matter: "If one method don't wake them up, let us try another." With new rituals and often with new theological emphases, nineteenth-century revivalism shared little in the Calvinism and sacramentalism that had informed the festal communions. The synthesis of conversionism and sacramentalism that the old way had embodied increasingly dissolved with the enshrinement of the new measures. The ritual of coming forward to the anxious bench or seat of decision became the sacramental focus of the new revivalism and dislodged the eucharist from its former centrality.

This modern revivalism thus wound up having only a vague resemblance to the sacramental revivalism that had gone before it.[72]

The new revivalism was not simply modern; it was also American, and in that way, too, it was inimical to the Scottish tradition. In the nineteenth century, America was indeed "a land of revivals," but more than that it was a land with its own kind of revivals. In 1839 a French commentator on American society and manners, Michael Chevalier, noted that the United States had already created its own "religious festivals"; he identified these festivals as being above all "the Methodist camp-meetings" and the "scenes of the *anxious bench*." Though somewhat bemused by the revivals, Chevalier saw them as America's great "festivals and spectacles" integral to the formation of "national character" and "American nationality."[73] How important the revivals were as "national festivals" remains arguable, but that the revivals became American and ceased to be recognizably Scottish is evident. While the Scottish communion, as an Old World festival, had clearly flourished in America, it had always remained somehow a transplant, tied less to American Christianity than to the Church of Scotland. Scottish patterns of revival had indeed contributed profoundly to the forging of America's evangelical tradition, but by the mid-nineteenth century American Protestants had gone far to solidify their own forms of renewal and, as Chevalier would have it, their own national and religious identity. In matters of revivalism, that identity came to center finally on camp meetings, anxious benches, protracted meetings, professional evangelism, inquiry rooms, and other new measures, not on the sacramental season.

More than simply eclipsing the old revivalism, the new American revivalism undermined one of the basic assumptions at the heart of the sacramental occasion, that of the Scottish Presbyterians as a covenanted people. Frankly interdenominational, the new revivalism drew its evangelists from Methodists like John Newland Maffitt to Baptists like Jabez Swan and Jacob Knapp to Congregationalists like Lyman Beecher to Presbyterians like Finney and Edward Norris Kirk. Though the sacramental occasion was never limited to Scots or Ulster Scots in its missionary outreach in America, it was nonetheless a notably ethnic tradition. A scene like the one in Scotland where a minister simply debarred "the English" from coming to the Lord's table was probably rarely repeated, but it remains emblematic of how Scottish Presbyterian insularity could be expressed through the communion season.[74] This was a revivalism aimed not only at conversion and mission, but also at the renewal of peoplehood.

If American revivalism could be as insular and ethnic as its Scottish counterpart, it became so at the expense of Scottish particularism. The formation of an American Protestant identity demanded the submersion of various ethnic forms of Protestantism. As John Mitchell Mason, advocate not only of frequency but also of assimilation, put the matter in 1810:

> *Generally*, we must *Americanize* our churches; that is, [we] must adapt the great and immoveable principles of church order to the circumstances of our own country. Native habits will swallow up foreign habits, as infallibly as national language swallows up a foreign one. We have nothing before us but to assimilate, in prudential arrangements, to these habits, or to be swept away.

To Mason, the emergence of America's own cultural Protestantism necessitated the attenuation of specific Old World traditions. Under such assimilationist principles and pressures, Scottish communions became American revivals.[75]

Ironically, the emergence of American forms of revivalism undermined Scottish tradition not only in America, but also in Scotland; for American patterns of evangelism and renewal were vigorously exported. The mother of a fair portion of American revivalism, Scotland often became an object of its daughter's mission as American evangelists took on Britain. Finney himself would travel to Scotland, and his *Lectures on Revivals* would be popular and influential there. Dwight L. Moody and Ira Sankey would follow, and in the twentieth century Billy Graham would make Scotland the locus of extensive crusades. As one Scottish observer tellingly noted, with the tour of Moody and Sankey in mind, "Scotland . . . has come to resemble America, where revivals are incidents of constant experience."[76] Even in Scotland, revivalism by the latter half of the nineteenth century had come to be associated not with communion seasons, but instead with America's various evangelists and their new measures.

By the second half of the nineteenth century what legacies remained from the old Scottish communions were fairly pallid and insubstantial. Modern revivalism had gone in directions that more often obscured this early modern precursor than drew attention to it. Some of the rituals survived here and there, but they were generally attended with little of the former festivity and excitement. Parts of the piety as well were to be found in nineteenth-century devotionals, but these were only pieces, not a whole. A more substantial legacy of the communions was their history. Most nineteenth- and twentieth-century Presbyterians and evangelicals never looked back, or, if they did, they settled their gaze on the Reformation or on Westminster and saw the intervening history as one of accretion and apostasy. Or more likely they celebrated modernity's advance on the superstitions of the past. They wondered at these "rude festivals"—so happily abandoned and so strangely remote.[77]

Yet amid the celebrations of change, there were unobtrusive, little-noticed sounds of lament. Some looked back and saw not gain, but loss.

"Those were golden days," the Reverend Richard Webster reminisced of the communion seasons, "when souls were enlightened with such a knowledge of Christ, as if the light of the sun had been sevenfold, as if the light of seven days had poured at once on the worshippers, with healing in every beam." Some laments were not simply nostalgic over traditions lost, but bitter over changes in worship that looked less like reform than declension. Pastor Joseph Smith of western Pennsylvania, for example, criticized the "paring and clipping away" of forms of worship that had been "highly appropriate and edifying." Angry at those liturgical innovators who had fostered "a fastidious dislike of our old-fashioned Presbyterian usages," Smith rebuked his generation for having so neglected the old ways of the sacramental season. "[Our forefathers] would have been greatly pained," he said, "at the way in which matters are often conducted on these 'high days' of the Church of God." His Scottish Presbyterian forebears, Smith was convinced, would have been "much disgusted at the brevity with which such services are hurried over in many places now-a-days."[78]

Smith's resentment was significant. He wanted to vindicate the sacramental season from its critics; he wanted to save its history. Though he conceded that "there was much, in all the circumstances of these meetings, calculated to produce a species of religious dissipation," he did not let this common reservation obscure the past significance of the communions:

> We cannot but believe they were eminently profitable and refreshing seasons, and greatly aided in extending the influence of the gospel through those early settlements. The extension of the services through several successive days contributed to suspend or lighten the influence of the [settlers'] worldly cares, and to break up, for a time, their anxieties and all their little petty vexations of domestic life. . . . Above all, they proved seasons of special intercourse with heaven, and of foretaste of its joys, to many of those greatly tried and often sorrowing Christians who, in their frontier life, were frequently in heaviness through manifold temptations. It is worthy of special notice, also, that a very large proportion of those who were brought from darkness to light, and from the power of Satan unto God—traced their first religious impressions to these sacramental seasons.

In recalling the past power of the sacramental season, Smith, and others like him, sought to perpetuate a faithful understanding of these waning events. Although "the taste and usages of modern days" had rendered the traditional forms tedious and antiquated, Smith saw this not as an indictment of the old way, but as an indication of the church's having yielded to the "wishes of an ungodly world." Smith held on to the memory of the tradition in order to lament the waywardness of his own generation.[79]

Sometimes such laments issued in a naive call for the resuscitation of tradition. Smith certainly thought that renewal of the traditional sacramental services over four days "merit[ed] serious enquiry." Others made the call for a return to tradition more explicitly. "It would be well," the Reverend Edward Parker commented in 1851, "in this case to inquire for the old paths; where is the good way. Such solemn and devout convocations, such assembling of the people for several consecutive days for prayer and praise and preaching, if the practice were revived by the churches, would happily serve it is believed, to promote their spirituality and bring down the divine influences in more copious effusions." Recalling how the "sacramental seasons" had been "times of refreshing from the presence of the Lord," Parker saw in their renewal the means to revival. Such communions, having been in the past "attended with most signal manifestations of the divine presence," would, if revived, invigorate the very churches that had abandoned them.[80]

This naive view of revitalization needed to be tempered by realism, and others provided that. James W. Alexander suggested the ambivalence with which even admirers of the sacramental season often recalled it. He knew that for two hundred years "times of communion" among Scottish Presbyterians had been to "a remarkable degree . . . times of increase." He remembered the tradition from John Livingston's sacramental meetings in Scotland and Ulster to those "vast assemblages which were attracted to sacramental services" in America under the Tennents, the Blairs, and the Smiths. But in recalling, he did not urge re-creation. "It is not intended, by these remarks," he qualified, "to reproduce the obsolete forms. . . . It would ensure no good end to restore four-days-meetings, fasts, successive tables, numerous addresses, or any measures or ceremonies, however proper, without the spirit which informed them." Alexander, like Mason and many others, wanted "earnest" and "affectionate" eucharists within the context of simple, frequent communions. He was drawn back to the refreshing power of the traditional rituals, even as he saw the necessity of the reforms and pushed them forward.[81]

Alexander, caught between his commitment to reform and tradition, saw that any attempt to revive the old sacramental occasions in the changed church of mid-nineteenth-century America would be in vain. Merging praise and penance, all he could do finally was offer wistful remembrances of traditions lost and contrite reflections on failed reforms:

The remark is frequently made, that sacramental occasions have not the same interest which they had in former years. It is believed by the writer, that the complaint is not unfounded. In ridding the ordinance of that burdensome extent of service, which was justly chargeable on the old Scottish method, the fast, the repeated preparatory services, the discourses on successive days, and the tedious serving of table after table, we have on the other hand lost much that was comely, and glowing, and delightful. How many of us recall, with a pensive satisfaction, the impressions made even on our infant minds by the solemnities of a sacrament, as dispensed in our earlier days, and particularly in those parts of the country where Scottish Presbyterianism most prevailed. . . . Aged Christians who may read these lines will acknowledge, that memory can recall no seasons in which there was so much of the manifestation of God in his sanctuary, as in these great sacramental gatherings. Whole assemblies were often bathed in tears, and moved as the trees of the wood are moved by the wind. . . . These were times of revivals; and it is by means of the extraordinary assemblages, and penetrating influence of such communions, that the chief advances of our church were made. These were days of gladness, when the beauty of Zion was admired of her sons, and when thousands were brought to acknowledge Christ. And, whatever may be thought of the admission, I hesitate not to own, that we have gained nothing as a church, by magnifying the convenience and the decorum of ordinances, at the expense of fervour and joyfulness and life.

Alexander wrote a memorial for the sacramental season and a confession for the Victorian church of which he was a part. He lamented what was lost and saw that all that was left—or at least all that was soon to be left—was remembrance.[82]

Alexander's memorial came in 1846. In another generation remembrance was barer, and the rituals and those that celebrated their faith through them were growing more distant. By 1900 few missed the festal communions of a hundred years earlier; former laments had largely settled into silence or given way to further relief and bemusement. Having once been dramatized with sermons and psalms, careful gestures and frenetic ones, long tables and consecrated elements, tokens and tears, thronged assemblies within churches and without, prayers secret and public, conversions and diversions, visions and meditations, these fair-days of the gospel receded—piecemeal and bloodless—into archives. History may enrich our memory of the motion and fervor, the words and actions, the drama and spectacle, but it is a poor substitute for a sacrament. Remembrance is not re-presentation, but it is what we are left with.

Retrospect

PERHAPS THE NARRATIVE should have ended there—in the loss of this tradition—without the scholar's afterword or coda. This tradition of sacramental festivity in Scotland and in America was reformed and abandoned, and that perhaps is the overriding conclusion. Nonetheless, to close with those who offered memorials and tolled the decline would be to give the story the wrong ending. Loss or lament are the wrong words for the last word. To end primarily with the decline of this tradition would suggest an overly simple conclusion. It would tend to obscure various complexities, problems, and issues that the long history of these holy fairs raises.

The fate of these festal communions should not be misconstrued or overemphasized. The forms of festivity, community, sacramentalism, and renewal embodied in these rituals were not somehow vestigial, paling in significance before familiar forces that scholars have found at play in the early modern period—privatization, antiritualism, the reform of popular religion, the social transformation of traditional communities, or the like. For two hundred years in Scotland and for a century in America, the sacramental season was a critical part of the religious culture of the evangelical Presbyterians. Enlightenment and then Victorian reforms came, but they were perhaps remarkable as much for the belatedness of their success as for the success itself. The clear vitality of these holy fairs in post-Reformation Scotland and in early America, more than the waning of this tradition, is what calls for final, retrospective reflection.

The very emergence and development of these festal communions reveals some interesting wrinkles on popular Protestantism and its relationship to Catholicism. In Scotland (and by extension in America) the communion occasions revealed the persistence and resilience of sacramental festivity, the capacity within popular culture and religion—to use Peter Burke's words—for "taking the new and transforming it into something very like the old." Though the reformers dismantled the rituals of the Easter season and levelled the pageantry of Corpus Christi, eucharistic mystery, spectacle, and solemnity survived and resurfaced in the festal communions of the Presbyterians. Catholic festivals and traditions were indeed repudiated, but popular festivity centering on the sacrament was rehabilitated and maintained in Reformed guise. Attracting thousands of communicants, wayfarers, pilgrims, and spectators, the sacramental season was indeed a holy fair with all the marks of a popular festival. These occasions seriously undermine the presumption that Protestantism simply levelled the festal rhythms of medieval piety and replaced it with a steady week-to-week observance of the Sabbath. In this case Reformed Protestantism created its own sacramental festival—one that was marked not only by an evangelical concern for conversion and revival, but also by familiar patterns of eucharistic devotion and renewal.[1]

The prevalence of eucharistic renewal in the Scottish Presbyterian tradition points historians to its presence in other evangelical Protestant traditions as well. In America the coincidence of sacrament and revival extended beyond the Presbyterians to other evangelical groups. For example, the Anglican Devereux Jarratt, in discussing the awakening in Virginia, pointed to renewed regard for the eucharist as marking the spread of the evangelical gospel. "The sacrament of the supper had been so little regarded, in Virginia, by what were called *Church people*," Jarratt related, "that generally speaking, none went to the *table*, except a few of the more aged, perhaps seven or eight at a church. The vast majority of all ages, sexes and classes seemed to think nothing about it." But with the advent of the evangelical awakening, Jarratt reported that communicants thronged his meetings, "hundreds conven[ing] from different quarters, joining devoutly in the divine service" with as many as "nine hundred or one thousand" people coming to the table. These "delightful seasons," he concluded, were "a little heaven upon earth—a prelibation of celestial joys."[2] Further accounts of "*Raptures* of Joy" in eucharistic celebration cropped up in other narratives of evangelical revivals in early America— for example, northward in Congregational New England at Lyme, Connecticut, and southward in pluralistic Georgia at Whitefield's Bethesda. Also in Methodist camp meetings, sacramental celebration, at least early on, was often a central part of the gatherings.[3] Though particularly prominent in the Scottish tradition, the synthesis of revivalism and sacramentalism was noteworthy in other evangelical traditions as well; certainly, any easy antithesis that pits, as an interpretive truism, "revivalists against sacramentalists" warrants reconsideration. Indeed, the communion season provides an occasion to rethink the way the relationship between eucharist and revival has at times been conceived. Far from oppositional, the two often coalesced in early modern Scotland and in early America. Like Catholic forms of renewal, Protestant revivalism could be richly sacramental in its emphases.[4]

Seeing the centrality of the eucharist in many evangelical revivals also suggests another way of viewing Protestant forms of renewal. Historians have long thought about revivalism mostly in terms of Great Awakenings, as epochal movements that dramatically shake up the religious and social landscape. But seeing how the sacrament was commonly woven into evangelical revivals reminds historians of how such renewal was often interrelated with familiar and regular patterns of worship, how religious rejuvenation was often tied into a calendrical rhythm. For Presbyterians this was marked especially in their annual gatherings for communion. For Methodists, Cumberland Presbyterians, Adventists, and other groups, it would be evident in annual camp meetings and protracted meetings. These special events were viewed as the high days of the year; as one southern observer noted in 1846, people saw these summer and early fall meetings "as *necessarily* the time of harvest for souls"—a time as regular as that of the harvest for "cotton and corn."[5] Similarly, in the evangelical colleges there would often be yearly revival meetings; as one commentator wryly remarked, "the annual revival" in the colleges was as much a part of the calendar as "the Junior exhibition."[6] For many evangelicals, revivals were not so much extraordinary and surprising outpourings, but year-to-year rituals of conversion and renewal, part of the very fabric of religious life. That is not to say, of course, that all revivals were upon a level. There were obviously years of unusual awakening—Shotts in 1630, Cambuslang in 1742–1743, Boston in 1740–1742, or Cane Ridge in 1801, for example, all stand out. But it is to say that there is another less appreciated, equally important side of evangelical renewal— its year-to-year, summer-in-summer-out influence on the lives of people, its steady and repeated impact on religion, society, and culture. Revivals, from this standpoint, less often constituted Great Awakenings than calendrical festivals.

Questions about evangelicalism, sacramentalism, and patterns of renewal are reflective of a larger issue about Protestantism and ritual. Protestantism, and evangelical Protestantism especially, has often been seen as antiritualistic, as epitomizing the devaluation of ritual in the early modern period. Peter Burke and others have argued that Protestantism, particularly of the more Puritan or evangelical stripe, contributed to a modern "repudiation of ritual." Attitudes toward religious ritual may well have become more "dismissive" in the course of the early modern and modern periods; modernity has indeed more often hollowed out than hallowed ritual.[7] But what seems noteworthy, at least if much of early modern Presbyterianism is any gauge, is that evangelical Protestantism often resisted this devaluative trend as much as contributed to it. Indeed, the evangelicals, looking to biblical and apostolic examples, generally embraced ritual and carefully constructed it. For the Presbyterians this embrace was especially evident in their sacramental rituals, Sabbath observances, and devotional lives. Other evangelicals, such as the early Methodists, Baptists, and Moravians, added other "apostolic" rituals to their worship—love feasts and watch nights, for example—as rich liturgical patterns emerged from their restorationist and scripturalist search.[8] Historians have a tendency to speak in grand terms about the Protestant impoverishment of ritual—about the Protestant "denial of the meaning-fulness of action" or about Protestants being "without ritual, . . . fac[ing] God across infinite lonely space."[9] But, in thinking in these ways, histo-rians have often missed much of Protestantism, especially in its popular forms. Evangelical Protestants, far from dismissing ritual, displayed a wide range of performative expression and a notable confidence in rituals to symbolize, and even to make manifest, the divine.

Evangelical ritualism, as evidenced in the sacramental occasion, ex-tended particularly to notions of spectacle, of seeing the Christian faith enacted. The Scottish tradition, like other Protestant traditions, put a pre-mium on the preaching of the Word. But this valuation of the Word did not mean a devaluation of the sacrament nor did it mean that the ear necessarily replaced the eye as the dominant sense of the faith. The sac-ramental occasion all along represented a complex visible gospel. People came not only to hear sermons, but also to see them performed, not only to listen to meditations on the sacrament, but also to watch its celebra-tion—the solemn procession of the elders carrying forward the elements, the careful eucharistic gestures, the red wine poured out, the bread bro-ken, the various actions of the communicants. There was undoubted spectacle in the all-day celebration of the sacrament, in the thronged meetings, in the tears of the repentant, in the ecstatic countenances or fainted bodies of the transformed, in the best clothes of the participants, in the brilliant white linens that covered the communion tables, and in the outdoor settings in groves, on hillsides, or in churchyards. There were sights, too, that came in visions and meditations as the eye of faith drew people to Golgotha, where they saw the sufferings of Christ in bloody detail. There were, of course, other senses at play as well—in the tasting or touching of the elements or in the handling of imprinted tokens. Words rang out in sermons, prayers, and exhortations, but seeing, watching, and envisioning were always vital parts of this evangelical faith. Word and sacrament, sermon and spectacle, vision and meditation were combined in the rituals of these festal communions.

As spectacles, these communions were grand public events. These oc-casions indeed gathered whole communities, even regions, together. The vital communalism and festivity displayed in the holy fair give pause. Connections are often drawn between Protestantism and the privatiza-tion of religion, between Protestantism and the diminution of Christian community, or between Protestantism and the triumph of individualism. And in both Scotland and America, as elsewhere, the decline of commu-nity, the ascent of individualism, and the waning of religious authority were often noted and often lamented aspects of modernity. The Scot Thomas Carlyle gave voice to this regret, when he spoke of "the cut-purse and cut-throat Scramble" of nineteenth-century society, "where Friendship, Communion, has become an incredible tradition; and your holiest Sacramental Supper is a smoking Tavern Dinner, with Cook for Evangelist." As urbanization, industrialization, and capitalism advanced, Carlyle wondered at a society that was losing its "sacred Tissues"—one where a "universal selfish discord" seemed to prevail and where "once-sacred Symbols" fluttered "as empty Pageants."[10] Through a number of forces, religion's role in the public realm and in the community had been to various degrees eroded.

A problem comes, however, in fitting evangelical Presbyterianism into this familiar picture. If anything, the Scottish communions stood in the way of these forces of change. They were envisioned as the bulwarks of Christian community, as the nodal events in a religion that was staged outdoors in wide-open public spaces for all to see and experience. Individual conversions and individual pilgrimages there were—and they were vitally important and strikingly variegated—but these private experiences and quests led back to the eucharist, to a communal feast, to commensality. Sharp boundaries were drawn around this Christian community, but, despite these important lines of exclusion, these sacramental festivals remained profoundly inclusive—gatherings in which people from over wide areas discovered a basis for Christian community and regional cohesion. If the realities of divisiveness, whether through sectarian strife, political turmoil, or social change, did at times undermine or even invert this communalism, there always remained the hope and vision of finding community through the festal sacraments, of bringing a communion of saints out of dispersion or factiousness. The Scottish sacrament in its grand, region-wide enactment stood in tension with the privatizing and domestic thrusts evident in the religious history of the early modern period.

This communal, regional, and public focus was true of much of evangelical Protestantism in America as well as in Scotland. This was the case obviously for America's own sacramental occasions, but it was also the case for the camp meetings and protracted meetings that gradually developed, often out of the communion seasons themselves. One advocate of camp meetings, who saw these occasions as being desirable "not only in the West, but also in the East, and the North, and the South," observed that such great gatherings were the best way to reach "*the whole mass of society*," to bring "the whole community" under the influence of the gospel. He chided those ministers who always wanted to stay "inside" their "houses of worship" and attend to "three hundred people," while never wanting to go outside where "five thousand" could be drawn together. The spectacle and festivity of camp meetings, he suggested, went hand in hand with the forging of a larger and more inclusive Christian community. In the ordinary way of indoor worship, "christians of different families," he argued, "may leave their homes, . . . go to the church and take possession of their different pews, hear a sermon, and when the congregation is dismissed, return home; thus they may attend at the same church for years, and have little, very little acquaintance, and consequently little interest in each other's welfare." Camp meetings, by contrast, held out the promise of greater mutuality and community. "Let those same people come and settle on the ground at the commencement of a camp-meeting, and they will be better acquainted, and form more christian attachments by the time the meeting closes, than they would have formed in many years on the ordinary plan." Evangelical Christians, in such festal gatherings as communion occasions and camp meetings, sought ways to engage "all the community," to preserve the "golden bonds of union" among people "over large districts of country." The traditional forms of Christian community would indeed be transformed in the course of the early modern and modern periods, but many evangelicals long resisted those processes of change. Scottish communions and American revivals, as popular evangelical traditions, were often the conservators of Christian mutuality and community in a world that found it ever harder to preserve such ideals.[11]

The communal quality of the sacramental occasions and camp meetings underscores once again the traditionalism of much of early modern evangelicalism. Often seen as the clear allies of middle-class values, the unblinking enemies of popular culture, and the heralds of a private, individualistic religion, the evangelicals were in actuality hard to pigeonhole. If much of early modern evangelicalism dovetailed with the emergent bourgeois culture, much of popular evangelicalism and its revivalism did not. Indeed, evangelical Presbyterians were often themselves the subjects of middle-class reform. The tent preaching, the enthusiasm, the lengthiness and crowdedness of the meetings, the sociability and conviviality, the communal festivity were all seen as in tension with the modern, capitalistic society that was emerging. In this context popular evangelicalism was not the purveyor of reform, but its object.

As grand religious gatherings, widely troubling to various reformers, the Scottish communions long presented a compelling combination of solemnity and festivity. Often crowded, bustling events, the sacramental occasions remained deeply solemn affairs. Those critics, who, in seeing the gregariousness of participants, dismissed the communions as "public diversions" or as "*gala day*[s] . . . not sacred, but social" in character, missed much of the point. If these gatherings had the social excitement of fairs, they were also holy. People ate, drank, conversed, and courted, but they also prayed, meditated, and covenanted. The sacred and the social were inextricably combined at these events, and this combination was a critical part of their power. By comparison, the fairs of the worldly remained simple things—"poor, little, sensual, painted pleasures"—without the religious mystery and ultimacy that empowered these fair-days of the gospels. All along the communion had given the conviviality meaning, and the conviviality had given the communion life.[12]

The Scottish communions or holy fairs loomed large throughout the early modern period. Vital to Scottish culture, the sacramental occasions were, in turn, prominent and influential in America as well. As an early modern festival, the Scottish sacrament reveals much about the evangelical tradition in the Old World and the New, about the long history of revivalism, about the spiritual complexity of popular devotion, about shared rituals and piety in the Atlantic world, about the pertinacity of tradition, as well as about the reform of popular religion. The bounties of this history may finally belie the warnings of these evangelicals about the bareness of historical remembrance. In the case of their own festal communions and holy fairs, history offers a rich and varied feast.

Notes

PROSPECT

1. Robert Burns, *The Poems and Songs of Robert Burns*, ed. James Kinsley, 3 vols. (Oxford: Clarendon Press, 1968), 1:128; Robert Wodrow, *The Correspondence of the Rev. Robert Wodrow, Minister of Eastwood, and Author of the History of the Sufferings of the Church of Scotland*, ed. Thomas McCrie, 3 vols. (Edinburgh: Wodrow Society, 1842–1843), 1:55.

2. Burns, *Poems and Songs*, 1:132–33.

3. John Cunningham, *The Church History of Scotland from the Commencement of the Christian Era to the Present Time*, 2d ed., 2 vols. (Edinburgh: James Thin, 1882), 2:423; Henry F. Henderson, *Religion in Scotland: Its Influence on National Life and Character* (Paisley: Alexander Gardner, [1920]), 137; Alexander Webster, *Burns and the Kirk: A Review of What the Poet Did for the Religious and Social Regeneration of the Scottish People* (Aberdeen: A. Martin, 1888), iii; George B. Burnet, *The Holy Communion in the Reformed Church of Scotland, 1560–1960* (Edinburgh: Oliver and Boyd, 1960), 253; Robert Lee, *The Reform of the Church of Scotland in Worship, Government, and Doctrine* (Edinburgh: Edmonston and Douglas, 1864), 194–96; Henry Grey Graham, *The Social Life of Scotland in the Eighteenth Century* (London, 1899; London: Black, 1928), 313. The role Burns played in the decline of these sacramental occasions is evaluated in chapter 4.

4. Graham, *Social Life of Scotland*, 302, 310, 313–14.

5. W. J. Couper, *Scottish Revivals* (Dundee: James P. Mathew and Co., 1918), 153–54; D[uncan] MacFarlan, *The Revivals of the Eighteenth Century, Particularly at Cambuslang* (London: John Johnstone, n.d.), 68. For rare secondary works, see Ian A. Muirhead, "The Revival as a Dimension of Scottish Church History," *Records of the Scottish Church History Society* 20 (1980): 179–96; John MacInnes, *The Evangelical Movement in the Highlands of Scotland, 1688 to 1800* (Aberdeen: University Press, 1951); Steve Bruce, "Social Change and Collective Behaviour: The Revival in Eighteenth-century Ross-shire," *British Journal of Sociology* 34 (1983): 554–72; Arthur Fawcett, *The Cambuslang Revival: The Scottish Evangelical Revival of the Eighteenth Century* (London: Banner of Truth, 1971). These useful works notwithstanding, Muirhead's conclusion about the study of Scottish revivalism stands: "It is an area in which very little satisfactory work has been done and not much has been attempted" (p. 179).

6. "Our Communions: Some Reflections on Them, No. I," *North Carolina Presbyterian*, 13 June 1866; Mary McWhorter Tenney, *Communion Tokens: Their Origin, History, and Use* (Grand Rapids: Zondervan, 1936), 157–64; Ernest Trice Thompson, *Presbyterians in the South*, 3 vols. (Richmond: John Knox Press, 1963–1973), 1:133–34, 226–34; Charles A. Johnson, *The Frontier Camp Meeting: Religion's Harvest Time* (Dallas: Southern Methodist University Press, 1955), 28–29; David A. Ramsey and R. Craig Koedel, "The Communion Sea-

son—An 18th Century Model," *Journal of Presbyterian History* 54 (1976): 203–16; Marilyn J. Westerkamp, *Triumph of the Laity: Scots-Irish Piety and the Great Awakening, 1625–1760* (New York: Oxford University Press, 1988), 161–62, 198, 203. Westerkamp's work does cover some of the territory that is explored in this study. Her book, though as noted, is only marginally concerned with the sacramental season. She offers relatively little interpretation of the rituals of these occasions and surprisingly, given her title, essentially excludes discussion of lay spirituality. Also the far longer time span covered in the present study is particularly critical for understanding the Catholic background of such festal gatherings as well as the eventual decline or reform of these popular festivals in the nineteenth century—aspects of this evangelical tradition that Westerkamp does not treat at all. Also Gwen Kennedy Neville makes some thoughtful points in passing on the old Scottish communions in Gwen Kennedy Neville and John H. Westerhoff, III, eds., *Learning Through Liturgy* (New York: Seabury Press, 1978), 13–18, which are reprinted in her most recent book, *Kinship and Pilgrimage: Rituals of Reunion in American Protestant Culture* (New York: Oxford University Press, 1987).

7. William G. McLoughlin, "Timepieces and Butterflies: A Note on the Great-Awakening Construct and Its Critics," in R. C. Gordon-McCutchan, ed., "Symposium on Religious Awakenings," *Sociological Analysis: A Journal in the Sociology of Religion* 44 (1983): 108. Most of those involved in this symposium side with McLoughlin's agenda, particularly the editor. See also William G. McLoughlin, *Revivals, Awakenings, and Reform: An Essay on Religion and Social Change in America, 1607–1977* (Chicago: University of Chicago Press, 1978); Richard L. Bushman, *From Puritan to Yankee: Character and Social Order in Connecticut, 1690–1765* (Cambridge, Mass.: Harvard University Press, 1967), esp. 135–232; Whitney R. Cross, *The Burned-over District: The Social and Intellectual History of Enthusiastic Religion in Western New York, 1800–1850* (Ithaca: Cornell University Press, 1950), esp. 3–109; Paul E. Johnson, *A Shopkeeper's Millennium: Society and Revivals in Rochester, New York, 1815–1837* (New York: Hill and Wang, 1978).

8. On "retrospective ethnography," see Charles Tilly, "Anthropology, History, and the *Annales*," *Review: A Journal of the Fernand Braudel Center for the Study of Economies, Historical Systems, and Civilizations* 1 (1978): 207–13. For outstanding examples of this cultural history, see Peter Burke, *The Historical Anthropology of Early Modern Italy: Essays on Perception and Communication* (Cambridge: Cambridge University Press, 1987); Robert Darnton, *The Great Cat Massacre and Other Episodes in French Cultural History* (New York: Basic, 1984), esp. 3–7, 257–63; Natalie Zemon Davis, *Society and Culture in Early Modern France: Eight Essays* (Stanford: Stanford University Press, 1975); Natalie Zemon Davis, "From 'Popular Religion' to Religious Cultures," in *Reformation Europe: A Guide to Research*, ed. Steven Ozment (St. Louis: Center for Reformation Research, 1982), esp. 325–26, 331–33; Henry Glassie, *Passing the Time in Ballymenone: Culture and History of an Ulster Community* (Philadelphia: University of Pennsylvania Press, 1982); Emmanuel Le Roy Ladurie, *Carnival in Romans*, trans. Mary Feeney (New York: Braziller, 1979); Richard C. Trexler, *Pub-*

lic Life in Renaissance Florence (New York: Academic Press, 1980); Susan G. Davis, *Parades and Power: Street Theatre in Nineteenth-Century Philadelphia* (Philadelphia: Temple University Press, 1986); and Rhys Isaac, *The Transformation of Virginia, 1740–1790* (Chapel Hill: University of North Carolina Press, 1982), esp. 323–57. For a superb exploration of ethnographic approaches to history outside Europe and America, see Greg Dening, *Islands and Beaches: Discourse on a Silent Land, Marquesas 1774–1880* (Honolulu: University Press of Hawaii, 1980). For valuable cultural anthropological counterparts of this ethnographic history, see particularly Stanley Jeyaraja Tambiah, *Culture, Thought, and Social Action: An Anthropological Perspective* (Cambridge, Mass.: Harvard University Press, 1985), esp. 123–66; John J. MacAloon, ed., *Rite, Drama, Festival, Spectacle: Rehearsals Toward a Theory of Cultural Performance* (Philadelphia: Institute for the Study of Human Issues, 1984); Victor Turner, ed., *Celebration: Studies in Festivity and Ritual* (Washington, D.C.: Smithsonian Institution Press, 1982); Clifford Geertz, *The Interpretation of Cultures* (New York: Basic, 1973), esp. 3–30, 412–53. For important sociological background, see notably Erving Goffman, *Interaction Ritual: Essays on Face-to-Face Behavior* (Garden City, N.Y.: Anchor, 1967).

9. Darnton, *Great Cat Massacre*, 3.

10. Thomas Prince, Jr., ed., *The Christian History*, 2 vols. (Boston: Kneeland and Green, 1744–1745), 2:309–10. For discussion of these issues, see Jon Butler, "The Future of American Religious History: Prospectus, Agenda, Transatlantic *Problématique*," *William and Mary Quarterly* 42 (1985): 167–83; Roger Chartier, "Intellectual History or Sociocultural History? The French Trajectories," in Dominick LaCapra and Steven L. Kaplan, eds., *Modern European Intellectual History: Reappraisals and New Perspectives* (Ithaca: Cornell University Press, 1982), esp. 22–32; Charles E. Hambrick-Stowe, *The Practice of Piety: Puritan Devotional Disciplines in Seventeenth-Century New England* (Chapel Hill: University of North Carolina Press, 1982); Carlo Ginzburg, *The Cheese and the Worms: The Cosmos of a Sixteenth-Century Miller*, trans. John and Anne Tedeschi (Baltimore: Johns Hopkins University Press, 1980), xiii–xxvi; George Selement, "The Meeting of Elite and Popular Minds at Cambridge, New England, 1638–1645," *William and Mary Quarterly* 41 (1984): 32–48; David D. Hall, "Toward a History of Popular Religion in Early New England," ibid., 49–55; William A. Christian, Jr., *Local Religion in Sixteenth-Century Spain* (Princeton: Princeton University Press, 1981); David Clark, *Between Pulpit and Pew: Folk Religion in a North Yorkshire Fishing Village* (Cambridge: Cambridge University Press, 1982); Barry Reay, "Popular Religion," in Barry Reay, ed., *Popular Culture in Seventeenth-Century England* (New York: St. Martin's Press, 1985), 91–128; James Obelkevich, ed., *Religion and the People, 800–1700* (Chapel Hill: University of North Carolina Press, 1979).

11. George Wemyss, "The Preface to the Reader," in John Spalding, *Synaxis Sacra; Or, A Collection of Sermons Preached at Several Communions; Together with Speeches at the Tables, both before, at, and after that Work* (Edinburgh: Andrew Anderson, 1703), preface unpaginated. The problem over diachronic and synchronic modes of historical interpretation is, of course, of long standing.

Within the field of American religious history, a classic juxtaposition of the perspectives comes in Perry Miller's two tomes, *The New England Mind: The Seventeenth Century* (Cambridge, Mass.: Harvard University Press, 1954) and *The New England Mind: From Colony to Province* (Cambridge, Mass.: Harvard University Press, 1953). Recently the problem has come increasingly to the fore in ethnography—a field in which synchronic studies have often held sway. See Renato Rosaldo, *Ilongot Headhunting, 1883–1974: A Study in Society and History* (Stanford: Stanford University Press, 1980), esp. 1–28.

12. For McGready, see *Western Missionary Magazine* 1 (1803): 174; for the other report, that of Rev. Thomas Robbins, see *Connecticut Evangelical Magazine* 4 (1803–1804): 314, 316. See also *New York Missionary Magazine* 3 (1802): 121, 310–12.

CHAPTER 1

1. *Western Missionary Magazine* 1 (1803): 173, 177.

2. William Croft Dickinson, ed., *John Knox's History of the Reformation in Scotland*, 2 vols. (London: Nelson and Sons, 1949), 2:141–42; *Calendar of Scottish Papers*, 13 vols. (Edinburgh: H. M. General Register House, 1898–1969), 2:149. This story is narrated in book 5 of Knox's history which was most likely not written by Knox himself. See Dickinson's "Bibliographical Note" for a critical discussion of authorship.

3. Dickinson, ed., *Knox's History*, 2:12, 48. See also 1:87, 120–21. For Catholic uses of eggs at Easter and for Protestant suspicions of these folk customs, see Venetia Newall, *An Egg at Easter: A Folklore Study* (London: Routledge and Kegan Paul, 1971), esp. 177–206.

4. For a broad discussion of the age of Reformation in Scotland, see Ian B. Cowan, *The Scottish Reformation: Church and Society in Sixteenth Century Scotland* (London: Weidenfeld and Nicolson, 1982). Also Gordon Donaldson's *Scottish Reformation* (Cambridge: Cambridge University Press, 1960) is especially useful for the debates on episcopacy and church government, though his work should be weighed alongside that of James Kirk, " 'The Polities of the Best Reformed Kirks': Scottish Achievements and English Aspirations in Church Government after the Reformation," *Scottish Historical Review* 59 (1980): 22–53. Kirk also valuably supplements the straight political reading of the Scottish Reformation in emphasizing the growing religious attachment to the Protestant cause before 1560. See his "The 'Privy Kirks' and Their Antecedents: The Hidden Face of Scottish Protestantism," in W. J. Sheils and Diana Wood, eds., *Voluntary Religion* (Oxford: Basil Blackwell, 1986), 155–70. The essential secondary source for Catholicism in this era in Scotland is David McRoberts, ed., *Essays on the Scottish Reformation, 1513–1625* (Glasgow: Burns, 1962), while the standard general work for this and subsequent periods remains T. C. Smout, *A History of the Scottish People, 1560–1830* (London: William Collins Sons and Co., 1969). For a recent and highly useful bibliographical essay on this period, see James Kirk, "The Scottish Reformation and Reign of James VI: A Select Critical Bibliography," *Records of the Scottish Church History Society* 23 (1987): 113–55. For a good collection of essays surveying the history of Scottish worship, see Duncan B.

Forrester and Douglas M. Murray, eds., *Studies in the History of Worship in Scotland* (Edinburgh: Clark, 1984).

5. James K. Cameron, ed., *The First Book of Discipline* (Edinburgh: St. Andrew Press, 1972), 204; *Confession of Faith*, in Dickinson, ed., *Knox's History*, 2:268–70; George Hay, *The Confutation of the Abbote of Crosraquels Masse* (Edinburgh: Robert Lekpreuik, 1563), 15v. For a comparison of Scottish eucharistic thought and practice with other traditions, see Yngve Brilioth, *Eucharistic Faith and Practice: Evangelical and Catholic*, trans. A. G. Herbert (London: S.P.C.K., 1956), 186–93. For one of the most cogent (as well as concise) discussions of Reformed eucharistic thought, see B. A. Gerrish, *The Old Protestantism and the New: Essays on the Reformation Heritage* (Chicago: University of Chicago Press, 1982), 106–30.

6. *Confession of Faith*, in Dickinson, ed., *Knox's History*, 2:270. For a broad discussion of such liturgical differences and symbols, especially as evidenced in early and medieval Christianity, see Philippe Rouillard, "From Human Meal to Christian Eucharist," *Worship* 53 (1979): esp. 45–54.

7. Originally the reformers had envisioned monthly communions, but soon settled for quarterly, semiannual, or even annual celebrations. On the frequency debate, see the section in chapter 4 on "Frequency versus Festivity."

8. Cameron, ed., *Book of Discipline*, 88, 204; Hay, *Confutation*, 43v. On the eucharistic piety and ritual of medieval Catholicism, see Dennis Steel Devlin, "Corpus Christi: A Study in Medieval Eucharistic Theory, Devotion, and Practice" (Ph.D. diss., University of Chicago, 1975). For a highly useful discussion of such devotion in medieval Scotland, see David McRoberts, "Scottish Sacrament Houses," *Transactions of the Scottish Ecclesiological Society* 15 (1965): 33–56.

9. David Calderwood, *The History of the Kirk of Scotland*, ed. Thomas Thomson, 8 vols. (Edinburgh: Wodrow Society, 1842–1849), 3:593; 4:656–66. See also 3:351–53, 357, 503–4. Calderwood (1575–1650) compiled his history from innumerable documents, many of which are among the best sources for the religious life of post-Reformation Scotland. See as well *Acts and Proceedings of the General Assemblies of the Kirk of Scotland, from the Year MDLX, Collected from the Most Authentic Manuscripts*, 3 vols. (Edinburgh: Bannatyne Club, 1839), 2:715–23. Of note in the secondary literature is W. McMillan, "Festivals and Saints Days After the Reformation," *Records of the Scottish Church History Society* 3 (1929): 1–21.

10. "Extracts from the Kirk-Session Register of Perth, 1577–1634" in James Maidment, ed., *The Spottiswoode Miscellany: A Collection of Original Papers and Tracts Illustrative of the Civil and Ecclesiastical History of Scotland*, 2 vols. (Edinburgh: Spottiswoode Society, 1845), 2:233–34, 264, 268, 275, 313–14.

11. Charles Phythian-Adams, "Ceremony and the Citizen: The Communal Year at Coventry, 1450–1550," in Peter Clark and Paul Slack, eds., *Crisis and Order in English Towns, 1500–1700: Essays in Urban History* (London: Routledge and Kegan Paul, 1972), 78–80. On the different liturgical rhythms and calendars, see also Horton Davies, *Worship and Theology in England*, 5 vols. (Princeton: Princeton University Press, 1961–1975), 2:215–52; Natalie Zemon

Davis, "The Sacred and the Body Social in Sixteenth-Century Lyon," *Past and Present* 90 (1981): 60–62.

12. Archibald Simsone, *A True Record of the Life and Death of Master Patrick Simsone*, in W. K. Tweedie, ed., *Select Biographies*, 2 vols. (Edinburgh: Wodrow Society, 1845–1847), 1:97.

13. Steven Ozment, *The Age of Reform, 1250–1550: An Intellectual and Religious History of Late Medieval and Reformation Europe* (New Haven: Yale University Press, 1980), 436–38.

14. French sociologist Roger Caillois quoted in Peter Burke, *Popular Culture in Early Modern Europe* (New York: Harper and Row, 1978), 179.

15. John Bossy, *Christianity in the West, 1400–1700* (Oxford: Oxford University Press, 1985), 140–41. See also Bossy, "The Mass as a Social Institution 1200–1700," *Past and Present* 100 (1983): 29–61; Mervyn James, "Ritual, Drama and Social Body in the Late Medieval English Town," *Past and Present* 98 (1983): 3–29. James offers an impressive social and structural analysis of Corpus Christi as well as keen insight into the decline of the "folk festivals" of medieval Catholicism and the subsequent "privatization" of religion thereafter.

16. [Alexander Barclay], *In the Honor of ye Passion of our Lorde* (London: Robert Copland, 1522); [Alexander Barclay], *The Doctrynall of Mekenesse with Other Devout and Goodly Prayers* (London: Robert Copland, 1529); Daniel Campbell, *Sacramental Meditations on the Sufferings and Death of Christ*, 4th ed. (Edinburgh: Anderson, 1703); Daniel Campbell, *The Frequent and Devout Communicant, or A Treatise Concerning the Sacrament of the Lord's Supper* (Edinburgh: Anderson, 1703). The prominence of the Virgin in Barclay's texts and her absence in Campbell's reminds us again of discontinuity amid continuity. For valuable discussion of the issue of continuities, see William McMillan, "Medieval Survivals in Scottish Worship," *Church Service Society Annual* 4 (1931–1932): 21–34. For more on the Presbyterian devotional tradition, see chapter 3.

17. H. J. Schroeder, ed., *Canons and Decrees of the Council of Trent* (St. Louis: B. Herder Book Co., 1941), 80; Cameron, ed., *Book of Discipline*, 183; John Sage, *The Fundamental Charter of Presbytery, as It Hath Been Lately Established, in the Kingdom of Scotland, Examin'd and Disprov'd* (London: C. Brome, 1695), 372. The focus in the scholarly literature has been on the Presbyterians as dour Sabbatarian levellers and destroyers of "the old pattern of commemoration, festival and fast that made the Christian year" with far less appreciation of the eventual evangelical capacity for festivity. See, for example, Rosalind Mitchison, *Life in Scotland* (London: B. T. Batsford, 1978), with quotation on p. 34.

18. Robert Heron, *A Memoir of the Life of the Late Robert Burns* (Edinburgh: T. Brown, 1797), 13; *A Letter from a Blacksmith to the Ministers and Elders of the Church of Scotland in which the Manner of Public Worship in that Church is Considered; Its Inconveniences and Defects Pointed Out; and Methods for Removing of Them Humbly Proposed* (London, 1759; New Haven: Oliver Steele, 1814), 20.

19. John Livingston, *A Brief Historical Relation of the Life of Mr. John Livingston Minister of the Gospel* (n.p.: n.p., 1727), 8–9; William Cunningham, ed., *Sermons by the Rev. Robert Bruce, Minister of Edinburgh. Reprinted from the*

Original Edition of M.D.XC. and M.D.XCI. with Collections for his Life, by the Rev. Robert Wodrow, Minister in Eastwood (Edinburgh: Wodrow Society, 1843), 140; Robert Fleming, *The Fulfilling of the Scripture* (Rotterdam, 1669; Boston: Rogers and Fowle, 1743), 394; Robert Wodrow, *Analecta: Or, Materials for a History of Remarkable Providences; Mostly Relating to Scotch Ministers and Christians*, 4 vols. (Edinburgh: Maitland Club, 1842–1843), 1:271; James Robe, *Narratives of the Extraordinary Work of the Spirit of God, at Cambuslang, Kilsyth, &c. Begun 1742* (Glasgow: David Niven, 1790), 217–18.

20. For the traditional line on the beginnings of these events see, for example, George W. Sprott, *The Worship and Offices of the Church of Scotland* (Edinburgh: Blackwood and Sons, 1882), 104–5; Thomas Burns, *Old Scottish Communion Plate* (Edinburgh: R. and R. Clark, 1892), 37–38; William McMillan, *The Worship of the Scottish Reformed Church, 1550–1638* (London: Clarke, [1931]), 196–97, 228–29; George B. Burnet, *The Holy Communion in the Reformed Church of Scotland, 1560–1960* (Edinburgh: Oliver and Boyd, 1960), 125–27. The last goes so far as to claim that the Shotts revival was "an entirely isolated and unexpected event" and that "there was no attempt to repeat the Shotts technique for twenty years" (p. 126). A fuller account of Shotts can be found in W. J. Couper, *Scottish Revivals* (Dundee: James P. Mathew and Co., 1918), 33–39. The best in a long line of evangelical histories, Couper's book has been rarely noticed in the historiography, as much because of its scarcity as its shortcomings; only thirty-seven copies were printed.

21. For background on Episcopal and Presbyterian conflict, see Kirk, " 'The Polities of the Best Reformed Kirks' "; George I. R. McMahon, "The Scottish Courts of High Commission, 1610–1638," *Records of the Scottish Church History Society* 15 (1966): 193–209; David Stevenson, "Conventicles in the Kirk, 1619–1637: The Emergence of a Radical Party," *Records of the Scottish Church History Society* 18 (1974): 99–114; William Roland Foster, *The Church before the Covenants: The Church of Scotland, 1596–1638* (Edinburgh: Scottish Academic Press, 1975). For a still standard survey of the religious history of seventeenth-century Scotland, see G. D. Henderson, *Religious Life in Seventeenth-Century Scotland* (Cambridge: Cambridge University Press, 1937).

22. James Kirkton, *The Secret and True History of the Church of Scotland, from the Restoration to the Year 1678*, ed. Charles Kirkpatrick Sharpe (Edinburgh: Bannatyne Club, 1817), 26; Livingston, *Brief Historical Relation*, 10; Cunningham, ed., *Collections for his Life*, 15–16, 140, 145; Robert Bruce, *Sermons upon the Sacrament of the Lords Supper* (Edinburgh: Robert Walde-grave, 1590), sermon 1, unpaginated. Besides his great preaching, Bruce's gifts were reputed to include healing and prophetic powers. See Fleming, *Fulfilling of the Scripture*, 407–8.

23. Cunningham, ed., *Collections for his Life*, 123–28, 130–34, 140–41. See also Calderwood, *History*, 6:291; 7:545.

24. [James Kirkton], *The History of Mr. John Welsh, Minister of the Gospel at Ayr*, in Tweedie, ed., *Select Biographies*, 1:4–6; Robert Wodrow, *A Short Account of the Life of the Rev. David Dickson*, also in Tweedie, ed., *Select Biographies*, 2:7–8; Livingston, *Brief Historical Relation*, 10; Robert Rollock, *Select*

Works of Robert Rollock, Principal of the University of Edinburgh, ed. William M. Gunn, 2 vols. (Edinburgh: Wodrow Society, 1844), 2:13–329.

25. It is perhaps noteworthy that already in the 1540s the itinerant George Wishart had laid claim to the fields and churchyards, reportedly pronouncing that "Christ Jesus is as mightie upon the feilds as in the church." Perhaps later leaders, such as John Livingston, were tapping into a still larger popular preaching tradition within folk Christianity of taking the gospel to the fields. On Wishart's evangelistic activities, see Calderwood, *History*, 1:188.

26. Livingston, *Brief Historical Relation*, 4–5; Fleming, *Fulfilling of the Scripture*, 407. On William Livingston, see *The Register of the Privy Council of Scotland, 1545–1625*, 14 vols. (Edinburgh: H. M. General Register House, 1877–1898), 7:541; 8:2n. William Livingston's troubles with the powers that be began from his first years as a preacher in the late 1590s. See Glasgow Presbytery Records, Strathclyde Regional Archives, the Mitchell Library, Glasgow, 32:139, 151. For a suggestion of large eucharistic gatherings already in about 1610 in Burntisland, see Andrew Edgar, *Old Church Life in Scotland: Lectures on Kirk-Session and Presbytery Records*, 2 vols. (Paisley: Alexander Gardner, 1885–1887), 2:379n.

27. Calderwood, *History*, 7:196.

28. The Articles of Perth are reprinted in several sources. I have used the copy in *Original Letters Relating to the Ecclesiastical Affairs of Scotland, Chiefly Written by, or Addressed to, His Majesty King James the Sixth, After his Accession to the English Throne*, 2 vols. (Edinburgh: Bannatyne Club, 1851), 2:658–60. On the articles, see P. H. R. MacKay, "The Reception Given to the Five Articles of Perth," *Records of the Scottish Church History Society* 19 (1977): 185–201; Ian B. Cowan, "The Five Articles of Perth," in Duncan Shaw, ed., *Reformation and Revolution* (Edinburgh: St. Andrew Press, 1967), 160–77.

29. David Calderwood, *A Dispute upon Communicating at Our Confused Communions* (n.p.: n.p., 1624), 29, 70; David Calderwood, *An Exhortation of the Particular Kirks of Christ in Scotland to their Sister Kirk in Edinburgh* (n.p.: n.p., 1624), 10, 12; David Calderwood, *An Epistle of a Christian Brother Exhorting an Other to Keepe Himselfe Undefiled from the Present Corruptions Brought in to the Ministration of the Lords Supper* (n.p.: n.p., 1624), 7–9. For a defense of kneeling, see John Michaelson, *The Lawfulnes of Kneeling, in the Act of Receiving the Sacrament of the Lordes Supper* (St. Andrews: Edward Raban, 1620).

30. John Spottiswoode, *The History of the Church of Scotland, Beginning the Year of our Lord 203, and Continued to the End of the Reign of King James the VI*, 3 vols. (London, 1665; Edinburgh: Oliver and Boyd, 1851), 3:257, 268; Calderwood, *History*, 7:359, 380, 457; Livingston, *Brief Historical Relation*, 5.

31. Calderwood, *Dispute*, 68, 71; Calderwood, *History*, 7:359–60; Calderwood, *Epistle*, 7.

32. Kirkton, *Secret and True History*, 16, 18–19; Thomas McCrie, ed., *The Life of Mr Robert Blair, Minister of St. Andrews, Containing His Autobiography, from 1593 to 1636, with Supplement to his Life, and Continuation of the History of the Times to 1680, by his Son-in-Law, Mr William Row, Minister of Ceres*

(Edinburgh: Wodrow Society, 1848), 19, 50; Fleming, *Fulfilling of the Scripture*, 393–94.

33. Wodrow, *Short Account*, 7; David Dickson, *Select Practical Writings* (Edinburgh: John Grieg, 1845), li, 76–197, esp. 83, 85, 92–95, 133, 150, 157, 167; Samuel Rutherford, *Letters of Samuel Rutherford*, ed. Andrew A. Bonar (Edinburgh: Oliphant, Anderson, and Ferrier, 1891), 58–59, 66–67, 69, 95, 113–14, 124, 128; Samuel Rutherford, *Fourteen Communion Sermons*, ed. Andrew A. Bonar (Glasgow: Charles Glass and Co., 1877). Many of Rutherford's communion sermons were preached in the early 1630s at Kirkcudbright, a parish that had been the locus of much of John Welsh's work. Dickson's sacramental sermons, published from a manuscript dated 1635, are helpful for understanding the revivals at Irvine. These sermons suggest a form still in flux. The Saturday and Monday services, for example, were already clearly evident, but also the waning practice of celebrating the communion over two successive Sabbaths was still apparent. The sermons indicate as well that a day of "Humiliation" and fasting before the communion may have already been known among the radicals at this early date (pp. 76–89).

34. Livingston, *Brief Historical Relation*, 6–9.

35. McCrie, ed., *Life of Blair*, 58.

36. Ibid., 70; Andrew Stewart, *The History of the Church in Ireland since the Scots Were Naturalized*, in Patrick Adair, *A True Narrative of the Rise and Progress of the Presbyterian Church in Ireland*, ed. W. D. Killen (Belfast: Aitchison, 1866), 317. Both the work of Adair and of Stewart are seventeenth-century manuscript histories that found publication only in the nineteenth century. For a recent treatment of the Ulster revivals, see Marilyn J. Westerkamp, *Triumph of the Laity: Scots-Irish Piety and the Great Awakening, 1625–1760* (New York: Oxford University Press, 1988), 15–42.

37. McCrie, ed., *Life of Blair*, 70–74; Stewart, *History*, 316.

38. Adair, *True Narrative*, 12; McCrie, ed., *Life of Blair*, 84–86, 89–90, 119–21. For a good compilation of materials on communions in Ulster, see John M. Barkley, "The Evidence of Old Irish Session-Books on the Sacrament of the Lord's Supper," *Church Service Society Annual* 22 (1952): 24–34.

39. McCrie, ed., *Life of Blair*, 86, 131, 148, 156, 167; Livingston, *Brief Historical Relation*, 12–14, 23, 28; Robert Stevenson, *The Communion and Some Other Matters in Dunfermline, in the Seventeenth Century* (Dunfermline: A. Romanes, 1900), 19.

40. Livingston, *Brief Historical Relation*, 13; McCrie, ed., *Life of Blair*, 90; *The Register of the Privy Council of Scotland, 1625–1660*, 2d series, 8 vols. (Edinburgh: H. M. General Register House, 1899–1908), 5:421–22.

41. Gilbert Burnet, *Bishop Burnet's History of His Own Time*, 2 vols. (London: Thomas Ward and Joseph Downing, 1724–1734), 1:63–64.

42. Burnet, *Holy Communion*, 127.

43. Robert Baillie, *The Letters and Journals of Robert Baillie, A.M.*, 3 vols. (Edinburgh: Bannatyne Club, 1841–1842), 2:195, 204. See also Burnet, *Holy Communion*, 105–11.

44. See *A Directory for the Publique Worship of God, throughout the Three*

Kingdoms of England, Scotland, and Ireland (London: Evan Tyler, Alexander Fifield, Ralph Smith, and John Field, 1644), 48–56; *Acts of the General Assembly of the Church of Scotland, M.DC.XXXVIII–M.DCCC.XLII* (Edinburgh: Edinburgh Printing and Publishing Co., 1843), 120–21. On the issues of popular versus official religion, see the first three sections of chapter 4.

45. Livingston, *Brief Historical Relation*, 28, 42; McCrie, ed., *Life of Blair*, 166–67; William Muir, *Memoir and Letters of the Rev. William Guthrie, Author of "The Christian's Great Interest"* (Edinburgh: Oliphant, 1827), 17–18, 41–43; Baillie, *Letters and Journals*, 3:48–49, 53.

46. Livingston, *Brief Historical Relation*, 41; Archibald Johnston, *Diary of Sir Archibald Johnston of Wariston, 1650–1654*, ed. David Hay Fleming (Edinburgh: Scottish History Society, 1919), 95, 194–95, 236–39, 279, 294–99, 312–13; [William A. Clarke], *Memoirs of the Life of Mr. Thomas Hog, Minister of the Gospel at Kiltearn, in Ross* (Edinburgh: Stevenson, 1756), 43; Kirkton, *Secret and True History*, 54–55. See also John Lamont, *The Diary of Mr. John Lamont of Newton, 1649–1671* (Edinburgh: Maitland Club, 1830), 15, 31–32, 38–39, 42, 55, 77, 99–100, 117–18, 125; Andrew Hay, *The Diary of Andrew Hay of Craignethan, 1659–1660*, ed. Alexander George Reid (Edinburgh: Scottish History Society, 1901), 29–32, 34–38, 78–84, 103–8. For a sampling of sermons preached at these communions in the 1650s, see "A Collection of Twelve Seventeenth-Century Sermons ca. 1655," National Library of Scotland manuscripts, 90–202.

47. [James Wood], *A True Representation of the Rise, Progresse, and State of the Present Divisions of the Church of Scotland* (London: n.p., 1657), 2, 35–36; Baillie, *Letters and Journals*, 3:220, 245.

48. McCrie, ed., *Life of Blair*, 322–23. See also Burnet, *Bishop Burnet's History*, 64.

49. See, for example, Smout, *History*, 68–69; Burnet, *Holy Communion*, 135–37.

50. McCrie, ed., *Life of Blair*, 559, 561; John Howie, ed., *A Collection of Lectures and Sermons, Preached upon Several Subjects, Mostly in the Time of the Persecution* (Kilmarnock: Crawford, 1809), 538. See also Burnet, *Holy Communion*, 147–56. For a valuable general treatment of the Covenanters in this period, see Ian B. Cowan, *The Scottish Covenanters, 1660–1688* (London: Gollancz, 1976).

51. John Blackader, "Mr. Blacader's Memoirs," Wodrow manuscripts, National Library of Scotland, 21v, 22r, 25v, 40r, 40v, 63v, 68v, 69r, 77r, 79r, 79v. For Blackader, historians have usually relied on Andrew Crichton, *Memoirs of Rev. John Blackader; Compiled Chiefly from Unpublished Manuscripts, and Memoirs of his Life and Ministry Written by Himself While Prisoner on the Bass*, 2d ed. (Edinburgh: Tait, 1826). Crichton's editing of Blackader's memoirs is often unreliable, however. He freely abridges, amends, and augments Blackader's own language.

52. Ibid., 77r–82v.

53. Ibid., 88r–91v. See also Gabriel Semple, "Autobiography," National Library of Scotland manuscripts, 22–23, 52–54; [Clarke], *Memoirs of Hog*, 44–45;

Kirkton, *Secret and True History*, 343, 379–80; James Wodrow, "Sermons Preached by the Rev. James Wodrow at Conventicles at Mauchline and Kilmarnock, 1674," National Library of Scotland manuscripts, 20.

54. Ibid., 93v–94r. This means attendance at this sacrament must have been estimated as being in excess of eight thousand people, for not many pages earlier in his "Memoirs" Blackader had spoken of a meeting with "8000 people present" (p. 72r).

55. Ibid., 103r.

56. James McGready, *The Posthumous Works of the Reverend and Pious James M'Gready, Late Minister of the Gospel in Henderson, K[entuck]y*, ed. James Smith (Nashville: J. Smith's Steam Press, 1837), 317.

57. John Willison, "Five Sacramental Sermons," in W. M. Hetherington, ed., *The Practical Works of the Rev. John Willison* (Glasgow: Blackie and Son, [1844]), 326. Even as distant a New England cousin as Harriet Beecher Stowe marvelled at the endurance of the Covenanters. In a tour of Scotland she visited the studio of the Scottish artist George Harvey. "I saw there," she related, "his Covenanters celebrating the Lord's Supper—a picture which I could not look at critically on account of the tears which kept blinding my eyes." Harvey's painting depicted "a bleak hollow of a mountain side" where a band of "hunted fugitives nestle themselves beneath the shadow of their Redeemer; . . . all gathering for comfort around the cross of a suffering Lord." See Harriet Beecher Stowe, *Sunny Memories of Foreign Lands*, 2 vols. (Boston: Phillips, Sampson, and Co., 1854), 1:186–87. The painting, now in the National Gallery of Scotland, is another evidence of the hallowing of the Covenanters' communions.

58. William McCulloch, "An Account of the Second Sacrament at Cambuslang," in Robe, *Narratives of the Extraordinary Work*, 33–38.

59. John Scot, "Memoir, 1729–1803," Strathclyde Regional Archives manuscripts, Mitchell Library, Glasgow, 4.

60. Robe, *Narratives of the Extraordinary Work*, 140–45.

61. Ibid., 61–62; William McCulloch, "Examinations of Persons Under Spiritual Concern at Cambuslang During the Revival in 1741–42," 2 vols., Edinburgh University manuscripts, New College Library. For more on the McCulloch materials see especially chapter 3. McCulloch and Robe also both published a number of sermons, many of which were sacramental ones. See William McCulloch, *Sermons on Several Subjects* (Glasgow: David Niven, 1793); James Robe, *Counsels and Comforts to Troubled Christians, in Eight Sermons* (Glasgow: John Robertson, 1749); James Robe, *A Second Volume of Sermons in Three Parts, for the Most Part Preached at the Celebration of the Lord's Supper* (Edinburgh: R. Fleming, 1750); James Robe, *A Third Volume of Sermons for the Most Part Preached at the Celebration of the Lord's Supper* (Glasgow: J. Bryce and D. Paterson, 1756).

62. John Willison, *A Sacramental Catechism: Or, A Familiar Instructor for Young Communicants* (Edinburgh, 1720; Edinburgh: Samuel Willison and Co., 1756), xiii; John Anderson, *A Defence of the Church-Government, Faith, Worship & Spirit of the Presbyterians* (Glasgow: Hugh Brown, 1714), 280.

63. Sage, *Fundamental Charter*, 370–71, 373; Clydesdale Synod Records, 6

April 1697, 4 October 1705, Scottish Record Office, Edinburgh, 1:170; 2:48. See also Thomas Rhind, *An Apology for Mr Thomas Rhind* (Edinburgh: Robert Freebairn, 1712), 182–85.

64. Thomas Boston, *A General Account of My Life*, ed. George C. Low (London: Hodder and Stoughton, 1908), 46; Robert Paul, ed., "The Diary of the Rev. George Turnbull, Minister of Alloa and Tyninghame, 1657–1704," in *Miscellany of the Scottish History Society, Publications of the Scottish History Society* 15 (1893): 328, 335, 354, 362, 364, 368–69, 372–73, 403–4, 419–22, 444; Robert Wodrow, *The Correspondence of the Rev. Robert Wodrow, Minister of Eastwood, and Author of the History of the Sufferings of the Church of Scotland*, ed. Thomas McCrie, 3 vols. (Edinburgh: Wodrow Society, 1842–1843), 1:30, 46, 55, 165; 2:294; 3:74–75, 452; Wodrow, *Analecta*, 1:20–21, 178; 4:4.

65. George Wemyss, "The Preface to the Reader," in John Spalding, *Synaxis Sacra; Or, A Collection of Sermons Preached at Several Communions; Together with Speeches at the Tables, both before, at, and after that Work* (Edinburgh: Andrew Anderson, 1703), preface unpaginated; *Dan; An Adder in the Path: Or, Issachar Couching under a Burden. Containing, Some Considerations upon the New Scheme of Communions Introduced in the Presbytery of Edinburgh* (Edinburgh: n.p., 1720), 21; *Dan in Beersheba: Or, The Idolatry of Communion Sermons, in a Few Reflections on that Pamphlet, Dan an Adder in the Path, &c.* (Edinburgh: William Brown and Co., 1721), 8.

66. A good study of Scottish Presbyterian piety has not appeared, though Adam Philip's *Devotional Literature of Scotland* (London: Clarke, 1922) makes an attempt. This devotional tradition is accorded further attention in chapter 3.

67. For the estimation of Willison's popularity, see Henry Grey Graham, *The Social Life of Scotland in the Eighteenth Century* (London, 1899; London: Black, 1928), 318–19. For a sample of Willison's influence, see McCulloch, "Examinations," 1:485, 489, 546; 2:639, 661; Hetherington, ed., *Practical Works of Willison*, vii. For his influence on the American side, see, for example, John Barr, *Early Religious History of John Barr, Written by Himself, and Left as a Legacy to his Grand-children* (Philadelphia: Presbyterian Board of Publication, 1852), 23–24, 35; James W. Alexander, *The Life of Archibald Alexander, D.D.* (New York: Charles Scribner, 1854), 49. See as well the various American printings of several of Willison's works. There had been, for example, at least eight American editions of his *Sacramental Meditations* to 1821 and ten American editions of his *Young Communicant's Catechism* to 1839. For rare recognitions of Willison in the secondary literature, see Henry F. Henderson, *Religion in Scotland: Its Influence on National Life and Character* (Paisley: Alexander Gardner, [1920]), 219–25; Stephen Albert Woodruff, III, "The Pastoral Ministry in the Church of Scotland in the Eighteenth Century, with Special Reference to Thomas Boston, John Willison and John Erskine" (Ph.D. diss., University of Edinburgh, 1965).

68. Mary Somervel, *A Clear and Remarkable Display of the Condescension, Love and Faithfulness of God, in the Spiritual Experiences of Mary Somervel* (Glasgow: George Caldwell, 1782), 8–13, 25–30, with quotation on p. 27; Elizabeth Cairns, *Memoirs of the Life of Elizabeth Cairns, Written by Herself Some Years before Her Death; and Now Taken from Her Own Original Copy with*

Great Care and Diligence (Glasgow: John Greig, n.d.), 19–23, 36–37, 100–102, 111–12, 127–30, 140–52, 193–99, 203, 211–12, with quotations on p. 129. See also John Ronald, *The Reality and Efficacy of the Work of the Spirit of God, Manifested in the Experiences of John Ronald, Late Lorimer in Edinburgh* (Edinburgh: John Gray and Gavin Alston, 1767); Margaret Bruce, *Spiritual Earnestness; As It Was Manifested in the Life and Experience of Margaret Bruce, a Scottish Peasant Girl* (London: Nisbet and Co., 1855); "Jonet Pollock's Diary" in Wodrow, *Analecta*, 1:78–81. See the full discussion of lay piety in chapter 3.

69. Elisabeth West, *Memoirs, Or Spiritual Exercises of Elisabeth West: Written by her Own Hand* (Edinburgh: Ogle and Aikman, 1807), 34–35, 45–46, 51–56, 65–76, 90–91, 108–9, 112–19, 126–28, 135–40, 151–53, 159–61, 169–70, 185–86, 197–99, with quotations on pp. 69–71, 136.

70. Elizabeth Blakader, "A Short Account of the Lords Way of Providence towards me in my Pilgrimage Journeys," National Library of Scotland manuscripts, 9v–11r, 23v.

71. Ibid., 7r–7v, 14v–15v, 19r–20r, 23v.

72. Wodrow, *Analecta*, 2:284; 4:67; Wodrow, *Correspondence*, 1:55–59.

73. Donald Fraser, *The Life and Diary of the Reverend Ralph Erskine, A. M. of Dunfermline* (Edinburgh: William Oliphant and Son, 1834), 57–58, 232–33; Scot, "Memoir," 5–10, 13–14. For revivals after 1750, mostly in the early nineteenth century, and often still connected with sacramental occasions, see Couper, *Scottish Revivals*, 88–129.

74. West, *Memoirs*, 70–71; Ronald, *Reality and Efficacy*, 27.

75. Blakader, "Short Account," 7v, 19r.

76. Livingston, *Brief Historical Relation*, 15, 18–20; McCrie, ed., *Life of Blair*, 104–8, 145.

77. For a recent assessment of the colonization of Ulster, see Raymond Gillespie, *Colonial Ulster: The Settlement of East Ulster, 1600–1641* (Cork: Cork University Press, 1985).

78. Here I am following George Pratt Insh's general discussion of Scottish efforts at colonization in *Scottish Colonial Schemes, 1620–1686* (Glasgow: Maclehouse, Jackson and Co., 1922). An excellent study of the Scottish colonization of East Jersey is to be found in Ned C. Landsman, *Scotland and Its First American Colony, 1683–1765* (Princeton: Princeton University Press, 1985). Landsman carefully considers the social, religious, and ethnic contours of Scottish settlement in that region.

79. [Francis Borland], *Memoirs of Darien Giving a Short Description of that Countrey, with an Account of the Attempts of the Company of Scotland, to Settle a Colonie in that Place* (Glasgow: Hugh Brown, 1715), 11–14, 34, 38, 51–52, 56, 93. See also Francis Borland, "Memorialle of My Pilgrimage and the Providences of Ye Lord Toward Me in All My Charges to this Day," Edinburgh University Library manuscripts.

80. For standard accounts of this exodus, see R. J. Dickson, *Ulster Emigration to Colonial America, 1718–1775* (London: Routledge and Kegan Paul, 1966); Ian Charles Cargill Graham, *Colonists from Scotland: Emigration to North America, 1707–1783* (Ithaca: Cornell University Press, 1956). For more recent

and far-ranging works in the field, see, for example, Landsman, *Scotland and Its First American Colony*; Kerby A. Miller, *Emigrants and Exiles: Ireland and the Irish Exodus to North America* (New York: Oxford University Press, 1985); J. M. Bumsted, *The People's Clearance: Highland Emigration to British North America, 1770–1815* (Edinburgh: Edinburgh University Press, 1982); Bernard Bailyn (with the assistance of Barbara DeWolfe), *Voyagers to the West: A Passage in the Peopling of America on the Eve of the Revolution* (New York: Alfred A. Knopf, 1986).

81. See Landsman, *Scotland and Its First American Colony*, 3–5, 227–55.

82. The still standard account of the development of colonial Presbyterianism is Leonard J. Trinterud, *The Forming of an American Tradition: A Re-examination of Colonial Presbyterianism* (Philadelphia: Westminster Press, 1949). Trinterud makes little mention of the communions and emphasizes how "frontier conditions" caused "all the old traditions, mores, conventions, and customs of the homeland" to be "sloughed off" (pp. 36–37). *Pace* this older frontier school, the persistence of Old World traditions was quite pronounced.

83. A narrative of the sacramental occasions in New Hampshire can be found in Edward L. Parker, *The History of Londonderry, Comprising the Towns of Derry and Londonderry, N. H.* (Boston: Perkins and Whipple, 1851), 130–31, 142–46. Parker's numbers were garnered from church records that apparently are no longer extant. Evidence of the continuing power of these events in these Presbyterian settlements is sprinkled throughout Parker's volume. See pp. 136, 156–57, 164, 176–77, 201. For a sacramental sermon of one of Londonderry's pastors, see David McGregore, *The True Believer's All Secured* (Boston: Kneeland and Green, 1747). On Booth Bay, see Thomas C. Pears, Jr., ed., "Sessional Records of the Presbyterian Church of Booth Bay, Maine, 1767–1778," *Journal of the Presbyterian Historical Society* 16 (1935): 314–15.

84. Thomas Prince, Jr., ed., *The Christian History*, 2 vols. (Boston: Kneeland and Green, 1744–1745), 2:309–10.

85. Ibid., 2:252, 294. Further testimony on the sacramental occasion in this period in the middle colonies can be gathered from the sermonic literature. See, for example, Gilbert Tennent, William Tennent, and Samuel Blair, *Sermons on Sacramental Occasions by Divers Ministers* (Boston: Draper, 1739); William Tennent, Sr., "William Tennent's Sacramental Sermon," ed. Thomas C. Pears, Jr., *Journal of the Presbyterian Historical Society* 19 (1940): 76–84; William Tennent, Sr., "Sermons," Presbyterian Office of History manuscripts, Philadelphia; Gilbert Tennent, *A Sermon upon Justification: Preached at New-Brunswick, on the Saturday before the Dispensing of the Holy Sacrament* (Philadelphia: Franklin, 1741).

86. Jonathan Edwards, *The Life of David Brainerd*, ed. Norman Pettit (New Haven: Yale University Press, 1985), 295–96, 305–6, 334–35, 383–89, 405–7, 413–14, 419–20, 431–33, with quotations on pp. 296, 305. See also David Brainerd, *Mirabilia Dei inter Indicos, or the Rise and Progress of a Remarkable Work of Grace amongst a Number of the Indians in the Provinces of New-Jersey and Pennsylvania* (Philadelphia: Bradford, 1746), 53–56, 143–53, 165–67, 184, 248.

No one, as far as I know, has ever taken stock of Brainerd's sacramental revivals and seen just how thoroughly Presbyterian in this matter he had become.

87. Brainerd, *Mirabilia Dei*, v–vi, 143–53; Edwards, *Life of Brainerd*, 383–89.

88. Brainerd, *Mirabilia Dei*, 165–67, 248; Edwards, *Life of Brainerd*, 405–7.

89. Brainerd, *Mirabilia Dei*, 184.

90. Samuel Davies, *The State of Religion among the Protestant Dissenters in Virginia* (Boston: Kneeland, 1751), 8–9, 17, 23–24; John Gillies, ed., *Historical Collections Relating to Remarkable Periods of the Success of the Gospel* (Edinburgh, 1754; Kelso: Rutherfurd, 1845), 501–6.

91. Gillies, *Historical Collections*, 505–6, 520; William Henry Foote, *Sketches of North Carolina, Historical and Biographical, Illustrative of the Principles of a Portion of her Early Settlers* (New York: Robert Carter, 1846), 100, 219, 235–36. For further indication of the prevalence of sacramental occasions in Virginia, see William Henry Foote, *Sketches of Virginia, Historical and Biographical*, 1st series (Philadelphia: William S. Martien, 1850), 353, 362–69, 384, 421–24, 468, 496, 536; 2d series (Philadelphia: J. B. Lippincott and Co., 1855), 31, 46–49, 53–54, 123–24, 137, 139, 188, 211–12, 357–60, 569–73, 588–91.

92. On the structure of Scottish agrarian communities, see Landsman, *Scotland and Its First American Colony*, 17–47. In effective social analysis, Landsman argues that regional communities were created out of isolated hamlets or "farmtouns" through high geographic mobility among tenants and through extended kinship networks. I would add the sacramental occasion as an important ingredient in the maintenance of community in such a dispersed, mobile society. The reverse was also true, of course: this sort of agrarian culture was ideal for the furthering of the communion occasion. All along, though, the festal communions were not simply agrarian events, but often throve in more populous areas as well. For more on the interrelationship between these festal occasions and community, see chapter 2 on ritual.

93. John Cuthbertson, "Diary," Clifford E. Barbour Library manuscripts, Pittsburgh Theological Seminary, 39v. I have also consulted the typescript of this diary at the Presbyterian Office of History in Philadelphia which usefully decodes much of Cuthbertson's minuscule, abbreviated hand. For this passage in the typescript, see p. 62. For additional notations on sacramental occasions, see pp. 3, 9–10, 17, 24–25, 29–30, 36, 42, 52, 57, 72, 78, 87, 90–91, 97, 101, 106, 111, 115–16, 124, 128, 132, 137, 142, 146–47, 151–52, 156, 160, 164–65, 172–73, 175–76, 179 in the typescript.

94. Samuel Houston, "Journal, 1777–1782," Samuel Rutherford Houston Papers, Presbyterian Study Center manuscripts, Montreat, North Carolina, 12, 23–24, 56.

95. For the best general history of this revival, see John B. Boles, *The Great Revival, 1787–1805: The Origins of the Southern Evangelical Mind* (Lexington: University Press of Kentucky, 1972). Though he offers little discussion of the communions, his treatment of the overall movement is excellent. See also Charles A. Johnson, *The Frontier Camp Meeting: Religion's Harvest Time* (Dallas: Southern Methodist University Press, 1955).

96. *Western Missionary Magazine* 1 (1803): 289; McGready, *Works*, 26.

McGready has received a fair amount of attention as a revivalist, but none as a sacramentalist. His emphasis on both conversion and communion, however, is evident in his sermons. See McGready, *Works*, 65, 88, 174–79, 277–307, 354–55, 359–75, 458–69. For an attempt to get at McGready's thought, see John Opie, Jr., "James McGready: Theologian of Frontier Revivalism," *Church History* 34 (1965): 445–56.

97. David Elliott, *The Life of the Rev. Elisha Macurdy* (Philadelphia: Martien, 1848), 55–78, with quotation on p. 75; *Connecticut Evangelical Magazine* 4 (1804): 313–19. See also *Western Missionary Magazine* 1 (1803): 287–98; John Moodey, "Diary of Rev. John Moodey, 1776–1857, Pastor of Middle Springs Presbyterian Church, Cumberland County, Pa.," Presbyterian Study Center manuscripts, Montreat, North Carolina, 13–15, 55–57, 65–66, 97–100, 132–33; Joseph Badger, *A Memoir of Rev. Joseph Badger* (Hudson, Ohio: Sawyer, Ingersoll, and Co., 1851), 50–54; Dwight Raymond Guthrie, *John McMillan, The Apostle of Presbyterianism in the West, 1752–1833* (Pittsburgh: University of Pittsburgh Press, 1952), 211–57; Joseph Smith, *Old Redstone; Or, Historical Sketches of Western Presbyterianism, its Early Ministers, its Perilous Times, and its First Records* (Philadelphia: Lippincott, Grambo, and Co., 1854). Guthrie appends to his work McMillan's journal which records, like Cuthbertson's diary, communion season after communion season. In 1788 McMillan noted that McGready was one of his assistants at the "Sacrament of the Supper" at Pidgeon Creek (p. 233).

98. Foote, *Sketches of Virginia*, 1st series, 419–24, 466–68, 536; 2d series, 103–4, 572; Foote, *Sketches of North Carolina*, 288.

99. Foote, *Sketches of North Carolina*, 226–27, 235–36, 327–28, 372–75, 378–79, 390; "Letter XIX. from the Reverend Moses Waddel" in "Appendix" to William B. Sprague, *Lectures on Revivals of Religion* (Albany: Packard and Van Benthuysen, 1832), 146; *Western Missionary Magazine* 1 (1803): 139–44; "Our Communions: Some Reflections on Them, No. I," *North Carolina Presbyterian*, 13 June 1866.

100. McGready, *Works*, vii–xi; *Western Missionary Magazine* 1 (1803): 100, 172–77. See also McGready, *Works*, 471–72; *Western Missionary Magazine* 1 (1803): 45–54, 99–103; *New York Missionary Magazine* 4 (1803): 74–75, 151–55, 192–99, 234–36.

101. *New York Missionary Magazine* 3 (1802): 82–83; John Lyle, "Narratio factorum," Kentucky Historical Society manuscripts, Frankfort, 24–25. For another spiritual relation at Cane Ridge suggestive of Presbyterian traditionalism, see Edward P. Humphrey and Thomas H. Cleland, *Memoirs of the Rev. Thomas Cleland, D.D., Compiled from his Private Papers* (Cincinnati: Moore, Wilstach, Keys, and Co., 1859), 53–56. For further evidence of the perpetuation of the traditional rituals and forms of address, see Robert Marshall, "Sermons, 1796–1832," Shane Collection, Presbyterian Office of History manuscripts, Philadelphia, especially the sacramental ones dated 10 June 1798, 9 June 1799, 29 September 1799, 1 June 1800, 5 September 1802, 13 June 1806; John Newton, "Papers, 1784–1797," Presbyterian Study Center manuscripts, Montreat, North Carolina, especially the eucharistic sermons dated 20–27 September 1789, 15 August 1790, 14 August 1791, 9–12 August 1792, 13 July 1794, 7 August 1795, 16

October 1796; John McMillan, "Sermons," Washington and Jefferson College manuscripts, Washington, Pennsylvania; John McMillan, "Communion Address Delivered June 1821 and February 1829," Washington and Jefferson College typescript, Washington, Pennsylvania.

102. Lyle, "Narratio factorum," 41, 44, 51–52, 91; *New York Missionary Magazine* 3 (1802): 118–22. For a compendium of accounts of sacramental meetings in this period, see William W. Woodward, ed., *Surprising Accounts of the Revival of Religion in the United States of America* (Philadelphia: Woodward, 1802), 34–39, 43–46, 51–53, 56–58, 107, 131–33, 158, 160–63, 225–27, 229–30, 242.

103. For a Scottish example, see Fraser, *Life and Diary of Ralph Erskine*, 55.

104. The nomenclature, sacramental camp, is from Henry Christopher McCook, *The Latimers: A Tale of the Western Insurrection of 1794* (Philadelphia: George W. Jacobs and Co., 1898), 130. This phrase is suggestive of the way in which the camp meetings often evolved out of the traditional sacramental occasions. For Methodist precursors of the camp meeting, see Russell E. Richey, "From Quarterly to Camp Meeting: A Reconsideration of Early American Methodism," *Methodist History* 23 (1985): 199–213. Richey points out that the earlier quarterly meetings help explain the Methodist embrace of camp meetings. Camp meetings indeed became a quintessential expression of American Methodism, more so than of American Presbyterianism. One reason for this may be that the Presbyterians already had their festival and were often closely bound to it, while the Methodists were still in the process of creating their own tradition of festivity.

105. Peter G. Mode, *The Frontier Spirit in American Christianity* (New York: Macmillan, 1923), ix, 13–14. The common line on the Americanness of these "frontier" revivals is evident in a range of interpreters from Catharine Cleveland to Dickson Bruce. See, for example, Catharine Cleveland, *The Great Revival in the West, 1797–1805* (Chicago: University of Chicago Press, 1916), esp. xi, 120–21; Peter G. Mode, "Revivalism as a Phase of Frontier Life," *Journal of Religion* 1 (1921): 337–54; William Warren Sweet, *Revivalism in America: Its Origin, Growth, and Decline* (New York: Scribner, 1944); William Warren Sweet, *Religion in the Development of American Culture, 1765–1840* (New York: Scribner, 1952), 134–53; Dickson D. Bruce, Jr., *And They All Sang Hallelujah: Plain-Folk Camp-Meeting Religion, 1800–1845* (Knoxville: University of Tennessee Press, 1974). This line of interpretation is epitomized in Bruce's view that the camp meetings "simply 'grew up' with the frontier" or that they were "the frontier's unique contribution to Christian practice," marking a sharp departure from "Old World religious traditions" (pp. 11, 51). Behind this frontier school of American revivalism lay, of course, the seminal work of Frederick Jackson Turner. See his *The Frontier in American History* (New York: Holt, 1920), esp. 1–38.

106. This western traditionalism versus eastern innovation on the issues of Presbyterian sacramentalism and revivalism is evident, for example, in Smith, *Old Redstone*, 16–17, 62, 65–66, 152–55, 220–21, 224, 290–96; Jacob van Vechten, *Memoirs of John M. Mason, D.D., S.T.P. with Portions of his Correspondence* (New York: Robert Carter and Brothers, 1856), 366, 487–88.

107. This lithograph appeared with said title in Smith, *Old Redstone*, opposite p. 310.

108. Foote, *Sketches of North Carolina*, 227, 379. These counties in North Carolina are the only area for which I have seen mention of such cabins in connection with the sacrament. This suggests that this otherwise unidentified drawing may be of a communion gathering in that region. The caption, *A Communion Gathering in the Olden Time*, appears below this undated work.

109. Isaac Reed, *The Christian Traveller. In Five Parts. Including Nine Years, and Eighteen Thousand Miles* (New York: J. and J. Harper, 1828), 212, 228–30.

110. Ibid., 228–30.

CHAPTER 2

1. John Willison, *A Sacramental Catechism: Or, A Familiar Instructor for Young Communicants* (Edinburgh, 1720; Edinburgh: Samuel Willison and Co., 1756), 33; John Livingston, "The Exhortation after Two Tables Were Served," in John Howie, ed., *A Collection of Lectures and Sermons, Preached upon Several Subjects, Mostly in the Time of the Persecution* (Kilmarnock: Crawford, 1809), 528, 530; "The Substance of viii. Sermons that were preached at the Administration of the Lords Supper at Stenton by severall Ministers And Taken from their Mouthes, by the Short-hand-character. Upon 15, 18, 19, 20. Jully In the Year of God MDCCII," Edinburgh University Library manuscripts, 109–10.

2. Thomas C. Pears, Jr., ed., "Sessional Records of the Presbyterian Church of Booth Bay, Maine, 1767–1778," *Journal of the Presbyterian Historical Society* 16 (1935): 203–40, 243–88, 308–55. The critical pages for the sacramental occasion are pp. 234–40, 243–53 from which the ensuing narrative is developed unless otherwise noted. For details on Beath's responsibility for this history, see pp. 253, 315.

3. See George Hay, *The Architecture of Scottish Post-Reformation Churches, 1560–1843* (Oxford: Clarendon Press, 1957), esp. 22, 24–26, 131–33, 178–84; Harold Wickliffe Rose, *The Colonial Houses of Worship in America Built in the English Colonies Before the Republic, 1607–1789, and Still Standing* (New York: Hastings House, 1963), 136; James H. Smylie, *American Presbyterians: A Pictorial History* (Philadelphia: Presbyterian Historical Society, 1985), 29. The last work was published as numbers 1 and 2 in volume 6 of the *Journal of Presbyterian History* for 1985.

4. These later sacraments are reported in Pears, ed., "Sessional Records," 260–62, 285, 308, 314–15.

5. Willison, *Sacramental Catechism*, 33, 85. Rhys Isaac, whose work has greatly influenced this chapter, makes a similar argument in a different context in *The Transformation of Virginia, 1740–1790* (Chapel Hill: University of North Carolina Press, 1982), 81n, 323–57. The aim, as Isaac says, is to gain some grasp of "the total communications repertoire of a society" (p. 325). On the particular importance of the visual in the process of communication and the failure of most historians to incorporate it into their interpretations of Christianity, see Margaret R. Miles, *Image as Insight: Visual Understanding in Western Christianity and Secular Culture* (Boston: Beacon Press, 1985). For a study that recognizes the

richness of radical Protestant forms of communication, see Clarke Garrett, *Spirit Possession and Popular Religion from the Camisards to the Shakers* (Baltimore: Johns Hopkins University Press, 1987), esp. 3–5, 23–26, 215–16.

6. For the appellation "retrospective ethnography," see Charles Tilly, "Anthropology, History, and the *Annales*," *Review: A Journal of the Fernand Braudel Center for the Study of Economies, Historical Systems, and Civilizations* 1 (1978): 207–13.

7. Isaac, *Transformation of Virginia*, 166–68. This focus on social significations is evident as well in Dell Upton's excellent work *Holy Things and Profane: Anglican Parish Churches in Colonial Virginia* (Cambridge, Mass.: MIT Press, 1986), notably in the treatment of the eucharist. For a reading of the sacramental occasions as "a ceremony of solidarity," see Gwen Kennedy Neville, "Community Form and Ceremonial Life in Three Regions of Scotland," *American Ethnologist* 6 (1979): 98–99. For a critique of the functionalist preoccupations of many of the historical interpretations of religion in the early modern period, see Stuart Clark, "French Historians and Early Modern Popular Culture," *Past and Present* 100 (1983): esp. 86–93.

8. On "the fan of meanings" in symbol and ritual, see Michael G. Lawler, "Christian Rituals: An Essay in Sacramental Symbolisms," *Horizons* 7 (1980): 7–35. On the multivocality of symbolic action, see Victor Turner, *The Forest of Symbols: Aspects of Ndembu Ritual* (Ithaca: Cornell University Press, 1967). On the importance of "thickness" in interpretation and redescription, see Clifford Geertz, *The Interpretation of Cultures* (New York: Basic, 1973), esp. 3–30, 412–53. For two highly useful theoretical discussions of ritual, see Stanley Jeyaraja Tambiah, "A Performative Approach to Ritual," in his *Culture, Thought, and Social Action: An Anthropological Perspective* (Cambridge, Mass.: Harvard University Press, 1985), 123–66; Gilbert Lewis, *Day of Shining Red: An Essay on Understanding Ritual* (Cambridge: Cambridge University Press, 1980). For a recent and insightful anthropological look at eucharistic ritual and food symbolism in late antiquity, see Gillian Feeley-Harnik, *The Lord's Table: Eucharist and Passover in Early Christianity* (Philadelphia: University of Pennsylvania Press, 1981).

9. John Willison, *A Sacramental Directory, Or A Treatise Concerning the Sanctification of a Communion-Sabbath* (Edinburgh, 1716; Aberdeen: George and Robert King, 1846), 76, 90.

10. Sacramental fasts in various forms among the Scottish Protestants—on the day of the communion itself, in private, or even during the whole week before— were prevalent as early as the 1560s, evidence that the penitential and Lenten practices of their Catholic forebears were never wholly set aside. Only gradually in the course of the seventeenth century, however, did the fast become a fixed part of the sacramental occasion, and only slowly did Thursday emerge as the day most often sanctified for this purpose. On the early development of sacramental fasts in Reformation Scotland, see William McMillan, *The Worship of the Scottish Reformed Church, 1550–1638* (London: Clarke, [1931]), 197–98, 226–28.

11. Willison, *Sacramental Directory*, 121–22; *A Directory for the Publique Worship of God, throughout the Three Kingdoms of England, Scotland, and Ire-*

land (London: Evan Tyler, Alexander Fifield, Ralph Smith, and John Field, 1644), 75.

12. Pears, ed., "Sessional Records," 243–44; John Brown, "Memorandum Book of Rev. John Brown, Pastor of the Congregations at Timber Ridge and New Providence, 1753–1797," Presbyterian Office of History manuscripts, Philadelphia, unpaginated. The latter includes, toward the beginning, a fast day sermon before "the G[rea]t work" of the sacrament.

13. Willison, *Sacramental Catechism*, 178; Willison, *Sacramental Directory*, 121–22; James McGready, *The Posthumous Works of the Reverend and Pious James M'Gready, Late Minister of the Gospel in Henderson, K[entuck]y*, ed. James Smith (Nashville: J. Smith's Steam Press, 1837), 374–75; John Willison, *A Treatise on the Sanctification of the Sabbath* (Edinburgh, 1722; Edinburgh: J. Pillans, 1819), 140. See also Brown, "Memorandum Book" and Gilbert Tennent, William Tennent, and Samuel Blair, *Sermons on Sacramental Occasions by Divers Ministers* (Boston: Draper, 1739), 21.

14. Brown, "Memorandum Book"; *Directory for Publique Worship*, 75.

15. William Henry Foote, *Sketches of Virginia, Historical and Biographical*, 2d series (Philadelphia: J. B. Lippincott and Co., 1855), 572; William McCulloch, "Examinations of Persons Under Spiritual Concern at Cambuslang During the Revival in 1741–42," 2 vols., Edinburgh University manuscripts, New College Library, 1:458; Willison, *Sacramental Directory*, 226, 288–90. On the McCulloch manuscripts, see the first section of the next chapter.

16. Willison, *Sacramental Catechism*, 178; John Gillies, ed., *Historical Collections Relating to Remarkable Periods of the Success of the Gospel* (Edinburgh, 1754; Kelso: Rutherfurd, 1845), 521. An anonymous eighteenth-century critic spoke of the Presbyterians' "sacramental face" during these seasons—one of "gloom" and "penance" and of "groaning, sighing, and weeping." See *A Letter from a Blacksmith to the Ministers and Elders of the Church of Scotland in which the Manner of Public Worship in that Church is Considered; Its Inconveniences and Defects Pointed Out; and Methods for Removing of Them Humbly Proposed* (London, 1759; New Haven: Oliver Steele, 1814), 25, 30–31.

17. Willison, *Treatise*, 224; McGready, *Works*, 314; Willison, *Sacramental Directory*, 161–65.

18. Willison, *Sacramental Directory*, 80–81, 165; Tinicum Presbyterian Church, Red Hill, Pennsylvania, "Congregational Records, 1768–1838," Presbyterian Office of History manuscripts, Philadelphia, 8.

19. McGready, *Works*, 149; Willison, *Treatise*, 224–26; Zacharie Boyd, *Two Sermons, for These Who Are to Come to the Table of the Lord* (Edinburgh: John Wreittoun, 1629), 94.

20. McCulloch, "Examinations," 1:347; 2:499; Joseph Smith, *Old Redstone; Or, Historical Sketches of Western Presbyterianism, its Early Ministers, its Perilous Times, and its First Records* (Philadelphia: Lippincott, Grambo, and Co., 1854), 154, 164–65; McGready, *Works*, 181; Willison, *Treatise*, 147. See also Henry Grey Graham, *The Social Life of Scotland in the Eighteenth Century* (London, 1899; London: Black, 1928), 15, 180–81, 214–15, 308; Thomas Pennant, *A Tour in Scotland; 1769*, 5th ed., 2 vols. (London: Benjamin White, 1790),

1:102. Rhys Isaac has observed for colonial Virginia: "Symbols and practical necessities were combined in the conventions of dress" (*Transformation of Virginia*, 43).

21. Smith, *Old Redstone*, 154, 164–65; Graham, *Social Life of Scotland*, 214–15; Foote, *Sketches of Virginia*, 2d series, 206.

22. Smith, *Old Redstone*, 155; John Willison, *Sacramental Meditations and Advices, Grounded upon Scripture-Texts, Proper for Communicants, to Prepare their Hearts, Excite their Affections, Quicken their Graces and Enliven their Devotions on Sacramental Occasions* (Edinburgh: S. Willison and M. Jarvie, 1761), 323, 333; Willison, *Sacramental Directory*, 84; McGready, *Works*, 52, 182, 247–48, 370–71; Willison, *Treatise*, 147, 229; Pears, ed., "Sessional Records," 243.

23. Foote, *Sketches of Virginia*, 2d series, 358, 569; William Henry Foote, *Sketches of North Carolina, Historical and Biographical, Illustrative of the Principles of a Portion of Her Early Settlers* (New York: Robert Carter, 1846), 203.

24. Smith, *Old Redstone*, 154; Henry Christopher McCook, *The Latimers: A Tale of the Western Insurrection of 1794* (Philadelphia: George W. Jacobs and Co., 1898), 152; Pears, ed., "Sessional Records," 245; Samuel Rutherford, *Fourteen Communion Sermons*, ed. Andrew A. Bonar (Glasgow: Charles Glass and Co., 1877), 25; Willison, *Sacramental Directory*, 79; Willison, *Sacramental Meditations*, 335; McGready, *Works*, 371. In places I have admitted Henry McCook's novel *The Latimers* as evidence on the rituals of the sacramental occasion. Chapters 16–18 (pp. 130–56) of his novel are largely devoted to describing "a sacrament in the woods" (p. 149). McCook was steeped in the customs of his Ulster Scottish forebears in western Pennsylvania; his work was envisioned as a historical novel. When used critically, it is particularly helpful for confirming customs that are mentioned in less detail in earlier sources.

25. McGready, *Works*, 371; Willison, *Sacramental Directory*, 179, 211, 223.

26. Willison, *Sacramental Catechism*, 106; Willison, *Sacramental Directory*, 43, 45.

27. Willison, *Sacramental Catechism*, iv–vi; McCulloch, "Examinations," 1:2, 254–55, 300, 316, 362, 372, 453, 455, 472, 577; 2:25–26, 85, 199, 349, 456, 523, 549, 586; Walter Steuart, *Collections and Observations Methodiz'd; Concerning the Worship, Discipline, and Government of the Church of Scotland* (Edinburgh: Andrew Anderson, 1709), 132; John Barr, *Plain Catechetical Instructions for Young Communicants, Designed to Assist Them in Forming Scriptural Views of the Lord's Supper* (Glasgow, 1824; Philadelphia: Presbyterian Board of Publication, 1842), 20.

28. Willison, *Sacramental Catechism*, iv–vi; Willison, *Sacramental Directory*, 155–56; *The Constitution of the Presbyterian Church in the United States of America Containing the Confession of Faith, the Catechisms, the Government and Discipline, and the Directory for the Worship of God* (Philadelphia: Thomas Bradford, 1789), 199–200. See also McCulloch, "Examinations," 1:9, 18, 39, 577; 2:199, 349, 456.

29. McCulloch, "Examinations," 1:9, 577; John Leyburn, "Weymouth Sacrament Days," in Foote, *Sketches of Virginia*, 2d series, 572.

30. James Oliphant, *A Sacramental Catechism, Designed for Communicants*

Old and Young, 5th ed. (Glasgow: John Bryce, 1783), 57–64; John Willison, *The Young Communicant's Catechism: Or, A Help Both Short and Plain, for Instructing and Preparing the Young to Make a Right Approach unto the Lord's Table* (Edinburgh: Thomas Lumisden and John Robertson, 1734), v; *Constitution of the Presbyterian Church*, 199–200.

31. Willison, *Sacramental Directory*, 54.

32. Thomas C. Pears, Jr., ed., "A Journal of Two Missionary Tours Made in Kentucky and Tennessee by the Rev. Joseph P. Howe in the Years 1813 and 1814," *Journal of the Presbyterian Historical Society* 16 (1935): 386–87; Joseph Badger, *A Memoir of Rev. Joseph Badger* (Hudson, Ohio: Sawyer, Ingersoll, and Co., 1851), 59–60; Willison, *Sacramental Catechism*, 36–60, with quotations on pp. 46, 60; *Constitution of the Presbyterian Church*, 41–42, 193–94; John Cuthbertson, "The Diary of the Rev. John Cuthbertson," Presbyterian Office of History typescript, Philadelphia, 62. Baptism as a part of the sacramental occasion appears to have been more common in America than in Scotland. In sparsely settled, underchurched areas the communion season tended to become all the more a religious catchall.

33. Willison, *Sacramental Directory*, 61, 176; David Hogg, *Life and Times of the Rev. John Wightman, D.D. (1762–1847), Late Minister of Kirkmahoe* (London: Hodder and Stoughton, 1873), 48, 50. See also McCulloch, "Examinations," 1:328; John N. Macleod, *Memorials of the Rev. Norman Macleod* (Edinburgh: Douglas, 1898), 78.

34. John Dun, *Sermons in Two Volumes*, 2 vols. (Kilmarnock: J. Wilson, 1790), 1:200–201; Willison, *Sacramental Catechism*, vii. For an example of a woman who faced death with "great peace" because of her sweet experiences "at the Table," see Robert Wodrow, *Analecta: Or, Materials for a History of Remarkable Providences; Mostly Relating to Scotch Ministers and Christians*, 4 vols. (Edinburgh: Maitland Club, 1842–1843), 3:312–13.

35. Robert Burns, *The Poems and Songs of Robert Burns*, ed. James Kinsley, 3 vols. (Oxford: Clarendon Press, 1968), 1:132–33; *Letter to a Blacksmith*, 22–24, 31–34. On this evangelical Presbyterian preaching style, see also Graham, *Social Life of Scotland*, 292–96.

36. Leyburn, "Weymouth Sacrament Days," in Foote, *Sketches of Virginia*, 2d series, 572–73.

37. William Wirt, "Mr. Wirt's Description of James Waddell—As It Appears in the British Spy," in Foote, *Sketches of Virginia*, 1st series, 381–82.

38. McCulloch, "Examinations," 2:153; Willison, *Sacramental Directory*, 205, 224, 227, 233; Willison, *Sacramental Meditations*, 229. For the procession in with the elements, see also Macleod, *Memorials*, 34–35; McCook, *Latimers*, 152; McCulloch, "Examinations," 2:529.

39. Willison, *Sacramental Directory*, 231. See also Willison, *Sacramental Catechism*, 65–77, 222–23.

40. Willison, *Sacramental Catechism*, 78–81, 357–85.

41. McGready, *Works*, 22–23, 362–65, 377–82.

42. Willison, *Sacramental Meditations*, 229–33; Willison, *Sacramental Directory*, 205.

43. Willison, *Sacramental Directory*, 244–46.

44. Gillies, ed., *Historical Collections*, 525–26.

45. D[uncan] MacFarlan, *The Revivals of the Eighteenth Century, Particularly at Cambuslang* (London: John Johnstone, n.d.), 69; McGready, *Works*, viii.

46. Willison, *Sacramental Directory*, 43–44; *Western Missionary Magazine* 1 (1803): 173, 177, 222; 2 (1804): 360; Smith, *Old Redstone*, 156; McGready, *Works*, 448.

47. Willison, *Sacramental Directory*, 172; McGready, *Works*, 174–79.

48. Willison, *Sacramental Directory*, 48; McCulloch, "Examinations," 2:196.

49. James W. Alexander, *The Life of Archibald Alexander, D.D.* (New York: Charles Scribner, 1854), 50–53, 56–57, 62. For a Scottish example, see John Thomson, *Letters Addressed to the Rev. John Mason, A.M. of New-York, in Answer to His Letters on Frequent Communion* (Glasgow, 1799; Troy, N.Y.: R. Moffitt and Co., 1801), 15.

50. *Connecticut Evangelical Magazine* 4 (1803–1804): 313–14; Isaac Reed, *The Christian Traveller. In Five Parts. Including Nine Years, and Eighteen Thousand Miles* (New York: J. and J. Harper, 1828), 230. See also Increase N. Tarbox, ed., *Diary of Thomas Robbins, D.D., 1796–1854*, 2 vols. (Boston: Beacon Press, 1886), 1:212. In a separate, but analogous case, Rhys Isaac has said of the rituals of court day in early Virginia: "Only when it came together did the scattered community attain full existence" (*Transformation of Virginia*, 90). William Robertson Smith, a nineteenth-century scholar and theologian who came out of the Scottish evangelical tradition, was one of the first interpreters to analyze "public feasts" and "sacrificial festivals" in terms of community. See his *Lectures on the Religion of the Semites*, rev. ed. (London: Adam and Charles Black, 1901), esp. 244–68.

51. *Western Missionary Magazine* 1 (1803): 262–63, 336–37. See also McCook, *Latimers*, 134–35.

52. Paisley Kirk Session Records, Scottish Record Office, Edinburgh, 14 August 1713, 16 October 1713, 46(2): unpaginated; Cambuslang Kirk Session Records, Scottish Record Office, Edinburgh, 1: unpaginated collection lists; John McMillan, "Journal," in Dwight Raymond Guthrie, *John McMillan, The Apostle of Presbyterianism in the West, 1752–1833* (Pittsburgh: University of Pittsburgh Press, 1952), 217–18; Carnock Kirk Session Records, Scottish Record Office, Edinburgh, 7 July 1727, 2:45–46. For further discussion of collections and the poor, see Graham, *Social Life of Scotland*, 237–42. Also for an indication of the importance of these collections in Ulster communions, see John M. Barkley, "The Evidence of Old Irish Session-Books on the Sacrament of the Lord's Supper," *Church Service Society Annual* 22 (1952): 24–34.

53. Willison, *Treatise*, 100; Willison, *Sacramental Directory*, 230–31, 245–46.

54. Willison, *Treatise*, 100; *Directory for Publique Worship*, 83–84; *The Modes of Presbyterian Church-Worship Vindicated: In a Letter to the Blacksmith* (London, 1763; Newburyport: John Mycall, 1789), 8.

55. Cuthbertson, "Diary," 10, 25, 29, 30, 36, 42, 52, 57, 62; *The Psalms of David in Metre: According to the Version Approved by the Church of Scotland, and Appointed to be Used in Worship* (Oxford: Oxford University Press, n.d.),

12; McCulloch, "Examinations," 1:583; 2:153, 567. See also Macleod, *Memorials*, 34. Besides Psalm 24, another that was consistently sung at the communions was Psalm 103. Though the tradition of Scottish psalmody and the styles of performance were long cherished, differences and innovations in music were numerous, especially after 1800 and especially in America. Corporate psalm singing increasingly lost its centrality in Presbyterian worship and was often eclipsed by hymn singing and eventually choirs. See Millar Patrick, *Four Centuries of Scottish Psalmody* (London: Oxford University Press, 1949).

56. Dun, *Sermons*, 1:208.

57. Willison, *Sacramental Catechism*, 109, 193–95; Willison, *Sacramental Directory*, 63; Pears, ed., "Sessional Records," 319; McCulloch, "Examinations," 1:127. For a recent liturgical discussion of the Lord's Supper as "the symbol of community," see Jerome Theisen, "Images of the Church and the Eucharist," *Worship* 58 (1984): 118–29.

58. Pears, ed., "Sessional Records," 245; Smith, *Old Redstone*, 153–54. This organization of space with its central focus on the communion table sharply distinguished these Presbyterian revivals from those of other evangelicals, particularly those who adopted the revivalistic techniques that in many cases replaced the sacramental season, notably the new measures of the New School Presbyterians. In these forms the spatial focus was on the anxious seats or mourners' benches that occupied the central space in front of the pulpit.

59. Willison, *Sacramental Catechism*, 70–76; Oliphant, *Sacramental Catechism*, 40.

60. Willison, *Sacramental Meditations*, 348–49.

61. McGready, *Works*, 368–69. See also Hogg, *Life of Wightman*, 48–50.

62. Jonathan Edwards, *The Life of David Brainerd*, ed. Norman Pettit (New Haven: Yale University Press, 1985), 405; John Lyle, "Narratio factorum," Kentucky Historical Society manuscripts, Frankfort, 96, 98; Mary McWhorter Tenney, *Communion Tokens: Their Origin, History, and Use* (Grand Rapids: Zondervan, 1936), 84, 87, 92. The two different tokens for white and black members are in the Oliver Keith Rumbel Church Token Collection, Presbyterian Study Center, Montreat, North Carolina.

63. Helen Bruce Wallace, *Historic Paxton Her Days and Her Ways, 1722–1913* (n.p.: n.p., 1913), 96; McCook, *Latimers*, 154. Edward L. Parker in *The History of Londonderry, Comprising the Towns of Derry and Londonderry, N. H.* (Boston: Perkins and Whipple, 1851) also suggested that "the more elderly portion of the church" communed first during the communion seasons among the Scottish Presbyterians in New England (p. 144). Still the vast majority of sources, including Beath's session records and Smith's full chronicle in *Old Redstone*, made no indication that such distinctions in the order of communicating were operative.

64. Burns, *Poems and Songs*, 1:131. The ideal of an egalitarian feast was expressed in Walter Steuart's important eighteenth-century book of Presbyterian rubrics, *Collections and Observations Methodiz'd*, 141, 176–77. He also contrasted the open seating at the Lord's table with the hierarchical arrangements of pew assignments.

65. McGready, *Works*, 36, 178–79, 250, 276, 350, 366–67, 427, 437.

66. Willison, *Treatise*, 102–5, 112–15, 158, 188; Willison, *Sacramental Catechism*, 90; Willison, *Sacramental Directory*, 267–68; Wodrow, *Analecta*, 2:335. For a discussion of the patriarchal dominance of the ceremonies of dining in early Virginia, see Isaac, *Transformation of Virginia*, 75–78. For the Scottish side, see Graham, *Social Life of Scotland*, 9, 25.

67. Thomas Burns, *Old Scottish Communion Plate* (Edinburgh: R. and R. Clark, 1892), 14 n.4; Foote, *Sketches of Virginia*, 2d series, 358; McCook, *Latimers*, 152, 154; Pears, ed., "Sessional Records," 286, 315; "Our Communions: Some Reflections on Them, No. II," *North Carolina Presbyterian*, 20 June 1866. Indicative of male dominance of the household's economic transactions, Mr. Herrinden received the money for Mrs. Herrinden's work. Also even tending to the eucharistic linen could be an exclusively male activity as the elders set up for the rite. See Barony Kirk Session Records, Strathclyde Regional Archives, Mitchell Library, Glasgow, 7 June 1767, 27 June 1768, 16 June 1769, 6: unpaginated.

68. Isaac, *Transformation of Virginia*, 46. On tea and wheaten bread, see Graham, *Social Life of Scotland*, 8–11, 173.

69. On these other feasts, see Dickson D. Bruce, Jr., *And They All Sang Hallelujah: Plain-Folk Camp-Meeting Religion, 1800–1845* (Knoxville: University of Tennessee Press, 1974), 27–28.

70. Second Presbyterian Church, Philadelphia, "[List] of Communicants Phil. April the 2d 1744. Memorandum of Persons Spoken with in order to Communion of," Presbyterian Office of History manuscripts, Philadelphia; Second Presbyterian Church, Philadelphia, "Communicants of the Second Church as They were in Decem[be]r 1831," Presbyterian Office of History manuscripts, Philadelphia; Archibald Cameron, "A Sketch of Presbyterian Church History in Shelby County," Shane Collection, Presbyterian Office of History manuscripts, Philadelphia; Pears, ed., "Sessional Records," 237, 239–40, 327–29. For numbers on Cambuslang, see T. C. Smout, "Born Again at Cambuslang: New Evidence on Popular Religion and Literacy in Eighteenth-Century Scotland," *Past and Present* 97 (1982): 114–27. Whether women were actually two-thirds of the communicants at Cambuslang is, of course, impossible to say. There were several thousand communicants at these revivals in 1742. McCulloch only recorded the experiences of about 110 participants—of which at least seventy-four were women. For other communicant lists suggesting a preponderance of women, see also John McMillan, "A Memorandum Book of Such as Have Been Admitted to the Sacrament of the Supper in the Congregation of Chartiers from June 1815 to February 1830," Private Collection, typescript; Ballantrae Kirk Session Records, "Communion Rolls, 1753–1754, 1761–1768," Strathclyde Regional Archives, Mitchell Library, Glasgow, 16: unpaginated; Nicholas Baggs, *History of Abington Presbyterian Church, Abington, Pa.* (Hatsboro, Pa.: Robinson Publishing Co., 1914), 43–44; Tinicum Presbyterian Church, "Congregational Records," 29. Patricia Bonomi has also put together some broad-ranging evidence for the feminization of membership in the colonial churches in *Under the Cope of Heaven: Religion, Society, and Politics in Colonial America* (New York: Oxford University Press, 1986), 111–15. For women and revivals in the early nineteenth century, Mary P.

Ryan's *Cradle of the Middle Class: The Family in Oneida County, New York, 1790–1865* (Cambridge: Cambridge University Press, 1981) is excellent.

71. *New York Missionary Magazine* 4 (1803): 236. For two more examples, see Gillies, ed., *Historical Collections*, 521. For a Scottish writer who was convinced that evangelical Presbyterian women were controlling the religious lives of their "hen-peckt Husbands," see Thomas Rhind, *An Apology for Mr Thomas Rhind* (Edinburgh: Robert Freebairn, 1712), 205–6.

72. McCulloch, "Examinations," 1:14; *Western Missionary Magazine* 1 (1803): 50–51; Foote, *Sketches of Virginia*, 1st series, 364, 423.

73. *New York Missionary Magazine* 4 (1803): 235. Dickson D. Bruce, Jr., in his analysis of the rituals of camp meetings makes some similar points on role reversal and status negation. See his *And They All Sang Hallelujah*, 85–87.

74. Pears, ed., "Sessional Records," 244–45. Among the very best collections of communion tokens anywhere is the Oliver Keith Rumbel Collection at the Presbyterian Study Center in Montreat, North Carolina, which is the primary collection that I have used. Study of communion tokens has been confined by and large to antiquarians and numismatists. The richness of the symbols on these tokens bears further study. For example, the use of the pierced heart at Anwoth suggests a Protestant parallel to Catholic devotion dedicated to the sacred heart—devotion that was particularly prominent after the late seventeenth century. Any extended study of the tokens would be helped along by work already done by earlier researchers and collectors. See, for example, H. A. Whitelaw, *Communion Tokens, with Illustrated and Descriptive Catalogue of those of Dumfrieshire* (Dumfries: Council of the Dumfries and Galloway Natural History and Antiquarian Society, 1911); Robert Shiells, *The Story of the Token as Belonging to the Sacrament of the Lord's Supper*, 2d ed. (Edinburgh: Oliphant, Anderson, and Ferrier, 1902); A. A. Milne, *Communion Tokens of the Presbyterian Church in Ireland* (Glasgow: Fraser, Asher, and Co., 1920); Fred Bowman, *Communion Tokens of the Presbyterian Church in Canada* (Toronto: Mission Press, 1965); George A. MacLennan, *The Story of the Old Time Communion Service and Worship, also the Metallic Communion Token of the Presbyterian Church in Canada, 1772–* (Montreal: n.p., 1924); Tenney, *Communion Tokens*; Alexander J. S. Brook, "Communion Tokens of the Established Church of Scotland—Sixteenth, Seventeenth, and Eighteenth Centuries," *Proceedings of the Society of Antiquaries of Scotland* 41 (1906–1907): 453–604. The last work is the most extensive in its illustrations. Tenney's work is the best for the American side.

75. Ibid.

76. Smith, *Old Redstone*, 158–59; "Substance of viii. Sermons," 188–97; Willison, *Sacramental Catechism*, 362–64; *Connecticut Evangelical Magazine* 4 (1803–1804): 314. This ritualized litany, developed in Scotland and Ulster, passed readily to America. Besides Smith's *Old Redstone*, see Robert Marshall, "Fencing Tables, Geor[ge]town, June 9, 1799," in "Sermons, 1796–1832," Shane Collection, Presbyterian Office of History manuscripts, Philadelphia.

77. "Substance of viii. Sermons," 188–97; Willison, *Sacramental Catechism*, 362–64; Marshall, "Fencing Tables."

78. "Recollection of Two Years of Worship, By One who Frequented this Cor-

ner, 1816–17–18," in Foote, *Sketches of Virginia*, 2d series, 590. See also Tennent, Tennent, and Blair, *Sermons on Sacramental Occasions*, 59.

79. [James Wood], *A True Representation of the Rise, Progress, and State of the Present Divisions of the Church of Scotland* (London: n.p., 1657), 36; Robert Wodrow, *The Correspondence of the Rev. Robert Wodrow, Minister of Eastwood, and Author of the History of the Sufferings of the Church of Scotland*, ed. Thomas McCrie, 3 vols. (Edinburgh: Wodrow Society, 1842–1843), 1:479, 481; 2:284. A classic example of strife issuing out of a large field communion was the battle at Mauchline Moor in 1648. See Robert Baillie, *The Letters and Journals of Robert Baillie, A.M.*, 3 vols. (Edinburgh: Bannatyne Club, 1841–1842), 3:48–49, 53. In such a context Natalie Zemon Davis's reflections on "The Rites of Violence" are most apt. For her exploration of the connections among violence, riot, and religious ritual, see her *Society and Culture in Early Modern France: Eight Essays* (Stanford: Stanford University Press, 1975), esp. 169–70.

80. John Craig, "Autobiography," Presbyterian Study Center manuscripts, Montreat, North Carolina, unpaginated; "Description of Cabbin Creek Church, Kentucky, ca. 1797–1808," Shane Collection, Presbyterian Office of History manuscripts, Philadelphia, unpaginated. See also Andrew McClelland, Jr., "Letter to James Welch," 3 July 1792, James Welch Papers, Shane Collection, Presbyterian Office of History manuscripts, Philadelphia; B. W. McDonnold, *History of the Cumberland Presbyterian Church* (Nashville: Board of Publication of the Cumberland Presbyterian Church, 1893), 109; Guthrie, *John McMillan*, 162–63.

81. Willison, *Sacramental Directory*, 66, 264; "Substance of viii. Sermons," 100.

82. Willison, *Sacramental Directory*, 274–75; *Western Missionary Magazine* 1 (1803): 222.

CHAPTER 3

1. Thomas Prince, Jr., ed., *The Christian History*, 2 vols. (Boston: Kneeland and Green, 1744–1745), 2:253–54; *The Psalms of David in Metre: According to the Version Approved by the Church of Scotland, and Appointed to be Used in Worship* (Oxford: Oxford University Press, n.d.), 45. On Blair and his congregation, see J. D. Edmiston Turner, "Reverend Samuel Blair, 1712–1751," *Journal of the Presbyterian Historical Society* 29 (1951): 227–36; W. B. Noble, *History of the Presbyterian Church of Fagg's Manor, Chester County, Pennsylvania, 1730–1876* (Parkesburg, Pa.: Potts, 1876); Joseph Brown Turner, ed., "The Records of Old Londonderry Congregation, Now Faggs Manor, Chester Co., Pa.," *Journal of the Presbyterian Historical Society* 8 (1916): 343–79.

2. Prince, ed., *Christian History*, 2:254–56.

3. Ibid., 2:255–57; John Willison, *A Sacramental Catechism: Or, A Familiar Instructor for Young Communicants* (Edinburgh, 1720; Edinburgh: Samuel Willison and Co., 1756), iii.

4. Prince, ed., *Christian History*, 2:244. The congregational records for these years for Blair's church attest to the prevalence of the standard sins: drunkenness, swearing, backbiting, and sexual misconduct. See Turner, "Records of Old Londonderry Congregation," 345–52.

5. Ibid., 2:253.

6. See William McCulloch, "Examinations of Persons Under Spiritual Concern at Cambuslang During the Revival in 1741–42," 2 vols., Edinburgh University manuscripts, New College Library. For further descriptions of the manuscripts, see D[uncan] MacFarlan, *The Revivals of the Eighteenth Century, Particularly at Cambuslang* (London: John Johnstone, n.d.), 105–12, 173; Arthur Fawcett, *The Cambuslang Revival: The Scottish Evangelical Revival of the Eighteenth Century* (London: Banner of Truth, 1971), 1–8; T. C. Smout, "Born Again at Cambuslang: New Evidence on Popular Religion and Literacy in Eighteenth-Century Scotland," *Past and Present* 97 (1982): 114–15. Also Ned Landsman, in an article in press simultaneously with this book, makes effective use of the Cambuslang manuscripts to explore popular responses to evangelical preaching. See the *Journal of British Studies* for 1989. It should be noted that five cases in the first volume of the manuscripts are repeated in the second; three of the narratives in the first volume are fragments. These cases have led in the past to some confusion in tabulating how many cases there are. For the record, I have not counted duplicate cases, but have included the three fragmentary cases in my calculation. I have also found one of McCulloch's narratives in published form that no longer survives in the manuscripts. See Margaret Bruce, *Spiritual Earnestness; As It Was Manifested in the Life and Experience of Margaret Bruce, a Scottish Peasant Girl* (London: Nisbet and Co., 1855). This case would run the total to 109. For American researchers, I have deposited a microfilm copy of the manuscripts at Speer Library, Princeton Theological Seminary.

7. McCulloch, "Examinations," 1:316.

8. Ibid., 1:319.

9. Ibid., 1:320. The diction here echoes Zechariah 12:10: "They shall look upon me whom they have pierced, and they shall mourn for him." This verse, a pervasive part of this sacramental piety, is also echoed in John 19:37.

10. Ibid., 1:321. This is the first of many visionary statements that raised the suspicions of the ministerial editors. They marked it for deletion. The significance of this sort of editing as indicative of a possible division between the mental world of the laity and that of the ministers is discussed in the section "Popular Visions and Ministerial Revisions."

11. Ibid., 1:322–23. The ministers were wary of her diction here and marked the "Marriage Covenant" phrase for deletion. This is not easily explained. One of the foremost catechists and sacramentalists of the period and perhaps one of the editors of the Cambuslang manuscripts, John Willison, regularly applied such terms to the Lord's Supper. The theme of taking Christ as one's husband in this rite was standard in the minds of most clerics and congregants alike. See Willison, *Sacramental Catechism*, 9, 64, 123–24, 218, 223–25, 288, 297, 300, 322–23, 361, 376. Also see the discussion of this motif in the section "Communion and Consummation."

12. Ibid., 1:323–24.

13. Ibid., 1:324. The ministers consistently bracketed passages detailing such voices and visions for expunction.

14. Ibid., 1:325. The ministers would have deleted this revealing detail of her rising time and again to look at the Lord's table.

15. Ibid. The visionary elements in this passage received clerical censure.

16. Ibid., 1:337–39, 342.

17. Ibid., 1:329, 332, 334, 339, 343. Almost all mention of these dramatic visions and voices would have been expunged.

18. Ibid., 1:344.

19. John Dun, *Sermons in Two Volumes*, 2 vols. (Kilmarnock: J. Wilson, 1790), 1:207–8.

20. The historiography of Scottish Presbyterian piety is extremely thin. Adam Philip's summary work, *The Devotional Literature of Scotland* (London: Clarke, 1922) provides a basic discussion of some of the leading ministerial works. Puritans and Anglicans have fared far better than their Presbyterian counterparts. For discussions of Protestant devotion in England or New England, see Charles E. Hambrick-Stowe, *The Practice of Piety: Puritan Devotional Disciplines in Seventeenth-Century New England* (Chapel Hill: University of North Carolina Press, 1982); Charles Lloyd Cohen, *God's Caress: The Psychology of Puritan Religious Experience* (New York: Oxford University Press, 1986); Barbara Kiefer Lewalski, *Protestant Poetics and the Seventeenth-Century Religious Lyric* (Princeton: Princeton University Press, 1979), 147–78; Jerald C. Brauer, "Types of Puritan Piety," *Church History* 56 (1987): 39–58; C. J. Stranks, *Anglican Devotion: Studies in the Spiritual Life of the Church of England Between the Reformation and the Oxford Movement* (London: S.C.M. Press, 1961); Helen C. White, *The Tudor Books of Private Devotion* (Madison: University of Wisconsin Press, 1951); Helen C. White, *English Devotional Literature (Prose) 1600–1640* (Madison: University of Wisconsin Press, 1931); Louis L. Martz, *The Poetry of Meditation: A Study in English Religious Literature of the Seventeenth Century* (New Haven: Yale University Press, 1954); Gordon S. Wakefield, *Puritan Devotion: Its Place in the Development of Christian Piety* (London: Epworth Press, 1957). Of these works, only those of Hambrick-Stowe and Cohen inquire into popular as well as ministerial piety; most focus on ministerial works. For a highly engaging piece on the mentality of a prominent New England layman, see David D. Hall, "The Mental World of Samuel Sewall," *Proceedings of the Massachusetts Historical Society* 92 (1980): 21–44.

21. Baird Tipson, "The Elusiveness of 'Puritanism,' " *Religious Studies Review* 11 (1985): 250.

22. *A Letter from a Blacksmith to the Ministers and Elders of the Church of Scotland in which the Manner of Public Worship in that Church is Considered; Its Inconveniences and Defects Pointed Out; and Methods for Removing of Them Humbly Proposed* (London, 1759; New Haven: Oliver Steele, 1814), 18–38. Extended discussion of this *Letter* and Burns' poem, "The Holy Fair," is offered in the next chapter.

23. Cambuslang Kirk Session Records, Scottish Record Office, Edinburgh, 1 November 1744, 2:327; Stranraer Kirk Session Records, Scottish Record Office, Edinburgh, 10 July 1704, 1:241–42; Ayr Kirk Session Records, Strathclyde Regional Archives, Mitchell Library, Glasgow, 30 July 1750, 12: unpaginated; Bar-

ony Kirk Session Records, Strathclyde Regional Archives, Mitchell Library, Glasgow, 9 July 1758, 5: unpaginated. For more on drink and the issue of reforming the communions, see chapter 4.

24. Ayr Kirk Session Records, 13 August 1750, 27 August 1750, 17 September 1750, 2 March 1752, 12: unpaginated.

25. Carnock Kirk Session Records, Scottish Record Office, Edinburgh, 12 February 1748, 2:173. On the Blain and McBlain case, see Stranraer Presbytery Records, Scottish Record Office, Edinburgh, 13 August 1712, 2:237; Galloway Synod Records, Scottish Record Office, Edinburgh, 2:334, 344–45; 3:10–11, 23, 132. The Ballantrae session records evidently do not survive for these years, but the case was taken up by the presbytery and the synod.

26. Paisley Kirk Session Records, Scottish Record Office, Edinburgh, 20 May 1701, 46(1):12r–12v; John Lyle, "Narratio factorum," Kentucky Historical Society manuscripts, Frankfort, 41–42, 45–46.

27. Barony Kirk Session Records, 27 August 1766, 24 September 1766, 6: unpaginated; Govan Kirk Session Records, Strathclyde Regional Archives, Mitchell Library, Glasgow, 22–23 July 1733, 3 August 1733, 4:20–22; Culross Kirk Session Records, Scottish Record Office, Edinburgh, 29 July 1736, 17 August 1736, 23 November 1736, 10:14–15, 21.

28. Ayr Presbytery Records, Strathclyde Regional Archives, Mitchell Library, Glasgow, 18 December 1765, 7:183–84.

29. John Witherspoon, "Seasonable Advice to Young Persons," in *The Works of John Witherspoon, D.D., Sometime Minister of the Gospel at Paisley, and Late President of Princeton College, in New Jersey,* 9 vols. (Edinburgh: Ogle and Aikman, 1804–1805), 5:90–95.

30. Ibid.

31. Ibid., 5:93.

32. McCulloch, "Examinations," 2:49–50.

33. Ibid., 2:51.

34. Ibid., 2:52–54.

35. Ibid., 2:52, 55. Inexplicably some of the narratives in the second volume simply drop off. Perhaps in such cases McCulloch could tell they were unsuitable for publication and simply did not bother to complete them. The accounts in the second volume were, after all, never prepared for publication. They tended to represent a second tier behind the more exemplary saints of the first volume.

36. Ibid., 2:483–84. See Carlo Ginzburg, *The Cheese and the Worms: The Cosmos of a Sixteenth-Century Miller,* trans. John and Anne Tedeschi (Baltimore: Johns Hopkins University Press, 1980). Robert Wodrow in his *Analecta: Or, Materials for a History of Remarkable Providences; Mostly Relating to Scotch Ministers and Christians,* 4 vols. (Edinburgh: Maitland Club, 1842–1843) recorded an interesting story similar to this soldier's. John Broun—an "unlearned," but "exercised Christian"—was subjected at one communion in particular to "horride suggestions to doubt of all religion." "Ther wer soe many [religions] in the world, he knew not which of them was best; and what was in his religion more then in Popery, Mahumetanism, &c.?" (1:70–71). Like McCulloch's soldier, Broun overcame these temptations to unbelief.

37. Ibid.

38. Ibid., 2:26. On such tensions between these evangelicals and their employers, see also 1:53, 73–74, 182, 190; 2:86, 357, 476, 542.

39. Ibid., 2:445. On the conflict between the Protestant or bourgeois ethic and these lengthy sacramental occasions, see chapter 4.

40. John Barr, *Early Religious History of John Barr, Written by Himself, and Left as a Legacy to his Grand-children* (Philadelphia: Presbyterian Board of Publication, 1852), 31; McCulloch, "Examinations," 1:94; 2:202, 348; "Our Communions: Some Reflections on Them, No. II," *North Carolina Presbyterian*, 20 June 1866.

41. William Carse's painting was based upon a painting by his father, Alexander, done about 1816 and called *Mauchline Holy Fair.* William's work, though closely derivative, is less formal and stylized than his father's painting. Alexander's work was essentially a rendering of Burns' poem, while William's is a slightly freer and livelier genre scene. For the painting by Alexander Carse, see Stanley Cursiter, *Scottish Art to the Close of the Nineteenth Century* (London: George G. Harrap and Co., 1949), 107.

42. McCulloch, "Examinations," 1:355; 2:86, 140, 308, 312. See also 1:10–11, 223, 256, 262, 522, 524, 534; 2:9–10, 39, 76, 85, 124–27, 342, 344, 429.

43. Ibid., 2:677–78. See Richard Vines, *A Treatise of the Institution, Right Administration, and Receiving of the Sacrament of the Lords-Supper* (London: A.M., 1657).

44. Ibid., 1:7–8; Willison, *Sacramental Catechism*, 112–14, 143–50, 357; Henry Duncan, "The Most Memorable Passages of the Life of M. H. D. Containing Many Instances of Divine Goodness of Holy Wise and Powerful Providences towards a Sinner the Most Unworthy and Undeserving of the Leist of Gods Mercies Begun to be Extracted out of my Diary this 19th of May 1708," Wodrow manuscripts, National Library of Scotland, Edinburgh, 19. See also John Willison, *The Young Communicant's Catechism: Or, A Help Both Short and Plain, for Instructing and Preparing the Young to Make a Right Approach unto the Lord's Table* (Edinburgh: Thomas Lumisden and John Robertson, 1734), 48–51; McCulloch, "Examinations," 1:219, 353; 2:199, 523; Barr, *Early Religious History*, 24–28; Thomas Boston, *Memoirs of the Life, Time, and Writings of the Reverend and Learned Thomas Boston, A.M.*, ed. George H. Morrison (Edinburgh: Oliphant, Anderson, and Ferrier, 1899), 43, 276, 283–85.

45. Willison, *Young Communicant's Catechism*, 48–51; John Barr, *Plain Catechetical Instructions for Young Communicants, Designed to Assist Them in Forming Scriptural Views of the Lord's Supper* (Glasgow, 1824; Philadelphia: Presbyterian Board of Publication, 1842), 60–72, 90–96; Willison, *Sacramental Catechism*, 112.

46. McCulloch, "Examinations," 1:223–24; 2:141. See also 1:232, 236, 331, 335; 2:42, 254, 484.

47. Willison, *Young Communicant's Catechism*, 60–64; Willison, *Sacramental Catechism*, 120–21.

48. Willison, *Young Communicant's Catechism*, xi–xvii. For examples of these personal covenants, see the "Notebook of Colin Alison, 1684–1726," Edinburgh

University Library manuscripts, especially the lengthy section entitled "Formes of Personal Covenanting" which cites ten different covenants in full, including transcriptions of exemplary ones from such Scottish divines as William Guthrie, John Willison, Alexander Shields, and Thomas Boston as well as a covenant of "a Private Christian" signed 16 July 1726. An excellent example also survives in the papers of an eighteenth-century Scottish woman, Anne Stewart, who from year to year renewed her personal covenant before going to the Lord's table by subscribing to the document anew each time. See *Selections from the Family Papers Preserved at Caldwell*, 3 vols. (Glasgow: Maitland Club, 1854), 1:256–58; 2:5n. On the American side, for the personal covenant of Frances Blair (dated 14 August 1763), see William Henry Foote, *Sketches of Virginia, Historical and Biographical*, 2d series (Philadelphia: J. B. Lippincott and Co., 1855), 86–87. For another American case, see James W. Alexander, *The Life of Archibald Alexander, D.D.* (New York: Charles Scribner, 1854), 72–73.

49. Duncan, "Memorable Passages," 19–20; McCulloch, "Examinations," 1:229.

50. Willison, *Sacramental Catechism*, 214; McCulloch, "Examinations," 1:610.

51. John Moodey, "Diary of Rev. John Moodey, 1776–1857, Pastor of Middle Springs Presbyterian Church, Cumberland County, Pa.," Presbyterian Study Center manuscripts, Montreat, North Carolina, 13–15; McCulloch, "Examinations," 1:238; John Willison, *An Example of Plain Catechising upon the Assembly's Shorter Catechism* (Edinburgh, 1744; Pittsburgh: Loomis, 1832), 255, 257.

52. McCulloch, "Examinations," 2:141.

53. Willison, *Sacramental Catechism*, 207–9.

54. McCulloch, "Examinations," 2:151; Willison, *Sacramental Catechism*, 208, 219; Willison, *An Example of Plain Catechising*, 232–33. For a diary that is especially revealing on the herculean efforts to attain "fixedness" in preparing for the sacrament, see George Brown, *Diary of George Brown, Merchant in Glasgow, 1745–1753* (Glasgow: Thomas Constable, 1856), esp. 1–3, 96–100, 103–9, 143–46, 181–203, 245–47, 320–35.

55. Barr, *Early Religious History*, 35. The material on "John Chestnuts Catechism" is in Thomas Vincent's *Explicatory Catechism* (Glasgow: James Duncan, 1788) at Speer Library, Princeton Theological Seminary.

56. Boston, *Memoirs*, 43.

57. McCulloch, "Examinations," 1:215. See also 1:57, 216, 228, 230; 2:26, 142, 377, 540. For devotional directions to this effect, see Daniel Campbell, *Sacramental Meditations on the Sufferings and Death of Christ*, 4th ed. (Edinburgh: Anderson, 1703), 107.

58. Ibid., 1:59. The ministers looked askance at her kissing of the Bible and would have deleted mention of this gesture that probably smacked to them of papistry. It may also have suggested an old controversy surrounding "the *Idolatrous Kiss*[ing]" of the Bible as a form of oath taking. See [Gabriel Wilson], *The New Mode of Swearing in Scotland, Touching and Kissing of the Gospels, Consider'd* (n.p.: n.p., 1719).

59. Ibid., 2:661. See also, for example, 1:485, 487, 489, 546; 2:30, 254, 331,

639; Barr, *Early Religious History*, 23–24, 27, 35. Reading skills among the saints at Cambuslang were nearly universal. Literacy made the devotionals viable, and conversely the devotionals (as did the catechisms, the psalms, and the Bible) provided major incentives to acquire reading skills. On popular religion and literacy, see Smout, "Born Again at Cambuslang," 121–27.

60. Ibid., 2:331; John Willison, *A Treatise on the Sanctification of the Lord's Day* (Edinburgh, 1722; Edinburgh: J. Pillans, 1819), 123.

61. John Spalding, *Synaxis Sacra; Or, A Collection of Sermons Preached at Several Communions, Together with Speeches at the Tables both before, at, and after that Work, Fitted for the Whole Occasions Relating Thereto* (Edinburgh, 1703; Glasgow: James Meuros, 1750), unpaginated subscription list at front of 1750 edition; James Robe, *A Third Volume of Sermons for the Most Part Preached at the Celebration of the Lord's Supper* (Glasgow: J. Bryce and D. Paterson, 1756), unpaginated list of "Subscribers Names" in front matter.

62. See, for example, the New College Library's copy of John Gillies, *A Catechism upon the Sufferings of the Redeemer. Compiled for the Use of Young Communicants* (Glasgow: John Orr, 1763); and the British Library's copy of Robert Craighead, *Advice to Communicants for Necessary Preparation, and Profitable Improvement of the Great and Comfortable Ordinance of the Lords Supper* (Edinburgh: William Dickie, 1695).

63. McCulloch, "Examinations," 2:30. In addition to his *Sacramental Meditations*, Campbell also published *The Frequent and Devout Communicant, or A Treatise Concerning the Sacrament of the Lord's Supper* (Edinburgh: Anderson, 1703). Since the latter was three times as long as the former, it is doubtful that the reference in the Cambuslang manuscripts to Campbell's "little Book on the Sacrament" was to the larger treatise. The meditations were more popular and went through several editions, being reprinted, for example, at least three times in America—in 1740, c. 1785, and 1792.

64. Campbell, *Sacramental Meditations*, preface and pp. 18, 25, 29, 33, 39, 41. This last estimate about the nauseating effect of the sight Campbell borrowed from an unidentified author. Campbell garnered images from a wide range of authors—from Tertullian to Augustine to Bernard to the Carthusian Ludolphus of Saxony to the Puritan Isaac Ambrose. For continuities between Reformed devotionals and Catholic ones, see especially Hambrick-Stowe's discussion in *The Practice of Piety*, 25–39.

65. Ibid., 52–54; McCulloch, "Examinations," 1:359. Surprisingly, given manuals like Campbell's, the ministers thought this saint's fascination with the cross as rack excessive and thus marked this passage for expunction. The popular devotional writer John Flavel observed succinctly: "The Cross was a Rack, as well as a Gibbet." See his *The Cursed Death of the Cross Described and Comfortably Improved* (Boston: Harrison, 1743), 5. Flavel's work also carried an illustrative wood-cut of Christ's crucifixion; Scottish devotionals, like Campbell's, were not illustrated in this way, however.

66. Campbell, *Sacramental Meditations*, 92, 96, 98.

67. Ibid., 53–54, 107–8.

68. Boston, *Memoirs*, 275. The use of such pictorial images apparently was not

as easily reformed as Presbyterians would have liked. In 1612, for example, the presbytery of Glasgow had to deal with three painters who had "painted the crucifix in many houses." See Glasgow Presbytery Records, Strathclyde Regional Archives, the Mitchell Library, Glasgow, 35:248–49, 251, 317.

69. McCulloch, "Examinations," 1:292–93. This passage detailing his sight of Christ on the cross was bracketed for deletion.

70. Ibid., 1:217. See also 1:97, 106, 261, 283, 306, 383, 464, 494, 517; 2:356, 374, 379, 584. In some cases this very disavowal was bracketed for deletion, perhaps because it intimated that others had fainted and had visions.

71. Ibid., 1:514.

72. Ibid., 1:13; 354. For other visions or voices, especially for those that were seen or heard at the Lord's table, see 1:230, 278, 292–93, 324–25, 334, 339, 342, 356, 513–14, 534, 599; 2:151, 351, 421–22, 449–52, 474, 594.

73. Ibid., 1:134–38, 142. One suspects that the "as it were" phrase was an editorial gloss by McCulloch. The phrase, which serves to lessen the starkness and vividness of the scene, seems to crop up too consistently in these accounts to have been part of the diction of so many different people, but instead would appear to be the words of the scribe.

74. Ibid., 1:599; 230; 289, 292, 314, 325; 2:450. For a supporting text, see also James Robe, *Narratives of the Extraordinary Work of the Spirit of God, at Cambuslang, Kilsyth, & c. Begun 1742* (Glasgow: David Niven, 1790), 227–35. Robe himself took an unusually lenient stand toward ecstatic religious experience, including visions. But in a revealing passage on how one woman's spiritual autobiography was bowdlerized for publication by the Seceders, he remarked: "Wherever there is a vision, it is either altogether omitted, or turned into a faith's view of what, she says, she really saw with her bodily eyes" (p. 227). What Robe, in trying to score a point against the Seceders who were opposing the revival at Cambuslang and Kilsyth, failed to note was that these editorial principles were generally shared by his evangelical colleagues in the Church of Scotland.

75. Willison, *Sacramental Catechism*, 301, 317–18, 373.

76. James McGready, *The Posthumous Works of the Reverend and Pious James M'Gready, Late Minister of the Gospel in Henderson, K[entuck]y*, ed. James Smith (Nashville: J. Smith's Steam Press, 1837), 120, 348–58.

77. Ibid., 101, 354, 385, 405–6.

78. Duncan, "Memorable Passages," 15–17; McCulloch, "Examinations," 1:466.

79. Lyle, "Narratio factorum," 53.

80. Duncan, "Memorable Passages," 15–17.

81. Ibid., 16.

82. McCulloch, "Examinations," 1:150, 190, 254–55, 257, 265–66.

83. Ibid., 1:255; David Calderwood, *A Dispute upon Communicating at Our Confused Communions* (n.p.: n.p., 1624), 18.

84. Gilbert Goudie, ed., *The Diary of the Reverend John Mill* (Edinburgh: Scottish History Society, 1889), 19. See also James Oliphant, *A Sacramental Catechism, Designed for Communicants Old and Young*, 5th ed. (Glasgow: John Bryce, 1783), 63–64. For a particularly harsh estimate of "the general prevalency

of Ignorance" and "gross Mistakes" among the laity on eucharistic matters, see [James Hog], *A Letter to a Friend, Containing Diverse Remarks Concerning the Sacrament of the Lord's Supper* (Edinburgh: James Watson, 1706), 47–48.

85. Spalding, *Synaxis Sacra*, 180.

86. Galston Kirk Session Records, 6 July 1703, 7:70; 11 July 1703, 8: unpaginated, Scottish Record Office, Edinburgh; Henry Paton, ed., *Dundonald Parish Records: The Session Book of Dundonald, 1602–1731* (Edinburgh: Morrison and Gibb, 1936), 582. For another case of a man "taking away the bread from the table," see William Cramond and Stephen Ree, eds., *The Records of Elgin, 1234–1800*, 2 vols. (Aberdeen: New Spalding Club, 1908), 2:228.

87. On such popular beliefs and practices surrounding the eucharist, see Keith Thomas, *Religion and the Decline of Magic: Studies in Popular Beliefs in Sixteenth and Seventeenth Century England* (London: Weidenfeld and Nicolson, 1971), 33–36, 53–57; Dennis Steel Devlin, "Corpus Christi: A Study in Medieval Eucharistic Theory, Devotion, and Practice" (Ph.D. diss., University of Chicago, 1975), 236–40.

88. Willison, *Sacramental Catechism*, 209, 372–73.

89. McCulloch, "Examinations," 1:598.

90. Ibid., 1:191–92, 200, 231.

91. Ibid., 2:385, 452–53.

92. Ibid., 2:358, 445.

93. *Letter from a Blacksmith*, 50–51.

94. McCulloch, "Examinations," 2:311, 458, 499.

95. Ibid., 1:69–70, 413.

96. Ibid., 1:14; "Our Communions: Some Reflections on Them, No. I," *North Carolina Presbyterian*, 13 July 1866; Lyle, "Narratio factorum," 58.

97. McCulloch, "Examinations," 1:110; Willison, *Sacramental Catechism*, xii, 158, 274–75; Willison, *Treatise*, 178. See also 1:374, 473; 2:519, 533 in the McCulloch volumes.

98. Elisabeth West, *Memoirs, Or Spiritual Exercises of Elisabeth West: Written by Her Own Hand* (Edinburgh: Ogle and Aikman, 1807), 66, 70. As suggested, in *The Practice of Piety* Charles Hambrick-Stowe makes some similar observations about the importance of life-long pilgrimage and preparation in Puritan spirituality in the seventeenth century. Here I extend his perceptive analysis to the evangelical Presbyterians of both the seventeenth and eighteenth centuries.

99. Willison, *Sacramental Catechism*, iv, 172–75, 220.

100. McCulloch, "Examinations," 2:383, 531. See also 1:2, 19, 35, 68, 189–90, 216, 255–57, 312, 432, 513; 2:42, 152, 199, 254, 325, 357, 401, 456, 479–80, 665–67. See also Barr, *Early Religious History*, 32–33.

101. "Sermons Att the Communion att the West Port, October 1688," National Library of Scotland manuscripts, Edinburgh, 1–2; Goudie, ed., *Diary*, 19; Wodrow, *Analecta*, 1:110, 344–45; 2:66–67; Spalding, *Synaxis Sacra*, 15–16, 25.

102. McCulloch, "Examinations," 2:162.

103. Ibid., 1:68. See also 1:2, 5–7, 9, 83–84, 109–10, 220, 285, 302, 307, 372–

73, 388–92, 409–13, 453–54; 2:27, 74, 79, 154, 289–90, 307–8, 405, 510–12, 561.

104. Willison, *Sacramental Catechism*, 304–5. See also *Western Missionary Magazine* 2 (1804): 40; John Willison, *A Sacramental Directory, Or A Treatise Concerning the Sanctification of a Communion-Sabbath* (Edinburgh, 1716; Aberdeen: George and Robert King, 1846), 118, 183.

105. Spalding, *Synaxis Sacra*, 21–24; Boston, *Memoirs*, 285.

106. Mary Somervel, *A Clear and Remarkable Display of the Condescension, Love and Faithfulness of God, in the Spiritual Experiences of Mary Somervel* (Glasgow: George Caldwell, 1782), 28.

107. Quoted in Henry Grey Graham, *The Social Life of Scotland in the Eighteenth Century* (London, 1899; London: Black, 1928), 342.

108. McCulloch, "Examinations," 1:205, 580. See also 1:6–7, 13, 119, 134, 189, 195, 211–14, 246–48, 396–97, 455–58, 513–14, 530–32, 606–7; 2:61, 96, 145, 262–64, 290–95, 565–70.

109. Ibid., 1:293, 472–73, 580; 2:586; Willison, *Sacramental Meditations*, 64, 376. See also 1:59, 100, 260, 293, 323–24, 254, 396–97, 550; 2:163, 291, 325, 358, 500, 566–67, 576 in the McCulloch volumes.

110. McCulloch, "Examinations," 1:245, 247; 2:587.

111. Ibid., 2:19, 94.

112. Ibid., 1:327, 343; Willison, *Sacramental Catechism*, 301.

113. For wide-ranging historical and theoretical discussion of such issues, see Caroline Walker Bynum, *Holy Feast and Holy Fast: The Religious Significance of Food to Medieval Women* (Berkeley: University of California Press, 1987); Caroline Walker Bynum, Stevan Harrell, and Paula Richman, eds., *Gender and Religion: On the Complexity of Symbols* (Boston: Beacon Press, 1986); Caroline Walker Bynum, "Women Mystics and Eucharistic Devotion in the Thirteenth Century," *Women's Studies* 11 (1984): 179–214.

114. For examples of women who spoke of Christ as husband or Bridegroom, see McCulloch, "Examinations," 1:13, 59, 69, 230, 323–24, 327, 391, 395–96, 530, 580–81; 2:142, 541, 553, 566–67, 570. For examples of men, see 1:7, 132, 151, 354, 549–50; 2:163, 325.

115. Elizabeth Cairns, *Memoirs of the Life of Elizabeth Cairns, Written by Herself Some Years before Her Death; and Now Taken from Her own Original Copy with Great Care and Diligence* (Glasgow: John Greig, n.d.), 5, 100–102; Somervel, *Clear and Remarkable Display*, 9, 27–28; West, *Memoirs*, 35.

116. McCulloch, "Examinations," 1:13, 530; 2:566–70. I follow Caroline Walker Bynum on the continuity in these symbols for women. See especially Bynum, *Holy Feast*, 24–26, 276–89.

117. Bynum, *Holy Feast*, 25.

118. McCulloch, "Examinations," 1:404, 549–50.

119. Ibid., 2:163.

120. Ibid., 2:578–79. This last passage echoes Song of Solomon 2:17.

121. Ibid., 2:150; Gilbert Tennent, William Tennent, and Samuel Blair, *Sermons on Sacramental Occasions by Divers Ministers* (Boston: Draper, 1739), 59, 113.

122. Willison, *Sacramental Catechism*, 16, 97–98, 322–23; McCulloch "Examinations," 2:566; Bruce, *Spiritual Earnestness*, 59.

123. McCulloch, "Examinations," 1:12, 343; Willison, *Sacramental Catechism*, 164.

124. Willison, *Sacramental Catechism*, 97, 221, 373. See also "Sermons Att the Communion att the West Port," 87, 96, 107, 178–80.

CHAPTER 4

1. Edward P. Humphrey and Thomas H. Cleland, *Memoirs of the Rev. Thomas Cleland, D.D., Compiled from his Private Papers* (Cincinnati: Moore, Wilstach, Keys and Co., 1859), 41–44, 53–56, 102–5.

2. [Archibald Newton], *Uldericus Veridicus, sive, De Statu Ecclesiae Scoticanae, Dialogus* (Edinburgh: n.p., 1657), translated and quoted in *Dan in Beersheba: Or, The Idolatry of Communion Sermons, in a Few Reflections on that Pamphlet, Dan an Adder in the Path, &c.* (Edinburgh: William Brown and Co., 1721), 24–25; John Sage, *The Fundamental Charter of Presbytery, as It Hath Been Lately Established, in the Kingdom of Scotland, Examin'd and Disprov'd* (London: C. Brome, 1695), 373; Thomas Rhind, *An Apology for Mr Thomas Rhind* (Edinburgh: Robert Freebairn, 1712), 159, 182–85, 190, 197–98. See also [James Wood], *A True Representation of the Rise, Progresse, and State of the Present Divisions of the Church of Scotland* (London: n.p., 1657), 35–37; Gilbert Burnet, *Bishop Burnet's History of His Own Time*, 2 vols. (London: Thomas Ward and Joseph Downing, 1724–1734), 1:63–64.

3. On Burns' early and immediate acclaim in America, see Anna M. Painter, "American Editions of the *Poems* of Burns before 1800," *Library* 12 (1932): 434–56. As Painter comments, "wherever Scotsmen had gone, the poems and fame of Burns followed" (p. 434). His *Poems, Chiefly in the Scottish Dialect* were first published in Kilmarnock in 1786. Editions from Edinburgh, London, Philadelphia, New York, Dublin, and Belfast were out by 1788. Dissemination of the Blacksmith's *Letter* was similarly widespread. By the 1820s there had been at least seven American editions and double that in Britain.

4. For recent studies of the Scottish Enlightenment, see Nicholas Phillipson, "The Scottish Enlightenment," in Roy Porter and Mikuláš Teich, eds., *The Enlightenment in National Context* (Cambridge: Cambridge University Press, 1981), 19–40; Charles Camic, *Experience and Enlightenment: Socialization for Cultural Change in Eighteenth-Century Scotland* (Chicago: University of Chicago Press, 1983); Richard B. Sher, *Church and University in the Scottish Enlightenment: The Moderate Literati of Edinburgh* (Princeton: Princeton University Press, 1985). An old standard is William Law Mathieson, *The Awakening of Scotland: A History from 1747 to 1797* (Glasgow: J. Maclehose and Sons, 1910). For the American side, see, for example, Henry F. May, *The Enlightenment in America* (New York: Oxford University Press, 1976); Mark A. Noll, "The Irony of the Enlightenment for Presbyterians in the Early Republic," *Journal of the Early Republic* 5 (1985): 149–75.

5. Robert Burns, *The Poems and Songs of Robert Burns*, ed. James Kinsley, 3 vols. (Oxford: Clarendon Press, 1968), 1:113; G. Ross Roy, ed., *The Letters of*

Robert Burns, 2 vols. (Oxford: Clarendon Press, 1985), 1:88; "Preface," in Robert Burns, *Poems Chiefly in the Scottish Dialect* (Philadelphia: Peter Stewart and George Hyde, 1788), iv. On Burns' relationship to the traditional culture of Ayrshire, see James Kinsley, "Burns and the Peasantry, 1785," *Proceedings of the British Academy* 60 (1974): 135–53; Rosalind Mitchison, "The Rural Setting of Burns's Youth," *Scotia: American-Canadian Journal of Scottish Studies* 7 (1983): 16–24. As Kinsley says, Burns saw "the rustic society about him with the sympathy and critical clarity of a Brueghel" (p. 138).

6. Burns, *Poems and Songs*, 1:114, 124–26; Roy, ed., *Letters*, 1:135, 303; Henry Mackenzie, "Surprising effects of Original Genius, exemplified in the Poetical Productions of Rob't Burns, an Ayrshire Plowman," *Lounger*, 1786, reprinted in Donald A. Low, ed., *Robert Burns: The Critical Heritage* (London: Routledge and Kegan Paul, 1974), 70. For good discussions of Burns' religion, see Thomas Crawford, *Burns: A Study of the Poems and Songs* (Edinburgh: Oliver and Boyd, 1960), 25–76; A. Burns Jamieson, *Burns and Religion* (Cambridge: W. Heffer and Sons, 1931). Both see Burns as an enlightened skeptic who nevertheless remained intrigued by the traditional Calvinism he rejected. The sensitivity of both to Burns' religious searching is matched, however, by an insensitivity to the popular evangelical faith he deserted.

7. That is, streaked red and white.

8. A sloe is a blackthorn shrub or its fruit—the former known for its prickles and the latter for its astringency.

9. Burns, *Poems and Songs*, 1:128–37. This citation is to the whole poem, and thus these pages can be consulted as well for subsequent quotations from "The Holy Fair." The illustration by Wright and Rogers is from Robert Burns, *The Works of Robert Burns*, 2 vols. (Edinburgh: James Inglis, [1865]), 1:195. For other illustrations of Fun and her grim counterparts, Superstition and Hypocrisy, see Robert Burns, *The Poetical Works of Robert Burns; with his Life*, 2 vols. (Alnwick: Catnach and Davison, 1808), 1:89; James Currie, ed., *The Works of Robert Burns, with an Account of his Life*, 4 vols. (London: T. Cadell and W. Davies, 1820), 3:30.

10. The photograph of this engraving was taken from [G. Gleig], *A Critique on the Poems of Robert Burns* (Edinburgh: John Brown, 1812), opposite p. 19.

11. George B. Burnet, *The Holy Communion in the Reformed Church of Scotland, 1560–1960* (Edinburgh: Oliver and Boyd, 1960), 248–55; Mary Ellen Brown, *Burns and Tradition* (Urbana: University of Illinois Press, 1984), 15; John Strawhorn, *Ayrshire: The Story of a County* (Ayr: Ayrshire Archaeological and Natural History Society, 1975), 135; "Extract of Letter, from Gilbert Burns to Dr. Currie," in James Currie, ed., *The Works of Robert Burns* (Edinburgh, 1800; Philadelphia: Crissy and Markley, 1853), 239; Jamieson, *Burns and Religion*, 50. When interpreters have moved beyond Burns' own description of the holy fair, they have usually fallen back on the Blacksmith as corroboration of Burns' perspective or have relied upon the depiction of the late nineteenth-century historian Henry Grey Graham. See, for example, Crawford, *Burns*, 68–70; Jamieson, *Burns and Religion*, 50–55.

12. "The Minutes of the Kirk Session of Mauchline, 1783–1789," Strathclyde

Regional Archives photostat, Mitchell Library, Glasgow, 22, 68, 127, 171–72, 213, 239. In 1785, for the communion upon which Burns was said to have based his poem, the session noted simply: "The Sact. of our Lords Supper having been dispensed in this place upon Sabbath last. Communicants about 1242" (p. 127).

13. Burke quoted in Thomas Bender, *Community and Social Change in America* (New Brunswick, N.J.: Rutgers University Press, 1978), 10.

14. Burns, *Poems and Songs*, 1:131.

15. On this Scottish form, see Kinsley, "Burns and the Peasantry," 140–47; Allan H. MacLaine, "The Christis Kirk Tradition: Its Evolution in Scots Poetry to Burns," *Studies in Scottish Literature* 2 (1964–1965): 3–18, 111–24, 163–82, 234–50. Quotations are from MacLaine, pp. 11, 13; and Kinsley, p. 142.

16. Hamilton Paul, ed., *The Poems and Songs of Robert Burns, with a Life of the Author, Containing a Variety of Particulars, Drawn From Sources Inaccessible by Former Biographers* (Ayr: Wilson, M'Cormick and Carnie, 1819), xxiv–xxviii, xxxix; [Gleig], *A Critique on the Poems of Burns*, 16–17; Robert Heron, *A Memoir of the Life of the Late Robert Burns* (Edinburgh: T. Brown, 1797), 13. See also MacKenzie, "Surprising Effects of Original Genius," reprinted in Low, ed., *Burns: The Critical Heritage*, 70.

17. Jamieson, for example, dismissed orthodox responses to "The Holy Fair" as "utterly worthless but affording much amusement to the present-day reader." See Jamieson, *Burns and Religion*, 56.

18. [William Peebles], *Burnomania: The Celebrity of Robert Burns Considered: In a Discourse Addressed to All Real Christians of Every Denomination* (Edinburgh: G. Caw, 1811), 5–8, 25; John Dun, *Sermons in Two Volumes*, 2 vols. (Kilmarnock: J. Wilson, 1790), 1:257; James Maxwell, "On the Ayr-shire Ploughman Poet, or Poetaster, R.B.," reprinted in Low, ed., *Burns: The Critical Heritage*, 93; Fergus Ferguson, *Should Christians Commemorate the Birthday of Robert Burns? A Discourse* (Edinburgh: Andrew Elliot, 1869), 5, 24–25.

19. [Peebles], *Burnomania*, 19, 22; Burns, *Poems and Songs*, 1:133–34. See also Maxwell, "On the Ayr-Shire Ploughman Poet," in Low, ed., *Burns: The Critical Heritage*, 94; J. G. Lockhart, *Life of Robert Burns* (Edinburgh: Constable and Co., 1828), 100–101; Dun, *Sermons*, 1:197–208, 256–59. Dun's powerful addresses to communicants (pp. 197–208) provide substance to his repudiation of "The Holy Fair" (pp. 256–59). Also for one of Peebles' communion sermons, see his *Sermons on Various Subjects* (Edinburgh: George Caw, 1794), 133–55.

20. This common ascription of the *Letter* has been followed by most, though Witherspoon's principal biographer, Varnum Lansing Collins, long ago rejected it. See Collins, *President Witherspoon: A Biography*, 2 vols. (Princeton: Princeton University Press, 1925), 2:266. The attribution evidently first appeared in a 1791 London review of one of the many editions of the *Letter*, probably more as an Anglican barb than a serious ascription. Though Witherspoon later turned to the moral philosophy of the Scottish Enlightenment, in 1759, when the *Letter* was published, he was an arch-critic of those moderates who were moving toward *éclaircissement*. As a champion of the popular party, he satirized the taste of the polite and the enlightened—those who, among other things, were contemptuous of "evangelic enthusiasm," were disdainful of "the common people," advocated

"a rational way of preaching" and praying, and found the sacramental services "tedious and tiresome." See *Ecclesiastical Characteristics, or the Arcana of Church Policy* in *The Works of John Witherspoon, D.D., Sometime Minister of the Gospel at Paisley, and Late President of Princeton College, in New Jersey*, 9 vols. (Edinburgh: Ogle and Aikman, 1804–1805), 6:166, 168, 175–77, 188–90. All along Presbyterian respondents assumed that though the *Letter* was written "under Presbyterian colours" it had been composed by "an Episcopalian." See [Samuel Miller], "On the Use of Liturgies," *Biblical Repertory and Theological Review* 2 (1830): 389–407, with quotation on p. 390; *The Modes of Presbyterian Church-Worship Vindicated: In a Letter to the Blacksmith* (London, 1763; Newburyport: John Mycall, 1789), 11n, 13n, 14n, 22n, 53n.

21. *A Letter from a Blacksmith to the Ministers and Elders of the Church of Scotland in which the Manner of Public Worship in that Church is Considered; Its Inconveniences and Defects Pointed Out; and Methods for Removing of Them Humbly Proposed* (London, 1759; New Haven: Oliver Steele, 1814), 7, 11, 18–38.

22. Ibid., 21; *Modes of Presbyterian Church-Worship Vindicated*, 9–12, 14n. This answer to the Blacksmith was widely disseminated, going through editions in Scotland, Ireland, and America.

23. *Letter from a Blacksmith*, 18–19, 38–39, 42, 104–5, 119, 129, 137. See *Modes of Presbyterian Church-Worship Vindicated* for an extended defense of "the liberty of unfettered devotion" (p. 22).

24. Ibid., 17–18; Millar Patrick, *Four Centuries of Scottish Psalmody* (London: Oxford University Press, 1949), esp. 149–63, 191–94, 220–21, with quotation on p. 193; James Beattie, *A Letter to the Rev. Hugh Blair, D.D., One of the Ministers of Edinburgh, on the Improvement of Psalmody in Scotland* (Edinburgh: R. Buchanan, 1829), 27; Joseph Smith, *Old Redstone; Or, Historical Sketches of Western Presbyterianism, its Early Ministers, its Perilous Times, and its First Records* (Philadelphia: Lippincott, Grambo, and Co., 1854), 163–64.

25. *Letter from a Blacksmith*, 85–87; *Modes of Presbyterian Church-Worship Vindicated*, 35, 48.

26. Peter Burke explores the increasing gap between popular and learned culture in early modern Europe. He makes a case for what he terms "the withdrawal thesis"—that is, the withdrawal of learned elites from engagement with the culture of the common people. He documents this gap in several facets of culture—language, manners, education, medicine, and religion. Though he spends little time on Scotland, he intimates that this growing withdrawal of the elites was going on there as elsewhere, especially after 1750. This view is borne out by enlightened attitudes toward the festal communions. See Peter Burke, *Popular Culture in Early Modern Europe* (New York: Harper and Row, 1978), 270–81, 326.

27. James MacGregor, "Preface," in Thomas Burns, *Old Scottish Communion Plate* (Edinburgh: R. and R. Clark, 1892), xv; editorial note in the 1844 Spottiswoode edition of John Sage, *Fundamental Charter*, 368; Alexander Webster, *Burns and the Kirk: A Review of What the Poet Did for the Religious and Social Regeneration of the Scottish People* (Aberdeen: A. Martin, 1888), 22.

28. *Letter from a Blacksmith*, 28–30.

29. On the frequency issue within the medieval church, see Dennis Steel Devlin, "Corpus Christi: A Study in Medieval Eucharistic Theory, Devotion, and Practice" (Ph.D. diss., University of Chicago, 1975), 5–7, 137–43. Devlin casts the coincidence of increasing eucharistic devotion with declining frequency of lay reception as "one of the great paradoxes of medieval spirituality" (p. 137). With the sacramental occasion as an early modern parallel, the coincidence hardly seems paradoxical. Infrequency bred solemnity, mystery, and awe. See John Bossy, *Christianity in the West, 1400–1700* (Oxford: Oxford University Press, 1985), 70–72 for a perspective on the frequency issue in the late medieval period similar to mine on early modern Presbyterianism.

30. On the Westminster Directory, see the third section of chapter 1.

31. Clydesdale Synod Records, Scottish Record Office, Edinburgh, 1:70, 74, 100, 170, 179, 327; 2:48, 108, 115, 136, 181, 194, 200–201, 209, 214, 255, 306; 3:118–19, 145, 385, 388; Irvine Presbytery Records, Scottish Record Office, Edinburgh, 3:478. The synod included the presbyteries of Glasgow, Ayr, Hamilton, Lanark, Irvine, Paisley, and Dunbarton; only Lanark reported much success at complying with the plans for reform. Some synods and presbyteries, such as the Galloway Synod, simply left the issue alone, but others, as did Clydesdale, actively promoted greater frequency. For other efforts, see Edinburgh Presbytery Records, Scottish Record Office, Edinburgh, 10:301–2; Stranraer Presbytery Records, Scottish Record Office, Edinburgh, 4:124, 338; Argyll Synod Records, Scottish Record Office, Edinburgh, 6:168, 322–23, 331, 341–42, 347–53, 7:8–10, 20, 23–24, 30–31, 36–37, 48, 57–58, 68–69, 77–78, 93, 105–6, 118, 125–26, 137–38. The Synod of Argyll in its efforts at reform, which centered mostly on the 1750s and 1760s, was modestly trying to move from bi-annual sacraments in various parishes in its domain to annual ones and did so with wide success. The synod also was less modestly attempting to streamline the communions, cutting back on the number of sermons and week-day services; this part of their reform effort, however, was plagued by controversy.

32. *Acts of the General Assembly of the Church of Scotland, M.DC.XXXVIII–M.DCCC.XLII* (Edinburgh: Edinburgh Printing and Publishing Co., 1843), 458, 471–72, 568, 705; [Thomas Randall], *A Letter to a Minister from his Friend, Concerning Frequent Communicating, Occasioned by the Late Overture of the Synod of Glasgow and Air upon that Subject* (Glasgow: n.p., 1749), 36; *An Address to the Christian People, under the Inspection of the Reformed Presbytery, Concerning the More Frequent Dispensing of the Lord's Supper* (Glasgow: n.p., 1795), 55. For the continued pursuit of the frequency issue at official levels, see the summary of acts in John Wilson, *Index to the Acts and Proceedings of the General Assembly of the Church of Scotland from the Revolution to the Present Time* (Edinburgh: William Blackwood and Sons, 1863), 225–28, and also *Case of the Kirk Session of St. Mary's Parish, Edinburgh, Relative to More Frequent Communion* (Edinburgh: A. Balfour, 1832).

33. *A Draught of the Form of the Government and Discipline of the Presbyterian Church in the United States of America* (New York: S. and J. Loudon, 1787), 79, 84–85; *The Constitution of the Presbyterian Church in the United States of America Containing the Confession of Faith, the Catechisms, the Government*

and Discipline, and the Directory for the Worship of God (Philadelphia: Thomas Bradford, 1789), 195, 198. For a discussion of the draft and the subsequent constitution, see Julius Melton, *Presbyterian Worship in America: Changing Patterns Since 1787* (Richmond: John Knox Press, 1967), 16–27. Melton discusses the differences over the sacramental season on pp. 26–27. Ministers John Rodgers of New York City, Alexander MacWhorter of Newark, James Wilson of Philadelphia, and Alexander Miller of Morristown, New Jersey, constituted the committee responsible for the draft that urged departure from the old way.

34. Ayr Presbytery Records, Strathclyde Regional Archives, Mitchell Library, Glasgow, 1 March 1749, 6 March 1750, 6:48–49, 58.

35. See [Randall], *A Letter to a Minister from his Friend*; John Erskine, *A Humble Attempt to Promote Frequent Communicating* (Glasgow: Robert Urie, 1749). John Willison also early on urged more frequent communion, but without suggesting that the sacramental season should be significantly abridged. His vision was one of celebrating the high days of the summer season throughout the year. Other advocates of frequency saw clearly that the lengthiness of the traditional sacramental occasions stood in the way of quarterly communions and hence moved to pare down the extended rituals in order to make frequency feasible. Willison, by contrast, thought that frequency would demand greater stringency in observing "fast, preparation, and thanksgiving days" in order to preserve the due solemnity of the sacrament. See, for example, John Willison, *A Sacramental Directory, Or A Treatise Concerning the Sanctification of a Communion-Sabbath* (Edinburgh, 1716; Aberdeen: George and Robert King, 1846), v–xxviii, with quotation on p. xviii. For an early prescriber of weekly communion, see the work of the Scottish sectary John Glas, *A Treatise on the Lord's Supper* (Edinburgh, 1743; London: Sampson, Low, Marston, Searle, and Rivington, 1883).

36. John M. Mason, *Letters on Frequent Communion: Addressed Originally to the Members of the Associate-Reformed Church in North America*, in *The Complete Works of John M. Mason, D.D.*, ed. Ebenezer Mason, 4 vols. (New York: Baker and Scribner, 1849), 1:420, 425, 461–62, 497.

37. Ibid., 1:418–20, 469, 472.

38. John Thomson, *Letters Addressed to the Rev. John Mason, A.M. of New-York, in Answer to his Letters on Frequent Communion* (Glasgow, 1799; Troy, N.Y.: R. Moffitt and Co., 1801), 10, 28–29, 31. For an American pastor's concurrence with Thomson in the debate with Mason, see John Anderson, "Of Humiliation-days before, and Thanksgiving-days after, the Administration of the Lord's Supper," in his *Vindiciae Cantus Dominici* (Philadelphia: David Hogan, 1800), 301–21. Anderson, citing Thomson repeatedly, follows him almost to the letter. For another Scot who weighed in on Thomson's side, see [Alexander Duncan], *A Disquisition on the Observance of the Lord's Supper, with a View to the Defence of the Presbyterian Plan of Administrating that Ordinance. Appendix. A Short Review of Mr Mason's Letters on Communion* (Edinburgh: Thomas Turnbull, 1805). For further indication of the resistance that advocates of reform met, see John Ronald, *The Reality and Efficacy of the Work of the Spirit of God, Manifested in the Experiences of John Ronald, Late Lorimer in Edinburgh* (Edinburgh: John Gray and Gavin Alston, 1767), vi–vii, 50; *Dan; An Adder in the*

Path: Or, Issachar Couching under a Burden. Containing, Some Considerations upon the New Scheme of Communions Introduced in the Presbytery of Edinburgh (Edinburgh: n.p., 1720); James Russell, *Reminiscences of Yarrow*, 2d ed. (Selkirk: George Lewis and Son, 1894), 148.

39. Ibid., 29.

40. Jacob van Vechten, *Memoirs of John M. Mason, D.D., S.T.P. with Portions of his Correspondence* (New York: Robert Carter and Brothers, 1856), 68–69. Van Vechten provides a basic description of the gradual, though difficult, triumph of Mason's views. For examples of how Mason's views were assimilated and became a part of Presbyterian wisdom on the sacrament, see [James W. Alexander], "The Sacrament of the Lord's Supper," *Biblical Repertory and Princeton Review* 12 (1840): 18–20; John Brown, *Hints on the Permanent Obligation and Frequent Observance of the Lord's Supper* (Edinburgh: W. Matheson, [1832]), 34, 43.

41. Mason, *Letters*, 1:499. See, for example, *The Celebration of the Lord's Supper Every Lord's Day, Shewn to be the Duty and Privilege of Every Christian Church* (Edinburgh: Ritchie, 1802); John Brown, *An Apology for the More Frequent Administration of the Lord's Supper* (Edinburgh: J. Ritchie, 1804); *A Letter to the Members of the General Assembly of the Church of Scotland, Concerning the Present Mode of Administering the Lord's Supper, and Intended for the Perusal of Presbyterians in General* (Edinburgh: William Blair, 1818); *View of the Mode of Celebrating the Lord's Supper, in the Presbyterian Churches in Scotland* (Edinburgh: Wardlaw and Co., 1830); "Our Communions: Some Reflections on Them, Nos. I–V[I]," *North Carolina Presbyterian*, 13 June 1866 to 18 July 1866.

42. Van Vechten, *Memoirs of John Mason*, 68; Willison, *Sacramental Directory*, xv–xvi; Thomson, *Letters*, 15; John Livingston, *A Brief Historical Relation of the Life of Mr. John Livingston Minister of the Gospel* (n.p.: n.p., 1727), 11.

43. Thomas Burns in *Old Scottish Communion Plate* openly hailed the church's efforts "to have these great assemblages suppressed" and regretted that the church had for a long time been "unable to suppress the custom of communicants travelling in crowds to a Sacrament." Insisting on "stated and regular celebration in every parish," Burns surmised, had been the church's primary means of "discouraging these large Communion gatherings" (pp. 94, 115).

44. Thomson, *Letters*, 37. See also [Duncan], *Disquisition*, 72–73. For broad theoretical discussion of the issue of community, see, for example, Bender, *Community and Social Change* as well as the classic exposition of Ferdinand Tönnies, *Community and Society (Gemeinschaft und Gesellschaft)*, trans. Charles P. Loomis (East Lansing: Michigan State University Press, 1957).

45. "Sacramental Meetings," *Watchman and Observer* 3 (1848): 202; *Address to the Christian People*, 59. On the reform of popular culture, which included the control of popular festivals, see Burke, *Popular Culture in Early Modern Europe*, 207–43, 272–73. Also on the decline of religious festivity in the modern West, see Roger Caillois, *Man and the Sacred*, trans. Meyer Barash (Glencoe, Ill.: Free Press, 1959), 127–31, 163–64; Harvey Cox, *The Feast of Fools: A Theological Essay on Festivity and Fantasy* (Cambridge, Mass.: Harvard University Press, 1969), 3–47.

46. On the emergence of bourgeois culture and its ethic of self-control, discipline, and industry, see, for example, Burke, *Popular Culture in Early Modern Europe*, 211–14, 272–73; Robert D. Storch, ed., *Popular Culture and Custom in Nineteenth-Century England* (New York: St. Martin's Press, 1982), esp. 1–19; Carroll Smith-Rosenberg, *Disorderly Conduct: Visions of Gender in Victorian America* (New York: Oxford University Press, 1985), 79–89; Paul E. Johnson, *A Shopkeeper's Millennium: Society and Revivals in Rochester, New York, 1815–1837* (New York: Hill and Wang, 1978). Of course, Max Weber's *Protestant Ethic and the Spirit of Capitalism*, trans. Talcott Parsons (New York: Charles Scribner's Sons, 1958) remains the seminal text for discussion of the Protestant dimensions of this bourgeois ethic.

47. *Letter from a Blacksmith*, 26–28.

48. Henry Grey Graham, *The Social Life of Scotland in the Eighteenth Century* (London, 1899; London: Black, 1928), 160–62; editorial note in the 1844 Spottiswoode edition of Sage, *Fundamental Charter*, 369; John Courtas, *A Letter Addressed to the Community of Old Dissenters* (Glasgow: E. Miller, 1797), 75–76; Samuel Miller, *The Worship of the Presbyterian Church* (Philadelphia: Presbyterian Board of Publication, n.d.), 13. Whether Calvinism promoted a spirit of capitalism in Scotland is debated, but Victorian heirs of the traditional Presbyterians usually perceived the old faith as having been backward and hostile to economic change. For extended discussion of how Weber's thesis fares in the Scottish context, see Gordon Marshall, *Presbyteries and Profits: Calvinism and the Development of Capitalism in Scotland, 1560–1707* (Oxford: Clarendon Press, 1980).

49. *View of the Mode*, 17, 30–31, 45–46, 57–59; Courtas, *Letter*, 75–76.

50. William Henry Foote, *Sketches of North Carolina, Historical and Biographical, Illustrative of the Principles of a Portion of her Early Settlers* (New York: Robert Carter, 1846), 196; Smith, *Old Redstone*, 250–53, 264–65; *Letter from a Blacksmith*, 22. On the importance of drinking in everything from courting to commerce, from pastoral visits to craft initiations, see Ian Donnachie, "Drink and Society, 1750–1850: Some Aspects of the Scottish Experience," *Journal of the Scottish Labour History Society* 13 (1979): 5–22.

51. Courtas, *Letter*, 35–37; Kilsyth Kirk Session Records, Strathclyde Regional Archives, Mitchell Library, Glasgow, 2 August 1741, 16 August 1741, 27:137–38. For an interesting parallel case, see Barony Kirk Session Records, Strathclyde Regional Archives, Mitchell Library, Glasgow, 30 July 1766, 6: unpaginated.

52. Editorial note in the 1844 Spottiswoode edition of Sage, *Fundamental Charter*, 368–69; James Russell, *Reminiscences of Yarrow*, 7. See also Smith's *Old Redstone* (pp. 250–65) for an indication of how religion and drink were divided from one another—in this case even by a minister who was a traditionalist on many other points.

53. David Calderwood, *The Pastor and the Prelate, or Reformation and Conformitie Shortly Compared* (n.p.: n.p., 1628), 15–16; Cambuslang Kirk Session Records, Scottish Record Office, Edinburgh, 1: unpaginated treasurer's account; John Cuthbertson, "Diary," Clifford E. Barbour Library manuscripts, Pittsburgh Theological Seminary, 11r. For this last item, see also John Cuthberston, "The Diary of the Rev. John Cuthbertson," Presbyterian Office of History typescript,

Philadelphia, 17. On the abundant supply of wine at the early modern sacraments in Scotland, see Burnet, *Holy Communion*, 30–31, 194–95, 263–64; A. Mitchell Hunter, "The Celebration of Communion in Scotland since the Reformation," *Records of the Scottish Church History Society* 3 (1929): 169–70.

54. I. N. Hays, *An Appeal to the Authorities in the Presbyterian Churches on behalf of the Communion Wine Question* (n.p.: n.p., 1891), 2–3, 6–7; James Gall, *The Use of Wine at the Lord's Supper Not Sanctioned in Scripture*, 2d ed. (Edinburgh: Andrew Elliot, 1874), 3–4, 14–16. On nineteenth-century efforts in Scotland to substitute grape juice for wine, see Burnet, *Holy Communion*, 287–88. The primary literature on communion wine and related questions is extensive. For some of the earlier pieces, see, for example, [Samuel Miller], "Suggestions in Vindication of the Temperance Society," *Biblical Repertory and Theological Review* 3 (1831): 44–60; [William B. Sprague], *Dr. Sprague's Reply to Professor Stuart's Letter Addressed to him through the American Temperance Intelligencer of August, 1835, Relative to his Late Sermon on the Exclusion of Wine from the Lord's Supper* (Albany: Packard and Van Benthuysen, 1835); [John MacClean], "Bacchus and Anti-Bacchus," *Biblical Repertory and Princeton Review* 13 (1841): 267–306. For an indication of how the communion wine question was played out on a local level, see Glenn C. Altschuler and Jan M. Saltzgaber, *Revivalism, Social Conscience, and Community in the Burned-Over District: The Trial of Rhoda Bement* (Ithaca: Cornell University Press, 1983), 55–56, 101–8.

55. *Letter from a Blacksmith*, 20, 22, 25; Livingston, *Brief Historical Relation*, 17; Smith, *Old Redstone*, 156. Helping the saints to marry in the Lord and specifically to wed within the fold of Scottish Presbyterianism, the communion season assisted in keeping the courtship of young saints within the bounds of a religious and ethnic community. That the sacramental occasion may have helped foster endogamy would appear especially important for immigrant Scots. On the perpetuation of "in-group marriage" through such events, see Gwen Kennedy Neville, "Kinfolks and the Covenant: Ethnic Community among Southern Presbyterians," in John W. Bennett, ed., *The New Ethnicity: Perspectives from Ethnology* (St. Paul: West Publishing, 1975), 258–74.

56. *Letter from a Blacksmith*, 25.

57. T. Williams, *The Song of Songs which is by Solomon. A New Translation: with a Commentary and Notes* (London: Whittingham, 1801), 66–75; Moses Stuart, *Critical History and Defence of the Old Testament Canon* (Andover: Allen, Morrill and Wardwell, 1845), 374. On such changes in evangelical hymns, see Mary G. De Jong, " 'I Want to be Like Jesus': The Self-Defining Power of Evangelical Hymnody," *Journal of the American Academy of Religion* 54 (1986): 464–69. On Rutherford, see Alexander Duff, "Introduction," in Thomas Smith, ed., *Letters of the Rev. Samuel Rutherford* (Edinburgh: Oliphant, Anderson, and Ferrier, 1881), 13–18; G. W. Sprott's entry (1897) in *Dictionary of National Biography*, s.v. "Rutherford, Samuel."

58. *Letter from a Blacksmith*, 24.

59. Ibid., 20–21; *Dan in Beersheba*, 6, 23. For another blast at the "field or tent preaching," see Paul, ed., *Poems and Songs of Burns*, xxxix. The Edinburgh Presbytery was one of the first to attempt to curb outdoor preaching. In an act in

1720 the presbytery proposed eliminating sermons in the churchyards and admonished that everyone was "to keep to their own Parish Church, and not to come and throng others" during communions. This act, evidently concocted by a handful of ministers, was designed as "a Copy for the whole Church to imitate." This effort set the tone for future reforms that would take more than a century to realize. For the act and response to it, see *Dan an Adder*, 6–7, 22, 30–32.

60. David Hogg, *Life and Times of the Rev. John Wightman, D.D. (1762–1847), Late Minister of Kirkmahoe* (London: Hodder and Stoughton, 1873), 48, 50–53.

61. Burnet, *Holy Communion*, 253; *Dan an Adder*, 20.

62. Jethro Rumple, *The History of Presbyterianism in North Carolina: Reprinted from the North Carolina Presbyterian, 1878–1887 with Appendixes* (Richmond: Library of Union Theological Seminary in Virginia, 1966), 181, 186–87. On issues of public order and popular gatherings in the nineteenth century, see, for example, Storch, ed., *Popular Culture and Custom*; Susan G. Davis, *Parades and Power: Street Theatre in Nineteenth-Century Philadelphia* (Philadelphia: Temple University Press, 1986), esp. 30–48, 164–65. On the concepts of the public and the private, see S. I. Benn and G. F. Gaus, eds., *Public and Private in Social Life* (New York: St. Martin's Press, 1983), esp. 19–23.

63. Burns, *Poems and Songs*, 1:149–50; Webster, *Burns and the Kirk*, 18–19, 66–68. See also Jamieson, *Burns and Religion*, 54–55; Henry F. Henderson, *Religion in Scotland: Its Influence on National Life and Character* (Paisley: Alexander Garden, [1920]), 139, 226.

64. "Preface" to Robert Burns, *The Cotter's Saturday Night* (Philadelphia: Porter and Coates, 1872); Colleen McDannell, *The Christian Home in Victorian America, 1840–1900* (Bloomington: Indiana University Press, 1986), 152. The Chapman and Filmer illustration is taken from the above American edition of "The Cotter's Saturday Night," opposite p. 33, while the Carse and Scott work is taken from Robert Burns, *Poems*, 2 vols. (Kirkcaldy: J. Crerar, 1802), 1: opposite p. 30. See also Lindsay Errington, *The Artist and the Kirk* (Edinburgh: National Gallery of Scotland, [1979]), 4, 18–19; C. Kurt Dewhurst, Betty MacDowell, and Marsha MacDowell, *Religious Folk Art in America: Reflections of Faith* (New York: E. P. Dutton, 1983), 43, 46; Duncan Macmillan, *Painting in Scotland: The Golden Age* (Oxford: Phaidon Press, 1986), 180–82. The number of nineteenth-century illustrations, drawings, and paintings of "The Cotter's Saturday Night" is legion: indeed, it appears to have been the most commonly illustrated of Burns' works as evidenced in the index available at the Robert Burns Collection, Mitchell Library, Glasgow. About fifty illustrations akin to the two shown here have been indexed. The single most famous rendering, however, came in 1837 in David Wilkie's masterful painting of the scene.

65. Bossy, *Christianity in the West*, 142–43. On the growing importance of pews in Scottish churches after 1750, see Graham, *Social Life of Scotland*, 289. On pew assignments, see Guy Soulliard Klett, *Presbyterians in Colonial Pennsylvania* (Philadelphia: University of Pennsylvania Press, 1937), 92–93; Walter Steuart, *Collections and Observations Methodiz'd; Concerning the Worship, Discipline, and Government of the Church of Scotland* (Edinburgh: Andrew Ander-

son, 1709), 141, 176–77. This move can also be seen in the context of the anglicization of Scottish Presbyterian worship; for receiving the sacrament in the pews rather than at the table represented a marked acquiescence to Independent or Congregational forms of worship. For the move from table to pew, see William D. Maxwell, *A History of Worship in the Church of Scotland* (London: Oxford University Press, 1955), 171–72.

66. For discussion of some of the Presbyterian communion cups in early America as well as an indication of their replacement by individual glasses, see Ledlie I. Laughlin, "The Pewter Communion Services of the Presbyterian Historical Society," *Journal of Presbyterian History* 44 (1966): 83–88. For the Scottish side, see Burnet, *Holy Communion*, 294–96. For a picture of the traditional communion cups beside the new individual ones, see Market Street Presbyterian Church, Lima, Ohio, *Centennial Souvenir, 1833–1933* (Lima, Ohio: Parmenter Printing, [1933]), unpaginated. For the careful debate over this change in one congregation, see Walnut Street Presbyterian Church, Philadelphia, "Session Records, 1891–1901," Presbyterian Office of History manuscripts, Philadelphia, entries for 17 March 1898 and 15 May 1898.

67. Robert Lee, *The Reform of the Church of Scotland in Worship, Government, and Doctrine* (Edinburgh: Edmonston and Douglas, 1864), 194–96; Andrew Edgar, *Old Church Life in Scotland: Lectures on Kirk-Session and Presbytery Records*, 2 vols. (Paisley: Alexander Gardner, 1885–1887), 1:173. See also George W. Sprott, *The Worship and Offices of the Church of Scotland* (Edinburgh: Blackwood and Sons, 1882), 142; Robert Herbert Story, *The Reformed Ritual in Scotland* (Edinburgh: William Blackwood and Sons, 1886), 36–39. For liturgical revisions on the American side, see, for example, *The Church-Book of St. Peter's Church Rochester* (Rochester: Lee, Mann, and Co., 1855); [Charles W. Baird], *Eutaxia, or the Presbyterian Liturgies: Historical Sketches* (New York: M. W. Dodd, 1855); Samuel M. Hopkins, "The Presbyterian Cultus," *Presbyterian Review* 3 (1882): 40–61; [John W. Yeomans], "Forms of Worship," *Biblical Repertory and Princeton Review* 18 (1846): 487–514.

68. James W. Alexander, "Introduction," in Philip Doddridge, *Thoughts on Sacramental Occasions* (Philadelphia: William S. Martien, 1846), 20; Edward L. Parker, *The History of Londonderry, Comprising the Towns of Derry and Londonderry, N. H.* (Boston: Perkins and Whipple, 1851), 144–45. For an indication of the slow decline of the traditional rituals in Scotland over the course of the nineteenth century, see *Report of Committee of Free Presbytery of Edinburgh on Communion Seasons* (Edinburgh: Lorimer and Gillies, 1886). For evidence of persistence in some areas, see Trefor M. Owen, "The 'Communion Season' and Presbyterianism in a Hebridean Community," *Gwerin* 1 (1956): 53–66.

69. John W. Nevin, *The Mystical Presence: A Vindication of the Reformed or Calvinistic Doctrine of the Holy Eucharist* (Philadelphia: J. B. Lippincott and Co., 1846), 108n. See, for example, Hugh A. White, *The Communicant's Manual; Or, Sacramental Meditations*, 2d ed. (Richmond: Presbyterian Committee of Publication, 1899); William M. Baker, *The Life and Labours of the Rev. Daniel Baker, D.D., Pastor and Evangelist* (Philadelphia: Martien, 1858), 49–67; James W. Alexander, *Sacramental Discourses* (New York: Randolph, 1860); J. J. Janeway,

The Communicant's Manual; Or, A Series of Meditations Designed to Assist Communicants in Making Preparation for the Lord's Supper (Philadelphia: Presbyterian Board of Publication, 1848). The works of Willison also remained popular well into the nineteenth century.

70. "Sacramental Meetings," *Watchman and Observer* 3 (1848): 202.

71. On the new revivalism see, for example, Charles Grandison Finney, *Lectures on Revivals of Religion*, ed. William G. McLoughlin (Cambridge, Mass.: Harvard University Press, 1960), esp. 262–63; David O. Mears, *Life of Edward Norris Kirk, D.D.* (Boston: Lockwood, Brooks, and Co., 1877), esp. 75–79; Samuel Miller, *Letters to Presbyterians, on the Present Crisis in the Presbyterian Church in the United States* (Philadelphia: Anthony Finley, 1833), 151–91; Dwight Moody, *How to Conduct Evangelistic Services and Prayer-Meetings* (Springfield, Mass.: G. and C. Merriam, 1876). For secondary material see William G. McLoughlin, *Modern Revivalism: Charles Grandison Finney to Billy Graham* (New York: Ronald Press, 1959); W. J. Couper, *Scottish Revivals* (Dundee: James P. Mathew and Co., 1918); Ernest Trice Thompson, *Presbyterians in the South*, 3 vols. (Richmond: John Knox Press, 1963–1973), 1:226–34; Anne C. Loveland, "Presbyterians and Revivalism in the Old South," *Journal of Presbyterian History* 57 (1979): 36–49.

72. Finney, *Lectures*, 181; Moody, *Evangelistic Services*, 4.

73. Calvin Colton, *History and Character of American Revivals of Religion* (London: Frederick, Westley, and Davis, 1832), 59, 169; Michael Chevalier, *Society, Manners and Politics in the United States Being a Series of Letters on North America* (Boston, 1839; New York: Burt Franklin, 1969), 317–21.

74. John Lamont, *The Diary of Mr. John Lamont of Newton, 1649–1671* (Edinburgh: Maitland Club, 1830), 42. Ned Landsman highlights the nativistic potentialities of Scottish revivalism in "Revivalism and Nativism in the Middle Colonies: The Great Awakening and the Scots Community in East New Jersey," *American Quarterly* 34 (1982): 149–64.

75. Van Vechten, *Memoirs of Mason*, 71–72, 366–68, 487–88.

76. N. L. Walker quoted in Couper, *Scottish Revivals*, 15. See also R. B. Robertson, "When Billy Graham Saved Scotland," *Atlantic Monthly*, June 1957: 39–45; Tom Allan, ed., *Crusade in Scotland* (London: Pickering and Inglis, 1955).

77. Graham, *Social Life of Scotland*, 313.

78. Richard Webster, *A History of the Presbyterian Church in America, from its Origin until the Year 1760* (Philadelphia: Joseph M. Wilson, 1857), 124; Smith, *Old Redstone*, 156–58. For wistful recollections as well as attempts to salvage tradition on the Scottish side, see William Milroy, *A Scottish Communion* (Paisley: Alexander Gardner, 1882), vii–xxv; J. R. MacDuff, *Communion Memories* (London: James Nisbet, 1885), xiii–xix.

79. Smith, *Old Redstone*, 156. Recognition of the past revivalistic power of the sacramental season was common. See, for example, *Our Father's God; An Account of Our First National Revival of Religion* (Philadelphia: Presbyterian Board of Education, 1867).

80. Ibid.; Parker, *History of Londonderry*, 145.

81. Alexander, "Introduction," 18, 20–21. For Alexander's views on simplicity

and frequency, see his "Sacrament of the Lord's Supper," 14–30. For Alexander's extensive effort to reclaim Livingston's exemplary heritage, see his "The Life and Times of John Livingston," *Biblical Repertory and Theological Review* 4 (1832): 428–50.

82. Ibid., 16–18.

RETROSPECT

1. Peter Burke, *Popular Culture in Early Modern Europe* (New York: Harper and Row, 1978), 281.

2. Devereux Jarratt, *The Life of the Reverend Devereux Jarratt, Rector of Bath Parish, Dinwiddie County, Virginia* (Baltimore: Warner and Hanna, 1806), 101–4. It is worth noting that the Anglican Jarratt was working in close association with the Presbyterians, and his sacramental practices may have been influenced by them.

3. Thomas Prince, Jr., ed., *The Christian History*, 2 vols. (Boston: Kneeland and Green, 1744–1745), 2:103, 146–49; Isaac Reed, *The Christian Traveller. In Five Parts. Including Nine Years, and Eighteen Thousand Miles* (New York: J. and J. Harper, 1828), 230.

4. E. Brooks Holifield, *The Gentlemen Theologians: American Theology in Southern Culture, 1795–1860* (Durham: Duke University Press, 1978), 175; E. Brooks Holifield, *The Covenant Sealed: The Development of Puritan Sacramental Theology in Old and New England* (New Haven: Yale University Press, 1974), 229; E. Brooks Holifield, "Mercersburg, Princeton, and the South: The Sacramental Controversy in the Nineteenth Century," *Journal of Presbyterian History* 54 (1976): 238–57. Holifield sees the rise of evangelicalism in the eighteenth century as sparking the demise of the "sacramental renaissance" that had been fostered by late seventeenth-century Puritanism. "The Great Awakening and its aftermath," Holifield concludes in *The Covenant Sealed*, "severely inhibited the expansion of sacramental piety. . . . This antisacramental mood became characteristic of American revivalism" (p. 229). A position similar to Holifield's is taken by Doug Adams in *Meeting House to Camp Meeting: Toward a History of American Free Church Worship from 1620 to 1835* (Saratoga: Modern Liturgy Resource Publications, 1981), 108, 146. Some of American revivalism, of course, was antisacramental; much, however, was not. On the sacramental renewal of Catholics, see Jay P. Dolan, *Catholic Revivalism: The American Experience, 1830–1900* (Notre Dame: University of Notre Dame Press, 1978).

5. "Protracted Meetings," *Watchman and Observer* 5 (1849): 14–15. See also B. W. Gorham, *Camp Meeting Manual, A Practical Book for the Camp Ground; in Two Parts* (Boston: H. V. Degen, 1854), 23–24, 28–32. The emphasis in this quotation is mine.

6. "Protestant Revivals and Catholic Retreats," *Brownson's Quarterly Review* 3 (1858): 295.

7. Peter Burke, *The Historical Anthropology of Early Modern Italy: Essays on Perception and Communication* (Cambridge: Cambridge University Press, 1987), 223–38.

8. For a primary text describing some of these other evangelical or restoration-

ist rituals, see Redmond Conyngham, "History of the Mennonists and Aymneists or Amish," *Register of Pennsylvania* 7 (1831): 129–32, 150–53; for a secondary account, see Frank Baker, *Methodism and the Love-Feast* (London: Epworth Press, 1957).

9. For such generalizations in two excellent books, see Richard C. Trexler, *Public Life in Renaissance Florence* (New York: Academic Press, 1980), xvii; Paul E. Johnson, *A Shopkeeper's Millennium: Society and Revivals in Rochester, New York, 1815–1837* (New York: Hill and Wang, 1978), 96.

10. Thomas Carlyle, *Sartor Resartus* (London: J. M. Dent and Sons, 1908), 161–62, 174–75.

11. "On Camp-Meetings," *Calvinistic Magazine* 4 (1830): 301–7; Gorham, *Camp Meeting Manual*, 33. See also "Four Days' Meetings," *Charleston Observer* 5 (1831): 137; "Presbyterian Camp Meeting," *Watchman and Observer* 5 (1849): 22. Ongoing tensions in American Protestantism between individualism and community are discussed in Gwen Kennedy Neville, *Kinship and Pilgrimage: Rituals of Reunion in American Protestant Culture* (New York: Oxford University Press, 1987).

12. "Our Communions: Some Reflections on Them, No. I," *North Carolina Presbyterian*, 13 June 1866; Margaret Bruce, *Spiritual Earnestness; As It Was Manifested in the Life and Experience of Margaret Bruce, a Scottish Peasant Girl* (London: Nisbet and Co., 1855), 22.

Index